A Church at War

A Church at War

MacKay Presbyterian Church, New Edinburgh, and the First World War

Alan Bowker

Mercury Series
History Paper 65
Canadian Museum of History
and the University of Ottawa Press

© 2024 Canadian Museum of History

Legal Deposit: First Quarter 2024
Library and Archives Canada

All rights reserved. No part of this book may be reproduced or transmitted in any form or by any means electronic or mechanical, including photocopying, recording, or any retrieval system, without the written permission of the publisher.

Co-published by the **Canadian Museum of History** *and the* **University of Ottawa Press**

Production Team

Copyediting	Valentina D'Aliesio
Proofreading	Robbie McCaw
Typesetting	Transforma
Cover design	Bianca Daudelin

The University of Ottawa Press gratefully acknowledges the support extended to its publishing list by the Government of Canada, the Canada Council for the Arts, the Ontario Council for the Arts, the Federation for the Humanities and Social Sciences through the Awards to Scholarly Publications Program, and the University of Ottawa.

Library and Archives Canada Cataloguing in Publication

Title: A church at war : MacKay Presbyterian Church, New Edinburgh, and the First World War / Alan Bowker.
Names: Bowker, Alan, author.
Series: Mercury series. History paper ; 65.
Description: Series statement: Mercury series. History paper ; 65 | Includes bibliographical references and index.
Identifiers: Canadiana (print) 20230569102 |
  Canadiana (ebook) 20230569145 |
  ISBN 9780776642154 (softcover) |
  ISBN 9780776642161 (PDF)
Subjects: LCSH: New Edinburgh (Ottawa, Ont.) |
  LCSH: MacKay United Church (Ottawa, Ont.) |
  LCSH: Soldiers—Ontario—Ottawa. |
  LCSH: World War, 1914-1918—Social aspects—Ontario—Ottawa. | LCSH: Ottawa (Ont.)—Church history—20th century.
Classification: LCC FC3096.52 .B69 2024 | DDC 971.3/84—dc23

The Mercury Series

The best resource on the history, archaeology, and culture of Canada is proudly published by the Canadian Museum of History and the University of Ottawa Press.

La collection Mercure

Le Musée canadien de l'histoire et Les Presses de l'Université d'Ottawa publient avec fierté la meilleure ressource en ce qui a trait à l'histoire, à l'archéologie et à la culture canadiennes.

For this book/Pour ce livre

Series Editor/Direction de la collection
  Pierre M. Desrosiers
Editorial Committee/Comité éditorial
  Tim Foran, Teresa Lacobelli, Laura Sanchini, Janet Young
Managing Editor/Responsable de l'édition
  Robyn Jeffrey
Coordination
  Pascal Scallon-Chouinard

How To Order

All trade orders must be directed to the University of Ottawa Press:

  Web: www.press.uottawa.ca
  Email: puo-uop@uottawa.ca
  Phone: 613-562-5246

All other orders may be directed to either the University of Ottawa Press (as above) or to the Canadian Museum of History:

  Web: www.historymuseum.ca/shop/
  Email: publications@historymuseum.ca
  Phone: 1-800-5550-5621 (toll-free) and 819-776-8387 (National Capital Region)
  Mail: Mail Order Services
    Canadian Museum of History
    100 Laurier Street
    Gatineau, QC, K1A 0M8

Pour commander

Les libraires et les autres détaillants doivent adresser leurs commandes aux Presses de l'Université d'Ottawa :

  Web : www.presses.uottawa.ca
  Courriel : puo-uop@uottawa.ca
  Téléphone : 613-562-5246

Les particuliers doivent adresser leurs commandes soit aux Presses de l'Université d'Ottawa (voir plus haut), soit au Musée canadien de l'histoire :

  Web : www.museedelhistoire.ca/magasiner
  Courriel : publications@museedelhistoire.ca
  Téléphone : 1-800-5550-5621 (numéro sans frais) ou 819-776-8387 (région de la capitale nationale)
  Poste : Service des commandes postales
    Musée canadien de l'histoire
    100, rue Laurier
    Gatineau (Québec) K1A 0M8

Land Acknowledgement
Reconnaissance territoriale

The Canadian Museum of History and the University of Ottawa Press are located on the traditional, unceded territory of the Algonquin Anishinabeg. This land has held, and continues to hold, great historical, spiritual, and sacred significance. We recognize and honour the enduring presence of the Algonquin people. We also know that you, our readers, are joining us from many places near and far, and we acknowledge the traditional owners and caretakers of those lands.

Le Musée canadien de l'histoire et Les Presses de l'Université d'Ottawa sont situés sur le territoire traditionnel non cédé des Anishinabeg (Algonquins). Ce territoire a eu, et continue d'avoir, une grande importance historique, spirituelle et sacrée. Nous reconnaissons et honorons la présence pérenne du peuple algonquin. Nous avons aussi conscience que notre lectorat provient de nombreux endroits, proches et lointains, et nous reconnaissons les gens qui sont les propriétaires et les gardiens traditionnels de ces terres.

Abstract

One hundred and forty-one people from MacKay Presbyterian Church served in the First World War, and their church and their families at home steadfastly supported the war through four years of privation, suffering, and grief. MacKay church served New Edinburgh, a community with roots in the lumber industries at the Rideau Falls, where Rideau Hall was located and which was home to a growing number of public servants and a large German-speaking minority, as well as boasting a rich tradition of athletics and militia service. MacKay church embraced the conviction that an immanent God was working in history, and that Christians had a duty to realize the Kingdom of God on Earth through evangelism and social and moral reform. They regarded the British Empire as the apogee of Christian civilization bringing peace and progress to the world. They were thus convinced that in defending their country and Empire against German aggression and autocracy they were fighting for "justice, truth, and righteousness, and for the Glory of God". This book weaves together the stories of those men who served, their families at home, and their church as they responded to a terrible war. This volume focusses on the 19 men who fell in the war—some as heroes in desperate battles, others in tragically random circumstances or from illness, several who have no known grave—as well as their siblings who also served; the widows they left to cope as best they could, the children who would grow up without fathers, and the families whose pride in their sacrifice was mixed with heartbreak at their loss. The last chapters describe the return of the survivors and their adjustment, along with their families, to a changed world, as they launched new careers or returned to old jobs, started new families, and in some cases struggled with permanent injuries and painful memories. MacKay Presbyterian Church became MacKay United Church, re-affirming its Christian faith while remembering those who made the Supreme Sacrifice. This study of a church at war deepens our understanding of the social history of Canada's response to a global war, using new methods, including online research and the tools of genealogical study, to bring to life people who did not leave a rich legacy of information on their lives and families.

Résumé

Cent quarante et un membres de l'église presbytérienne MacKay ont combattu au cours de la Première Guerre mondiale. Au pays, leur église et leurs familles ont soutenu sans relâche l'effort de guerre à travers quatre années de privations, de souffrances et d'affliction. L'église MacKay desservait New Edinburgh, une communauté liée à l'industrie forestière des chutes Rideau, où l'on retrouvait Rideau Hall, un nombre croissant de fonctionnaires et une importante minorité germanophone, et qui s'enorgueillissait d'une riche tradition d'athlétisme et de milice. Les membres de l'église MacKay embrassaient la conviction qu'un Dieu immanent œuvrait au sein de l'Histoire et que les chrétiens avaient le devoir d'établir le Royaume de Dieu sur Terre à l'aide de l'évangélisme et de la réforme morale et sociale. Ils voyaient l'Empire britannique comme l'apogée de la civilisation chrétienne, apportant la paix et le progrès au monde entier. En conséquence, ils étaient convaincus qu'en défendant leur pays et l'Empire face à l'agression et à l'autocratie germaniques, ils luttaient pour « la justice, la vérité et le bien, et pour la gloire de Dieu ». Cet ouvrage entremêle l'histoire des combattants, celle de leurs familles restées au pays et celle de leur église face au défi d'une terrible guerre. Il s'intéresse particulièrement aux 19 hommes qui sont tombés à la guerre – certains morts au combat de manière héroïque, d'autres victimes d'accidents tragiques ou de maladie, et dont plusieurs n'ont pas de sépulture connue – ainsi qu'à leurs frères également combattants, aux veuves abandonnées à leur sort, aux enfants privés de pères et aux familles partagées entre la fierté de leur sacrifice et le déchirement de leur deuil. Les derniers chapitres sont consacrés au retour des survivants et à leur adaptation, et à celles de leurs proches, à un monde transformé, alors qu'ils abordaient une nouvelle carrière ou reprenaient leur emploi et fondaient de nouvelles familles, plusieurs devant composer avec des lésions permanentes ou des souvenirs traumatiques. L'église presbytérienne MacKay est devenue l'église unie MacKay et réaffirme sa foi chrétienne tout en honorant la mémoire de ceux qui ont accompli le sacrifice suprême. Cette étude sur une église en guerre enrichit notre compréhension de l'histoire sociale de la participation du Canada à la Première Guerre mondiale et met à profit de nouvelles méthodes, incluant la recherche en ligne et les outils de recherche généalogique, pour donner vie à des personnes qui ont laissé peu de documentation sur leur vie et leur famille.

Table of Contents

Land Acknowledgement/Reconnaissance territoriale v

Abstract vii

Résumé viii

List of Figures xi

Acknowledgements xvii

Abbreviations xxi

Introduction 3

Chapter 1
New Edinburgh 15

Chapter 2
MacKay Presbyterian Church 33

Chapter 3
A Church at War: 1914–1915 53

Chapter 4
Charles Albert Wendt: A German-Canadian Patriot 71

Chapter 5
A Church at War: 1916 81

Chapter 6
Victor and Theresa Coker: A Good Man, a Christian Woman,
and Her Two Sons at the Front 95

Chapter 7
The Bothwell Family: War Claims Lives and
Destroys Families 103

Chapter 8
Charles Edward Trotter and the Jackson Family: "Lovable Disposition and
Fine Character" 119

Chapter 9
The Robertson Family: "There Is no Other Woman in
Ottawa Who Has Given so Gloriously to the Cause" 131

Chapter 10
Gordon Maynard Porteous: "Quite a Few Homes … Will Be
Sad After This" 147

Chapter 11
Henry James Mayo: A "Home Boy" Serves His Country 153

Chapter 12
A Church at War: 1917 163

Chapter 13
The Stalker Family and the Many Faces of Courage 175

Chapter 14
The Ryan Family: "Who Played the Game Through" 195

Chapter 15
Reginald Isambard Brunel: Engineer and Artilleryman 213

Chapter 16
The Tubman Families: "Conspicuous Gallantry and
Devotion to Duty" 221

Chapter 17
Erland Dauria Perney: "Sorrow Which Is Almost Intolerable" 239

Chapter 18
A Church at War: 1918 253

Chapter 19
John Marshall: A Chauffeur in Egypt 259

Chapter 20
Homère Joliat: "A Brave Soldier, Having Won the
Military Medal" 267

Chapter 21
Irwin Kelly: "Blessed Are Those that Have Not Seen, and
Yet Have Believed" 281

Chapter 22
The McKenzie Brothers: Service and Sacrifice 289

Chapter 23
Arthur Frank Hawke and the War Against TB 299

Chapter 24
1919: The Men Come Home 309

Chapter 25
Aftermath 325

Epilogue 339

Bibliography 343

Notes 361

Index 389

List of Figures

Introduction 1.1.	In Memoriam plaque	2
Figure 1.1.	P. Checkly, *Mills at New Edinburgh,* c. 1895	16
Figure 1.2.	Rideau Hall, Ottawa c. 1926	17
Figure 1.3.	Map of Thomas MacKay estate showing lands available for sale and development including present-day Rockcliffe and Manor Park	18
Figure 1.4.	"Sash and Door Factory, Ottawa at the Rideau Falls," taken from "W. C. Edwards & Co. Ltd. Saw Mills and Lumber Yards c. 1897"	19
Figure 1.5.	"Saw Mill at Ottawa," taken from "W. C. Edwards & Co. Ltd. Saw Mills and Lumber Yards	20
Figure 1.6.	New Edinburgh and environs in 1912	21
Figure 1.7.	Map showing houses in New Edinburgh inhabited by families with German names	22
Figure 1.8.	Skating on the Rideau River c. 1914	26
Figure 1.9.	New Edinburgh Rugby Football Club City Champions, 1911	27
Figure 1.10.	Ottawa Seconds, winner of the City Hockey League Championship, 1908	28
Figure 1.11.	Floods in New Edinburgh (near Crichton and Keefer Streets) c. 1898	29
Figure 2.1.	New Edinburgh/MacKay Presbyterian Church, 1875–1910	34
Figure 2.2.	Interior of the first MacKay Presbyterian Church, c. 1900	35
Figure 2.3.	A page from MacKay's Communion Rolls	36
Figure 2.4.	Rev. P. W. Anderson	39
Figure 2.5.	Program for an "Entertainment" in the Sunday School hall at MacKay Presbyterian Church	41
Figure 2.6.	Cast of one of Mrs. Anderson's plays	42
Figure 2.7.	MacKay Presbyterian Church Hockey Team, Champions, Senior League, 1912	44
Figure 2.8.	John George Shearer, the leading Presbyterian voice for Sunday observance, Prohibition, and social reforms, who was greatly admired by Rev. Anderson	48
Figure 2.9.	"Patriotic Play" by Mrs. Anderson staged at MacKay Presbyterian Church	50

Figure 2.10.	MacKay Presbyterian Church, new sanctuary, built in 1910	51
Figure 2.11.	Modern interior of MacKay United Church	52
Figure 3.1.	"Your Chums are Fighting, Why aren't You?"	55
Figure 3.2.	Panoramic view of Valcartier Camp, 1916	56
Figure 3.3.	The Western Front	59
Figure 3.4.	38th Battalion: Company inspection before going overseas, c. 1915	61
Figure 3.5.	"'B' Company, 77th Overseas Battalion, C.E.F., Ottawa, Can, June 7, 1916"	65
Figure 3.6.	"Artillery Heroes at the Front Say 'Get into a Man's Uniform'"	66
Figure 4.1.	Charles A. Wendt	72
Figure 4.2.	Family tree of the Wendts	72
Figure 4.3.	Wilhelm "Billy" Wendt, 1900	73
Figure 4.4.	Albert Wendt as a member of the Ottawa Police Force, May 23, 1932	78
Figure 4.5.	Bailleul Communal Cemetery Extension	79
Figure 4.6.	Bailleul Communal Cemetery Extension	80
Figure 4.7.	Bailleul Communal Cemetery Extension	80
Figure 5.1.	Fire at the Parliament Buildings, February 3, 1916	82
Figure 5.2.	77th infantry Battalion colours presentation ceremony on Parliament Hill	84
Figure 5.3.	Recruiting poster for forestry units	87
Figure 5.4.	Illuminated list of MacKay soldiers who enlisted before June 1916	91
Figure 6.1.	George Victor Coker	96
Figure 6.2.	R. E. Farm Cemetery	100
Figure 6.3.	R. E. Farm Cemetery	100
Figure 6.4.	Mrs. G. V. Coker, in one of Mrs. Anderson's plays, in the early 1920s program	101
Figure 7.1.	Bothwell House at 61 MacKay Street in 1914	104
Figure 7.2.	"Lumber & In Yard of Sash and Door Factory." From W. C. Edwards & Co. Ltd. Saw Mills and Lumber Yards c. 1897	105
Figure 7.3.	John and George Bothwell, c. 1902	105
Figure 7.4.	Katie (?) and John Bothwell MacKay Street, Ottawa, c. 1900	106
Figure 7.5.	George S. Bothwell	107
Figure 7.6.	Canadian Ammunition Column passing 6" naval guns, July 1918	108
Figure 7.7.	Poperinghe New Military Cemetery	111

List of Figures xiii

Figure 7.8.	Poperinghe New Military Cemetery	111
Figure 7.9.	Page from William Bothwell Family History	113
Figure 7.10.	John Robert Bothwell	115
Figure 8.1.	Charles Edward Trotter	120
Figure 8.2.	Jackson house in Rockcliffe c. 1912	120
Figure 8.3.	The Jackson family, c. 1912	121
Figure 8.4.	Charles Trotter in uniform	122
Figure 8.5.	Thomas Isaac Jackson, 1916	125
Figure 8.6.	Thomas Nicholas Jackson	126
Figure 8.7.	Thomas Isaac Jackson during his rehabilitation	127
Figure 8.8.	Étaples Military Cemetery	128
Figure 8.9.	Étaples Military Cemetery	129
Figure 8.10.	Étaples Military Cemetery	129
Figure 8.11.	Étaples Military Cemetery	130
Figure 9.1.	Daniel Robertson Sr. before the war	132
Figure 9.2.	Daniel Robertson Jr. as a boy	132
Figure 9.3.	Daniel Robertson Jr. as a soldier, 1914	134
Figure 9.4.	George Robertson, 1915	136
Figure 9.5.	Daniel Robertson Sr. as a soldier, 1916	138
Figure 9.6.	Soldiers and staff at Fettercairn Island	141
Figure 9.7.	William Robertson and his mother, Mary, at Fettercairn Island, 1917	141
Figure 9.8.	Menin Gate, Ypres	143
Figure 9.9.	Interior of Menin Gate, Ypres	144
Figure 9.10.	Stairway at Menin Gate	145
Figure 9.11.	Vimy Memorial	145
Figure 9.12.	Vimy Memorial	146
Figure 9.13.	Mother Canada	146
Figure 10.1.	The Porteous Children, c. 1905	148
Figure 10.2.	Canadian troops returning from the trenches, Battle of the Somme, November 1916	151
Figure 10.3.	Vimy Memorial	152
Figure 11.1.	Henry James Mayo	154
Figure 11.2.	Knowlton Distributing Home c. 1890	155
Figure 11.3.	Knowlton Distributing Home, side view, c. 1905	155
Figure 11.4.	Villers Station Cemetery	162
Figure 11.5.	Villers Station Cemetery	162
Figure 12.1.	Prohibition parade, 1916	166
Figure 12.2.	Stretcher-bearers bringing wounded through mud	172
Figure 13.1.	Stalker family tree	176
Figure 13.2.	Robert Stalker in the early 1900s	177
Figure 13.3.	Robert Stalker c. 1914	177

Figure 13.4.	Page from the war diary of the 102nd Battalion, which records the death of Robert Stalker	181
Figure 13.5.	Villers Station Cemetery	182
Figure 13.6.	Villers Station Cemetery	182
Figure 13.7.	Andrew Douglas Stalker	184
Figure 13.8.	Doug Stalker	186
Figure 13.9.	Judgement in favour of Martha Kenny and custody of Stalker children	188
Figure 13.10.	British Columbia Order in Council 437/1927	189
Figure 13.11.	Doug Stalker and the 1919 Ottawa Rough Riders	191
Figure 13.12.	Fred Stalker in his military uniform in the 1920s	192
Figure 13.13.	Moray Stalker	193
Figure 13.14.	Arthur Stalker	193
Figure 14.1.	John T. McElroy served as team manager for many New Edinburgh and MacKay sports teams	196
Figure 14.2.	Jack Ryan	198
Figure 14.3.	Mathew William Ryan	199
Figure 14.4.	Jack Ryan, 1916	200
Figure 14.5.	Royal Aircraft Factory F.E.2.b	204
Figure 14.6.	Jack Ryan's obituary	206
Figure 14.7.	Editorial honouring Jack Ryan	207
Figure 14.8.	Dickebusch New Military Cemetery	208
Figure 14.9.	Dickebusch New Military Cemetery	209
Figure 14.10.	Achiet-le-Grand Military Cemetery	210
Figure 14.11.	Achiet-le-Grand Military Cemetery	210
Figure 15.1.	An 18-pounder and its crew; this artillery piece was the mainstay of the British field artillery	215
Figure 15.2.	MacKay United Church Choir, c. 1930	218
Figure 15.3.	Écoivres Military Cemetery	219
Figure 15.4.	Écoivres Military Cemetery	219
Figure 15.5.	Écoivres Military Cemetery, showing Brunel's headstone	220
Figure 16.1.	Tubman family tree	222
Figure 16.2.	Sam Hughes reviews 2nd Canadian Infantry Battalion, August 1916	224
Figure 16.3.	Photo of four soldiers at Ploegsteert	225
Figure 16.4.	Leslie Tubman's Military Cross citation	228
Figure 16.5.	Leslie Tubman's medals	229
Figure 16.6.	Ray Tubman	230
Figure 16.7.	Elmer "Joe" Tubman	232
Figure 16.8.	Reed Tubman; Ottawa Seconds Football Club	233
Figure 16.9.	Ste. Catherine British Cemetery	236

Figure 16.10.	Ste. Catherine British Cemetery	236
Figure 16.11.	Ste. Catherine British Cemetery	237
Figure 17.1.	Erland Dauria Perney	240
Figure 17.2.	Bristol F2B Fighter aircraft of the Royal Flying Corps	242
Figure 17.3.	Faubourg d'Amiens Cemetery, Arras	248
Figure 17.4.	Flying Services Memorial courtyard	249
Figure 17.5.	Flying Services Memorial	250
Figure 17.6.	1924 ONECC War Canoe team	251
Figure 17.7.	Perney-Tubman Trophy	252
Figure 18.1.	"The Morning of Armistice Day, The Plazza [sic], Ottawa, 1918"	258
Figure 19.1.	The Sinai campaign	262
Figure 19.2.	Wellshill Cemetery, Perth, Scotland	264
Figure 19.3.	Wellshill Cemetery, Perth, Scotland	265
Figure 19.4.	Area of Wellshill Cemetery where Marshall is buried	266
Figure 20.1.	Émile Joliat as Ottawa Police Chief, 1932	268
Figure 20.2.	Original Brutinel armoured machine gun batteries	270
Figure 20.3.	Military medal citation for Homer Joliat, December 1917	273
Figure 20.4.	German offensives, 1918	274
Figure 20.5.	Canadian Motor Machine Gun Brigade waiting alongside the Arras-Cambrai Road, August 1918	276
Figure 20.6.	Aurèle Joliat	278
Figure 20.7.	St. Pierre Cemetery, Amiens	278
Figure 20.8.	St. Pierre Cemetery, Amiens	279
Figure 20.9.	St. Pierre Cemetery, Amiens	279
Figure 20.10.	St. Pierre Cemetery, Amiens	280
Figure 21.1.	Irwin Kelly	282
Figure 21.2.	Canada's Hundred Days, Phase I (August–September 1918)	284
Figure 21.3.	Tigris Lane Cemetery	287
Figure 21.4.	Tigris Lane Cemetery	287
Figure 21.5.	Tigris Lane Cemetery: headstone of Irwin Kelly	288
Figure 22.1.	Alex Lyon McKenzie	290
Figure 22.2.	Jack McKenzie	291
Figure 22.3.	Military Medal citation for Alex Lyon McKenzie; in the last year of the war	294
Figure 22.4.	Jack McKenzie after his wound	295
Figure 22.5.	Sains-les-Marquion British Cemetery	296
Figure 22.6.	Sains-les-Marquion British Cemetery	297

Figure 22.7.	Sains-les-Marquion British Cemetery, headstone of Sandy McKenzie	298
Figure 23.1.	Haak family tree	300
Figure 23.2.	Page from Arthur Hawke's medical file	304
Figure 23.3.	Haak family plot, Beechwood Cemetery, with Arthur Hawke's headstone in the Commonwealth design	307
Figure 24.1.	Edward, Prince of Wales	310
Figure 24.2.	Pages from Ray Tubman's album from Siberia	313
Figure 24.3.	Victory parade in Ottawa	315
Figure 24.4.	MacKay Presbyterian Church Honour Roll plaque	316
Figure 24.5.	Admission ticket to service of unveiling of the memorial plaques, November 10, 1919	317
Figure 24.6.	Program of service, November 10, 1919	318
Figure 24.7.	The three Ralph sisters, Isabel, Edna, and Elizabeth, taken 1896 or 1897	319
Figure 24.8.	Clifton Springs Sanitorium and Clinic—School of Nursing, Graduating Class of 1910	319
Figure 24.9.	Elizabeth Ralph, 1910	320
Figure 24.10.	Studio portrait of Elizabeth Ralph by J. Alex Castonguay, likely at the time of her wedding	322
Figure 24.11.	The Olney family; the picture was likely taken shortly before Elizabeth's death	323
Figure 25.1.	Young Peoples' Memorial plaque	327
Figure 25.2.	50th anniversary souvenir program	330

Acknowledgements

The impetus for this project came from Tim Cook, military historian *sans pareil,* who has done so much to stimulate private scholarship and public history concerning the experience of Canada, its soldiers, and its people, in war. In 2014 after the Remembrance Sunday service at MacKay United Church, Tim pointed out to me that with the attestation papers for soldiers in the Canadian Expeditionary Force (CEF) from the First World War then coming online, it would be possible to know more about the men from MacKay who had fallen in the war, to bring them to life after a century as real people, not just names on a wall. Each year for the following four years on Remembrance Sunday, I told the stories of the soldiers who had fallen a century earlier, using an ever-wider range of sources as they became available and as my research progressed. While facing his own challenges, Tim was unstintingly generous in his advice, assistance, encouragement, and support, prodding me to delve ever deeper and expand this work into an academic publication. I join the many others whose work he has encouraged over the years in expressing my profound gratitude.

Rev. Peter Woods and the congregation of MacKay United Church have heard my yearly talks on Remembrance Sundays, encouraged me to continue, and above all affirmed that this work has a value to them and to the church that goes beyond that of a mere work of history. I acknowledge with gratitude and affection the late Dorene Hirsch, who introduced me to the documentary resources available in the church archives, and Susan Pitt, who provided invaluable assistance in ferreting out pictures, artifacts, and documents from their hiding places.

Pierre Desrosiers, editor of the Mercury series, and its editorial board, have my heartfelt thanks for believing in this project and seeing it to fruition, with suggestions and excellent advice but also a degree of freedom. I am also grateful to Pascal Scallon-Chouinard of the Canadian Museum of History for his assistance, and to Martin Llewellyn and the editorial staff of the University of Ottawa Press for their care and professionalism. And not least to the anonymous readers of the original manuscript, whose comments provoked serious re-thinking—if not always agreement—and made this a better book.

Janet Uren shared some of her research for her forthcoming history of New Edinburgh, including a typescript memoir by Judge Walter Schroeder, and provided helpful advice, comments, and corrections. Beverley Mathesius at St. John Lutheran Church provided documents and background on the German community in New Edinburgh. Joy Heft, archivist at Lisgar Collegiate, supplied documents on those MacKay men who were students at

Ottawa Collegiate Institute. Stephen Cunliffe provided information on his grandfather, Thomas Isaac Jackson, and Martha Edmond gave permission to use the photograph of the Jackson house that she acquired in preparing her excellent history of Rockcliffe. I wish to thank Bob Cleary for memories of his grandfather John MacKenzie. I am also grateful to Dr. Kym Bird for her research on Clara Anderson, which brought to light the importance of her plays and the contribution they made to enhancing the role of women in the church. Thanks also to Dr. Eric Story for reading the draft chapter on Arthur Hawke.

Special mention must here be made of the information and knowledge gathered, and the generous assistance provided, by members of the Canadian Expeditionary Force Study Group, The Aerodrome Forum (theaerodrome.com), and other online fora. These meticulous researchers corrected mistakes, criticized interpretations, and pointed the way to sources both primary and secondary. Dwight Mercer of the CEF Study Group shared his extensive research on the Borden Motor Machine Gun Battery, as well as the manuscript "Reminiscences of Pte. Richard Wm. Mercer, 911016." Les Fowler in the same group, with others, transcribed the 900-page previously unpublished history of the Canadian Machine Gun Corps. "Regular 122" on the Aerodrome Forum steered me to a source of information crucial to investigating the fate of Erland Perney. I was also fortunate to share information with Tony Kellett, co-writer of an outstanding history of the Royal Canadian Hussars (Montreal) which contains a chapter on the 1st Canadian Motor Machine Gun Brigade. Brian Northgrave arranged to have some of my research posted on the website *Just Ottawa*, which led to meeting useful contacts and receiving useful information. Articles on the Stalker family appeared in 2018 on the *War and Society* Web Series of the Laurier Centre for the Study of Canada.

Descendants or relatives of several of the nineteen men from MacKay church who fell in the war provided information and pictures and corrected errors, and they were often pleased in turn to learn new things about their forebears. It was a surprise to find that one of the nineteen, George Selkirk Bothwell, was the uncle of Robert Bothwell, an old friend from our student days at the University of Toronto, who allowed me to use the materials in the Robert Bothwell Fonds at the University of Toronto Archives and shared information and memories. Without information provided by a descendant of Ella Bothwell Marion in Philadelphia, I would not have known her story after she left Ottawa. Ian and Linda Parker of Falkirk, Scotland, provided information on the Robertson family from Scottish records and corrected mistakes in my research; Walter Robertson, son of William Robertson, provided information on his family and some pictures; and Sheila Gauthier shared background on the Gaitens family. Pat Allen, Richard Porteous, and Steve McKenzie were sources on the Porteous family. Jeanne Mayo and

Colleen Mayo shared memories, insight, and crucial information to fill in the story of their grandfather Henry James Mayo, and of his widow's life after 1920. Without the help of Barbara Sheppard of Prince Rupert, I would never have learned of the second marriage of her grandfather Robert Stalker and her great-grandmother's fight for custody of his children; and I am grateful to Deborah Wawryk for information and Stalker family pictures. Cathryn Crocker enhanced my knowledge of the Crowe and Ryan families and corrected some mistakes in my draft. David Bluestein shared photographs of Leslie Tubman's medals. William Borland of Liverpool, with whom I connected through the kindness of Joy Heft, generously sent me copies of papers from the UK National Archives which he had gathered for his own research on Ewan Blackledge, who was Erland Perney's Observer on his fateful last flight. I am grateful to Jeff Smith for providing information, assistance, and pictures, on Jack McKenzie and his brother Sandy.

I have been, like so many others, the fortunate beneficiary of researchers and archivists who, especially during a time of pandemic, walked the extra mile to provide access to records and pictures. Helen Edwards of Victoria, British Columbia, researched information in the British Columbia Archives on the legal battle of Edith Stalker for custody of the Stalker children. Gary Thomson of the Dundee City Archives in Scotland shared his information on John Marshall and his family and researched Dundee and Perth city directories, and Alistair Tough furnished important background on the Dykebar Hospital. Alan McCullough of the Ottawa New Edinburgh Canoe Club provided a picture and information on the Perney-Tubman Trophy. Sue Warren of the Chaffey's Lockmaster's House Museum facilitated access to images from their marvellous collection of pictures of the rehabilitation centre on Fettercairn Island. Joseph Inverso of the Clifton Springs Historical Society quickly responded to requests for information on the nursing school attended by Elizabeth Ralph and a picture of her 1910 graduating class; Melanie Morin-Pelletier provided information and advice to flesh out Ralph's story; and just as this book was in its final editorial stages, Stephen Ralph Olney provided information and pictures of his step-grandmother. The staff of the Canadian War Museum Library made research over many weeks a pleasure; they were helpful in locating files and teaching me how to use databases. Special thanks to Shannyn Johnson of the CWM for locating and reproducing pictures. Thanks also to Claire Sutton, Signe Jeppesen, Glenn Charron, Olga Zeale, Katy Hull, and others behind the scenes at the Ottawa City Archives who steered me to documents and sources, assisted my research visits, and provided photos. The staff of Library and Archives Canada, Grant Vogl of the Bytown Museum, Anne-Marie Charuest of the Brome County Historical Society, and Charles Campbell of the Hockey Hall of Fame provided exemplary cooperation in response to requests for photographic material.

Most of all I want to express my profound gratitude to my wife, Carolyn, who not only encouraged me through this book's long gestation but brought her ruthless proof-reading and editorial skills to bear to ensure that, in spite of the large cast of characters and the inevitable technical detail, the prose would be accessible to a lay reader. She also took hundreds of pictures of Commonwealth Cemeteries and War Memorials which we visited on our memorable journey in the fall of 2015 to the places where MacKay soldiers are buried or memorialized, as well as during a visit to Perth, Scotland, in 2017. She continued to provide support and assistance during the last phase of editorial preparation even as she recovered from serious heart surgery. This book is dedicated to her, with all my love.

Lastly, I want to pay tribute to our daughters Elizabeth and Sarah, our friends and neighbours, and the pastoral care team at MacKay United Church, who stepped up to support us in so many ways at a difficult time. They exemplify the belief so profoundly held by the congregants of MacKay Presbyterian Church a century ago, that the truest expression of Christian faith is in acts of kindness, service, and love.

It goes without saying that all mistakes and *bêtises* that appear in this book are solely my responsibility.

Abbreviations

1 CMMGB	1st Canadian Motor Machine Gun Brigade
4 CMR	4th Canadian Mounted Rifles
8 CMR	8th Canadian Mounted Rifles
AWOL	Absent Without Leave
BASC	British Army Service Corps
CAC	Catholic Apostolic Church
CAMC	Canadian Army Medical Corps
CASC	Canadian Army Service Corps
CCS	Casualty Clearing Station
CEF	Canadian Expeditionary Force
CFA	Canadian Field Artillery
FP No. 1	Field Punishment No. 1
IRFU	Interprovincial Rugby Football Union
MT	Motor Transport
NCO	Non-Commissioned Officer
NECC	New Edinburgh Canoe Club (before 1915)
ONECC	Ottawa New Edinburgh Canoe Club (after 1915)
QAINS	Queen Alexandra's Imperial Nursing Service
OCI	Ottawa Collegiate Institute (Today Lisgar Collegiate)
OER	Ottawa Electric Railway
PF	Patriotic Fund
RAF	Royal Air Force
RCR	Royal Canadian Regiment
RFC	Royal Flying Corps
TB	Tuberculosis
VD	Venereal Disease

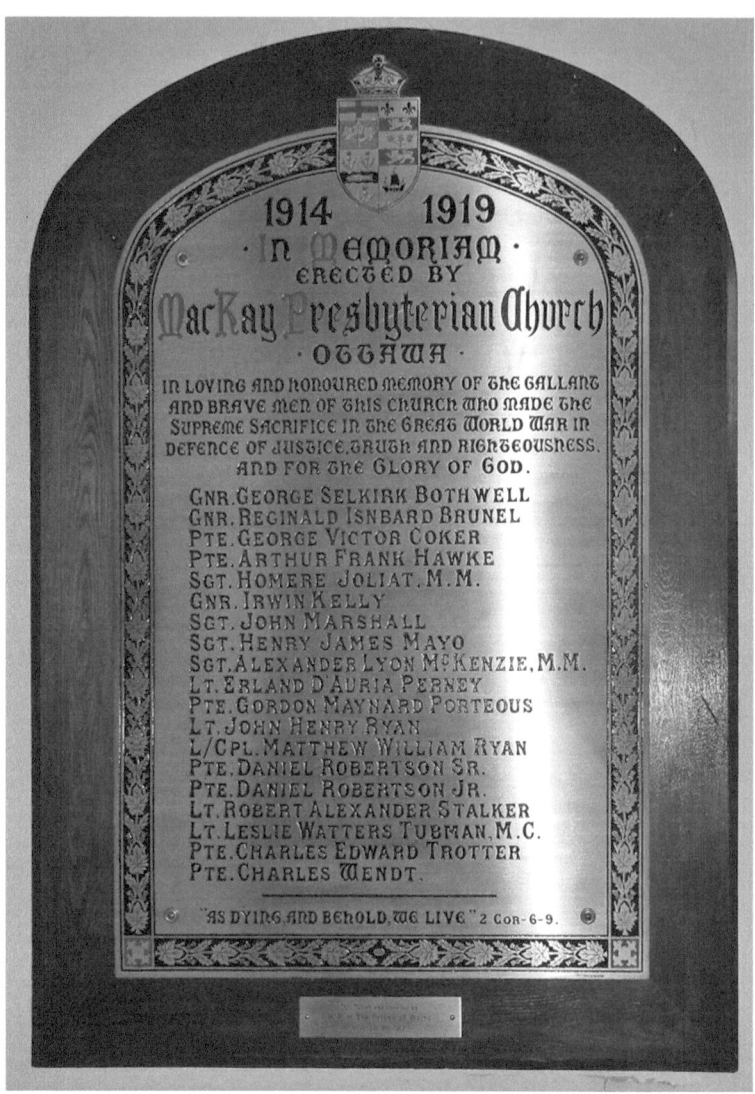

Introduction 1.1. In Memoriam plaque.
Source: MacKay United Church.

Introduction

On the walls of the Sanctuary at MacKay United Church in New Edinburgh, Ottawa, are two brass plaques on wooden tablets. One, the "Honour Roll," lists the names of the 140 men and one woman from what was then MacKay Presbyterian Church who served in the First World War. The other, "In Memoriam," gives the names of the nineteen of those who fell in the conflict. That 141 people enlisted in this war, out of a congregation of 364 members plus some three times more adherents, is an astonishing record of service, though by no means unique in Canada.

Who were these people? What was it about them, their church, and their community, that impelled them to fight in a far-off war? What did they experience on the battlefields of Europe? What was the impact of the war on their families, their church, and their community? The involvement of MacKay Presbyterian Church in the First World War is a story worth telling in itself, as the following pages will show. But it was also a small part of a great national enterprise that was strongly supported by the Protestant and English-speaking Catholic churches, and its experience paralleled that of thousands of other congregations, families, and communities throughout Canada. A detailed examination of a single church, the community it served, the soldiers it sent to war, and their families thus enriches our understanding not only of church history but also of the broader social history of Canada's experience of the First World War.

Such a study must begin by recognizing the profound conviction of the people of MacKay Presbyterian Church that they were fighting a just war for a cause they understood.[1] In the secular society of today, and after a century of vigorous debate about the causes, conduct, and meaning of the First World War, many people may be skeptical about this. But the basic requirement of any study of history will always be the need—as far as it is humanly possible—to enter that other country that is the past with an open mind, to walk with the people in it, to try to understand them as they were—in the words of Othello, "nothing extenuate, Nor set down aught in malice." In examining the experience of this church and its community at war, this means accepting the reality and recognizing the power of the ideals, faith, and beliefs that led so many men and their families at MacKay Presbyterian Church, and throughout Canada, to endure so much in what they were convinced was a just cause.

Though challenged by science and secularism, Christianity in the early twentieth century was still central to the Canadian experience.[2] Its stories, symbols, and vocabulary permeated every area of culture, discourse, and daily life. Religious leaders, teachers, and public intellectuals were influential figures in shaping the nation, defining its identity, and guiding its response to the social and moral issues of the day.[3] The available evidence indicates that the minister and leading congregants of MacKay Presbyterian Church fully embraced the conviction of their denomination that an immanent God was working in history. They subscribed to the Social Gospel belief that Christians should seek to realize the Kingdom of God on Earth through evangelism, moral reform, the redemption of individuals through the power and example of Christ, and through legislated social reforms, such as temperance and Sabbath observance, that would create a more Godly society.

Christian teachings went hand in hand—indeed, were intertwined—with another powerful conviction: that Canada and the British Empire represented the apogee of progress and Christian civilization, and that the Empire was, in the words of historian Carl Berger, "a providential agency, the greatest secular instrument for good in the world," with an evangelical mission to bring peace, progress, and prosperity to every land.[4] This conviction had been manifested in New Edinburgh in the form of overwhelming support for the Boer War; it was reinforced by the nearby presence of Rideau Hall and the staff of the Governor General; it was extolled in the schools and by the popular press; and it was expressed in patriotic ritual, militia participation, and cadet training. Although they maintained their Calvinist conviction that the church was the conscience of the people and the judge of the state, Presbyterians by 1914 had come to make, in the words of Stuart Macdonald, "little distinction between Empire and God's Kingdom, between what was the will of King George and what was the will of King Jesus."[5]

Thus, although Presbyterians had earnestly preached peace among nations, they were not pacifists. When war broke out, they had no doubt that they had a solemn duty to take up arms. Germany's militarism, its defiance of international order, and its savage treatment of innocent Belgium had to be punished. The Empire and all it stood for had to be defended. Justice, righteousness, and peace had to be restored to the world. This was not a duty they could evade or wish away. It was not a question of whether God was on their side, but whether they would be on the side of God. At the same time, they could hope that the service, suffering, and sacrifice called forth by war would purge their society of its selfishness and materialism, redeem their people, and bring closer the realization of the Kingdom of God on Earth.

Of course, churchgoers were not theology professors or public intellectuals and we cannot know what every individual in this (or any) church actually thought. Some of those who enlisted in the war, especially older recruits, were full members of the church—regular attendees with deep Christian faith. Others, especially young men, might not have been as religious or attended church as regularly (though their parents and, in many cases, their sisters might have). It is a truism that in this, as in all wars, young men sign up for a wide variety of reasons, mixed and matched in varying combinations—animal spirits, desire for adventure, need to prove oneself, peer and societal pressure, perhaps the need for a job or support for one's family, among many others. Most MacKay men who signed up in 1914 and early 1915 would probably not have been able to say much more than something like: "it was what you did," or "I just felt I had to." But all had been reared in Christian homes. Most had gone to Sunday School, many were part of church clubs or organizations—including sports teams, which were sponsored by the church as a means of channeling masculine energy in a wholesome direction and moulding "manly" Christians. In a myriad of ways, whether or not they always lived up to them, they had absorbed and been shaped by the Christian beliefs and values that surrounded them.

Whatever the mix of motivations for each individual, it is undeniable that belief in God, country, and Empire was a powerful element, not only for men to sign up but for their families and church to support and encourage them. As the war entered its second year, many of the factors that might have motivated men to sign up earlier in the conflict no longer existed. There were now plentiful jobs, with good pay, at home. With living costs rising rapidly, soldiers could no longer assume that their families would cope on their assigned pay and a separation allowance. Any naïve ideas they might earlier have held about the nature of modern war had long since been dispelled. Thousands of men had been killed. Letters and news from the front, however censored, had made it clear that there was nothing glorious or romantic about the dirty and dangerous world of trench warfare. The experience of the men at the front—literally and figuratively far from home—had profoundly changed them. Those at home could not fully comprehend this, but they were not unaware of it either. Yet in spite of all this, men from MacKay continued to enlist until the pool of suitable manpower began to dry up. Families remained steadfast in their support for the war, even as it claimed more lives, destroyed more families, led to privation and social unrest, and divided the nation.

A year after the war ended, the congregation of MacKay church expressed in symbolic form the faith and patriotism that had inspired and sustained them through the long conflict, in the In Memoriam plaque they created to honour those who had fallen. At the top is the Canadian coat of arms capped with a crown; the border consists of alternating maple leaves and thistles; an inscription above the names declares that these "gallant and brave men" had "made the Supreme Sacrifice in the Great World War in defence of justice, truth, and righteousness, and for the Glory of God"; and a verse from 2 Corinthians 6—"as dying, and yet behold we live"—indicates that they had suffered to advance the Kingdom of God, redeemed themselves and the world, and would not be forgotten. A sign below the plaque says that it was unveiled by the Prince of Wales, the living embodiment of the Empire and its ideals for which they had fought. The evidence is that in the years that followed, this plaque continued to reflect their belief.

Those who attended MacKay Presbyterian Church comprised over half the population of New Edinburgh, and the church and its minister reached out to and served this community in many ways that went well beyond its Sunday services. New Edinburgh was a neighbourhood in transition, within a city that was itself evolving from a lumber village into the political capital of a nation undergoing unprecedented expansion. Its roots were in the lumber industry and the factories at Rideau Falls, but it also contained Rideau Hall and was becoming a suburb for professional people; and neighbouring Rockcliffe was beginning to develop as an upscale parkland village. Pioneer settlers and wealthy families mingled with a flood of new immigrants and a substantial German community. Most of its residents were people of modest means who took pride in their work, their integrity, and their family values. New Edinburgh produced an astonishing number of excellent athletes, and it had a strong tradition of militia service. At this moment in history, balanced between the past and the future, New Edinburgh had a unique sense of community, continuity, and local identity. As the story of a community at war, seen through the lens of its largest church, this book adds to a body of literature about the experience of communities in the First World War, ranging from provinces to large cities, townships, small towns, villages, and churches.[6]

But it does not confine itself to the home front. Central to this book, as they were to the church and its community, are the nineteen men who fell in the war, and their families. Twelve of them served with the infantry, three with the artillery, two with the Royal Flying Corps, one with the Borden Motor Machine Gun Battery, and one with the British Army Service Corps. The first to die was killed near Ypres in the autumn of 1915; the last, a tuberculosis patient, was probably a victim of the Spanish Flu a few days before the end of the war—and both of these men came from the large German community in New Edinburgh. Four were officers, including Lt. Leslie Watters Tubman, an inspiration to his men who was promoted in the field. Two won the Military Medal and one the Military Cross. Some fell in desperate battles, like Homère Joliat who fought against overwhelming odds to slow the German offensive in March 1918; or dogfights in the air, like John Henry Ryan during "Bloody April" 1917 in the Arras Sector; or artillery duels, like Irwin Kelly at the Drocourt-Quéant Line during the Hundred Days. Others, like George Victor Coker or Mathew William Ryan, died with tragic randomness, victims of artillery or sniper fire, or, like Daniel Robertson Sr. and Gordon Porteous, lost forever in the hideous mud and carnage on the last day of the Battle of the Somme. John Marshall succumbed in a Scottish hospital to the complications of sunstroke suffered while serving in Egypt. Their sacrifice in this great cause was celebrated in the church, which pledged that their example and their memory would be treasured forever. But for their heartbroken families, pride was mingled with profound sorrow. Six of them left widows to cope as best they could, five of whom had children who would grow up without their fathers. One chapter of this book will thus be devoted to each of these men, in the order that they fell. It will include the stories of their family members who also served (which together with the nineteen who fell comprise almost 30 percent of the total of those from MacKay who enlisted) and of their families. Focusing on these soldiers and their families allows us to explore the main themes of this book in depth.

In life, these men had been parts of a vast war machine. In death, most of them became components of a network of Imperial and Commonwealth war cemeteries and memorials in France and Belgium which convey powerful messages about this and all wars, about service and sacrifice, as well as about sorrow and loss. Some of these cemeteries, designed by famous architects, are huge and awe-inspiring; some are small and intimate; some are in busy urban centres; others are engulfed by suburban housing, or in parks near battlefields, or in remote areas and open fields. But once inside the gate, the quasi-religious symbolism of the Great Cross and the Stone of Remembrance, the rows of identical stones, the ordered design of the spaces, and the beauty of trees and gardens, transform these symbols of sorrow into oases of peace, calm reflection, and inspiration.[7]

My wife and I visited all the cemeteries where the fallen from MacKay church are buried, or the memorials containing the names of the four men who have no known graves (including the Menin Gate in Ypres where, on October 14, 2015, I had the honour of reciting the Exhortation at the nightly Last Post ceremony). In our search we met many Canadians, including young people at the Vimy Memorial, who said that for the first time they understood what it means to be a Canadian. But we were also uncomfortably aware that this was not an experience that most of the families of the MacKay fallen would have shared. The governments of the British Empire had decided that no soldiers' bodies would be repatriated; all would lie near where they fell, and there would be no special memorials to individuals. Families were allowed, and encouraged, to provide a short and often moving epitaph for their loved one's headstone—and several MacKay families did so. But most could not afford transatlantic travel and they had, in effect, lost their son or husband twice. In telling the stories of these nineteen soldiers, it therefore seemed not only appropriate but essential to provide a brief description, with pictures, of the cemetery or memorial which most of their families never got to see.[8]

In addition to the fallen are the stories of the other soldiers of MacKay church who served, in whatever capacity, who came back, wounded or whole, with good memories of comradeship and recurring nightmares of what they had endured. I have examined CEF service files for 128 of the 141. There is also substantial information on the two who served in the Royal Flying Corps, one who was in the Royal Canadian Navy, and two who served in the British Army. Only eight are "unknown": six who attended the church and enlisted before the middle of 1915, but on whom we have no information regarding how or where they served or what happened to them afterward, and two others on whom we have no information whatever. The soldiers from MacKay church were a microcosm of the thousands of citizen soldiers who served in the various branches of the Canadian and British forces during the First World War, and their collective experience of the war mirrors that of the CEF as a whole. But in some ways, they were significantly different. Half of them signed up during the first year of the war, and most of the rest before the middle of 1916. Two-thirds of those who enlisted were Canadian-born, including many whose families had lived in New Edinburgh for decades. There are almost two dozen examples of two, three, or four brothers enlisting, as well as several fathers and sons (or stepsons). Since they generally belonged to infantry battalions and artillery batteries recruited from the Ottawa area (as well as specialist units, like forestry battalions), the men from MacKay church were more heavily involved in some actions than in others.

Behind all the stories of soldiers—and the bedrock of any study of a church and a community at war—are the stories of their families. For the most part the women of MacKay church, whatever they considered their social status, saw themselves primarily as Christian wives and mothers, helping each other and their community with private support and charity. Wives and daughters were more likely than their husbands and sons to be members of the church, and they played an important, though subservient, role. Through these church organizations and activities, women, including unmarried daughters living at home, could have independent and respected roles, and could wield some political influence on causes like temperance.[9]

They, like their community and their church, were in a time of transition when they suddenly faced the life-defining challenge of war. Church women held bazaars and bake sales, gave concerts, and performed plays to raise funds for war work; they made jam for the hospital and sewed garments for the Red Cross; they supported their local battalions; they sent Christmas parcels to soldiers. Those with children and absent husbands faced increasingly straitened circumstances. We have no record of the role of the Patriotic Fund (PF) in assisting families at MacKay; church women raised money for the PF and many in the congregation contributed, but there was no official link with the PF. Some families probably got PF assistance or some form of private support, and some lived with other families or relatives. There is no evidence at MacKay church that any of this was seen as demeaning or what Desmond

Morton and Nancy Christie describe as moral regulation of working-class women.[10] The women of MacKay church, whatever their social rank or role, and whatever their anguish over its consequences, were as patriotically committed as the men, and as staunch in their belief in the rightness of the war. And one, Elizabeth Ralph, a member of a prominent church family who had carved out a career as a trained nurse, actually served—first as a nursing sister with a British organization and then with the Canadian Army Medical Corps.

Each in their own way, they coped with war, sickness, and grief—including the official notice, often late and usually in agonizingly vague detail, that their loved one had fallen, or had been wounded, "somewhere in France." Clarinda Stalker lost one son at Vimy, another was seriously wounded at Passchendaele, another suffered illness and fought in the Hundred Days. Jennie Tubman had four sons and a nephew in uniform, one of whom was wounded and one killed. Mary Robertson saw four sons and her husband go off to war; her husband and one son were killed, and another son was seriously wounded. May Mayo, whose husband was killed at Vimy, raised two boys after the war while working as a cleaner in the Parliament Buildings. Another widow, Ella Bothwell, left her three children to be raised by their grandparents. Margaret Perney's grief was almost intolerable as she waited for months after the war for confirmation that her flying officer son was not coming home.

And while the war raged in Europe, there were tragedies at home as well. Mabel McElroy, having lost her two brothers in the war, died at age 38, a few weeks after the birth of a daughter (who also died a few weeks later)—perhaps, as one death notice suggested, of grief. Elizabeth Lamb, an Indigenous Canadian who had come from the interior of Quebec to work as a domestic in the minister's home, and had married at the church, died at age 26 giving birth to her fourth child, who also died. Tuberculosis claimed the lives of a great number of people, including many members of the Haak family and three daughters of Clarinda Stalker. Outbreaks of diseases like diphtheria and typhoid fever were a constant threat due to inadequate water and sewage treatment, and influenza ravaged the community even as the war was drawing to a close.

The impact of war did not end for these families on November 11, 1918. The soldiers coming back from Europe had to learn, with the help of their families, to readjust to civilian and family life. Some men had seen hard service. Others had worked behind the lines or had been discharged because of ill health. Some men would never recover from injuries and would die at a young age. Others suffered permanent disabilities. Some had memories of the war that would not go away, and their families also shared their pain. Others renewed their athletic activities. Some men launched careers, became successful businessmen, pillars of the church, and in several cases city aldermen.

Others simply returned to what they had been—honest, hard-working tradesmen, skilled and unskilled workers. They married, started families, and in many cases left New Edinburgh to move into newer, postwar housing. New Edinburgh changed as it adjusted to the new world of the 1920s and MacKay Presbyterian became MacKay United Church. A surprising number of the returned men continued to be affiliated with the military, as reservists, clerks, or serving soldiers.[11]

The experience of war profoundly changed the church and the men who fought in it. No one could think about war in 1919 as they had done in 1914. War had undoubtedly challenged their faith, and in some cases destroyed it. Nonetheless, the MacKay church experience appears to support the conclusions of Ian Miller, Jonathan Vance, Stuart Macdonald, and others, that for most, the basic elements of their faith remained and were even reinforced by the war. They continued to believe that the war had been a just one, and that their husbands, sons, brothers, and fathers had not died in vain. And when the Second World War broke out, 189 men and women from MacKay church answered the call, including several sons and daughters of those who had fought in the First World War, and even a few veterans. In all the years since 1919, MacKay church has continued to commemorate Remembrance Day, no longer as the aching memory of a fallen soldier or the recollection of service in a distant war, but as an acknowledgement of a time in history that shaped the country in which they lived, and of the sacrifice, courage, and resilience that made possible the world we live in today.[12]

This book begins with introductory chapters describing the community and the church. There follow chapters on the church at war—including the soldiers who enlisted and the families at home—during each year of the conflict. Interspersed with these are chapters on the men who fell in each year of the war—which include not only their war experience but the stories of family members who also served; of families who had to watch and wait and endure sorrow; and of parents, family members, and children who had to cope with loss. Final chapters describe the return of the men; their readjustment, and that of their families, to a changed world, new responsibilities, and the memory of a life-altering experience; the evolution of the church as it became MacKay United Church; and the enduring memory of those who had made the supreme sacrifice.

A Note on Sources and Methods

The decision to write about the war experience of a particular church, its families, its soldiers, and the community of which it was a part—rather than choosing a story because a body of evidence was available—presented a serious research challenge. That it was possible at all is a tribute to the wealth of digitized source material now online, and to the search engines and algorithms available on web portals, which allow this material to be accessed in a way that could not have been done even two decades ago (and certainly not, in the final stages of this research, during a pandemic). This project thus provides a good example of how new sources and methods can be used to bring to life, however imperfectly, people who did not leave a rich legacy of information on their lives and families. It may provide a useful road map for scholars—public historians, historians of churches, communities, businesses, schools, or military regiments or services—and genealogists or family historians, who are tasked with telling a story where the subject, and not the sources, is the starting point.[13]

The archives of MacKay United Church contain the Communion Rolls; wedding, baptismal, and burial registers and minutes of the Session, the Board of Managers, the Ladies' Aid, and the Annual General Meetings of MacKay Presbyterian Church, as well as pictures and artifacts. These provide important information on the governance and workings of the church and the makeup of its congregation. But, beyond a novel and some plays written by the minister's wife, there is little on theology; no box of collected sermons of its minister; no treasure trove of records about the thoughts and feelings of the people, such as soldiers' diaries, extensive published memoirs, or trunks full of family letters; not even the records of the many other church organizations that played such a central role in the life of the church and the broader community. The story of a church and a community at war had largely to be built, layer by layer, from the stories of the soldiers and of dozens of families—stories that had to be assembled from the often-fragmentary sources available.

Of course, this study accessed a variety of archival materials, published documents and memoirs, and secondary sources, as indicated in the bibliography and notes, as well as materials in local history and church repositories. It also benefited from the information and knowledge gathered, and the generous assistance provided, by the thousands of dedicated amateur military historians in the CEF Study Group, The Aerodrome Forum, and other online fora—a truly amazing resource which shows the contribution individual people, working together and connected by technology, can make to our understanding of the past. I was fortunate to make contact—often through some of these groups—with descendants of several soldiers from MacKay. They provided information and, in some cases, helped me learn things I could not have found out in any other way. They are listed in the acknowledgements.

But most of the primary sources concerning the people whose stories comprise this book were located through the growing databases of digitized records and the increasingly sophisticated search engines and algorithms in a number of key portals. For the stories of the soldiers, the information now available online—the service files of the soldiers, Circumstances of Death Registers, war diaries, citation records, and other information on the CEF which is itemized in endnotes—is a testament to the ongoing project of Library and Archives Canada of digitizing these records. I was able to get British military records by applying to the National Archives, Kew, and from the online Royal Flying Corps People Index, Casualty Cards, and information obtained through the online portal Forces War Records, as well as the Commonwealth War Graves Commission website. Ancestry.ca provided a portal to a cornucopia of birth, marriage, and death records; immigration records and ships' registers; census information; electoral registers; and other sources not only in Canada but in the United States, England, Scotland, and Ireland. The search engines in newspapers.com made it possible to search newspapers, including 80 years of the two daily newspapers in Ottawa, to locate relevant articles including obituaries, and to cross-reference sources and information and explore ancillary topics, in a way that would have been impossible otherwise. The Beechwood Cemetery Registers, digitized and with search assistance, provided information on the hundreds of people from the community who are buried there.

All these portals allowed me to assemble mini-biographies for each of the hundreds of people involved, drawn from service records, city directories, birth records, census documents, newspaper obituaries, and church records—all but the latter accessible online. For each soldier in the CEF, his or her service record was accessed, and for each family, city directories over several years, fire insurance maps, and the MacKay Communion Rolls were consulted. The records of the MacKay Session and Ladies' Aid are the basis for discussion of the activities of the church. The volume of information thus gathered raises another problem, namely that if every source were cited for each fact, endnotes would proliferate to the point of absurdity. I have therefore decided not to provide references to service files, city directories, and church documents such as Communion Rolls and minutes of Session, unless there is a particular reason to do so. These sources are all itemized in the bibliography (including the service number for each soldier so that their online files can be easily found).

Needless to say, information from online sources had to be used with care. Only documentary information accessed through ancestry.ca and other portals was used as source material. Family trees and commentaries were often useful but were varied in their reliability and were never treated as definitive sources. Documents available online are documents like any others and have to be used critically. Soldiers lied about their ages on their attestation papers. Census takers sometimes got it wrong. City directories and other sources misspelled names. Newspapers are seldom an infallible source, though the standard of accuracy in, for example, obituaries, was generally pretty good.

The staff of Beechwood Cemetery helped me to discover that Arthur Hawke was really August Haak, and that the Commonwealth War Graves information about the location of his burial place was wrong—this has now been corrected. However, the quantity of information in the databases of online portals, and their algorithms and search engines, also made it possible to correct mistakes that otherwise might have been made—as an example, to verify the real birthdate of a soldier by reference to birth, marriage, census, and death information and where applicable, immigration and ship's records.

As with any research, none of this was necessarily simple or straightforward. There are mistakes in the transcription of documents in databases and search engines do not catch everything. There is often a complex bit of sleuthing required to track down a document that does not show up in an ordinary search, and documents or leads on one subject pop up when one is looking for something else. Searching out documents and sources online has its own set of techniques which one learns with experience, but in concept it is not different from looking for "hard documents" in the "real world." It is just that hundreds of hours in one's study in front of a computer, making contacts through websites, and communicating by e-mail, have made possible research that would otherwise have taken several lifetimes—for that is what it would have taken to search out in archives in many different locations the documents and sources used in this book, if indeed it could have been done at all.

In the end, there remains the uncomfortable reality that there was much that I do not and will probably never know. I could not contact descendants of all the soldiers who fell. Family recollections differ in their accounts, depending on distance and points of view—and there are limits on how far one should intrude into family stories. Documents provide only a fragmentary picture. To craft what might appear a more interesting narrative, one is sorely tempted to fill in the gaps, to extrapolate beyond what can be documented from evidence, to imagine what people thought or put words in their mouths. I have chosen as far as possible to resist these temptations, not only because I am an historian and not a novelist, but also because, as it turns out, this story needs no embellishment.

Annex: The Names of those from MacKay Presbyterian Church who served in the First World War, as they appear on the Honour Roll

Those who fell are marked with an asterisk.

Nursing Sister Elizabeth K. Ralph

John F. Askwith	William Gaitens	Russell E. Muhlig	William B. Slinn
John R. Bothwell	Thomas K. Gerard	Alfred Merrit	S. Shirley Slinn
*George S. Bothwell	Nairn Grant	Fred Munro	John I. Slinn
Ernest Benedict	Dr. David M. Graham	William H. Milne	William F. Stevenson
*Reginald I. Brunel[14]	Robert Hill	Chas. G. R. Mathieson	Robert B. Smith
A. Ivan Brunel	Gordon Hughes	F. H. Myles[15]	B. Cleveland Stevenson
Horace E. Barnes	*Arthur F. Hawke	Elmer A. Moodie	Thomas E. Samways
Levi D. Boston	Joseph A. Hillas	*Alex L. McKenzie	George A. Sayles
George F. Beardsley	Andrew Inch[16]	John L. McKenzie	Arthur Sproule
*G. Victor Coker	*Homère Joliat	D. Kenneth McKenzie	*Robert A. Stalker
James Cairncross	Thomas I. Jackson	John McGillivray	G. Fred. Stalker
Gordon H. Clark	Thomas N. Jackson	John McKenzie	A. Douglas Stalker
Alex O. Clark	Arch. M. Jardine	Dr. Neil McLeod[17]	George H. F. Silsby
Norman Cameron	Andrew Jardine	A. Stuart McLaurin	William Silsby
George Cruickshank	Fred. J. Jamieson	Dalton McCarthy	John E. J. Simpson
Albert H. Currie	A. Reginald Johnston	Gerald F. McLatchie	*Leslie W. Tubman
William A. Currie	*Irwin Kelly	K. Wallace McPhail	T. Raymond Tubman
Robert H. Curtis	Samuel J. Kelly	John McGowan	W. Reed Tubman
Robert L. Drake	Albert R. Kendall	Olaf Olsen	N. Harry Tubman
Jason S. Davidson	Dr. Carson J. Kendall	John Powers	Elmer Tubman
Clifford L. Erskine	Herbert C. Love	George Powers	*Charles E. Trotter
John Edwards	James Leach	Alfred Philp	William A. Williams
George B. English	Walter S. Lindsay	*Erland D. Perney	Stanley Williams
Angus Edwardson	William H. Lanceley	Cecil E. Putman	Norman K. Wilson[18]
Clifford E. Earl	Percy B. Lister	*Gordon M. Porteous	Thomas Winton
R. Elliott	Alexander Masson	*John H. Ryan[19]	F. S. Wright
William J. Fallis	Joseph A. Munro	*M. William Ryan	William H. Wilson
George E. Farmer	*John Marshall	*Daniel Robertson Sr.	Arthur S. Wilson
William J. Farmer	Sidney B. Mansell	*Daniel Robertson Jr.	Russell Whyte[20]
Charles T. Foad	Percy T. Mansell	George Robertson	Edmund J. Watkins
William O. Finter	Emile A. F. May	William Robertson	Arthur K. Watkins
Robert H. Finter	Oscar V. A. May	John Regan	George T. Watson
Abraham Ferguson	*Henry J. Mayo	Herbert H. Rolt	A. John Wilson
Henry W. Ferguson	Gordon J. C. Munro	W. Harold A. Short	*Charles Wendt
T. Ernest Gardiner[21]	W. Douglas Munro	Milton D. Short	Charles W. Powers[22]

1 NEW EDINBURGH

MacKay Presbyterian (now United) Church is situated in New Edinburgh, a pleasant neighbourhood within the City of Ottawa. The oldest part of New Edinburgh is located between the Rideau River, where it empties into the Ottawa River at the Rideau Falls, and the grounds of Rideau Hall, the residence of the Governor General of Canada. It contains the official residence of the prime minister and several diplomatic missions, including those of France, Spain, Vietnam, and South Africa. North of Rideau Hall is Rockcliffe, a parkland village containing many ambassadorial residences and large houses. From the mid-nineteenth century on, New Edinburgh has been a popular place for public servants and business and professional people to live. In recent decades some of the older houses have been replaced or modernized, and the village itself has expanded north and east from its original boundaries. Yet for all the changes that have been made over the years, New Edinburgh retains much of the ambience of the small industrial village it once was, which owed its existence to three rivers and a canal.

The Ottawa River had been for many years a highway for commerce, on which rafts of square timber from the Upper Ottawa Valley floated down to markets in England and the United States. Emptying into the Ottawa opposite New Edinburgh is the Gatineau River, which provided access to the farms and rich timberlands of West Quebec. The Rideau River, flowing from the other direction, past New Edinburgh and around several islands before it drops into the Ottawa at the Rideau Falls, drains a system of lakes and rivers that form part of the Rideau Canal and Waterway connecting Ottawa with Kingston. But the lower part of the Rideau is too shallow and full of rapids to be navigable. It had to be bypassed by a spectacular set of eight locks that rise from the Ottawa River and a canal connecting them to the main river at Hog's Back Falls some 10 kilometres upstream. It was the construction of these locks that brought Thomas McKay to what was then called Bytown in 1826.[1] It was the industrial potential of the Rideau Falls that convinced him to stay and led him to create New Edinburgh.

Born in Perth, Scotland, McKay had come to Canada in 1817 and had worked on the Lachine Canal and other projects in Montreal. In 1826, with a partner, he was awarded the contract to build the first eight locks on the

Rideau Canal, and he was later contracted to build other projects. With the profits from these enterprises, he acquired 1,100 acres of land to the north and east of the Rideau Falls, comprising present-day New Edinburgh, Rockcliffe, Lindenlea, Manor Park, part of Beechwood Cemetery, and part of the former city of Vanier. He leased land around the Rideau Falls and over the years developed industries that used its water power, including a five-storey flour mill (the largest in Upper Canada at that time), a grist mill, a bakery, and the first textile mill in Ottawa, which was soon weaving a distinctive cloth that won a medal for quality at the 1851 Great Exhibition in London. He also built and leased out a distillery. In 1846 he and his son-in-law John MacKinnon built a sawmill which by the second year of its operation was producing 2.4 million board feet of lumber annually. Later factories made specialty products such as sashes, laths, doors, blinds, and shingles.

Figure 1.1. P. Checkly, *Mills at New Edinburgh*, c. 1895; watercolour on paper. Source: Bytown Museum P826.

To ship these products to the United States, a consortium in which McKay was an investor built the first railway into Ottawa from Prescott on the St. Lawrence River. This line cut across the southwest corner of New Edinburgh and crossed the Rideau River to its terminus near where the Lester B. Pearson building now stands.

For all these enterprises McKay recruited skilled workers, many from his native Scotland. In 1834, he began to lay out the village of New Edinburgh as a model industrial town, fronting on what has become Sussex Drive. In 1854, he built a house for his son-in-law John MacKinnon, which was later the home of Sir John A. Macdonald, who named it Earnscliffe; it is now the Official Residence of the British High Commission. For himself, McKay built a mansion, Rideau Hall, on 65 acres of forest which was later developed into gardens and parkland. When he died in 1855, he had not only achieved business success but had gained social prominence as a community builder, a justice of the peace, a colonel of militia, and Tory politician and member of the Legislative Council.[2]

Figure 1.2. Rideau Hall, Ottawa c. 1926; photographic postcard.
Source: Bytown Museum, P2017.

But many of his enterprises ran into trouble in his last years, and large debts—especially from the railway project that went in and out of bankruptcy until it became part of the Canadian Pacific system—threatened McKay's legacy. His last surviving son died a few years after McKay, and his son-in-law John MacKinnon died intestate, leaving further debts. It fell to another son-in-law, Thomas Coltrin Keefer, a pioneer engineer and visionary, to rescue the estate from disaster. The lumber mills were leased out and later sold off, and by 1894 the Rideau Falls operations were consolidated in the hands of the W. C. Edwards Company. In 1864, Rideau Hall was leased and then sold to the government to house the Governor General of Canada. Keefer himself bought a mansion, Rockcliffe Manor, where he also housed his mother-in-law and his widowed sister-in-law, Annie (MacKay) MacKinnon and her children. Three years after the death of his first wife, Elizabeth, he married Annie. Keefer began to develop the Rockcliffe portion of the MacKay estate as a parkland village outside the city limits.[3]

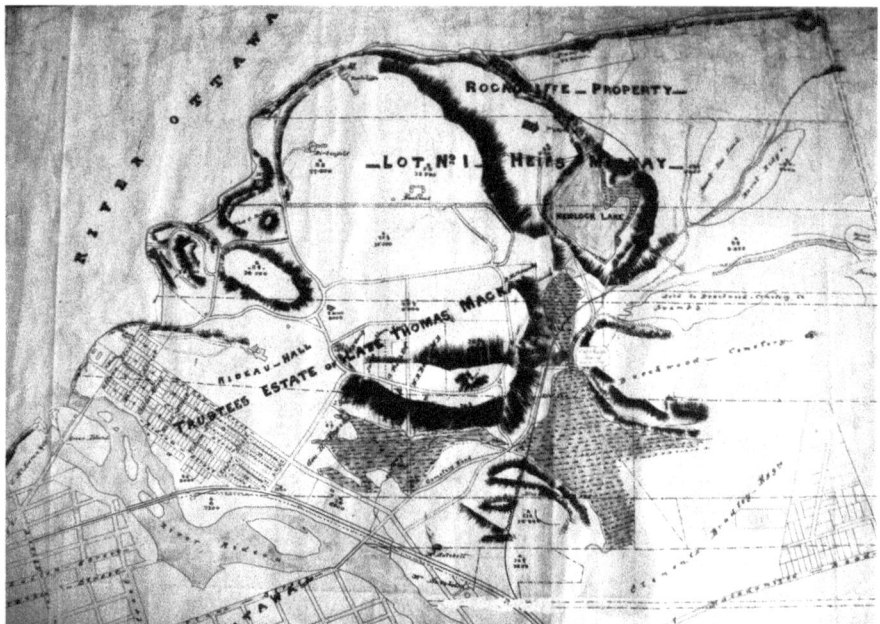

Figure 1.3. Map of Thomas MacKay estate, showing lands available for sale and development including present-day Rockcliffe and Manor Park. The original village of New Edinburgh is at the centre left, with streets laid out and house lots surveyed.
Source: MacKay United Church.

Most important for the immediate future was Keefer's aggressive promotion of New Edinburgh. He surveyed the land east of the original village, between Charles Street and what is now Dufferin Road, laying out new roads and building lots. These sold quickly as the village drew in not only industrial workers, but professional people and civil servants in the expanding government of what was now the Dominion of Canada. In 1870 Keefer inaugurated a horse-drawn tramway running along Sussex Street (later Sussex Drive) from Rockcliffe Park to downtown. In the 1890s the Ottawa Electric Railway, built by two Ottawa pioneers, Thomas Ahearn and Warren Soper, opened a main line to New Edinburgh along Beechwood Avenue. Its tracks ran down Crichton Street and connected to the Sussex line, which it absorbed and electrified, and it had an office and workshop on Sussex Street as well.[4] With easy transport to downtown businesses and government offices, New Edinburgh grew rapidly. Incorporated as a village with some 500 people in 1867, it had almost doubled its population when it was annexed to the City of Ottawa in 1887 as Rideau Ward.[5]

The industrial heart of New Edinburgh, and the source of direct or indirect employment to many of its residents, remained the complex of industries operated by W. C. Edwards at Rideau Falls. At its height, the Edwards lumber mill produced 50 million board feet per annum and employed up to 2,000 men at various times during the year. The Patterson and Law Caledonia Foundry, built to supply the mills with machinery, was by 1897 selling products throughout the country. But in 1907 the Edwards mills and factory complex caught fire, and its lumber piles burned for a week. Though it was rebuilt and a hydro-electric station at Rideau Falls was inaugurated, the company never regained its market share, and although the Edwards industries remained the major employer in the village, the balance began to shift away from large-scale industrial employment.[6] Smaller industries sprang up in various parts of New Edinburgh, such as a mica factory,[7] a metal works, a furniture factory, as well as rail sidings, warehouses, and workshops.

Figure 1.4. "Sash and Door Factory, Ottawa at the Rideau Falls," taken from "W. C. Edwards & Co. Ltd. Saw Mills and Lumber Yards c. 1897"; silver gelatin photograph.
Source: Bytown Museum p1839.

By 1914, Crichton Street (which during the period of this study was usually spelled Creighton) had become the "main street" of New Edinburgh. Sussex Street still had the workshops and offices of the electric railway, a post and telegraph office, a fire station, a grocery store, and other businesses. At the foot of John Street there was a wharf from which a steamer ran to Gatineau every 30 minutes. However, a growing number of small businesses on Crichton Street, sometimes in converted houses—a butcher shop, confectionery, drug stores, a Chinese laundry, a shoemaker, and other

Figure 1.5. "Saw Mill at Ottawa," taken from "W. C. Edwards & Co. Ltd. Saw Mills and Lumber Yards c. 1897"; silver gelatin photograph.
Source: Bytown Museum p1839.

businesses that came and went—provided convenient services to an expanding community. A grocery store at 42 Crichton Street was owned from 1883–1902 by William Tubman and was taken over in 1902 by William McCreery, whose family would operate it for eight decades. From 1896 to 1913, Breary Slinn operated a bakery, ice cream parlour, and soda fountain at 177 Crichton Street. A number of women also worked from their homes as dressmakers, hairdressers, and music teachers.

As New Edinburgh grew, newcomers from the region and from overseas added diversity to its older Scottish, Irish, and English population. Many people, including some French Canadians, came to New Edinburgh from West Quebec and the Upper Ottawa Valley because of the Edwards mills and factories. A growing demand for carpenters, bricklayers, plasterers, painters, and other trades attracted a wave of skilled British immigrants. A Chinese family opened a laundry on Crichton Street in 1904. Perhaps the most important minority was a growing German community. German settlers, mainly from Pomerania, had originally taken up land in Renfrew County, but by the 1880s many had migrated to Sandy Hill and New Edinburgh, where they were joined by newcomers from the old country.[8] They found work in the Edwards mills and other industries, and later many of them worked on the Ottawa Electric Railway. By 1914 this community had expanded from the older parts of the village to the newly opened streets to the south and east of Dufferin Road. Most were labourers with modest incomes and large families—the surviving houses from that period are small frame dwellings which, for the most part, the original Germans built and owned.

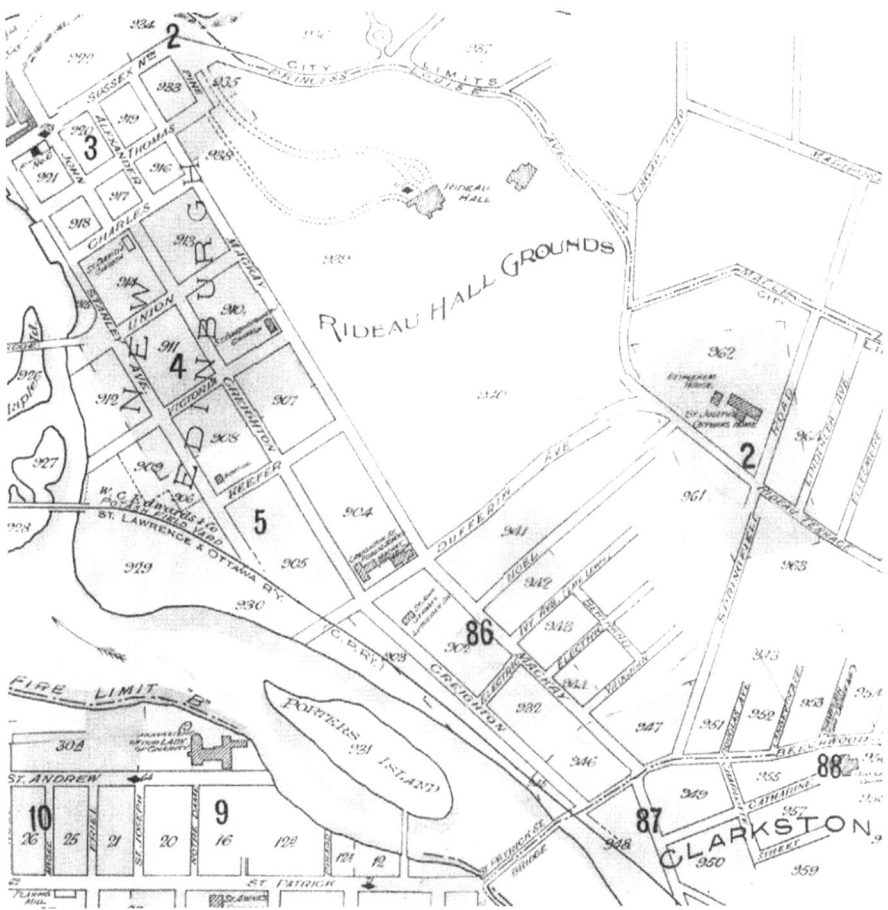

Figure 1.6. New Edinburgh and environs in 1912; settlement was spreading into the streets north and west of the original village.
Source: Drawn from insurance plan of the city of Ottawa, Ontario, Volume 1, September 1902, revised 1912, Map C. LAC MIKAN no. 3816030.

Figure 1.7 shows the approximate location in 1913 of households with German names in New Edinburgh.

Relations between different ethnic communities seem to have been generally amicable. Children would, as one old-timer recalled, fight as they went to their various schools, calling each other ethnic names ("German," "pea soup," etc.), and later would play together quite amicably in backyards.[9] But Frank Boucher, whose father was French Canadian and whose mother was Irish, recalled that in the first two decades of the twentieth century, local kids of all backgrounds eagerly awaited the annual picnic of the German community. "It didn't matter if we were Roman Catholics or Protestants; we were all welcome." After games, beer (for the men), and sewing or knitting

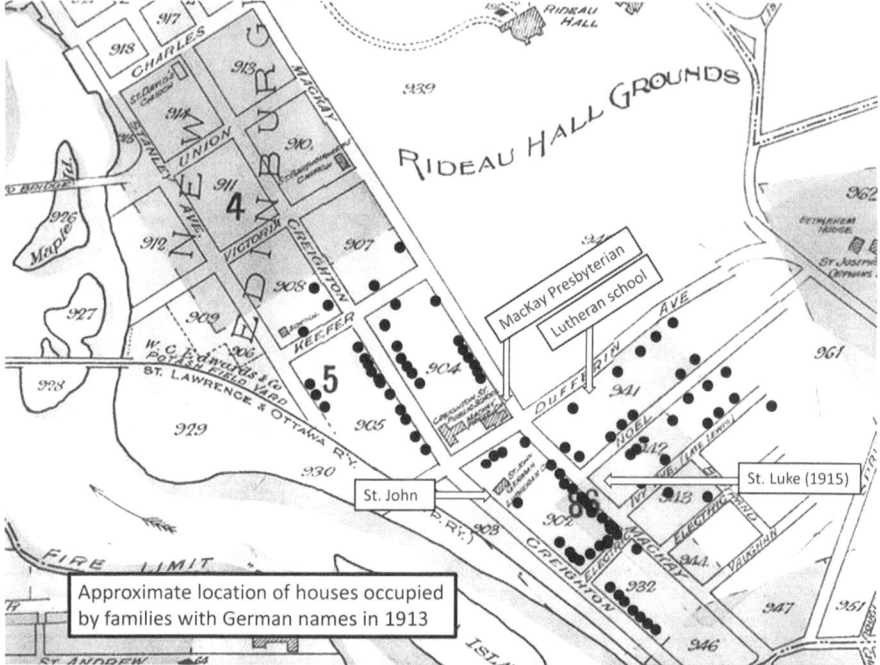

Figure 1.7. Map showing houses in New Edinburgh inhabited by families with German names. *Source:* Created by the author from insurance plan for the City of Ottawa LAC MIKAN no. 3816030 and information in Might's Ottawa Directory 1913.

(for the women), there were huge plates of food: "marvellous smoked meats and sausages, sauerkraut, cold mashed potatoes and potato salad with all kinds of breads and baked goods and pies as large and fat as pumpkins." Everyone would pitch in with cleaning up, and then sing German songs, "although none of us had the vaguest notion what the words meant—or even what they were."[10] The Lutherans built a skating rink with heated shacks and sometimes had a brass band for skating music. Families had to pay $5 for a yearly membership.[11] As Boucher recalls, the neighbourhood kids would work as shovellers just to get a chance to skate there. (Boucher later married a woman of German ancestry.)[12]

By 1900, settlement had spilled over the original boundaries of New Edinburgh to new developments north and east of MacKay Street and Dufferin Road as far as Beechwood Avenue. Beechwood Avenue was in fact the boundary between Ottawa/New Edinburgh and the village of Clarkstown, and the businesses on either side of this street, which included butcheries, stores, and a hotel and tavern, were in different municipalities. In 1908 Clarkstown and two adjacent villages combined to form the village of Eastview with about 2,500 people, and its main street was Montreal Road, which ran about a kilometre to the south and east of New Edinburgh. On the other side of Rideau Hall, Rockcliffe also remained a separate village. A few wealthy people had built large houses there in the decade before the war, like Warren Soper, co-owner of the Ottawa Electric Railway, whose mansion overlooking the Ottawa River has since become the residence of the American ambassador. But many other less wealthy people from New Edinburgh were also moving into the western part of Rockcliffe. Further east of Rockcliffe, on a large stretch of flat land, were a racetrack and a rifle range where shooting competitions were held. During the First World War some Ottawa regiments would train there.

With some exceptions (such as the upscale houses on Rideau Terrace and a few large houses throughout the village), the houses in New Edinburgh reflected a gradient of wealth from west to east. Wealthy people, mill owners, businessmen, senior civil servants, and managers in the mills lived at the older, western end of the village, in large stone or brick houses, many dating from the middle decades of the nineteenth century. All of these elite, and many middle-class families, had maids, gardeners, and servants. Skilled tradesmen, mill foremen, or mid-level civil servants, whose incomes were around $1,000 a year, lived in large frame houses with verandas and decorative woodwork. Lower-level civil servants and skilled workers, earning in the range of $500–800, lived in more modest dwellings in the older part of the village as well as some in the newer, eastern part. At the bottom of the economic ladder were labourers who tended to live in small frame houses. There were also single men, and some women, who boarded at houses throughout the village.[13]

Not everyone was a house owner; in fact, most people in New Edinburgh rented property, and there was a good deal of movement both into, out of, and within the community as incomes fluctuated and families sought cheaper rent. On the other hand, home ownership did not of itself reflect great wealth. A larger house might cost $3,000 to $4,000 to build, less if the owner did some of the work himself. However, anything but the most basic structure was out of reach for those with incomes of less than $1,000 a year. This amount—about $28,100 in today's dollars, but with no income tax or other deductions and modest sales taxes—was enough for a family to live on but with no frills. Those who earned less had to make some hard choices and, in some cases, to produce some of their own food in gardens, from fruit trees to chickens, or even cows and the occasional pig, in additions or outbuildings behind their houses.

Yet somehow they coped, and they raised families that were much larger than those of today—often six or seven children, or more. A house with four bedrooms might shelter not only the mother and father and minor children, but possibly one or more of: single working sons who were not yet married;

a married son or daughter, perhaps with small children, who were saving to strike out on their own; a widowed mother; or unmarried daughters who would live at home all their lives. Unmarried sons, and increasingly, daughters who could work as store clerks or at home as dressmakers, supplemented the family income. Those who had space, or needed the money, could also take in boarders or roomers; houses got more and more crowded the further down the income scale one went. At the bottom of the scale women and girls might work as laundresses or domestics. Even housework, without modern labour-saving devices, took a heavy toll on poorer housewives.

Central to the spiritual lives of New Edinburghers were the churches that served the village. Most families attended church, some more frequently than others, and only a tiny minority were willing to tell the census taker that they had no religion. In 1867 St. Bartholomew's Anglican Church, across MacKay Street from Rideau Hall, was constructed with the support of the Keefer and MacKay families. New Edinburgh (later MacKay) Presbyterian Church was built in 1875 on land donated by the MacKay Estate. In 1887, St. Bartholomew's suffered a serious blow when a third of its congregation, who opposed its "High Church" tendencies, broke away to found St. David's Reformed Episcopal Church at the corner of Crichton and Charles Streets. The early German settlers, "Old Lutherans" who adhered to the strict letter of the Augsburg Confession (which did not admit of any Calvinist or Reform ideas), at first had no church in New Edinburgh but worshipped at St. Paul Lutheran Church in Sandy Hill, a church under the aegis of the Missouri Synod in the United States. They, too, fell victim to a schism in 1894 when a faction started St. John Evangelical Lutheran Church, on Crichton Street just east of Dufferin Road, affiliated with the more liberal Canada Synod. But St. John did not remain liberal; in 1908 a new pastor committed to "strict discipline" forced some members out of the congregation, and by 1912 the church had declined to 12 voting members before it began to revive.[14] The majority who remained loyal to St. Paul had to trek to Sandy Hill until 1915, when that church established a daughter congregation, St. Lucas (later St. Luke) at MacKay and Noel Streets in a newer part of the village.[15] There were some Catholic institutions within New Edinburgh, including a junior school and an orphanage, but worshippers had to attend St. Brigid's or Notre Dame churches in Lower Town. Unquestionably, religious differences could be sources of sometimes bitter divisions between and within denominations. But churches could also bring people together, as community institutions where cultural events were held, and whose picnics, fairs, festivals, sports teams, and cultural activities attracted attendance from the whole community.

Also central to the life of New Edinburgh were its schools. A small Catholic school went up to Grade 5, after which the boys went to St. Brigid's School and the girls to Our Lady's School, both in Lowertown. There was also a small Lutheran school on Dufferin Road under the aegis of St. Paul church. But it was the Creighton Street Public School that played the central role, not only in providing elementary education (now both free and compulsory) but also in blurring class, ethnic, and social distinctions and shaping the unique character of New Edinburgh.[16] Founded in 1875 as a two-room brick structure at the corner of Crichton (Creighton) Street and Dufferin Road, rebuilt and successively enlarged in 1900 and 1906, this school, under a succession of outstanding principals and excellent teachers, provided most children in the village with a good basic education. Only a few—mostly boys—went on to high school, usually Ottawa Collegiate Institute (OCI, now Lisgar Collegiate), which required the payment of school fees. Only a handful of these students graduated or went on to university.[17] But the education they received at public school was sufficient to allow boys who left school at 14 to find work not only as labourers and semi-skilled factory hands, but as messengers or office boys in the public service, or as junior bank tellers or store clerks, where they could work their way up the ladder to management jobs. With high school education, on-the-job or night school training, and practical experience, some might even qualify as engineers or lawyers. Girls with education had more limited prospects, usually as teachers, nurses, or working in music.

Cultural activity for most people in New Edinburgh was largely what they created for themselves. True, theatres, music halls, and large hotels downtown provided regular entertainment, and there were amateur musical and theatre companies and, after 1906, a new Carnegie library. But for most women and girls, and for young men with neither the income nor inclination for frequent "downtown" entertainment, cultural activity largely consisted of local amateur plays and music, some dancing at community halls, musical and dramatic performances at churches (within the rules of decorum), as well as house parties. There was in fact a good deal of talent in the village, including amateur singers and pianists, and some of the most gifted ones had successful careers in music and culture.

The main outlet for the boys and young men of New Edinburgh was athletics. In the early twentieth century some prominent men from New Edinburgh founded the New Edinburgh Canoe Club that quickly won a reputation in local and national competition; it merged with the Ottawa Canoe Club just before the war. Almost every young athlete in New Edinburgh participated in races in or for the NECC/ONECC.[18] Boys played baseball down by the Rideau River or on the grounds of Rideau Hall, where the Governor General would often come out to watch their games. Sports clubs would canvass the neighbourhood to raise funds to buy equipment and always got a good hearing from the wealthier families like the Edwardses, and from the Governor General who would usually provide a five- or ten-dollar bill and often milk and cookies as well. "Depending on the season of the year," recalled Frank

Figure 1.8. Skating on the Rideau River c. 1914. Besides pleasure skating along the length of the river, there is a pick-up hockey game in the centre of the picture. The Edwards industrial complex is in the background, behind the Minto Bridges, which were built between 1900 and 1902, as part of a ceremonial route from Rideau Hall to the Parliament Buildings.
Source: City of Ottawa Archives MG397 – G00575 Box A2007-750. Glass neg. CA022224.

Boucher, "we played baseball, football, lacrosse, soccer, hockey, and even took part in track and field … it was an unusual one among us who didn't play all the sports."[19]

Hockey was especially popular, played on backyard rinks behind many houses and schools, and on the Rideau River where Frank Boucher grew up playing hockey. The boys would shovel a rink, clean it with homemade plows, and flood it by carrying pails of water from holes cut in the ice.

> On Saturdays, for instance, the first arrivals would start a game around 8 o'clock, dividing the available players evenly into two teams. As more boys came they joined one side or the other, always keeping the teams equal. Soon there'd be fifteen or twenty boys playing on each side, thirty or forty kids pursuing one puck. […] This game went on all day except for a halt at noon. We'd skate home, have our lunch in the kitchen without removing the skates, and then go back at it again. The game finally ended sharp at 9 P. M. when a Burg curfew bell sounded.[20]

When it got dark they lit the rink by setting fire to oil-soaked rags around it, or used the lights from the Minto Bridges on the river. The curfew, it appears, was set by the parents to bring the boys home and limit hijinks in the village, and it was respected.

New Edinburgh athletes won a wide reputation in this last golden age of amateurism. In 1911, the New Edinburgh Football Club was champion of the Ottawa Rugby League (see Figure 1.9). Jack Ryan (see Chapter 16) was one of the greatest athletes of his day; the Tubman brothers excelled in several sports; and their cousin Joe Tubman (see Chapter 14), starred with the Ottawa Rough Riders after the war. In 1915, members of the Ottawa New Edinburgh Canoe Club became the half-mile champions of Canada. Frank Boucher and his three brothers, Aurèle Joliat (see Chapter 20), and Eddie Gerard played hockey in the National Hockey League. Boucher, with the New York Rangers, centred one of the great lines in hockey history with Bill and Bun Cook and won two Stanley Cups. Gerard played for the Ottawa Senators, winning three Stanley Cups between 1920 and 1923. Boucher, Joliat, and Girard are all in the Hockey Hall of Fame.[21]

Figure 1.9. New Edinburgh Rugby Football Club City Champions, 1911. Note the presence of D. Stalker, A. P. Stalker, A. R. Kendall, R. Tubman, and J. T. McElroy as manager, Dr. Neil MacLeod presumably as team physician, and Jack Ryan as coach. All these men, except A.P. Stalker and McElroy, would appear on the Honour Roll at MacKay Presbyterian Church for their service in the First World War. G. Boucher would later play in the National Hockey League.
Source: MacKay United Church.

There was also a strong tradition of militia participation and military training. The presence of British military aides at Rideau Hall, and of senior

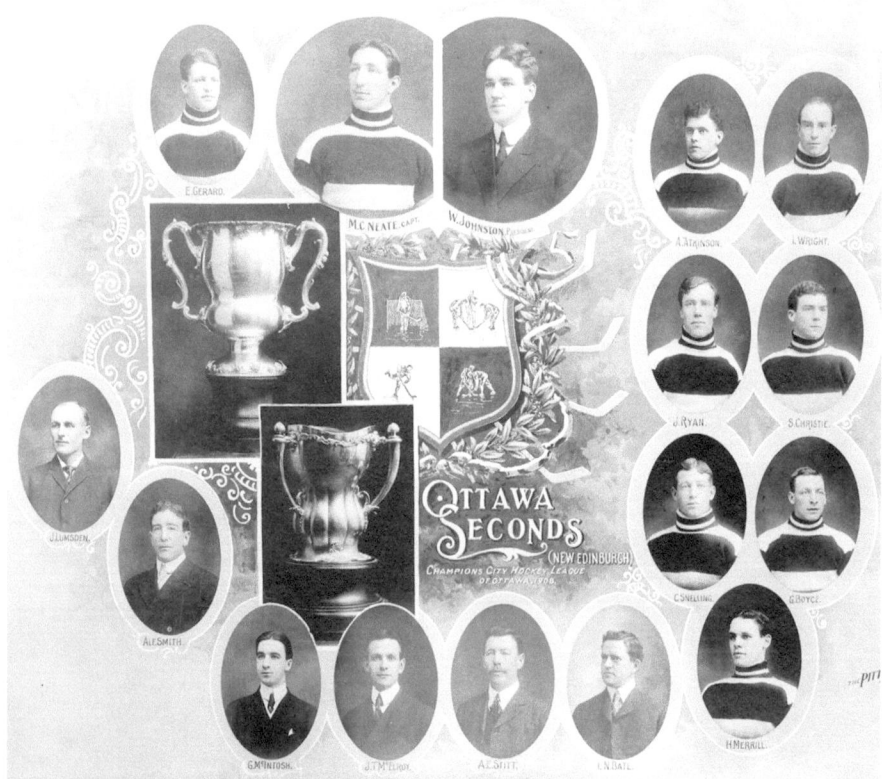

Figure 1.10. Ottawa Seconds, winner of the City Hockey League Championship, 1908. Several of these players, including Jack Ryan and Eddie Gerard, were star athletes from New Edinburgh, and A. E. Stitt and J. Lumsden were prominent New Edinburgh residents.
Source: City of Ottawa Archives, MG 101 Ernest Stitt Fonds, Box #A2012-0381.

militia officers and the British Chief of the General Staff, added colour and status at the top echelons; but military enthusiasm ran through the community at all levels. New Edinburgh strongly supported Canada's participation in the Boer War. When Wilhelm "Billy" Wendt, a Lutheran, returned from service in South Africa in 1900, he was hailed as a local hero and was presented by the Orange Lodge with an expensive mantle-clock.[22] Three young men from the village who enlisted for service in the Boer War in April 1902 were given silver drinking cups at a rousing send-off in the MacKay Sunday School hall.[23] Many young men from New Edinburgh belonged to militia regiments such as the Governor General's Foot Guards or the Duke of Cornwall's Own Regiment. Besides drills, they held regular shooting competitions in which New Edinburgh men often placed well. There was also a cadet program at Creighton Street Public School, which featured not only drill but also

Figure 1.11. Floods in New Edinburgh (near Crichton and Keefer Streets) c. 1898. Flood control measures would alleviate this problem in the early decades of the twentieth century, but water-borne diseases would continue to be a threat to the inhabitants of New Edinburgh. *Source*: Bytown Museum, P868a. William James Topley (attrib.); silver gelatin photograph.

shooting competitions for its boys. Like athletics, the cadet program reinforced the ideals of "manliness," which were also promoted in churches and schools.[24]

Like most of Ottawa in the years before the First World War, railways, sawmills, and industries made New Edinburgh a noisy and dirty place. Unpaved streets, soot, sawdust, animal waste, overcrowded housing, cold winters, spring floods, poor drainage, sanitation and sewage (the sewers exploded in 1916), food and water impurities, lack of refrigeration, and the prevalence of infectious diseases meant that at the turn of the twentieth century, child mortality and chronic disease were widespread. An outbreak of diphtheria in the late 1890s brought about the first use of individual glass cups for communion at MacKay Presbyterian Church. Typhoid was rife in Ottawa, as much of its water supply was drawn from the Ottawa River into which raw sewage was dumped. In the early years of the twentieth century, an average of 20 people a year died from the disease, including in 1907 the daughter of Governor General Earl Grey. In spite of public outrage, little was done, and the water situation remained a major scandal.[25] The register of nearby Beechwood Cemetery records a heartbreaking number of infant deaths and early mortality—for example, the page which covers July 27 to September 5, 1903, has, out of 55 names, 7 stillborn babies and at least 17 infants where the cause of death reflects an epidemic of intestinal infection that struck the east side of Ottawa in mid-summer, as well a 10-year-old who died from diphtheria. Many families lost a child in infancy or childhood. There was also the ever-present threat that the breadwinner might die, be crippled, or become chronically ill, as a result of an accident or conditions at work, leaving his family destitute unless he owned his home or had some life insurance (most men, according to the 1911 census, did have some form of life insurance, reflecting a very large investment of a labourer's wage). Doctors and medicines were expensive and families had to think twice before seeing a physician—though most appear to have found a way if they really needed it. Babies were delivered by midwives, and complications from childbirth were a not-infrequent cause of death.

Nutrition was also an issue. The attestation papers of 118 of the men from MacKay Presbyterian Church who enlisted in the First World War show that about half (66) were between five feet five inches and five feet eight inches tall with the largest number (26) around five feet seven inches. There were 30 men between five feet nine inches and five feet eleven inches and only three at six feet. And that is of those who met the minimum height requirements—eight men got in at five feet three inches or five feet four inches, one was under five feet three inches tall, and undoubtedly many smaller men were rejected. Some of these men were teenagers who grew a little during their service—most put on weight—but there was little difference between younger and older recruits or between recent immigrants and Canadian-born recruits. Smaller men were not necessarily weaker; several of the best athletes among the recruits were five feet seven inches tall, and two who became famous—Aurèle Joliat and Joe Tubman—were very short by today's standards.

The service records of MacKay soldiers also show many chronic health problems—heart murmurs, bronchial conditions, hernias, varicoceles, asthma—and the aftermath of diseases such as typhoid and rheumatic fever, not to mention the prevalence of venereal disease, that reinforce the conclusions of Nic Clarke and others about the poor state of health of many Canadians which was revealed by recruiting for war.[26] A related issue revealed by the war was poor dental health. Each soldier was given a dental examination because a requirement of enlistment was the ability to masticate food. Cavities, infections, and abscesses were probably sources of constant pain as well as deeper health problems. And the early deaths of so many residents of New Edinburgh from heart disease, strokes, and hypertension, may reflect, at least in part, a diet that was too high in fat, sugar, and carbohydrates.

Besides gastrointestinal and infectious diseases, a particular scourge resulting from dirty air, industrial pollution, and overcrowding in houses that were cold during the winter was tuberculosis. Tuberculosis ran through families, especially among the girls who were more vulnerable because they spent most of their lives indoors. In the decade before the war, public health agencies, volunteer bodies, and governments had begun to address this situation with public health measures and sanitoriums. But the assumption that tuberculosis was a disease of the poor and of immigrants—"a social disease with a medical aspect" in the words of Sir William Osler—often got in the way. Families like the Haaks (see Chapter 23) were working class, but others like the Stalkers (see Chapter 13) were middle class, as were many others (including the first minister of New Edinburgh [later MacKay] Presbyterian Church and his wife, who both died young from the disease). Tuberculin tests revealed exposure but not active cases; they were thus of very limited usefulness even if they had been widely available, since most people would have tested positive. X-rays were expensive and rare. For those with active cases, treatment in a sanitorium (one opened in Ottawa in 1911) was very expensive. Most patients were treated at home. Many were able to lead an active life for months or years, and some recovered; but still many eventually died a lingering death.[27]

By 1914 much progress had been made in alleviating at least some of these health problems. New Edinburgh was well ahead of its time in having access to electricity for street lighting, homes, and public buildings, made possible by abundant power generation (including after 1907 at the Rideau Falls) and the vision of men like Ahearn who pioneered electrification. (For example, the women of MacKay Presbyterian Church raised money as early as 1880 for electric lighting in the Sanctuary, and in the early 1900s money was being raised for tungsten lighting throughout the church.) Though some local people still sold fresh milk to customers in pails, Slinn and the larger dairies delivered pasteurized milk. Public health measures had greatly improved the health of the young people—virtually all the MacKay recruits had been vaccinated against smallpox. More people had access to doctors and a number of MacKay recruits had had minor surgery. The Protestant Hospital on Rideau Street, which had opened a nursing school in 1890, treated serious illnesses. New Edinburgh was less crowded and likely a healthier place than many urban environments in Canada, where 15 percent of children—20 in some places—did not live to see their first birthday.[28] Flood control had alleviated some outbreaks of water-borne diseases; nonetheless, the almost criminal inertia of the City of Ottawa in addressing the need for a clean water supply meant that contaminated water continued to cause illness and death. The quantum leaps in public health, hospitals, medical research, public education, water and sewage treatment, housing, and greater access to medical services that would greatly improve the length and quality of life in the succeeding decades would have to wait until after the war—indeed, they were stimulated by it.

By 1914 New Edinburgh was a community of more than 2,000 people in transition from an industrial village to a residential suburb, along with a growing exclusive enclave in Rockcliffe, within a city that had not yet fully evolved from what Goldwin Smith had called "a subarctic lumber village" into the capital of a rapidly growing and modernizing nation. While it contained some wealthy families, most of its residents were modest—but not poor—people who took pride in their trades and their family values. While there were differentials of wealth, class distinctions were blurred; an old family, a professional or business family, a skilled worker, a recent immigrant, a German family, and a labourer or clerk boarding with a family, might all live on the same block. Large families and recent immigration meant that there were many young men and women in New Edinburgh. Schools, athletic and cultural activities, and churches were focal points and meeting places for a growing and diverse community. In this transition period, New Edinburgh could find an equilibrium between its ties to the Ottawa Valley lumber industries, its streetcar connections to downtown, and the presence of Rideau Hall, which served as a constant reminder that it was also part of a transcontinental Dominion and a world-spanning Empire. In the age before the automobile and mass communications, New Edinburgh and its surrounding settlements could retain a sense of community, a continuity, and a distinct identity.

2 MACKAY PRESBYTERIAN CHURCH

Unlike the Lutheran and Reformed Episcopal churches in New Edinburgh, MacKay Presbyterian Church was the product not of a schism, but of the healing of one. Since 1840, Presbyterians had been divided by a bitter feud between the Free Church of Scotland, or "Free Kirk", which had seceded from it because of what they regarded as excessive influence of the state and the watering down of older religious beliefs and congregational independence. New Edinburgh had begun as a largely Scottish community; Thomas McKay had been a founder of St. Andrew's Presbyterian Church in downtown Ottawa and had taught Sunday School in a small school in New Edinburgh as early as 1845. But because of the division in the church, there was not the critical mass of believers to allow either faction to establish a viable church. All this changed in 1875 when, following Confederation, all the Presbyterian churches united to form the Presbyterian Church in Canada. This new national church not only brought together the provincial churches, but also healed the schism between the Canadian branches of the Free Kirk and the Church of Scotland (a quarter of a century before this happened in Scotland) and began a series of church unions that would culminate in the United Church of Canada. The way was now clear for Ottawa Presbytery to agree that establishing a Presbyterian Church in New Edinburgh would not adversely affect existing congregations. Under the leadership of Thomas McKay's grandson William MacKinnon, and with the strong support of McKay's widow, Annie MacKay, and his daughter, Annie (MacKinnon) Keefer, the New Edinburgh Presbyterian Church was founded in 1875. It built a long, low stone building on two lots donated by the MacKay estate at the corner of Dufferin Road and MacKay Street. In 1894 another of McKay's daughters, Christina MacKay, donated land and funds to build a manse next door to the church. In 1896, a new Sunday School wing provided not only classrooms but a meeting hall for the community at large. In 1900 the church recognized the contribution of the MacKay family by changing its name to MacKay Presbyterian Church.

By the turn of the twentieth century the church had 254 members from 108 families. Its governing body was the Session, consisting of ordained Elders (all men) elected for life by the Congregation. The Session examined and received new members, set policy for the church, and could (when necessary)

Figure 2.1. New Edinburgh/MacKay Presbyterian Church, 1875–1910. The original church was a small, low rubble-stone building. The corner of the Sunday School hall, built in 1896, is just visible at the left; to the right is the substantial manse donated by one of Thomas McKay's daughters in 1894.
Source: MacKay United Church.

reprove or discipline members for misconduct, or purge from the rolls the names of members who had ceased to attend for an extended period. The Board of Managers, a larger group of men in charge of day-to-day operations and upkeep, was elected for fixed terms at the Annual General Meeting of the Congregation. The Ladies' Aid, which elected its own executive committee, was a group whose regular membership seldom exceeded 20, but which could mobilize church women to conduct bazaars, rummage sales, garden parties and socials, and provide dinners or refreshments for church functions. These activities, and those of other church groups, raised funds for electric lights, for furniture and furnishings, for major repairs, for the interest on the mortgage on the church building, and for many other special projects.

The church held morning and evening Sunday services with different hymns and sermons for each (clearly many people were expected to attend both) and a prayer service on Wednesday evenings. Full membership in the church was taken very seriously. New members were accepted by Profession of Faith, which involved an examination of the candidate by the Session. Others might transfer from another Presbyterian church (or in some cases, from a church of another denomination), on the basis of a Certificate which attested that they had been members in good standing of that church. Attendance at Communion four

Figure 2.2. Interior of the first MacKay Presbyterian Church, c. 1900. Oil lamps were replaced in the 1880s by electric lights and were upgraded in the early 1900s, to brighten the dark interior.
Source: MacKay United Church.

times a year was an important obligation of membership and was recorded in the Communion Rolls. In addition to members, there were at least three times as many people who attended but did not formally join the church. Those who attended fairly regularly were classified as adherents and were entitled to participate fully in all the activities of the church, except that they could not hold senior positions in church governance or vote at Annual General Meetings.

Sunday School was one of the highest priorities for MacKay church, not only for Christian education but as an outreach to the broader community. There were classes for all ages, and some children from other faiths also attended. It was reported in 1900 that 150 children in 10 classes took part in its annual festival, and the number grew considerably in succeeding years.[1] The Women's Missionary Society supported the world mission of the church through education and fundraising, and supervised the Junior and Senior Mission Bands which introduced children to mission work. There was also a Young Peoples' Association and various ad hoc groups like the "Sunshine Girls." The church contributed to a French-language theological college at Pointe-aux-Trembles, Quebec, to the Protestant Hospital in Ottawa, and to homes for widows and orphans. It was particularly devoted to temperance, with a pledge book and stern treatment of its members who departed too obviously from sobriety. In 1899, the congregation supported a petition to abolish the New Edinburgh

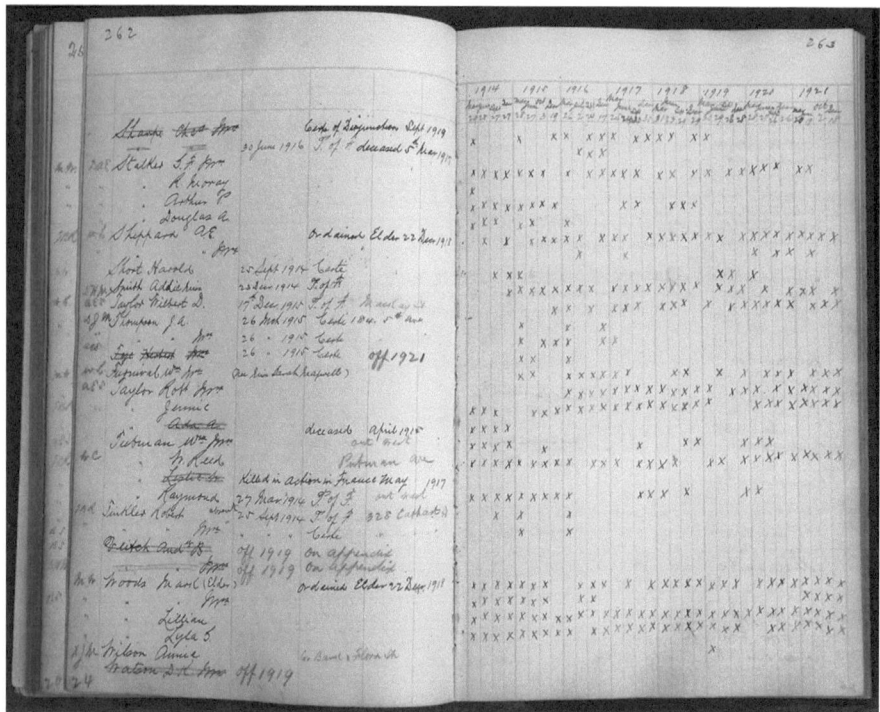

Figure 2.3. A page from MacKay's Communion Rolls. The Communion Rolls recorded the names of church members and their attendance at communion four times a year. This page includes the Stalker and Tubman families with a note recording the death of Leslie Tubman.
Source: MacKay United Church.

Tavern. As well, the church supported the demand by the Lord's Day Alliance in 1901 for federal legislation to observe the Sabbath.[2]

In the decade before the First World War, MacKay's members and adherents were a cross-section of the New Edinburgh community and its surrounding settlements. Some came from well-established families in the community, like the Askwith, Cherry, Dawson, English, Esdale, Lumsden, McElroy, Neate, Ralph, Rankin, Sherwood, and Tubman families, who often intermarried and created a web of influence in New Edinburgh. Others had more recently moved into New Edinburgh, including from West Quebec, or from Britain in the wave of immigration during the decade before the war. While most congregants lived in New Edinburgh, including the newer sections of the village that were opening up by 1914, a few lived in large houses along Rideau Terrace, or in Rockcliffe (where the first settlers were not always wealthy people), or even further out, like the Finter family that lived near the Rockcliffe Rifle Range (where the RCMP barracks are now, at the foot of St. Laurent Boulevard), or in Eastview, where some had small businesses and even farms.

Some were business leaders. Gordon Edwards, nephew of W. C. Edwards, was president of two of Edwards' companies and president or director of various other firms; he was also active in Liberal politics and was elected to Parliament in the 1926 federal election. (He inherited his uncle's house at 24 Sussex Drive, which later became the residence of the prime minister, and his brother owned the property at Harrington Lake which is now the summer residence of the prime minister.) James Hope's downtown store had one of the finest book departments in Canada; the Rankin family ran a prosperous hardware business; the Currie family operated greenhouses on Rideau Terrace; and the Powers family ran a leading men's furnishing business on Sparks Street. Donald Mackenzie owned a contracting business, as did Thomas Jackson, who lived just inside the border of Rockcliffe and was also Constable of that village; George Farmer, a newcomer to New Edinburgh in 1914, mined the sand and gravel quarries in Rockcliffe. There were also professional men (such as Frank Perney, principal of Creighton Street Public School, Thomas Henry Mansell, who was sent from England in 1907 to help establish the Royal Canadian Mint, and A. E. Stitt, who was secretary-treasurer of several companies), managers (such as William Bothwell, the yard foreman for W. C. Edwards, and William Gerard, a Scottish millwright who became superintendent of Edwards' sawmill), and a number of senior public servants and government experts. But the majority of the congregation were skilled tradespeople and mid-to-lower-level civil servants, or bookkeepers, junior managers, and craftsmen, as well as some newly arrived immigrants and labourers.

There were also widows and single mothers. Rachel Barnes came to New Edinburgh when her skilled tradesman husband died. Her sons found work as millwrights in the Edwards mill. Her oldest son married and had a daughter, but his wife died, and when he remarried and moved away, one of his daughters remained with Rachel. Her second son married and had four children, but his wife also died and he also brought the children to New Edinburgh to live with his mother. By 1909 this multigenerational family—Rachel, her daughters (including Gladys, an accomplished music teacher), and five grandchildren from her two sons—was living in a frame row house at 56 Stanley Avenue. The widow of John Munro, a retired soldier who had fallen to his death from a pile of lumber in 1885, lived in a small wood-frame house at 135 Crichton Street. One of her sons built a house next door and became a much-respected inspector with the street railway company, and his boys were well-known and popular athletes. Her daughters, Christina and Margaret, lived with her and worked at various times as laundresses and domestics. Though both were described as single, Christina had a son and a daughter, and Margaret adopted a son, Joseph, who had been an orphan.[3] There were others: blended families resulting from death or desertion; people in straitened circumstances or working their way up the ladder of education, skills, and trades; or girls working as dressmakers or clerks to contribute to the family income, who attended MacKay, its Sunday school, or another of its activities.

Wealth and social standing were less important than character in determining who would play leadership roles at MacKay. Wealthy men were usually generous donors and businessmen and professionals often played leading roles as Elders and managers, and some of their wives were prominent in the Ladies' Aid. But many church leaders were men of more modest means. Frederick Dawson, a carpenter, had worked as a skilled tradesman in the Edwards complex; Douglas Henry Macdonald had joined the civil service as a teenager and worked his way to a senior clerkship; William Lunan was a clerk or bookkeeper; William Cherry, who lived with his very large family on Rideau Terrace, had climbed the ranks of the Post Office to become an accountant; F. W. P. English was a clerk in the Post Office who also profited from mining ventures; Mark Woods was a carpenter who had come from England in 1896, built many public buildings and homes in the area, and devoted all his free time to the church. Bessie Hill Askwith, one of four siblings who grew up in the Protestant Orphans' Home after her mother died and her father could find only occasional work, married an electrician from a prominent family in New Edinburgh in 1912. She became a leading figure in the Ladies' Aid; her siblings and widowed father sometimes lived with or were assisted by her, and her sister joined MacKay by Profession of Faith. Theresa Coker, a twice-widowed woman of modest means (see chapter 6), played an important role in the Ladies' Aid, as did several unmarried younger women.

The same went for leadership in the wider community. Breary Slinn, William Cherry, Frank Perney, D. H. Macdonald, and David Esdale served as city aldermen for Rideau Ward at various times between 1898 and 1925. In fact, during most of this period at least one of the aldermen for the ward was a member or adherent of MacKay—and on occasion MacKay men ran against each other. James Hope was a school trustee and water commissioner. William Bothwell was well connected in the Liberal Party. George Farmer, even after he moved to New Edinburgh, remained Reeve of the nearby village of Eastview. Alexander Maginnes had a low-level job in the government printing bureau but as a man known to be "careful, thrifty, but above all upright in his business dealings,"[4] he served as a school trustee in New Edinburgh for many years. W. F. Drake, a government expert in irrigation and land reclamation, was a Rockcliffe pioneer who served on a plethora of organizations in that community. Rideau Hall played an important part in the life of New Edinburgh, and some MacKay people worked there as gardeners, chauffeurs, tradesmen, staff, and even as laundresses. But its church was St. Bartholomew's, and its glittering life, so captivatingly described by Sandra Gwyn, found little echo in MacKay Presbyterian Church.[5]

Figure 2.4. Rev. P. W. Anderson.
Source: MacKay United Church.

In 1904, 35-year-old Rev. Peter Anderson was called to be the minister of MacKay. A child of Scottish immigrants in Victoria County, Ontario, Anderson had taught for three years as a teenager and had then studied philosophy at the University of Toronto and theology at Knox College. He came to MacKay church from Shelburne, Ontario, where he had earned a splendid reputation.[6] A leading physician later recalled that Anderson

> was a great humanitarian and was never too tired or too busy to answer a call from anyone, church member or not. Often when I arrived at a home, I found that the family had sent for Dr. Anderson, too, for spiritual comfort. When we had done all we could, we would walk home together in the early hours of the morning. He was a quiet man who enjoyed an evening of good conversation and companionship.[7]

Within his church he deftly resolved disputes between congregants, such as a 1909 lawsuit brought by Dr. Dougall King, brother of the Minister of Labour, against W. B. Garvock, who had designed the building for the Sunday School and had been its superintendent for many years. By 1910 he could justifiably report to the church annual meeting on "the unity, harmony, and good will that pervaded the organization."[8] The congregation rewarded him in 1912 with a sabbatical to study in Edinburgh and travel to the Holy Land. He received an honorary Doctor of Divinity from Emmanuel College in 1930 and when he retired from MacKay in 1934, he was the only minister most congregants had known.

His wife, Clara Rothwell Anderson, was an accomplished woman in her own right. She had attended the Toronto Conservatory of Music and had been soloist at Trinity Methodist Church in Toronto. At MacKay, she was well known as the author of more than a dozen plays, designed for performance in churches by young peoples' groups, Ladies' Aids, and other small groups with limited acting experience or facilities for costumes or staging. By 1912 her plays were being produced not only in Ottawa but across Canada and she was earning substantial royalties. Her main characters were usually women, and the performances of her plays, especially as they were often accompanied by amateur musical recitals, not only allowed the women of the church an outlet for their talents but also highlighted their role in the church.

Some of her light-hearted "character sketches" poked (not always kindly) fun at ladies' groups in small villages for the amusement of urban middle class audiences. But her later plays were more serious, addressing the role of women in the family, the church, and a modernizing community. In some plays, set in a small town, a young, educated woman challenges older beliefs and persuades the men in authority to allow the women to play their full role in the church and society. Other plays asserted the need for a modern, urban, materialist society to rediscover the old-time values of the small town. In *Aunt Susan's Visit,* the title character rescues her family, which has moved to the city and become obsessed with social climbing, by reminding them of the simpler virtues of honesty, hard work, and going to church, while charming the sophisticated people the family had been afraid she would offend. Anderson's plays gave short shrift to pretentious suffragists, radical social reformers, or "men-hating" women. Her comic situations were usually resolved by marriage, engagement, or at least the renewal of marital relationships. In her only published novel, *John Matheson: A Wholesome Human Study of Canadian Rural Life* (1923), a talented singer who marries a rural minister makes clear to a skeptical friend that her only ambition is to "sing to an audience of *one* in an old, vine-covered manse [...] Perhaps, sometime, I might sing for a little, sick child, – to help him forget [...] You know I could never preach, but I wish I could make people feel the love of God—as I feel it when I am singing."[9] The role of woman was in the home, but she must not be confined to that sphere. The feminine virtues of motherhood,

A Unique Entertainment

WILL BE GIVEN IN

MacKay Church S.S. Hall

Cor. MacKay St. and Dufferin Ave.

ON

Tuesday Evening, Jan. 31st

at 8 o'clock

UNDER THE AUSPICES OF THE LADIES' AID

Tickets 25 Cents   Doors Open 7.30

Part I.
CONCERT

Miss Gladys Barnes	Piano Solo
Miss Hampshire	Vocal Solo
Miss Mabel Cole	Vocal Solo
Mr. Coleman	Musical Selection
Mr. Armstrong	Violin Solo
Mr. Collingwood	Reading
Miss Dillon	Recitation

Part II.

The Members of the Ladies' Aid will present—

"**An Old Time Ladies' Aid Business Meeting at Mohawk Cross-Roads**"

CHARACTERS

Mrs. Green *(Mrs. Anderson)*	Hostess
Mrs. De Lloyd Fitz-Hammond *(Mrs. Ellicott)*	From Boston and Guests of
Mrs. J. Algernon Kindly *(Mrs. Hope)*	the Hostess
Mrs. Smith *(Mrs. Gerard)*	President
Mrs. Gray *(Mrs. Splitt)*	Secretary, *Pro. tem.*
Mrs. Day *(Mrs. English)*	Treasurer

Miss Harpe *(Mrs. Woods)*		Mrs. Andrew Scott	
Mrs. Sampson Hoyt *(M. Askwith)*		Mrs. Roberts *(McLeod)*	
Mrs. Wise *(Mrs. Gordon)*		Mrs. Garibaldi Jones *(Mrs. Lipsey)*	
Mrs. Clower *(Mrs. Ralph)*		Mrs. Harris *(McDonald)*	
Mrs. Lowell *(Mrs. Glinn)*		Mrs. Bruce *(Sharpe)*	
Mrs. Brown *(Mrs. J.D. Sherwood)*		Mrs. Alphonso Hay	
Mrs. Ignatius Dale *(Mrs. A. Dawson)*		Mrs. Kane *(M. passoe)*	
Mrs. Henderson *(Wm peres)*		Mrs. White *(Sid Sherwood)*	
Mrs. Black *(Mrs. McDonald)*		Mrs. John Bain *(Mrs. McKenzie)*	

Figure 2.5. Program for an "Entertainment" in the Sunday School hall at MacKay Presbyterian Church. The first half of the program showcased the musical talent at MacKay, which often found its main outlet through church performances. Mrs. Anderson's play in the second half was presented by members of the Ladies' Aid, likely as a fundraiser.
Source: MacKay United Church.

empathy, and nurturing were those of the church, and women had a crucial role to play in exemplifying and promoting these ideals both in the church and in the wider society. Her play *Martha Made Over* recasts the biblical story of Mary and Martha. The modern Martha, ever encumbered with much serving, confined to a narrow sphere, conforming to outmoded norms, and pursuing unworthy ambitions, is redeemed by adopting the virtues of Mary, a woman of thought and agency, fully realizing and performing her feminine role in service to family, God, church, and community.[10]

Figure 2.6. Cast of one of Mrs. Anderson's plays. The play appears to be *The Young Village Doctor* from 1920; Mrs. Anderson is second from right, to the left of her husband, in the third row.
Source: MacKay United Church.

In reality, Mrs. Anderson was the ideal minister's wife, a helpmeet to her husband and mother to their children. She never sang at MacKay. She opened the manse and its lawn for church functions and engaged actively in Ladies' Aid work. She allowed her own congregation and deserving organizations, such as the IODE and others during the war, to perform her plays royalty-free. She was hardly typical of most women of New Edinburgh; with a maid to help look after her three children, and a small but independent income, she could play the role of Mary, befriend Ottawa writers like Madge Macbeth, hold an executive position in the Women's Press Club, and participate in other literary and dramatic activities. But in a period of transition, she opened up possibilities to the women of her church and showed them that they too had an important public role in building a Christian community.

Indeed, the MacKay church Communion Rolls show that the women of some families were more likely to become members of the church than the men, especially the young men, and more regular attendees at Communion. Several women, like Nan Slinn, Gladys Barnes, Ethel Dawson, and Margaret Askwith, were teachers and accomplished musicians or, like Isabel Ralph, devoted themselves to good works in the church and the community. The Elders and Managers made the big decisions, but the Ladies' Aid, in the recollection of some, actually ran the place. The Women's Missionary Society was a more diverse and active group that drew in a broader (and probably younger) range of membership to undertake social and charitable work as well as support for foreign and domestic missions. Women were equal members with men in the Young People's Association and, indeed, sometimes predominated. Even so, it was not until late in the war and into the 1920s that more independently minded groups involving younger women were formed to address more social issues and mission work; it would be many years before women played anything but a supporting role in the management of the church.

One area where women had a voice—literally—but men still made the decisions, was the church choir. Membership in the choir was substantial and there were a number of gifted singers in the church, as well as dedicated musicians such as Elizabeth Reid who gave of her time and talents over many decades. Choral recitals and performances were an outlet for talent and a form of outreach in New Edinburgh. But its primary purpose was always seen as the glorification of God and much attention was paid to discipline in the choir and the conduct of its members. These issues, and periodic dissatisfaction with choir directors, were perennial subjects of discussion in the Session, and there was a frequent turnover in the choirmaster position. In 1912 Mrs. Frances Brunel (see Chapter 15), who lived in New Edinburgh and was a very highly qualified pianist and choir director, was interviewed for the position and it was agreed to engage her at a rate considerably above what previous incumbents were paid. Apparently this fell through and another person was hired at a lower stipend, and issues with the choir continued to draw the concerned attention of the Session throughout the war.

An exclusively male preserve was athletics. Elder Frank Perney, an early member of the New Edinburgh Canoe Club, stressed athletics and military training as principal of Creighton Street Public School, and he took the lead in renting a vacant lot next to the manse for recreational skating in winter. There were active church hockey and football leagues in the city and MacKay Presbyterian Church was a powerhouse. Athletics was considered an important church program for young men, engaging them in wholesome activity which bred habits of temperance, discipline, and fair play and reinforced the church teachings of chivalry and service. In these and other activities that involved young men, MacKay was responding to a growing concern among Protestant churches that they were going too far in a "feminine" direction—that they risked losing their young men unless they showed that wholesome masculine activity also had its place in building healthy, "manly" individuals in a Christian society.[11] This concern was perhaps best exemplified at the neighbouring St. David's Reformed Episcopal Church, where between 1899 and 1909, Rev. C. Edward Russell ran what one newspaper described in 1904 as "one of the best organized boys' associations in the city of Ottawa." He described his Young Men's Guild as "non-sectarian" and "having a manly influence" on the young people of New Edinburgh. The boys played rugby and had gymnasium classes twice a week and Bible study on Sunday. They wore blue and white uniforms and had flags emblazoned with a Maltese Cross. The object of all this was to give boys "something good and clean to think about, and something manly to do" so they would feel that the church was not something foreign to them and that "a manly Christian is not something to be despised."[12] What is significant for our story is that his programs attracted a substantial number of young men whose families were or would become prominent members of MacKay Presbyterian Church, who continued their athletic activities at MacKay church after St. David's went into decline.

Figure 2.7. MacKay Presbyterian Church Hockey Team, Champions, Senior League, 1912. MacKay teams were very successful in the church leagues that were a prominent part of the Ottawa amateur athletic scene. The captain of the MacKay team, Sandy McKenzie (front row, centre) would be killed in the war (see Chapter 22).
Source: MacKay United Church.

MacKay also shared the strong military tradition of New Edinburgh. One long-time church member was a veteran of the North-West Rebellion. Another, Oscar May, had served for 35 years in the Governor General's Foot Guards and had been selected by his militia regiment to represent Canada at Queen Victoria's

Diamond Jubilee in 1897; his most prized possession was a faded Union Jack which was given to the group during that memorable occasion. Oscar's six sons had also served in militia regiments for a total of 74 years by 1914 (one, Emil May, had a tattoo on his arm that read "Death Before Dishonour").[13] Still another MacKay man was one of two militia soldiers from Ottawa at the coronation of George V in 1910. The Orange Lodge that feted "Billy" Wendt on his return from the Boer War undoubtedly contained many MacKay men. Boys and young men from MacKay frequently won top honours in shooting contests at the Rockcliffe Rifle Range, and at least 18 of the MacKay men who enlisted in the first year of the war claimed prior militia experience. William A. Williams, president of the Young People's Association and a delegate to the Ottawa Temperance Alliance, was a petty officer in the naval department, and Norman K. Willson, a refiner at the Royal Canadian Mint, was a sergeant-major in the permanent militia. Several recent British immigrants had done military service in the old country, and a few were still on the reserve list with their old regiments.

Church records provide a detailed picture of the organization and life of the church, but they have very little to say about theology. A prayer was said or a Bible passage read at the start of meetings of church organizations and attendance at Communion was expected. MacKay church undoubtedly adhered to the fundamental doctrines of the Presbyterian Church as expressed in the Westminster Confession of Faith, its Catechisms, and its Directory of Public Worship. "Most," says historian Phyllis Airhart,

> would have agreed with R. C. Chalmers's identification of Presbyterian principles: an emphasis on the sovereignty of God, salvation by grace through faith, the priesthood of all believers that found expression in a church ruled by presbyters, an approach to the sacrament of the Eucharist that avoided both Catholic and Lutheran "magic" and Zwingli's memorialism, and a recognition of the state as called to fulfill a divine purpose (and to be resisted only when it acted in violation of Christian conscience).[14]

But within this framework there was undoubtedly a variety of religious views. Some members were deeply rooted in the Free Kirk tradition and a few people so identified themselves as late as the 1911 census. Others were more liberal in their beliefs. Many were Orangemen, though how far most would have shared or openly professed the anti-Catholic bigotry displayed by some prominent members of the Order is an open question, and several MacKay people married Catholics and started or came from mixed-faith families. People undoubtedly came to church for very different reasons and sought different things; not every word from the pulpit reached every ear or moved every heart. But religious belief was unquestionably an important element in the lives of those who attended MacKay church regularly.

Rev. Anderson's sermons have not been preserved and we can only catch glimpses of the messages he delivered every week. His views well reflected the Christian idealism of the University of Toronto philosophy department, and of his mentors at Knox College. He was liberal in his interpretation of some Presbyterian doctrines including predestination, and he believed such things could be open to doubt and debate without surrendering the fundamentals of Christian faith. He embraced the "Higher Criticism" which saw the Bible as literature, situated in an historical context and thus open to analysis and interpretation. This might not have gone down well with everyone, as illustrated by a character in Mrs. Anderson's novel *John Matheson:* "I'll have the truth revealed in the way I want it, or I won't have it at all! I'll have the Bible written by the same folks and at the same time—and handed down all bound and ready for family worship! I'll have the world made in six days of twenty-four hours each, and finished Saturday night before sun down, so there's no breaking of the Sabbath day neither, and I *won't listen* to those heretics who would have it that it took thousands of years in the making!" It is unlikely that Anderson encountered this rock-ribbed opposition, but he must have shared the concerns the two fictional young ministers expressed in their earnest discussion that followed this outburst. Did they have the right to shake the staunch faith of simple people? But equally, did they have the right to pretend to believe things they knew were not true, or to "dumb down" religion and cheat those who wanted, and needed, more? The wise clergyman tempered his more contentious views, and Anderson undoubtedly saved his deepest thoughts for his closest friends.

Clara Anderson undoubtedly had her husband in mind when she put into the mouth of her main character an expression of his core beliefs:

> There is one thing sure. God is the same – *Infinite* – *Eternal* – and *Unchangeable*. Throughout the march of the centuries He has never ceased to reveal His beauty, truth, and goodness. [...] Through the long line of prophets and reformers – through the best in literature, in art, and in music (which are in themselves a revelation of God to man) – yes, and through the life of Christ, spent in ministering to mankind, do we discover an undying message, and we believe that if preacher and people alike endeavour to follow in the footsteps of One whose days were spent in loving service, any problem may safely be left, until solved by the searchlight of eternity.[15]

It was thus action, more than abstract theory or theological speculation, that would be the truest and most essential expression of Christian faith. As the fictional Anderson—John Matheson—put it: "Inasmuch as we interest ourselves in making of the community a place wherein little children and young people may reach their highest development, spiritually, mentally, and physically, we are fulfilling our mission as a church of Christ."[16] Or, as the real Peter Anderson told a gathering of Oddfellows and Rebekahs in 1906: "The air is vibrant with the spirit for the betterment of humanity. ... The world would be a better world in which to live if men would transform their theories into deeds."[17] Presbyterians, says church historian Brian Fraser, "united evangelical zeal with moderated reason in their attempt to establish a universal consensus on individual morality and social responsibility. Taken together, these qualities of character would reform in an ascending pattern, the family, the city, the province, the nation, and ultimately the world."[18] The Christian values of work, temperance, charity, and duty would bring personal regeneration and redeem an urban, materialist society. While he could angrily attack a businessman "of tender heart and emotional character," who had in his business dealings "reached out with one hand to steal from the father while giving biscuits to the child," who "crushes the life out of the heart of the widow" but "hangs the crepe upon the door and places new coppers upon the dead eyes," Anderson never indulged in radical attacks on capitalism or demands for wholesale social change. Christ, he insisted, had "proclaimed the last word in socialism in the parable of the Good Samaritan."[19]

Anderson greatly admired John George Shearer, who headed the Presbyterian Church Committee on Moral and Social Reform (which teamed up with a similar Methodist committee to form the Social Service Council in 1913). Shearer had founded the Lord's Day Alliance, whose success in getting provinces and cities to enact restrictive regulations led to what came to be known as "Presbyterian Sunday." His great crusade before the First World War was against "white slavery" and the victimization of innocent women, which he saw as rampant, especially in western Canada. In 1909, Anderson read to the Session a Petition "praying for the amendment of the Criminal Code to make all gambling and traffic in the white slave trade a punishable offence," and congregants were encouraged to sign it during Sunday service.[20] There was, he told his congregation in 1910, "sin in every Canadian city, on every street, and it was contaminating some of the most generous and warm-hearted citizens." Only the church could "keep the cities Christian." Anderson was a member of the Board of the Ottawa Mission and took a personal interest in the men it served, and he was known as a keen supporter of other charitable and social improvement initiatives. He was also on the Board of the Ottawa Ladies' College, which was affiliated with the Presbyterian Church. He paid tribute to the Boy Scouts in keeping boys in the right path and praised the work of those advocating a garden city and those fighting the liquor traffic.[21] The Session of MacKay church made regular reports to Shearer's Committee on Moral and Social Reform that were incorporated into presentations to the provincial legislature.

Figure 2.8. John George Shearer, the leading Presbyterian voice for Sunday observance, Prohibition, and social reforms, who was greatly admired by Rev. Anderson.
Source: United Church Archives 76.001/P5913.

By 1914, Shearer and other religious reformers had come to realize that moral reform would not of itself produce social reform and spiritual regeneration. Moral degradation resulted from poverty, ignorance, exploitation, and vice as much as it produced them, and eliminating them would require scientific study and state intervention.[22] Observing the Lord's Day might be a religious obligation, but it was also necessary to relieve the crushing burden of a seven-day work week and to make time for rest, family life, and self-improvement. Temperance, traditionally seen as personal morality, evolved into a crusade for the prohibition of the public sale of alcohol, and against the "liquor trade" which was destroying working men and their families. By 1911, a representative of the Dominion Alliance for the Total Suppression of the Liquor Traffic occupied the MacKay church pulpit once a year, and several Elders, as well as delegates from the Young Peoples' Association and the Ladies' Aid, represented MacKay church on inter-church committees to promote Prohibition. In 1913, Anderson preached a sermon in favour of reducing liquor licenses in Ottawa to make it the most moral city in Canada. "He took up the different arguments advanced against license reduction," said a newspaper account, "and referred especially to the claim that there would be just as much liquor consumed if the number of licenses were reduced. He asked why it was that the trade was so opposing the reduction."[23]

Anderson had no doubt that Protestantism represented the best hope for progress and reform in the world, and that Canada and the Empire, their national character informed by Protestant ideals and morality, were the highest manifestation of Christian civilization.[24] At a banquet in 1913 for the Young People's Association and the Young Men's Club, Anderson told the 140 attendees, including the guest of honour, Minister of Militia Sam Hughes, of his pride in his church, country, and Empire, and his happiness to be in "Ottawa, the Capital city of the greatest Dominion under heaven." He spoke of "the position the church had filled and is filling in the world—the separation of church and state, and her wonderful influence over the lives of men. Evangelization is civilization; the progressive state means a prosperous state."[25]

The Protestant churches could best perform this role, which Phyllis Airhart describes as "friendly service to the nation"[26] by not only working together to promote evangelism and reform, but actually uniting as one national Protestant church. Presbyterians, Methodists, and some others had been discussing Church Union as early as 1902. Anderson participated at the local level in these ongoing discussions. In 1912, MacKay's congregation voted overwhelmingly in favour of the Church Union questions that were put to each Presbyterian congregation, and in 1915 it voted strongly in favour of union.[27] While they thus served the nation from within, it followed that the churches would also rise to its defence if it was threatened from without.

Anderson put these views into action in New Edinburgh, reaching out to people of all faiths. "By common agreement he belonged to all of New Edinburgh, and his parish was really the whole of Ottawa," recalled a close friend. "I have met few more spiritual men. He was a real 'shepherd of the sheep' and as a pastor he was unexcelled in my experience."[28] Anderson provided evidence in court to allow a Chinese boy, abused by his uncles who ran the local laundry, to live with Irish/French Catholic Frank Boucher until his father's return from China—even though none of the actors in this drama were members of MacKay.[29] In the decade before the war, MacKay attracted many new congregants from Anglican, Episcopal, Methodist, Congregationalist, Baptist, Lutheran, and even Catholic churches, not to mention sects such as the Plymouth Brethren or the Catholic Apostolic Church. Indeed, the experience of New Edinburgh belies the commonly held view that the people of this time were dyed in their religious wool. Some families of mixed marriages attended both churches, or spouses and children might each attend their own

Figure 2.9. "Patriotic Play" by Mrs. Anderson staged at MacKay Presbyterian Church. The cast of this play included several young men who would enlist in the war, and one, Jack Ryan (at left, second row) who would be killed (see Chapter 14). The play's title or the occasion of its performance are not known, but it was likely staged in 1913 or 1914. The Union Flags, and the military uniforms and costumes, symbolic of representing the British Empire, convey the church's strong nationalism and imperial loyalty. *Source:* MacKay United Church.

church. The evangelical beliefs of St. David's were close to those of MacKay, and when it began to decline around 1909 a number of its members came to MacKay. Several Methodist and Baptist families attended MacKay because they did not have a church close by. People moved back and forth between MacKay and St. Bartholomew's, like the family of William Short (a founder of St. Bartholomew's), whose wife, Maria, was so incensed when the Rector reproved her for a misdemeanor committed by her sons that they marched down the street to MacKay Presbyterian, and most of the family stayed there for many years even as other family members remained Anglican stalwarts.[30] Fourteen names, including three who died, appear on the Honour Rolls of both St. Bartholomew's and MacKay, and two names are common to MacKay and St. David's.[31] There were also friendly relations with the many Lutherans who lived nearby, and with St. John Lutheran Church.[32] MacKay's Young Men's Association, founded in 1909, attracted a large membership, including many outside the church, for its discussions of social as well as moral and religious subjects. Anderson's inclusive, tolerant approach ran the risk of watering down what some might have considered essential doctrines and placing social engagement above pure evangelism. But the congregation supported and

Figure 2.10. MacKay Presbyterian Church, new sanctuary, built in 1910.
Source: MacKay United Church.

reflected the balance he struck. One man who began to attend MacKay in 1916 recalled it as "an excellent example of a Union Church" whose members were "of practically all shades of Protestant beliefs with the good old Scottish Presbyterians predominating of course, and leavening the whole."[33]

In March 1910, MacKay Presbyterian Church inaugurated a new Sanctuary. Planning had begun in 1904, over $2,500 had been raised by 1908, and construction had begun the following year. The new building, designed by Henry F. Ballantyne, quickly became a New Edinburgh landmark with its rubble stone exterior, distinctive offset bell tower, and Romanesque windows and doors. Inside, the Sanctuary was unpretentious yet elegant, combining hints of traditional church architecture with exposed wooden pillars and beams, plain walls and period chandeliers, a sloped floor under an amphitheatre of simple curved oak pews, a rostrum across the front with organ, choir, and pulpit, and Arts and Crafts stained-glass windows that on sunny days bathed the interior in a golden light. It seated 300 to 400 people and was often full twice on Sundays and even during the week.

MacKay was in a very strong position in 1914. Bolstered by British immigration, the Presbyterians had edged past the Methodists as the largest and most influential Protestant denomination in Canada.[34] The ceremony opening

Figure 2.11. Modern interior of MacKay United Church. The Sanctuary was originally hung with chandeliers, but other than its modern lighting and some accessories, today's church retains the open Arts and Crafts design of 1910, with curved wooden pews, wooden pillars and accents, and amphitheatre layout. The stained-glass windows were replaced in 1924 but were almost identical to the originals. *Source:* Photograph by the author.

the new Sanctuary had been attended by the Governor General, and one of the foremost Canadian Presbyterian theologians, Principal Gandier of Knox College, had delivered an address trumpeting the importance of the church in nation building.[35] The Sunday School, the Women's Missionary Society, the Young People's Association, the Young Men's Association, as well as the new building itself, were all attracting people to the church. The Session, Managers, Ladies' Aid, and other church organizations were working to pay off the debt through a combination of fundraising activities and some not-so-gentle persuasion, such as the yearly "request" that each head of a family put a dollar—a large portion of a labourer's daily wage—on the collection plate for the building fund. But the congregants attended, and for the most part they gave. Each annual report between 1910 and 1915 described the preceding year as the best yet. In 1914 there were 364 members in 160 families, which together with adherents, members of extended families, and participants in church activities, meant that MacKay was a spiritual home for over half the population of New Edinburgh, as well as many people from surrounding communities. This was a church, within a community, that was not particularly wealthy or powerful, but was confident, close-knit, and poised, though the congregation did not know it yet, to endure the trial of war.

3
A CHURCH AT WAR
1914–1915

The long weekend of August 1–3, 1914 would later be remembered as a golden time in an idyllic summer. Those in New Edinburgh who could afford it were at cottages or summer homes along the Ottawa River and in the Gatineau Hills. Others were at Britannia Beach, Rockcliffe Park, or other recreation spots easily reached by streetcar, or enjoying swimming, boating, or canoeing on the Rideau or Ottawa rivers. If they were simply relaxing at home, they would have experienced intense heat on the first day, then humidity and a thunderstorm on Sunday, together with the odour of smoke from nearby bush fires.[1] News reports in late July of impending war in Europe had not caused undue alarm. After all, Ottawa newspapers had reported several serious war scares in Europe over the past decade. All had been peacefully resolved. The assassination of an archduke, yet another war in the Balkans, and the rattling of sabres by the Great Powers, only seemed to be more of the same. Even when Europe began to mobilize, it seemed Britain might remain outside the fray. But then Germany invaded Belgium. The British government issued an ultimatum which the Germans ignored. On August 4, the British Empire was at war with Germany. This meant that Canadians, too, were now at war.

It took some days for people in Ottawa to fully absorb the meaning of all this. Most churches in all belligerent countries were quick to declare that their cause was just, and to invoke the support of the Almighty.[2] The churches in Canada and New Edinburgh were no exception. At St. Bartholomew's, the British aides to the Governor General departed to rejoin their regiments or ships, or to enlist in the newly formed Princess Patricia's Canadian Light Infantry.[3] Ten of these men would be killed, including two Lords and two others who had "Hon." before their names. Other parishioners of St. Bartholomew's, over 80 in all, joined the Canadian Expeditionary Force and six were killed. St. David's Reformed Episcopal Church had a smaller but still impressive Honour Roll.[4]

For the Lutherans, things were more complex. The younger generation, who had grown up in the New Edinburgh community, did not need to be told by the president of the Evangelical Lutheran Synod to be loyal to the "powers that be" and avoid "any act or word, breathing the spirit of rebellion, insubordination or treason."[5] Lutheran congregations contributed to war work and a number of Lutherans in New Edinburgh enlisted. There is little evidence that Germans in New Edinburgh were suspected of being saboteurs or spies. But there were some dissenters, and according to the history of St. John church, the war presented its pastor with the "biggest challenge in his ministry" in "maintaining a strong relationship with the community for his German congregation."[6] The pastor made regular visits to German internees at Fort Henry in Kingston, but none of these appear to have been members of his congregation. He was careful to assure a newspaper reporter that his main objective, beyond providing spiritual guidance and comfort, was to "do away with a lot of bitter animosity against Canada" and he praised the fair and humane treatment of them.[7] Perhaps a better indication of the mood of the community was a newspaper report of rumours in the fall of 1914 "that the former German-Canadian team of New Edinburgh proposed amalgamating with the McKay [sic] Church team" in the Church Hockey League. "Whether or not the McKay management will agree to this is a question. If they do, however, McKay will produce a team which will be hard to beat."[8] It does not appear that such a merger took place, but it is revealing that it was even talked about.

Presbyterian General Assemblies had for many years before the war supported resolutions calling for world peace, and even as storm clouds gathered, church leaders and newspapers had believed that a peaceful resolution might be possible. But Presbyterians were not pacifists, and Rev. Anderson was certainly not one. It is a safe bet, given his statements on other occasions, that on Sunday, August 3, 1914, and in his September 6 sermon on "The Church's Duty in the National Crisis," Anderson would have echoed the declaration of Charles W. Gordon (better known as the novelist Ralph Connor) that "[w]ith a clear conscience and a steadfast heart, we can invoke the God, not of battles, but the God of Righteousness and Truth to our aid."[9] He would have agreed with Rev. Herridge of St. Andrew's Presbyterian Church in downtown Ottawa that while Christ stood for peace, He abhorred injustice and expected Christians to take action to cleanse the world of the evil that now threatened both the Empire and the ideals and values of Western civilization. Germany had attacked a peaceful neighbour without provocation. It had trampled on sacred treaties and the international order. Germany's militarist, authoritarian regime had debased its Christian ideals in the service of a perverted science and a distorted *kultur*. Anderson would have been careful, like other leading Presbyterians, to make clear that this war was being waged not against the German people but against the pride and oppression of their rulers. The struggle would be long and difficult, and Christians must remain humble and trust in God. But Anderson would have assured his flock that an Allied victory would rescue Germany from the great evil that had overtaken it, and that the Canadian people would be redeemed by their sacrifice and service from the materialism, selfishness, and immorality he had been deploring for many years.[10]

Figure 3.1. "Your Chums are Fighting, Why aren't You?" This was one of many recruiting posters from the early days of the war encouraging young men to sign up.
Source: Library and Archives Canada C-029484.

Given the militia tradition of MacKay, its strong support for the South African War, and Anderson's national and imperial patriotism, it is unlikely that those who attended on those Sundays would have disagreed with any of this. Inspired by their religious beliefs, by the need to defend the Empire, and by the ideals of Christian manliness, and with the encouragement and support of their families, community, and church, it is little wonder that many young men from MacKay rushed to enlist in the first days of the war.

August–September 1914: The First Men Enlist

Brushing aside the mobilization plans prepared by his professional military staff, Minister of Militia Sam Hughes sent out telegrams to militia commanders across the country inviting them to bring their regiments to a newly created camp at Valcartier, Quebec. Chaos and confusion reigned when the men arrived in late August. An understaffed administration wrestled with the logistics of an unfinished camp, the paperwork required to attest the men, provide medical examinations, and create a pay and record system, and the organization of companies, brigades, and battalions and appointment of officers. In the first days of October, having received rudimentary training at best and with the ink hardly dry on the attestation papers, the 31,000 men of the First Contingent of the Canadian Expeditionary Force marched through Quebec City with bands playing and crowds cheering, boarded troopships, and sailed for England. Twenty men, or one-seventh of all those whose names would appear on the MacKay Honour Roll, enlisted in some fashion during August and September 1914.[11]

Figure 3.2. Panoramic view of Valcartier Camp, 1916. The camp is much the same as it would have appeared to the men who signed up between August 1914 and mid-1916.
Source: Canadian War Museum CWM 200030180-004, George Metcalf Archival Collection.

Twelve MacKay men joined local militia regiments that travelled to Valcartier in August:

- Three men were attested into the 2nd Battalion of infantry: **Leslie Watters Tubman**, 22, a bank clerk and civil servant from an old New Edinburgh family (his story is told in Chapter 14); **Thomas Winton**, 22, a florist/gardener who had come to Canada from Scotland in 1912; and **Oscar May**, 20, a furniture repairman whose father (a German-Canadian convert from Lutheranism) had represented his

militia regiment at Queen Victoria's Diamond Jubilee in London in 1897.
- Four men joined the Canadian Field Artillery (CFA): **Frederick Jamieson**, 27, a railway conductor, joined the 1st Battery; **William and George Farmer**, 20 and 21 respectively, sons of contractor George Farmer, joined the 2nd Battery; and **Robert Finter**, 22, son of a gardener for leading families in Rockcliffe, also joined the artillery.[12]
- Five men enlisted in other services: **John Bothwell**, 23, a printer, son of W. C. Edwards' yard foreman William Bothwell, joined the Canadian Army Service Corps as a medical assistant (his story is told in Chapter 7); Capt. **Dr. Neil MacLeod**, a 37-year-old physician who had practised in New Edinburgh since 1909 and was a medical officer in the militia, became a medical officer in the CEF; **Arthur Wilson**, 18, son of Mrs. Theresa Coker and stepson of George Victor Coker (see Chapter 6), joined the Canadian Army Service Corps as a driver; **George F. Beardsley**, 37, a civil service clerk who had just moved to New Edinburgh with his family, joined the Royal Canadian Dragoons; and **Emil May**, 23, brother of Oscar, enlisted as a bugler but later served in the infantry at the front.

Of the remaining eight:

- **William A. Williams,** a petty officer in the naval department, joined the crew of the cruiser HMCS *Niobe* in August 1914. One of two obsolete British ships in the fledgling Royal Canadian Navy, the *Niobe* had been taken out of service in 1911 but was reactivated when war broke out. It patrolled the Atlantic coast until it was declared unfit for service in 1915. There is no further information regarding Williams after 1915—he did not return to MacKay.
- **John MacKenzie**, a 32-year-old policeman who had emigrated from Scotland in 1907 and married a woman from the German community in New Edinburgh, was called back to Scotland to serve with the Seaforth Highlanders.[13]
- Three men who enlisted at the start of the war were not members of MacKay Presbyterian Church at the time, but they or their families would later join the church: **Alexander Masson**, 28, a Scottish rancher in Moose Jaw, enlisted in the Princess Patricia's Canadian Light Infantry at Ottawa;[14] **Daniel Robertson Jr.**, 24, a Scottish immigrant working as a plasterer in Saskatoon, enlisted in the 11th Battalion CEF (see Chapter 9); and **Archibald Stewart McLaurin**, 21, whose family joined MacKay church in 1915, was homesteading in Alberta when he enlisted with the 19th Alberta Dragoons.

- Three MacKay men were listed in a newspaper article as having signed up in the fall of 1914, but no records have been located of their service: **Stanley Williams** had played a leading role in one of Mrs. Anderson's plays in 1912; **John Edwards** joined MacKay with his wife in 1912 but disappears from the records in 1915; no record has been found for **G. T. Watson**.[15]

October 1914–February 1915: Recruiting the Second Contingent

The first two months of the war took a terrible toll on all fronts. In France, the British regular army was all but wiped out as the Germans advanced almost to the gates of Paris before being thrown back to the line of trenches that would, in spite of major offensives and bloody battles, remain largely static for many months to come. New armies would now have to be recruited and trained. No sooner had the First Canadian Contingent embarked for England than recruitment began for a Second.

Six men whose names would appear on the MacKay Honour Roll enlisted in the Second Contingent:

- Five MacKay men signed up in January and February 1915. **Robert Drake**, 20, a civil engineer who was a son of a government land reclamation expert, joined the 2nd Signal Company, Canadian Field Engineers. **Gordon Halcro Clark**, 19, a student draughtsman who was a son of one of the last steamboat captains on the Ottawa River, also joined the Canadian Engineers. **William Slinn**, 26, a "Physical Director" and the first of three sons of dairy owner Breary Slinn who would enlist, joined the Canadian Army Medical Corps as an orderly. **Carson Kendall**, 22, a medical student whose father was a millwright, also joined the Canadian Army Medical Corps (he served for a short time in a general hospital in France in 1915 but was soon sent back to Canada to finish his medical studies). **Norman K. Willson**, 31, married, a refiner at the Royal Canadian Mint, had served for over a decade in the permanent militia and went to Valcartier in March 1915 as a sergeant-major in the artillery; he was discharged in August "at his own request" and then signed up in October at the Niagara Camp with the 40th Battery, CFA, and served with that unit throughout the war.
- **Charles A. Wendt**, 21, a florist whose cousin would later join MacKay church, enlisted in the 21st Battalion in November 1914 (his story is told in Chapter 4).

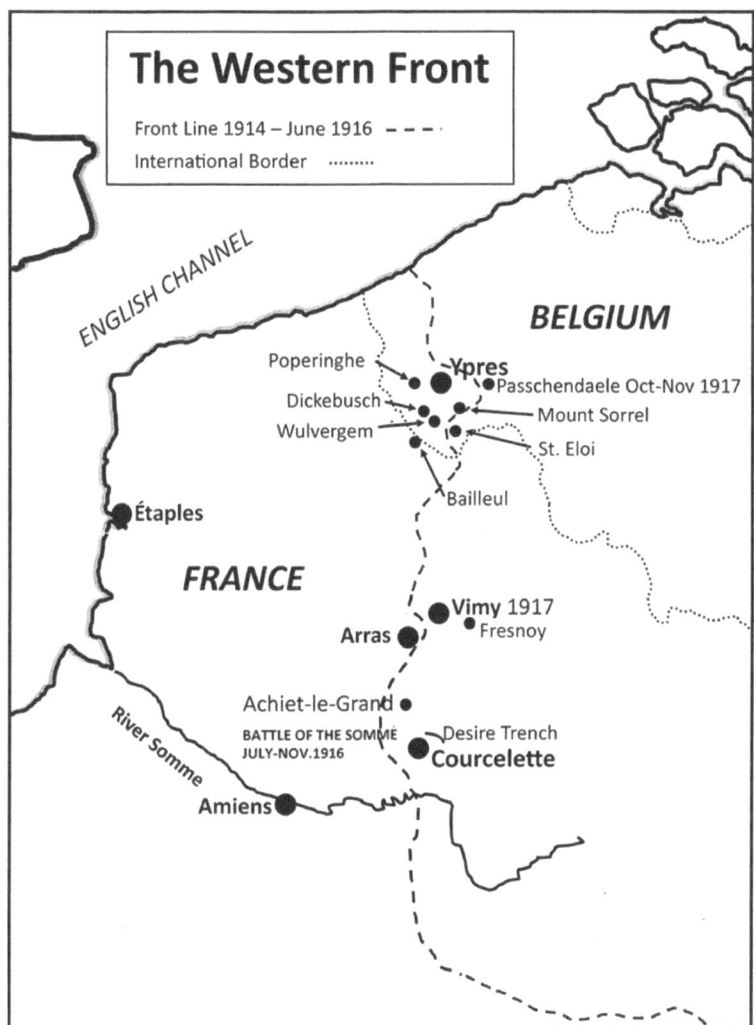

Figure 3.3. The Western Front. The front lines changed little between late 1914 and the Somme campaign in the summer of 1916.
Source: Created by the author.

January–June 1915: Recruiting the Third Contingent

In early 1915, recruitment began for a Third Contingent, which would be trained in Canada rather than rushed overseas as the first two had been. Two infantry battalions that were intended to form part of this contingent were raised in Ottawa during the first half of 1915: the 8th Canadian Mounted Rifles and the 38th Battalion.

8th Canadian Mounted Rifles

The Canadian Mounted Rifles were mounted infantry that would, it was thought, combine the mobility of cavalry with the firepower of infantry. Training for Ottawa's contribution, the 8th Canadian Mounted Rifles (8 CMR), began at Lansdowne Park in January 1915, though the horses did not arrive until April. In May, 8 CMR departed for further training in Kingston, then returned to Ottawa in October for one final parade before the Governor General on Parliament Hill, after which the men boarded special trains to begin their journey overseas. By the time they reached England, the military authorities, after long debate, had finally recognized that mounted infantry would have little value in trench warfare, and there were no plausible alternative uses for them. Four CMR regiments were therefore converted into infantry battalions and incorporated directly into the Third Canadian Division. The others, including 8 CMR, were broken up and the men were reassigned.

Ten men from MacKay enlisted and trained in 8 CMR. The list that follows includes the units they were assigned to when 8 CMR was broken up:

- **Homère Joliat**, 20, a clerk in the Ottawa water department, who was a son of an Ottawa police detective; **Albert Kendall**, 22, a surveyor (brother of Carson Kendall); and **Sidney Mansell**, 18, a clerk and son of a specialist in the Royal Canadian Mint; were assigned to the Borden Motor Machine Gun Battery (see Chapter 20).
- **James Cairncross**, 24, a printer who had emigrated from Britain, served in various units in Britain.
- **Harold and Milton Short**, 20 and 19, who enlisted together, became clerks in the 3rd Division Headquarters in France.
- **George and John Powers**, 21 and 20, sons of the owner of a men's furnishing store, and **Joseph Munro**, 18, a clerk who was the adopted son of Margaret Munro, were sent to the 27th Infantry Battalion (originally from Winnipeg) in the Second Division.
- **Ernest Gardner**, 34, a taxi business operator in Eastview, became an ambulance driver.

38th Battalion

The 38th Infantry Battalion began recruiting in January 1915, with serious training beginning in April. It was quickly oversubscribed. All new battalions were required to send advance drafts of 250 men to England to replace losses in the field, but the 38th was able to send two such drafts—one in May, and a second in June. Once the battalion was down to its proper size, it was sent to Kingston for training. Then on July 31, 1915, the 38th was paraded before the Governor General before being sent to Bermuda for garrison duty and further training by British professionals.

Figure 3.4. 38th Battalion: Company inspection before going overseas, c. 1915.
Source: History of Canada, public domain.

Ten men whose names appear on the Honour Roll enlisted in this battalion:

- Three MacKay men went to England in the June reinforcing draft: **G. Victor Coker**, 37, a labourer who had immigrated from Britain in 1907 and married widow Theresa Wilson; his stepson **William Henry Wilson**, 19 (their stories are told in Chapter 6); and **Robert Hill**, 18, who had grown up in the Protestant Orphans' Home with his sister Bessie who had married a prominent member of MacKay church. All three were sent to join the 2nd Battalion at the front.
- Five MacKay men went to Bermuda with the 38th: **George Cruikshank**, 31, a floor finisher, and **John McGillivray**, 28, a bank clerk, both Scottish immigrants and married with children; **Reginald Elliott**, 35, a butcher who had emigrated in 1911 from England and was the father of five; **Julius Hillas**, 41, an English immigrant painter and musician, who enlisted as a bandsman; and **Herbert Charles Love**, 37, a father of eight, who enlisted as a cook.
- Two men who were not members of the church, but whose names would appear on the Honour Roll, also went to Bermuda: **Gordon Porteous**, 20, a labourer from Buckingham, Quebec (his story is told in Chapter 10); and **Arthur Frank Hawke**, 25, a labourer from a German family in New Edinburgh (his story is told in Chapter 23).

Other Units

Six men enlisted in other units in the Third Contingent:

- **Samuel Thomas Samways**, 35, a street railway conductor with previous service in the British Royal Marines, enlisted in April in the Remount Depot which became part of the Canadian Army Veterinary Corps, and went to France in July where he rose to the rank of sergeant. (The CAVC was responsible for care of the 40,000 horses being used at any given time by various branches of the military.)
- **William Currie**, 46 (he lied about his age), a decorator in Brockville whose family owned greenhouses on Rideau Terrace, enlisted in the 156th Battalion in June but was discharged as medically unfit.
- **Mathew William Ryan**, 32, a street railway conductor, enlisted in July in the 59th Battalion and was assigned to the 24th Battalion when the 59th was broken up in England. (His story is told in Chapter 16.)
- Two other men who were not members of MacKay church, but whose families would join during the war, were **George Robertson**, 21, a stationer, who enlisted in the 59th Battalion (his story is told in Chapter 9); and **Russell White**, 19, a plumber, who joined the Canadian Engineers. A Baptist, White would join MacKay church on his return from overseas.
- There is no information on **Norman Cameron**, who joined the Third Contingent in March 1915.

March–June 1915: The War Develops

The written records of the church during the first months of the war make little reference to the ongoing conflict. It was business as usual: maintaining the church building, paying down the debt, managing the choir, canvassing for funds, distributing communion tokens, receiving new members, supporting temperance campaigns, and allocating funds to charities. Only the Ladies' Aid minutes refer to war work. The Presbyterian General Assembly in June passed resolutions deploring the barbaric treatment by the Germans of conquered peoples, declaring that Germany's conduct threatened the progress of Christianity and the peace of humanity, recognizing the heroism of the soldiers, and praying for peace.

But by early 1915 the war was assuming an increasingly central place in the life of MacKay church. At a "patriotic service" on March 7, 1915, a flag bearing the names of the men from the church who had enlisted up to that date was unfurled by Rev. Anderson. "After the service," read a newspaper account, "the flag was placed in the vestry, where it will remain." That evening at the manse the Young Peoples' Association held an at-home for those men still in training in the city.[16] A little over two weeks later Mr. H. B. Brophy, MP, speaking on "Britain and the War," extolled "the statesmanship of the men at the head of affairs in the Empire," as well as "the loyalty of the British people."[17]

In June, at a special service marking the end of the Sunday School season, Lt. Col. A. T. Thompson gave a thinly disguised recruiting pitch aimed at the older Sunday School boys. He lamented Britain's unpreparedness for war, her naïve trust in human goodness, and the perfidy of the German attack. He spoke of the magnificence and grand ideals of the Empire and Canada's share in both. But he warned that the past empires of Babylon and Rome had fallen and that the British Empire "will surely pass away and become food for antiquarians and historians unless we continue our fight for right principles and high ideals."[18]

Between these two patriotic services, news of the Battle of Second Ypres had made clear the terrible reality of war. After a miserable winter of training on Salisbury Plain, the First Canadian Division had been sent to the Ypres Salient, a bulge in the front line around the medieval city of Ypres, Belgium, which the British were determined to hold at all costs. On April 22, 1915, the Germans used chlorine gas for the first time on the Western Front, against a French colonial regiment to the left of the Canadians. With their flank suddenly exposed, the Canadians, including two MacKay men, covered their faces with cloths soaked in water or urine and fought desperately to avoid being surrounded and annihilated. When forced to retreat, they made an orderly withdrawal. The Canadians, once regarded as undisciplined colonials, had won a reputation for courage. But within days pride gave way to horror, as lengthy casualty lists began to fill the Ottawa newspapers. News reports and soldiers' letters home left little doubt as to the ordeal the men had endured. An Ottawa newspaper reported that Daniel Robertson Jr. (whose family would join MacKay in 1916) had described in a letter home "how, when they were retiring, the machine guns of the enemy played such havoc on their ranks that in the roll call which followed only about 330 answered to their names out of 1,000. He also gave several illustrations of the narrow escapes he and his chum had while under fire and his great thankfulness to be alive from it all."[19] Then in June the Battle of Festubert produced another long casualty list. The First Division had been effectively destroyed. No one could now have any doubt that this would be a long and terrible war.

July–November 1915: Recruiting Continues

Far from discouraging recruitment, the news from the front only seemed to make men more eager to enlist. When a new Ottawa infantry battalion, the 77th, began recruiting in July, men lined up at recruiting offices as they would for tickets at a hockey game, and the battalion soon had hundreds more men than it needed.[20] In addition, two batteries of field artillery were being raised in the city as the Canadian Corps struggled to shore up that crucial element of its forces; and there was every bit as much enthusiasm for this service as for the infantry.

The 77th Battalion

The 77th would be the first battalion to receive all its training in Ottawa. In August, the men went under canvas at Rockcliffe for instruction in musketry, signalling, first aid, trench work, and bayonet fighting, as well as long route marches. There were so many recruits that a draft of 250 men was sent directly overseas in October, and later in the year smaller drafts were sent to Bermuda and to reinforce a forestry battalion. Once down to its proper size, the 77th moved into winter quarters in downtown armouries and public buildings to continue its training, and it became the darling of the city. Patriotic societies, churches, politicians, and wealthy patrons fell over each other to donate guns, musical instruments, and clothing, and to provide concerts, musicales, carnivals, and suppers, and in all other ways to care for the men in uniform.[21]

Nine MacKay men (plus Robert Finter who enlisted for his second time and was once again quickly discharged as medically unfit) signed up in the 77th:

- Two, **Alfred Philp**, 19, an assistant machinist who had come to Canada in 1912 to live with his foster family, and **Charles Edward Trotter**, 37, an English bricklayer, were sent to England in the reinforcing draft in October 1915. Philp would join the 4th CMR and Trotter the 60th Battalion (his story is told in Chapter 8).
- Six men continued training in Ottawa with the 77th: **Henry J. Mayo**, 18, a lithographer, married and with a child (his story is told in Chapter 11); **James Leach**, 18, an English immigrant from a family of calico-weavers; **Frank Henry Miles**, 42 (he lied about his age), an English immigrant bricklayer; **William Fixter Stevenson**, 19, a clerk for the Ottawa Electric Company whose father was a gardener at Rideau Hall; **William Henry Lanceley**, 22, a clerk whose father was House Steward at Rideau Hall; and **John Simpson**, 31, a Scottish immigrant employed by the CNR, married with three children.
- **William Price Robertson**, 19, a clerk, was not a member of MacKay but his family would join the church in late 1916 (see Chapter 9).

Canadian Field Artillery (CFA)

Each Canadian Division was intended to have three brigades of mobile field artillery, as well as batteries of siege guns and companies of trench

Figure 3.5. "'B' Company, 77th Overseas Battalion, C.E.F., Ottawa, Can, June 7, 1916"; silver gelatin photograph. *Source:* Bytown Museum, P648.

mortars. Each field artillery brigade would consist of three batteries of four 18-pounder guns and one battery of howitzers. Each of these batteries comprised some 130–140 men, including six gunners operating each gun, drivers to manage the teams of horses drawing the guns and ammunition wagons, and an ammunition column to transport ammunition, food, and supplies to the front. The minimum height and weight requirements for gunners were higher than for the infantry, though smaller men might find a place as drivers or in the ammunition columns.

But the First Contingent had taken with it all the up-to-date guns and most of the trained gunners when it departed in the fall of 1914, so the artillery batteries for the Second and Third Divisions had to start from scratch. Without modern guns or proficient teachers, training was mostly physical training, lectures, signalling, and the management of horses, with some instruction on obsolete 12-pounders. Only when they got to England would these batteries get proper instruction on modern guns. Even then, they still had to wait before their own guns were manufactured and delivered, and they would thus not join their divisions until months after the infantry battalions had been sent to the front.

Figure 3.6. "Artillery Heroes at the Front Say 'Get into a Man's Uniform'". *Source:* Library and Archives Canada C-095377.

- Three MacKay men enlisted in the 25th Battery, CFA, which sailed for England in August 1915 as part of the 7th Brigade, CFA, in the Second Canadian Division: **Walter Samuel Lindsay**, 16 (he lied about his age), son of a foreman in the Edwards mills; **Clifford Leslie Erskine**, 18, an engineering draftsman with the City of Ottawa, also a son of a foreman with W. C. Edwards; and **Reginald Isambard Brunel**, 18, a clerk in the City Engineer's Office who was the son of an engineer in the public service (his story is told in Chapter 15).

- Five MacKay men joined the 32nd Battery, CFA, part of the 8th Brigade, CFA, in the Third Canadian Division, which went to Kingston for training (it would sail for England in February 1916): **Irwin Kelly**, 18, a clerk in the Royal Canadian Mint and son of a house-painter (his story is told in Chapter 21); **Alex Hobart Clarke**, 17 (he lied about his age), whose brother had already enlisted; **George Selkirk Bothwell**, 26, an electrician, married and with three small children, whose brother was already overseas (his story is told in Chapter 7); **Thomas Knight Gerard**, 23, an accountant whose father was a millwright and whose parents were both leading figures in the church; and **Robert Bruce Smith**, 50 (he lied about his age), a stationary engineer with a wife and six children.

Other Enlistments

Seven MacKay men enlisted during the second half of 1915 in other infantry battalions being raised outside Ottawa, or in specialist units:

- **Alex Lyon McKenzie** and **John Langsdale McKenzie**, 22 and 19, sons of a department store salesman, joined the 37th Battalion (Algonquin Rifles) (their stories are told in Chapter 22).
- **John Fotheringham Askwith**, 32, a clerk from a well-established New Edinburgh family, enlisted in Calgary in the 3rd University Company, 103rd Calgary Rifles, which was being recruited to reinforce the Princess Patricia's Canadian Light Infantry.[22]
- **Herbert Henry Rolt**, 35, a chauffeur who had come to Ottawa in 1913 to serve at Government House, enlisted as a driver in the second reinforcing draft for the Canadian Army Service Corps.
- **John Marshall**, 40, a Scottish chauffeur who had immigrated in 1910, enlisted in the British Army Service Corps Mechanical Transport Section (his story is told in Chapter 19).
- **Thomas Nicholas Jackson**, 19, a steamfitter in his father's contracting business, enlisted with the 3rd Division Canadian Engineers (see Chapter 8).
- **J. McGowan** enlisted in the summer of 1915 but there is no further information.

1915 Draws to a Close

On January 19, 1916, the Annual General Meeting of the congregation of MacKay Presbyterian Church was told, with some pride, that there were now 65 MacKay men in khaki. "This list," said a newspaper account, "includes the President of the Young Peoples' Association, Mr. T. K Gerard; five Sunday

School teachers; 14 scholars, and 18 ex-scholars. This is an excellent record considering the fact that the membership of the church totals 397."[23] According to the Communion Rolls, 25 of these men were full members of the church. 23 others were from families where one or both parents, and perhaps some siblings, were members; they undoubtedly attended church at least occasionally, and would probably have attended Sunday School and participated in other church activities. Seventeen were adherents—occasional or frequent churchgoers who had not formally joined, newcomers to the community, or members of other churches or denominations who attended MacKay.

But in fact, 76 men whose names would eventually appear on MacKay's Honour Roll—including men whose families would join the church later in the war—had enlisted by the end of 1915. Of these 76 men fifteen would die. Of the sixty-nine for whom such information is available, two were underage, seventeen were 18–19, twenty-five were 20–25, five were 26–30, fifteen were 31–39, and five were over 40. Only a handful had any high school education and only two appear to have attended university (both were in the medical corps). In contrast to the general pattern across the country, two-thirds (46) were Canadian-born and at least half of these had long and deep ties to New Edinburgh and MacKay church. Only one-third (23) had emigrated from Britain, all after 1907 and more than half after 1911.

Ten families had two sons who enlisted—in several cases at the same time—and other brothers of those already in uniform would join later in the war. Those under 18 had lied about their age, and their families must have known it—a phone call from his mother would have ended 16-year-old Walter Lindsay's enlistment before it began. Some men—we do not know how many—would have tried to enlist but were rejected as too short, too small, or medically unfit. Some of these men would find their way into uniform later in the war as standards were relaxed, or as the authorities increasingly recognized that less-than-fit men could still do useful service.[24] There is also evidence that some might have served in militia regiments or performed other quasi-military duties. There is no evidence to indicate whether economic motivations played any role in the decision to enlist; but most of these men appear to have been employed.

Married men, especially those with children, needed the permission of their wives to enlist until the middle of 1915. Of those who signed up before that time, only twelve were married; seven of these men had children but only four of them would serve in front-line units. After permission was no longer required, four married men, all with children, signed up and all were in combat roles. There is no record of any provision by the church for direct assistance to the women with children whose husbands were abroad (or widowed mothers who depended on their sons for support). Presumably, assigned and separation pay, together with assistance from the Patriotic Fund, were deemed sufficient. But some of the men—including some with militia service—who did not enlist at this point may have been needed to support families, including widowed mothers, or orphaned siblings.[25]

There is thus no question about the enthusiasm of the young (and some not-so-young) men of MacKay and their families for the war effort, nor about the commitment of the church. In November the Ladies' Aid "proposed to send a Christmas bag to each man from our Congregation who had enlisted for overseas service," and the following month this was broadened to include those still in Canada. The Ladies' Aid also agreed to a request from the Women's Auxiliary of the YMCA to entertain the 77th Battalion and engineers on a Sunday during the winter.

Indeed, there is something a bit chilling today in how proud the church was of the number of Sunday School teachers, graduates, and scholars who had marched off to war. By the end of 1915 the reality of the war had become apparent to all. One man well known at MacKay church, Charlie Wendt, had been killed. Fred Jamieson had been seriously wounded at Second Ypres. But only a small number of MacKay soldiers had been in the front lines; most were still in training and would not see action until 1916. For the present, MacKay families could take pride in seeing their boys in uniform, and they could be encouraged by upbeat letters from training camps in Kingston, Bermuda, or England. Still, they all knew that some of their names—perhaps many of them—would appear on casualty lists in the coming months. As 1915 drew to a close, sermons from the pulpit, and prayers from the people, might well have echoed what Lt. Col. Thompson said in June: "to those who had gone he fervently said, God save them; to those who are going, God speed them; and to those who anxiously wait, God comfort them."[26]

4

CHARLES ALBERT WENDT
A German-Canadian Patriot

It is ironic that, of the men whose names appear on the In Memoriam plaque in MacKay Presbyterian Church, the first and last to die were members of the large German Lutheran community in New Edinburgh. Though both men had strong ties to MacKay, neither was formally a member. Their presence on the Honour Roll is testament to the outreach of this Presbyterian church and its minister to people of other faiths and backgrounds, and of its willingness to recognize the sacrifice of all those who came within its orbit.

Charles Albert Wendt was part of an extended family descended from Heinrich Wendt (1818–1888) and his wife, who had come from Pomerania in the wave of German immigration to Renfrew County.[1] By 1891, two of their sons were living in New Edinburgh: Johann ("John") Wendt, whose son Albert Wendt will figure in our story; and Wilhelm ("Billy") Wendt, a motorman for the Ottawa Electric Railway who lived in a small attached frame house with his wife, Augusta Raabe, and their seven children: Louise (1889), Henry (1891), Charles (1893), Margaret (1895), Herbert (1897), and two younger children.[2] Several other members of the Raabe family were also in New Edinburgh, working for industries such as the Ottawa Electric Railway, the Edwards Sash and Door Factory, the Hull Brewing and Malting Company, and as labourers for the city and at Rideau Hall.

In 1900 Wilhelm "Billy" Wendt enlisted in the Royal Canadian Regiment for service in the Boer War, a war that had little support among German-Canadians. After a long journey to South Africa, he endured the difficult march across the veldt and participated in the disastrous battle at Paardeberg and the eventual victory at Cronje's Laager that ended the first phase of the war.[3] Though he escaped injury in battle, he and many other soldiers contracted severe gastroenteritis from drinking river water. After months in hospital he was invalided to London and then sent back to Canada. He and four comrades from Ottawa were greeted by cheering crowds when they arrived in Quebec in July 1900, and two days later, thousands of enthusiastic Ottawans met them at the station. For months afterwards, he was frequently visited by well-wishers, and the local Orange Lodge presented him with an expensive mantle-clock.[4] Billy Wendt remained a sergeant in the militia and frequently participated in its shooting competitions.

Figure 4.1. Charles A. Wendt.
Source: Ottawa *Citizen*, December 3, 1915.

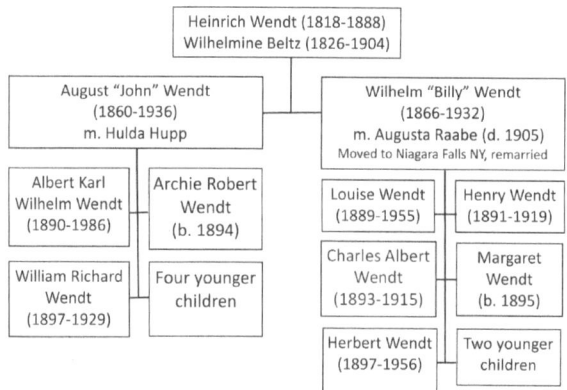

Figure 4.2. Family tree of the Wendts.
Source: Created by author.

Figure 4.3. Wilhelm "Billy" Wendt.
Source: Ottawa *Journal*, July 14, 1900.

Though the family remained Lutheran, several of Billy Wendt's children attended Sunday School at MacKay Presbyterian Church.[5] But his family was blown apart in 1905 when his wife died after an operation.[6] The following year, he moved to Niagara Falls, New York, with his youngest children and became a motorman on the street railway there. He married Sarah Tunstead (1874–1950), an Irish immigrant, and they had three more children as well as her two sons by her first marriage.[7] He never returned to Canada, but his two oldest children stayed behind in New Edinburgh.

Fourteen-year-old Henry and twelve-year-old Charles Wendt went to live with their late mother's parents, William Raabe, a carpenter, and his wife, Carolina. In 1911 they were both florists in the greenhouses on Rideau Terrace, working 60 hours a week for about $400 a year.[8] By 1913 two of their sisters had returned from Niagara Falls and were also living in New Edinburgh. The eldest, Louise, married Daniel O'Leary, a clerk for a company manufacturing stoves. The couple lived in a new brick row house at 33 Ivy Street with Louise's younger sister Margaret, a bookbinder, and it was Louise who was named on Charles's attestation papers as next of kin.[9] (The O'Learys later moved to a new brick double house at 364 MacKay Street, and then to Montreal before returning to Niagara Falls, where it appears that Daniel died in 1917.) "Charlie" Wendt was a well-known young man in the New Edinburgh community.

On November 6, 1914, 21-year-old Charles Albert Wendt enlisted in the 21st Battalion based in Kingston, in the Second Contingent of the Canadian Expeditionary Force. He was five feet nine and a half inches tall, with fair complexion, blue eyes, and light-brown hair. The 21st Battalion was being recruited from cities and towns in eastern Ontario, including French Canadians from "up the valley" and men who had missed out on the First Contingent. Its dynamic recruiting sergeant and its commanding officer, Lt. Col. William St. Pierre Hughes—a militia officer who had been inspector of penitentiaries and was a veteran of the 1885 North-West campaign (and was a brother of the Minister of Militia, Sir Sam Hughes)—portrayed the 21st as a regiment "on the go," willing to cut corners and move quickly. Evidence of this is that Wendt's attestation papers were approved in Ottawa on October 22 (more than two weeks before his formal enlistment) by Hughes himself; Wendt's "signature" is in the same handwriting as the rest of the form; Wendt is both declarant and witness to his oath; his religion is given as Anglican, which was the default entry when a recruiting officer did not ask or know the correct answer; and the magistrate who counter-signed all these papers in Kingston on November 6 was one W. S. Hughes! The battalion was over-subscribed when it began training in Kingston.[10] Wendt was assigned to G Company and later to the Machine Gun Section.

Rigorous training weeded out some unfit men, and the officers received training at the Royal Military College. But uniforms did not arrive until late November and nor did they yet have the latest version of the Ross Rifle—a Canadian-made weapon that would prove unreliable in combat and which would be replaced by the British Lee-Enfield rifle in 1916. Discipline was not all it should have been, and even sentences of 28 days in confinement did not altogether deter drinking and rowdiness, much less some misbehaviour at the social events provided by the people of Kingston.[11] Nonetheless, according to a postwar publication honouring the battalion, on May 5 "the '21st'" was accorded a rousing send-off by the people of Kingston, who most heartily showed their appreciation of the spirit and loyalty" of the battalion; at Brockville and Cornwall "the citizens assembled at the stations and wished all 'God speed' and a 'safe return.'"[12]

The 21st Battalion sailed from Montreal and after a "pleasant" 10-day voyage on the *Metagama*—this ocean liner had not yet been converted to a troop ship and there were nursing sisters from several hospital units on the voyage—arrived in England and settled in at the West Sandling Camp, Kent.

Here the cocky and undisciplined Canadians underwent a progressively more serious regimen of training, in musketry (where they began to find out the shortcomings of the Ross rifle) and trench warfare (where they were taught some of the harsh lessons learned on the battlefields at Ypres earlier in the year). They were inspected by Sir Robert Borden, Sir Sam Hughes—in both cases in a downpour—by Canadian-born British parliamentarian Bonar Law, and on September 2, by the King and Lord Kitchener. Then on September 14, 1915, they embarked for France as part of the Second Canadian Division. At Boulogne, after a hearty welcome by the local population, they began a long trek to the Ypres Salient in which, during an all-night march, their Canadian-made boots literally dissolved in the mud.[13]

The reality of war in the Ypres Salient was far worse than anything they could have imagined during their training. Private Donald Fraser, who was there at the same time, vividly recalled life in the salient: constant mud, rain, and frost; men marching over rotting duckboards; the ever-present threat of snipers and shells; non-stop work parties digging, draining, moving roads, trenches, and communications systems; men cold and soaked to the skin. Some of the older men had to be sent to the rear because they could not stand the cold and damp; others cracked under the strain.[14] The 21st Battalion was based near Dickebusch throughout the autumn of 1915. Its only real action was a "demonstration" on September 25, with machine gun fire and smoke, to support a British attack on Loos.[15] "Just a few lines," Charlie wrote his family in early November, "to let you know I am still alive and kicking and to hope you are the same. It is still very muddy out here; it's fierce the rain we get. We have had rain capes issued to us. It's a good thing too; they keep out most of the rain. War is about the same around our parts, merely exchanging shots."[16] But "exchanging shots" was hardly as trivial as the folks back home may have imagined. As the war diary of the battalion shows, men were killed or wounded on a daily basis, a process clinically described by the High Command as "wastage." Between December 1, 1915, and March 31, 1916, 10 percent of the Canadian soldiers at the front were killed, wounded, or missing, yet there were no major battles during that period.[17]

In trench warfare, it was the practice of the Canadian Corps to rotate men regularly in and out of the front lines. At any given time, two of the three brigades that formed a Division would be at the front, while a third was in "Divisional Reserve," well to the rear, where the men could refit, train, and rest. In each of the two brigades at the front, two battalions would be in the front-line trenches facing the enemy, a third would be in support trenches a little further back, with the fourth in "brigade reserve," still further back. Soldiers would thus typically spend about eight days a month in the front-line trenches, where they experienced the taut nerves of men exposed to constant danger. They would then have a week in positions half a mile back, where they dug trenches, repaired transport, equipment, and communications, and moved supplies, usually at night because they were still within artillery and even machine gun range. Only during the third week, in billets four or five miles behind the lines, could they truly relax, with games, sports, a bath (so-called, usually a few minutes in a tub or getting hosed down), dry clothes, and estaminets where Belgian families did a roaring business providing chips and eggs, and sometimes wine, beer, and other services, to the Canadian troops.[18]

This constant rotation was necessary to the morale, training, and well-being of the troops, but the men were exposed to great danger when they moved in and out of the front lines. Fraser has left a riveting account of what happened when his company had to go through an open stretch called "Suicide Road."

> When trenches are broken down, getting into the line is a ticklish business. An alert enemy can discern your paths and prepare for you at night time. He may let off a burst of fire every now and then at a certain spot on the off chance that there are passers by. Coming up Suicide Road stray bullets were whizzing fairly thick and we were feeling decidedly uneasy. I remember our section officer was leading, the sergeant second, a Lance Corporal third, and I was fourth, when a bullet crashed through the hedge [...] and caught Jimmy Rodgers in the arm with a loud smack. He was about three yards behind me. The bullet came in a slanting direction and brought Rodgers to earth with a cry. Dunstall of our Company was wounded the same night, getting into the line. We heaved a sigh of relief when we reached [the Company's assigned trench line] and had the friendly protection of the firing trench to keep the strays away.[19]

On November 14, 1915, a week after the incident Fraser describes, the 21st Battalion was moving in the opposite direction, company by company, from the front to Brigade Reserve. As his company was moving out of the trenches, a stray bullet caught Charles Wendt in the stomach.[20]

Wendt was in all probability taken by stretcher-bearers to a field ambulance, where he was given initial treatment and was then sent on a bumpy and painful journey by ambulance to Casualty Clearing Station (CCS) No. 3, just across the French border at Bailleul, France. Bailleul was a railhead, headquarters, and staging area for troops and supplies, and it had British, Canadian, and Australian CCSs with medical staff, nurses, and operating facilities. There, soldiers were treated for wounds, perhaps operated on, and then sent on by ambulance trains to base hospitals, and perhaps from there to England for treatment and rehabilitation. But those who died of their wounds at the CCS were buried in a specially created extension of the Bailleul Communal Cemetery.

Unfortunately, Wendt was among the latter group. He died on November 16, 1915, and was buried by Padre Rev. A. V. Hodges who also erected the cross on his grave. He was 22.[21] His brother Harry told the Ottawa *Citizen* that the family had just sent him a large Christmas package. "We were proud of our brother and did our best to make his Christmas in the trenches comfortable." In his last letter Charlie had written: "I wish we could make one big drive and end this business. Best regards to all. Au revoir. Charlie."[22] He was not the first, and would by no means be the last, to hope that one big push would end the war.

Harry Wendt posted a poem in the Ottawa *Citizen* on the first anniversary of his brother's death:

> Had I but seen him at the last,
>   Or watched his dying bed,
> Or heard the last sigh of his heart,
>   Or held his drooping head,
> My heart, I think, would not have felt
>   Such bitterness of grief:
> But God has ordained otherwise
>   And now he rests in peace.[23]

By then Harry had little incentive or wish to enlist, nor was his health up to it. Nevertheless, on November 10, 1917, he was conscripted under the Military Service Act. He did not report right away, and he was declared a "defaulter" and forfeited 19 days' pay when he did show up. He was then declared medically unfit for service and was discharged in February 1918. On August 31, 1918, he was married at St. Alban's Anglican Church.[24] Then in February 1919, he died from the Spanish Flu.[25]

Meanwhile, another of the Wendt brothers was serving in the First World War—but in the American, not the Canadian, army. A small child when his mother had died, Herbert Wendt had moved with his father to Niagara Falls and had grown up an American. In 1916 he joined the National Guard at age 18 and was briefly deployed on the Mexican border during the expedition against Pancho Villa. When the United States entered the war, his regiment became the 108th Infantry, which in November 1917 was grouped into the 54th Infantry Brigade. Arriving in France in May 1918, the 54th Brigade was attached to British forces for training. It fought alongside the British and Australians, first in the Ypres Salient from July to September 1918, then as part of the British Fourth Army on the Somme. On September 29, 1918, the American 54th Brigade attacked the Hindenburg Line in what has become known as the Battle of St. Quentin Canal. Overeager and badly led, the Americans penetrated the German defenses but suffered severe casualties and then faced a fierce enemy counterattack. The survivors were pulled out of the line on October 21, having suffered 1,763 casualties—including 331 dead—in three months of combat.[26] Herbert Wendt survived this battle,

Figure 4.4. Albert Wendt as a member of the Ottawa Police Force, May 23, 1932. Detail from a group photograph of the Ottawa Police.
Source: City of Ottawa Archives, Police Service Fonds: Photograph of the Ottawa Police Department CA001245.

became a corporal, and served overseas until March 1919—a Canadian-born American soldier who had served as part of a British Army in the salient that had claimed his brother's life. He spent the rest of his life in Niagara Falls and died in 1956.[27]

"Charlie" Wendt had not been a member of MacKay church, though he had attended Sunday School there as a boy, participated in some church activities, and undoubtedly had friends in the congregation. But in 1917 his first cousin (and boyhood friend), steamfitter Albert Charles Wendt, began to attend MacKay after he married Mary Jane Robertson, a Presbyterian who had immigrated from Scotland. In December 1920, Albert and Mary Wendt, now living at 35 Ivy Street, became full members of MacKay Presbyterian Church by Profession of Faith. Albert Wendt became a policeman with the Ottawa force, and the Wendts attended MacKay United Church for two decades. As someone who was now certainly part of the MacKay extended family, Charles Wendt was included on the Honour Roll and the In Memoriam plaques when these were created in 1919.

Charles Wendt rests in the Bailleul Communal Cemetery Extension, which is on a side street about 500 metres off the main road to Ypres, just outside the town centre, adjacent to the municipal cemetery and a French military cemetery. The cemetery is well laid out, with the Great Cross at one side and the Stone of Remembrance at one end on a slightly raised grass platform, with large trees and plants among the gravestones. It is marked off from the street and surrounding houses by a low wall on three sides and a hedge, with large trees. The men—about 1,700, including 291 Canadians—were buried in rows as they died in the hospitals, so Allied soldiers of all units and nationalities are mixed together. Behind the Great Cross are headstones for German soldiers who died in nearby battles in 1914 and 1918, or as prisoners of war in hospital, as well as some Chinese labourers who were brought to the Western Front in 1917 and 1918. Wendt is in one of two rows of soldiers, many with maple leaves on their headstones, who died in November and December 1915, which bear testimony to the steady stream of casualties from the southern Ypres Salient in what was nonetheless called a "quiet time."

Charlie's brother, Herbert, may well have visited his grave, before the cemetery was redesigned as an Imperial/Commonwealth War Cemetery. Charlie's 1914–15 Star, British War Medal, Victory Medal, scroll, and plaque, were sent to his father, "Billy" Wendt, Boer War veteran, now American citizen, whose sons had served two countries in the First World War.

Figure 4.5. Bailleul Communal Cemetery Extension.
Source: Photograph by Carolyn Bowker.

Figure 4.6. Bailleul Communal Cemetery Extension.
Source: Photograph by Carolyn Bowker.

Figure 4.7. Bailleul Communal Cemetery Extension.
Source: Photograph by Carolyn Bowker.

5

A CHURCH AT WAR
1916

On January 18, 1916, Mrs. Eugenia Ralph led the Ladies' Aid in prayer and read out letters of thanks from soldiers in the 38th Battalion for the parcels that had been sent to them in Bermuda. The ladies then arranged for materials provided by the Red Cross to be distributed to the women of the church for sewing into garments. The following month they provided a supper and entertainment at the YMCA for the soldiers of the 77th Battalion. Hymns were sung, Rev. Anderson gave a short address, Miss Ethel Dawson played a piano solo, and the MacKay church quartet sang. The ladies declared the evening a great success and made plans for bake and rummage sales to raise money, and to do more work for the Red Cross.[1]

The Session in February elected a member to serve on the Soldiers' Aid Commission, established in 1915 to assist wounded and disabled soldiers and their families. It went on record as "heartily supporting the bill for the abolition of the manufacture, importation, and sale of intoxicating liquors" and sent a copy of the resolution to the prime minister, the opposition leader, and the local MP.[2] The Session and the Managers raised funds to pay the church mortgage, mourned the passing of two Elders, supported a Boy Scout troop at the church, managed the choir, and worried about the deficit MacKay was now running. In May, the young people of MacKay presented a playlet written by Mrs. Anderson, *The Young Village Doctor*, with Mr. and Mrs. Blyth Macdonald, two prominent younger members of the congregation, in leading roles. On the same program Miss Margaret Askwith and Mr. Alex Nichol sang solos.[3] On February 3, the Parliament Buildings caught fire and men of the 77th Battalion, including some from MacKay, were called out to help with crowd control, assist firemen, rescue trapped people, and preserve valuable paintings and books.

Later that month the MacKay Death Register recorded shattering news: "Pte G. Victor Coker paid the supreme Sacrifice, 'somewhere in France', laying down his life for his Country & King." Theresa Coker, an active member of the Ladies' Aid, was now a widow for the second time and still had two sons on active service.

The Canadian Corps had spent the winter rebuilding its forces in the Ypres Sector after the losses of the previous year, and it had added a Third Division. Its first major action in 1916 came after the British exploded six

Figure 5.1. Fire at the Parliament Buildings, February 3, 1916.
Source: Library and Archives Canada r000240.

mines under German positions at St. Eloi on March 26, but then got lost and captured the wrong mine craters. During April 3–4, the Canadian Second Division was called on to pursue the attack, but the men also lost their way and were massacred. Two months later, at nearby Mount Sorrel, the Germans unleashed the heaviest bombardment yet seen, and then attacked on June 2. The 4th Canadian Mounted Rifles was all but annihilated. A hundred of its men were forced to surrender, and Alfred Philp became the first and only MacKay soldier to become a prisoner of war. On June 6, a bombardment severely wounded another MacKay soldier, Charles Trotter, who later died in hospital. By the time the Canadians regained the ground they had given up 10 days before, they had lost 8,000 men.

Long lists of casualties began to fill the Ottawa papers. John Powers, George Powers, Joseph Munro, and John L. McKenzie were wounded at St. Eloi. The MacKay church Death Register entered battle deaths with increasing frequency. "Pte George Bothwell died of wounds in Flanders, Gunner. Buried behind the lines. Another hero." "Corp. Charles E. Trotter died in Flanders from wounds on June 10, 1916—buried behind the lines, another hero." News that Philp had been taken prisoner doubtless came as a relief to his family and friends, even if being captured carried a stigma in some quarters.

By mid-1916 over 50 MacKay men were in France or Belgium within sound of the guns, but news reports from the front were filtered and vague. Soldiers' letters sometimes contained more details. But they were more likely to be upbeat and mundane, like the letter received by the family of John Powers, just before he and his brother were wounded, which said how glad they had been before the big battle to have had a bath in a pond behind the lines, and how lucky they were not to have been separated from each other.[4] It is unlikely that any of these men could have conveyed, in any terms the folks at home would have understood, their experience in the Ypres Salient, where the "very ground," in the recollection of one soldier, "seemed to speak and the night wind seemed to pluck at your sleeves and counsel you beware. [...] You could feel the presence of something not of this earth."[5] And letters might take weeks to reach a soldier at the front, with more weeks to get a reply. Wives and families were now beginning to realize that they might not see their husbands, fathers, or sons for years—if they would ever see them at all.

But the reality of the war was beginning to come home in a different form, as a few wounded soldiers began to return, bringing with them personal experience of the horrors of the front. In March, Alexander Masson, a soldier invalided home to recover in hospital, joined MacKay church and was married there. John MacKenzie returned from his service with the British Army in 1916, having been gassed at Ypres, and rejoined his wife and family in her family's home. (They would have two more children, and the whole family would attend MacKay church for the next two decades.) In September Dr. Neil MacLeod, suffering from battle fatigue after 18 months in front-line field ambulances, moved back into his former home and medical practice on Charles Street. "His condition is one of nervousness, and he is generally run down," read a medical report. "He is still unable to sleep properly and cannot concentrate his mind on his work." By December 1916 his condition was improving but he still slept badly at night, had a poor appetite and had lost weight, suffered a slight tremor of the hands, and at times severe headaches.

Recruiting for the Infantry

In the first half of 1916, recruiting drives continued apace. A late addition to the ranks of the 77th Battalion was **Daniel Robertson Sr.**, 48, a plasterer who had come from Scotland with his family just before the war. After he enlisted in April, his wife Mary and her remaining children moved to New Edinburgh and joined MacKay church (see Chapter 9). On June 8, the 77th received its colours—donated by the Ottawa Electric Company and the Ottawa Gas Company and presented by their Chairman, Thomas Ahearn—in a ceremony on Parliament Hill. Nine days later it marched through cheering crowds to Union Station to begin the journey to England. But once there, the battalion was broken up and its men were dispersed to reinforce existing units. Of the MacKay men in the 77th, Mayo was sent to the 50th Battalion, Robertson to the 87th Battalion, and Simpson to the 8th Battalion. Leach joined the Canadian Engineers; Stevenson was assigned to the Third Division Ammunition Column; Lancely went to the railway troops in France, while Miles remained in England due to a heart problem.

Figure 5.2. 77th infantry Battalion colours presentation ceremony on Parliament Hill.
Source: Canadian War Museum CWM 20070101-005_2, A, George Metcalf Archival Collection.

Meanwhile six MacKay men enlisted in three new infantry battalions that had begun recruiting in the Ottawa area: the 156th Battalion (based in Brockville), 154th Battalion (based in Cornwall), and the 136th Battalion (based in Kingston):

- **Thomas Isaac Jackson**, 45, a contractor, joined the 156th Battalion in February (see Chapter 8), as did **George Sayles**, 40, a construction worker who had immigrated from England in 1912, and Lt. **Albert Currie**, 35, a partner in a successful hardware business, who had enlisted for the Boer War in 1900 but had fallen ill in Halifax. (Currie's luck remained bad; he was hospitalized in England in September with Bright's disease—acute inflammation of the kidneys.)
- **Andrew Jardine**, 23, a carpenter, and **Archibald Jardine**, 19, a painter, who had immigrated from Scotland in 1913, enlisted together in March in the 154th Battalion.
- **Abraham Ferguson**, 51, a machine hand at one of the Edwards companies, enlisted in the 136th Battalion in March. He was discharged in September when doctors discovered valvular heart disease.

But the main recruiting drive in Ottawa, begnning in the spring of 1916, was for the 207th Battalion, organized by Lt. Col. Charles Wesley MacLean, who personally paid some of the recruiting costs. Like the 77th, this battalion would receive all its training in Ottawa, and its leaders hoped it would be as prominent in the community as the 77th Battalion had been. Its prowess in local sports earned it the nickname "MacLean's athletes." Its band provided concerts and played at public events, including at the laying of the cornerstone of the new Parliament Buildings. But the 207th Battalion never achieved the community response or the recruiting success the 77th Battalion had enjoyed. No advance drafts of men were sent to England, and indeed, the battalion was not up to full strength when it went overseas in 1917. Four MacKay men signed up for the 207th Battalion:

- **Andrew Douglas Stalker**, 22, a draughtsman and an engineering student at Queen's University, enlisted as a lieutenant in April, and became one of the foremost of "MacLean's athletes" (see Chapter 13).
- **Frederick Samuel Wright**, 25, an electrical lineman, was recruited in May into the battalion's 3rd special services company (what these "special services" were is not clear).
- **Elmer Moodie**, a 17-year-old "saw-filer" (he lied about his age) whose father was a blacksmith, enlisted in May.
- **Ivan Brunel,** a 13-year-old student, was formally attested but only to play in the band, and he was discharged a few months later.

Four other MacKay men enlisted in infantry units outside Ottawa:

- **William Fallis**, 45, a pressman in the government printing bureau, enlisted in the 108th Battalion at Selkirk, Manitoba, as a bandsman (he was later discharged as unfit for overseas service).
- **George Frederick Stalker**, 39, enlisted in British Columbia with the 196th Western Universities Overseas Battalion; and his brother, **Robert Alexander Stalker**, 37, enlisted at Prince Rupert as a lieutenant in the 102nd Battalion of Northern British Columbia (their stories, and that of Andrew Douglas Stalker, are told in Chapter 13).
- **Thomas Raymond Tubman**, 21, a clerk in the Department of Militia and Defence, enlisted as a lieutenant in the 139th Battalion, then resigned his commission to go to England with an artillery battery (see Chapter 16).

If recruitment for the infantry had become hard slogging, men were still signing up for other services, including forestry battalions and the artillery.

Forestry Battalions

A massive amount of lumber was needed on the Western Front, but when shipping shortages made it uneconomical to send Canadian lumber to Britain and France, the British requested that Canada recruit forestry battalions, which would develop these resources in Britain and France and manufacture lumber and wood products closer to the front. Two forestry battalions were recruited in Ottawa, with equipment provided by Canadian lumber companies. The 224th Battalion was recruited in February, reached Britain in April, and immediately began production of sawn lumber. The 238th Battalion went to Britain later in the year. Both battalions attracted men with experience in the lumber industries of the Ottawa Valley and in sawmills like the Edwards complex in New Edinburgh.

Five MacKay men signed up for these forestry battalions:

- **Edmund Watkins**, 23, whose father worked in the Edwards mills, joined the 224th Forestry Battalion.
- **Horace Barnes**, 34, a "saw filer" (a skilled trade that maintained the giant blades in sawmills that became warped or dull with use) in Arnprior, joined the 238th Forestry Battalion, as did **William Finter**, 29, **Alex Inch**, 45, a carpenter-joiner with four children who had immigrated from Scotland in 1913, and **Robert Henry Curtis**, 26, a "gas fitter" who had emigrated from England in 1912, boarded with Alex Inch, and married his daughter.

Once in England, these and other forestry battalions were reorganized into forestry companies and assigned to a series of projects throughout Britain and France. Finter and Inch were sent to forestry operations in the north of England, headquartered at Carlisle. The other three were sent to France and worked at forestry camps, sawmills, and factories in Burgundy, Normandy, and Picardy.

Artillery

The two batteries of field artillery that had been recruited in Ottawa in 1915 were still in England being trained and waiting for their own guns to arrive from the factories. By the time they were ready to go to France, many of the men in these batteries had already been deployed elsewhere. Walter Lindsay went to France in January with the Second Division Ammunition Column; George Bothwell was sent to the First Division Ammunition Column; Thomas Gerard was assigned to clerical duties in London (he would go to the front the following year). The other men were deployed to various artillery batteries as drivers or gunners as they were sent to the front in 1916.

Figure 5.3. Recruiting poster for forestry units.
Source: Canadian War Museum CWM 19900055-003 George Metcalf Archival Collection.

Between February and April three new batteries of artillery were being recruited for what would be the 13th Brigade Canadian Field Artillery. The 50th Battery drew from Queen's students, graduates, and friends; the 51st Battery drew on the Ottawa area; and the 52nd Battery was recruited in Cobourg, Peterborough, and Kingston. Nine MacKay men signed up for these batteries:

- **Cecil Eugene Putman**, 21, son of the Chief Inspector of Ottawa Public Schools; **Norman Henry Tubman**, 18, a student; and **Ernest Benedict**, 17 and a half, enlisted in the 50th Battery.
- **John Imrie Slinn**, 18; his brother **Shirley Slinn**, 20 (the third Slinn brother to enlist); and **Charles Foad**, 17 (he lied about his age), whose family had immigrated from England in 1910, joined the 51st Battery.
- **Russell Muhlig**, 18, a high school student and son of the head gardener at Rideau Hall, enlisted in the 52nd Battery.
- In addition, **Gordon James Campbell Munro**, 22, and **William Douglas Munro**, 21, champion athletes and sons of an inspector for the Ottawa Electric Railway, enlisted in the 80th Depot Battery which would supply men to the 13th Brigade CFA.

These three batteries left for England in September 1916. There, the 50th was disbanded and its men were dispersed among the other batteries. The 51st, 52nd, 53rd, and a howitzer battery, were formed into the 13th Artillery Brigade of the Fifth Canadian Division.[6] (Putman and Tubman were assigned to the 53rd Battery.)

By the summer of 1916, artillery batteries were being raised solely for the purpose of providing reinforcements for existing batteries in the field. Six MacKay men joined two batteries that were recruited in the area around Kingston:

- Three men enlisted in the 73rd Battery. **Alfred Merritt**, 18, like his father, worked at the Royal Canadian Mint. **Arthur Henry Sproule**, also 18, was the son of a pioneer settler in Nepean township and an Irish Catholic mother, who together ran a hotel in Lebreton Flats; he was passed around among relatives when his mother died and his father left for the Yukon, and in 1916 he was sharing lodgings with Merritt. **Olaf Olsen**, 29, had been raised in New Edinburgh by a single mother. The 73rd Battery went to England in November where the men were dispersed to other units. In 1917 Merritt would go to France with the 5th Division Ammunition Column, Sproule with the 3rd Division Ammunition Column, and Olsen with the First Division Ammunition Column.
- Three men joined the 72nd Battery, which remained in Canada until March 1917: **Dalton McCarthy**, 21, a clerk and son of a street railway motorman; **Elmer ("Joe") Tubman**, 19, a clerk with the Imperial Munitions Board; and **Donald Nairn Grant**, 19, a bank clerk and son of a prominent Ottawa lawyer. McCarthy would be sent to the

3rd Division Ammunition Column; Grant would end up with the 21st Battery at the front; Tubman would hold a series of clerical jobs in England and France.

Royal Flying Corps

Canada had no air force, but in 1915 British recruiters began seeking Canadians for the Royal Flying Corps and the Royal Naval Air Service (the two would be merged in 1918 into the Royal Air Force). Some 22,000 Canadians served with the British flying services during the war. Two MacKay men joined the Royal Flying Corps in 1916:

- **John Henry Ryan**, 30, a civil service clerk, was gazetted a 2nd Lieutenant in the Royal Flying Corps (RFC) on January 1. After training in England, he was assigned to 21 Squadron in France and fought during the autumn in the Somme campaign. (His story is told in Chapter 14.)
- **Erland Dauria Perney**, 21, son of the former principal of Creighton Street Public School, attended the Royal School of Artillery and then joined the 72nd Battery CFA in August; on October 12 he was accepted into the RFC and sent to England for training. (His story is told in Chapter 17.)

Specialist Services

Four other MacKay people joined the field ambulance and medical corps, the service corps, and the increasingly important signals corps.

- **Elizabeth Ralph**, 31, a trained nurse, went overseas in April to join the Queen Alexandra's Imperial Nursing Service (see Chapter 24).
- **Arthur Watkins**, 19, an elevator operator whose father was a timekeeper at the Edwards mills, enlisted in the Canadian Army Medical Corps Field Ambulance Depot.
- **Cleveland "Zeke" Stevenson**, 28, a clerk, enlisted in the Signals Training Depot. He would serve with the 1st Canadian Division Signals Company and would be awarded the Military Medal.
- **William Gaitens**, 40, a baker who had immigrated from Scotland in 1911, enlisted in the Army Service Corps and served in England and later with the First Canadian Field Bakery in France.

An Autumn of Tragedy

In all, 36 men (aged 18 and over), four boys, and one woman from MacKay Presbyterian Church enlisted for service in 1916. A few had had militia experience. There were more officers and men with high school education than the year before, but most had public school education only. Two-thirds were Canadian, most with roots in New Edinburgh. About half were full members of the church. Four sets of two or more brothers joined during this year, along with four other men whose brothers had enlisted in the previous year. There were also three fathers or stepfathers who joined their sons or stepsons in uniform.[7] Eleven men were married with children, but of these only George and Robert Stalker would serve in combat units, while three others would serve in forestry or railway units in France. An illuminated list (Figure 5.4), to which names of soldiers were added as they signed up, had filled up by the end of June with 102 names.

But by the fall of 1916 some uncomfortable truths were becoming apparent. There were no enlistments of MacKay men in the last third of 1916, and in the last two years of the war only 16 men from MacKay would enlist voluntarily for service in Europe, mostly in artillery and specialist units. Some men of military age who were members of MacKay church did not serve overseas, for reasons that cannot now be ascertained. The strong enthusiasm in the church and community for the war undoubtedly put pressure on men to enlist, but there is no evidence that those who did not do so suffered any repercussions—indeed, some of them were staunch supporters of the war and were supportive of the men who did sign up. Some may have been in the militia or home guard, or in essential services including the civil service; others may have been the sole support of their families—including several who had brothers at the front.

There is no way of knowing how many men might have been rejected for service, for chronic health conditions, for being too small, or for other infirmities including poor eyesight or chronic injury—which, oddly enough, included some leading athletes like Reed Tubman. It is indicative that more than a few of those who did enlist in 1916, and during the remainder of the war, were under- or over-age, under-sized, unfit, or unqualified—indeed, men who would have been (or had been) rejected earlier and should have been again. For example, recruiters accepted Ernest Benedict knowing that he was not yet 18, and at five feet two inches he was much shorter than what had previously been the height requirement for the artillery (he would be kept from the front until December and then assigned to the Canadian Cavalry Brigade which fought with the British Army). It is also indicative that only a handful of men from MacKay church would be conscripted in 1917. In short, by mid-1916 most of the MacKay men who would go to the front were already there or were on their way.

And the news from the front was getting worse, much worse. On August 10, 1916, the MacKay Death Register recorded that Mathew William Ryan had "paid the supreme Sacrifice in the field of battle and was buried

A Church at War 91

Figure 5.4. Illuminated list of MacKay soldiers who enlisted before June 1916. The names were added as men enlisted, and those at the bottom of the list date from about June 1916. It is not known whether another list was created for men who enlisted after that time—by the fall of 1916 voluntary enlistment had largely dried up.
Source: MacKay United Church.

with military honours 'somewhere in France'—another hero added to the list of the world's heroes." Thomas N. Jackson was wounded in August. Robert Stalker, Robert Drake, and Alex McKenzie were wounded at the Somme in September, followed by Norman Willson in October. Several other men suffered more mundane injuries—one hit by a truck, another hurt playing football—as well as infections, minor injuries, and illnesses. And there were further losses of a different sort: Dr. Neil MacLeod, Oscar May, and Russell White were treated for "battle fatigue," and Jack Ryan was sent back to England with "shell shock" after losing his brother and seeing an appalling number of his fellow pilots shot down in an unequal struggle against superior German aircraft and tactics.

In September, the Canadian Corps, using tanks for the first time in warfare, took the village of Courcelette, as always with heavy casualties. But after they failed, with severe losses, to take the next objective, Regina Trench, the depleted Canadian Corps was pulled back to regroup. It fell to the newly formed Fourth Canadian Division, still part of a British Army, to capture Regina Trench after two weeks of heavy fighting. Then on November 18, 1916, the 12th Brigade of the Fourth Division attacked the next line of German trenches, Desire Trench, under the most appalling conditions imaginable. The 38th Battalion from Ottawa, and the 87th Battalion, which had many Ottawa men in it, spearheaded this attack. Many of the men killed taking Desire Trench would never be found—dismembered by shellfire, lost forever in the muddy ooze, or buried unidentified as soldiers "known unto God." Gordon Maynard Porteous, whose parents would join MacKay in the following year, was among these, as was Daniel Robertson Sr. The Robertson family, new to MacKay, would feel even more keenly the pain of Desire Trench; not only was Daniel Sr. killed but his son William was severely wounded, and a month later the news would arrive that another son, Daniel Jr., had been killed earlier in the year. (See Chapter 9.) Irwin Kelly, in the artillery battery that supported the attack, was wounded.

For the families of the 17 MacKay men serving overseas who had wives and children, the struggle to pay the rent, food and fuel bills, clothing, and other expenses, was becoming increasingly acute. A few had the means to continue in reasonable comfort, but most had to live on a separation allowance of some $20 a month, assigned pay from their husband (usually $15, in some cases $20) and, perhaps, some assistance from the Patriotic Fund. Desmond Morton estimates that about three-quarters of the recipients of separation allowances also got help from the Patriotic Fund in 1916, and the average allowance for a family in Ottawa in that year was $16.63. There is no further information on Patriotic Fund assistance to war wives from MacKay church, but if Morton's analysis is correct, it is highly likely that some were in receipt.[8] Taken together, these allowances might have replaced the income of a labourer before the war, but they could no longer cope with wartime inflation. In a few cases war wives moved in with parents; in other cases families shared accommodations. Some moved to cheaper housing, often several times. Some left New Edinburgh altogether. A few moved to England or Scotland. The social conventions of the time prevented wives with children from working. Unmarried daughters might augment the family income by seeking employment, as many had done before the war, as seamstresses or store clerks; new opportunities were opening up in banks or as clerks in the expanding Department of Militia and Defence. In a tight-knit community like New Edinburgh, neighbours undoubtedly looked out for each other, helping with the storm windows, doing small repairs, making sure the wife or widowed mother of a soldier on duty had enough coal or wood.

MacKay, like the Presbyterian church as a whole, remained grimly determined to carry on the war, as it increasingly wrestled with issues of faith, death, and despair. From the pulpit, Anderson surely echoed the exhortations in the Presbyterian press to remain steadfast in their duty in spite of suffering, to take comfort in the assurance of eternal life for the fallen and of victory in the struggle, and above all, to resist hopelessness and to trust in God. As the Presbyterian *Record* put it in an editorial in June:

> The Third Factor in this war is God ... what part He takes, or where or how, we know not. That is His own affair. This we know: "The Lord reigneth" and whatever of ill may be wrought by the great Adversary of all good and his unholy train; and however sin and greed may for a time shadow and sadden our world, the wrong must meet its doom; and our part, in darkness as in light, is to link ourselves, by faith and trust and purpose and effort, with God; to follow His guidance and His will; till right shall triumph and the world's song of freedom have not one jarring note.[9]

The boast in the 1916 annual report of the Ladies' Aid that "notwithstanding the many demands on our members arising from the war, they have made this year more successful than any in the past" is as much a cry of defiance as it is a record of achievement. On October 10, the president of the Ladies' Aid reported that "eighty-two pairs of socks and a number of other articles" had been collected for soldiers' Christmas parcels. In its year-end report it noted: "One hundred and five parcels were sent to the men from our Congregation who have enlisted for over-seas service to fight for the great cause of Liberty and Justice."[10] That many families to wait, watch, hope, and pray.

6

VICTOR AND THERESA COKER
A Good Man, a Christian Woman, and Her Two Sons at the Front

The first MacKay soldier to fall in 1916 was George Victor Coker, a labourer for the City of Ottawa who had immigrated from Britain in 1907 after serving for 13 years in the Royal Marines. By all accounts a solid, steady, decent man, Coker had married a widow, Theresa Wilson, who was a decade his senior. She was also a British immigrant with two sons, H. William Wilson (1895) and Arthur S. Wilson (1897), and two daughters, Dora (1900) and Jessie (1904). Coker and his two stepsons, like many other British immigrants, enlisted early in the war in the expeditionary force of their adopted country. Coker, like Charles Wendt, became one of the many thousands of random victims of the endless "wastage" in the Ypres Salient. His widow Theresa supplemented her income by taking in boarders and maintained a respectable lifestyle as Mrs. G. V. Coker. She became a mainstay of the Ladies' Aid and other MacKay church activities.

Victor Coker was born on July 23, 1877, in Surrey, England, one of six surviving children of Frederick Coker and Jane Beagley Coker.[1] In 1893, at age 16, he joined the Royal Marines, Light Infantry. He served at the home base in Chatham until October 1898, when he embarked on the *Thetis*, a second-class protected destroyer then serving in the Mediterranean. After a short stint back at Chatham, he briefly served on the cruiser *Medusa*, and then, again after a short shore leave, he served between 1900 and 1904 on a series of cruisers in the Australia station. After another few months in Chatham, he embarked in July 1904 on the *Acheron*, which was part of the newly created Australian naval service. In July 1906, he returned to Chatham where he was discharged. Throughout his career his rating for both character and ability was consistently "V.G.," his performance on drills and tests was good, and his general character on discharge was "Very Good."[2] But he had acquired little education and had no skills useful for civilian life. As a labourer approaching 30, his future in England was not promising. He thus emigrated to Canada in 1907 and settled in New Edinburgh—still a labourer but with more opportunities and better pay than at home.

Figure 6.1. George Victor Coker.
Source: De Wolfe 1919, 66.

On June 10, 1910, Coker married Theresa Elizabeth Wilson at MacKay Presbyterian Church.³ She was born in Surrey, England, daughter of Henry Hupfeld, described in the 1871 British census as a "dealer in birds," and Annie Susman, both of whom were born in Germany. The family does not appear to have been wealthy, and the 1881 British census records her, at age 14, as living at the Clarence Street Industrial School in Richmond, Surrey, England, as a "pupil in domestic training." Sometime about 1890 she married William H. Wilson, described in the 1901 British census as a portrait painter.⁴ The couple appear to have moved often, and when William Wilson died in 1908, Theresa decided to join her sister Annie and her husband, Frederick Corp, a labourer, who had just moved to New Edinburgh.⁵ At age 40, with four children, she travelled steerage on the *Tunisian* out of Liverpool, arrived in Halifax on December 27, 1908, and then took the CPR train to Ottawa.⁶ In 1910 she and her children were living at 150 Stanley Avenue, New Edinburgh, one of a row of four small wood-frame houses. Next door were the Corps, at 148 Stanley Avenue. The Corps had a boarder, George Victor Coker.⁷

Coker was a bachelor and Theresa was a widow with children to support. Both took some pains to conceal their real ages, perhaps even from each other. On the MacKay church wedding register Victor, who was about 33, gave his age as 38, while Theresa, who was 43, gave her age as 40. In the 1911 census (where they may have been interviewed together), they again gave their ages as 38 and 40.[8] In the ship's records Theresa's religion was listed as Baptist, but she appears to have attended MacKay Presbyterian Church from the time she arrived in New Edinburgh, and she became a member by Profession of Faith in March 1911. Victor also joined MacKay church in June, but he only attended Communion once or twice and appears, like the Corps, to have also attended St. Bartholomew's Anglican Church—he is listed on their memorial plaque.

After their marriage, the Cokers moved to 134 Stanley Avenue, half of a larger wood-frame double house. Besides the Cokers and the four Wilson children, there were three lodgers: Annie Evans, 73, who was born in Ireland; another labourer for the City who was a recent immigrant from England; and a young member of the Dominion Police. By 1914 the family had moved to 58 Stanley Avenue, another wood-frame double house, together with other boarders including Annie Evans, who would board with Mrs. Coker for the rest of her life.[9]

When war broke out in 1914, the younger of Coker's two stepsons, Arthur Wilson, went to Valcartier with the Canadian Army Service Corps (CASC) and was attested into the CEF in September, two weeks shy of his eighteenth birthday. He was five feet seven inches tall, with dark complexion, hazel eyes, and light-brown hair, and he gave his occupation as upholsterer. The CASC, modelled on the British Army Service Corps, provided transportation and supply services to the Army; each Canadian Division had a CASC service train which carried ammunition and equipment. After training in England, Arthur Wilson was sent to France in February 1915 as a driver with the First Divisional Train. Though the service trains did use horse-drawn transport, Wilson was in all probability driving motor vehicles, and he was later assigned to the Divisional HQ, perhaps as a staff driver.

A few months later, in late February 1915, George Victor Coker and his elder stepson, William Henry Wilson, signed up with the 38th Battalion. William, who was attested four days before his stepfather, was five months shy of his twentieth birthday. He was five feet eight inches tall, with ruddy complexion, hazel eyes, and auburn hair. He gave his occupation as driver and claimed three years' militia experience in the artillery. Victor Coker, at 37, was a fit man, five feet seven inches tall, weighing 148 pounds, with good physical development, ruddy complexion, and black hair. He had a tattooed anchor, several dots, and a soldier on his left forearm, and a very indistinct scar on the back of his head. Both men were sent to England in June 1915 as part of the second reinforcing draft from the 38th Battalion, and in August 1915 they were sent to the dreaded Ypres Salient to join the 2nd Battalion, which was being completely rebuilt after the Battle of Second Ypres.[10] There, Victor wrote out a will on the form provided in his paybook, leaving his property and effects to Mrs. Theresa Coker.

Coker and Wilson spent a cold, wet fall in 1915 in the trenches near Ploegsteert, and in reserve and rest camps, working, trying to keep warm, and cursing the weather. Although the Canadians were not involved in any major battles in the fall and winter of 1915/16, desultory fighting, sniping, and shelling on both sides continued to take their gruesome toll. In February 1916, the 2nd Battalion staged trench raids which resulted in the loss of several officers and men, and the Germans made similar probing attacks.[11] On February 23, 1916, George Victor Coker was "killed in action," "North East of Wulverghem," which is about nine and a half kilometres south of Ypres.[12] The battalion's war diary records that some of its companies were in the trenches on that day and some were in reserve, and it is impossible to know where Coker was or whether he was killed by artillery, a sniper, a stray bullet, or in a raid.

Now approaching 50, Theresa Coker was again a widow. She was no longer receiving $15 a month from Victor's assigned pay, nor the $20 a month separation allowance; but she would have been eligible for a widow's pension and would later receive a $180 war gratuity, and Coker had a $500 life insurance policy. She was receiving $31 a month in assigned pay from her two sons overseas. Her daughters were living with her and had found work: Katie as a stenographer and Jessie as a stenographer and later a nurse. Her circumstances may therefore not have been unduly straitened, as she moved to a newly built brick row house at 289 Crichton Street and then to a new brick single house at 331 MacKay Street. She was also accompanied by her lodgers, Annie Evans and Harriet Twyman, a newly arrived English immigrant who worked as a clerk in the Records Department of Militia and Defence. Both these women, like their landlady, were faithful members of MacKay Presbyterian Church.

While grieving the loss of her husband, Theresa's main concern was her two sons still at the front. On September 6, William Wilson reported in a letter to his mother that a shell had exploded on top of the trench over his head, that he was blinded by flying dust, and that a portion of his ear was torn away. Fortunately, he cheerily informed her, his eyesight was not damaged, and he returned to the trenches 10 days later.[13] (His service file says that he was treated for a "bullet wound face" and the following day for a "wound head + dust in eyes" and "abrasion L. temple.") On April 26, 1916, the 2nd Battalion fought a sharp encounter with the Germans, suffering heavy casualties (following which Wilson was rewarded in May with a week's leave in Paris). Perhaps to spare Theresa the undue anxiety that other relatives had experienced when they had been notified, clumsily or erroneously, of the death or injury of a loved one, notes were placed on the personnel files of both sons that in case of casualty, Miss Twyman was to be notified first.

Theresa's concern may have been alleviated when in August 1916, just as the 2nd Battalion was about to leave for the Somme, William Wilson was transferred to join his brother Arthur in the First Divisional Train. One wonders whether Arthur, who would be awarded a good conduct badge in December 1916, might have pulled some strings, given his brother's wound and their stepfather's death. But military discipline and the strain of war were beginning to tell even on Arthur, in spite of his relatively "bomb-proof" job. In January 1917, he was sentenced to 14 days' confinement for being found in an estaminet after 8:00 p.m. His performance remained good enough to warrant a promotion to lance corporal in April 1917, and to corporal in July. However, in September 1918 he was reprimanded for "creating a disturbance at the railhead."

William Wilson remained with the First Divisional Train until February 22, 1918, but then went back to the front. Once again with the 2nd Battalion, he survived the bloody battles of the Hundred Days. After the 2nd Battalion lost half its men in the battle at Bourlon Wood on September 28, William was granted 14 days' leave, which had the unfortunate result that he contracted gonorrhea. His appears to have been a difficult case because he was treated in several hospitals over a period of 37 days (for which, as had become policy at this stage in the war, he was docked 50 cents per day of pay and his field allowance for the period) and again from November 17 to January 1, 1919 at 7 Canadian Stationary hospital (for which he forfeited a further 38 days of field allowance and 50 cents per day). When he was discharged in April 1919, his medical report affirmed that he no longer had any evidence of gonorrhea, and that despite an injury to his hand, he was in good health with no disability.

As for Arthur, he remained in France for five months after the end of the war, and in February 1919 he was granted "Leave to Ploegsteert," possibly to visit his stepfather's grave at R. E. Farm Cemetery, about nine and a half kilometres from Ypres.

This Commonwealth cemetery is just off a main road running out of the small town of Wulverghem, about a kilometre from the town. It is a small cemetery, one of several in this farm country, and it contains many Canadians. There is a Great Cross but no Stone of Remembrance, and though austere, it is carefully kept, with a few trees and flowers among the headstones. Its low brick wall defines the cemetery but also leaves it open to the broad, fertile fields of Belgium that surround it, and there are busy farm buildings right next door. In the distance can be seen the church spire of Wulverghem. In 1916 the town would have been rubble and the land would have been torn up by shelling, with the front just over the ridge. The peace and quiet of the countryside today, and the order and tranquility of the cemetery, contrasts with the terrible battles and destruction which surrounded it throughout the First World War. In Figures 6.2 and 6.3, which show the entrance to the cemetery, Coker's headstone is at the right of the second row.

Figure 6.2. R. E. Farm Cemetery.
Source: Photograph by Carolyn Bowker.

Figure 6.3. R. E. Farm Cemetery.
Source: Photograph by Carolyn Bowker.

Figure 6.4. Mrs. G.V. Coker, in one of Mrs. Anderson's plays, in the early 1920s; detail from program for an "Entertainment" in the Sunday School hall at MacKay Presbyterian Church. *Source:* MacKay United Church.

Theresa Coker continued in regular attendance at MacKay Presbyterian church and was a regular participant in Mrs. Anderson's plays. She played a leading role in the Ladies' Aid and a host of other activities for the next two decades. She seems to have made this work her life, being constantly involved with teas, bazaars, young people's groups, fundraising, and mission bands (she was president of the Junior Mission Band in 1927). In press reports and minutes of meetings she was always referred to as "Mrs. G. V. Coker." She was finally able to settle in a modest eight-room frame house at 171 Stanley Avenue which she rented for more than a decade and where she hosted meetings of the Ladies' Aid.[14] After his return in April 1919 her son Arthur, a "stenographer," continued to live with her for a number of years until he married later in life and moved elsewhere in New Edinburgh. Theresa's daughters, Kate and Jessie, lived with their mother until they married. Also living with her were her long-term lodgers and fellow churchgoers Annie Evans, who died in 1928 in her late 80s, and Harriet Twyman, who was very active in the work of MacKay United Church until her death in 1946. William Wilson never returned to the family home; he married and moved to a suburb of Detroit.

Theresa Coker had four grandchildren and two great-grandchildren and died at the home of her married daughter in 1956 at the age—correctly reported—of 89.[15]

# THE BOTHWELL FAMILY
War Claims Lives and Destroys Families

The stories told in this chapter poignantly illustrate how the death of a single soldier, George Selkirk Bothwell, in a far-off war profoundly altered the lives of dozens of people. Families were destroyed, people were broken, children grew up without parents, and the repercussions of this tragedy would be felt through several generations.

George Bothwell was the oldest son of Captain William Bothwell (1849-1928), the yard foreman for the W. C. Edwards Company. From an old Scots Quebec family (he and his wife both spoke French), William Bothwell had worked from the age of eighteen on river tugs and steamers in the rough-and-tumble world of the Ottawa Valley lumber trade, and had risen to be a captain of long-distance lumber barges. He and his brothers retained an interest in the steamboat and lumber trades, and in the 1890s they had run a lumberyard in Lachine. By 1901 William Bothwell had come to New Edinburgh to join the W. C. Edwards Company, and the family occupied a large brick attached house at 61 MacKay Street.[1]

Bothwell's position with W. C. Edwards was an important one. During the fire that destroyed the Edwards complex in 1907, he directed firefighting and salvage operations, liaising directly with Edwards, his son, and his nephew Gordon.[2] The Bothwells were especially close to Gordon Edwards, whose mansion at 55 MacKay Street (now the Vietnamese Embassy) was across the street—John Bothwell recalled years later that one of his earliest memories was driving home from the mill in Gordon Edwards's sleigh or buggy.[3] Captain Bothwell had substantial investments and owned rental properties, was active in Liberal Party politics, and was well connected in local business circles.[4]

Captain Bothwell and his wife Adelia Gale (1863–1939) had five children: George Selkirk (1889), John Robert (1890), Agnes (1892), Katie (1894), and Emma (1897). George and John were athletes and were great friends with the Tubman families who lived nearby. After public school education, George Bothwell went to work for the Edwards mills about 1909. Various records show him occupying a series of positions there—"shipper," "checker," and by 1914, "electrician"—which appear to have earned him about $1.50 a day.[5] His younger brother John Bothwell, also with public school education, became a

Figure 7.1. Bothwell House at 61 MacKay Street in 1914. *Source:* University of Toronto Archives, Robert Bothwell Fonds, B89-0044, Box 6, file 13.

lithographer with the Canadian Bank Note Company and was making $312 a year in 1911.

The three girls attended school (including high school in the case of Emma), took piano and singing lessons, and participated in concerts and plays at MacKay church. In 1910, Katie Bothwell represented the Mission Band as one of the MacKay delegates to the Annual Ottawa Convention of the Women's Foreign Missionary Society. In 1914 she played a lead role in a "character sketch" put on by the Young People's Association and the Young Men's Club—a play in three acts written by the players, with elaborate costuming and sets.[6] Emma became an accomplished pianist and Katie trained as a nurse. In Figure 7.4 the girls are shown in front of 61 MacKay Street, about 1914.

The Bothwell family attended St. David's Reformed Episcopal Church in the first decade of the twentieth century. John Bothwell was one of the young men involved with its Boys' Guild, and John and George played on sports

Figure 7.2. "Lumber & In Yard of Sash and Door Factory." From W. C. Edwards & Co. Ltd. Saw Mills and Lumber Yards c. 1897; silver gelatin photograph.
Source: Bytown Museum p1839.

Figure 7.3. John and George Bothwell, c. 1902.
Source: University of Toronto Archives, Robert Bothwell Fonds, Box 006, file 11, photo 13.

Figure 7.4. Katie (?) and John Bothwell MacKay Street, Ottawa, c. 1900.
Source: University of Toronto Archives, Robert Bothwell Fonds, Box 006 file 10, photo 14.

teams for that church. But about 1909–1910 the Bothwells were among several families who moved from St. David's church to MacKay Presbyterian. In 1910 Adelia and her daughters Agnes and Katie joined the church by Profession of Faith, and within a few years Adelia was playing a prominent role in the MacKay Ladies' Aid. William Bothwell joined in 1912 and Emma in 1915; George Bothwell's obituary says that he was a long-time member of MacKay church, but his name does not appear in the Communion Rolls.

On May 2, 1910, 21-year-old George Bothwell married Helen Eleanor "Ella" Robinson, 17, in an Anglican ceremony.[7] She came from a relatively poor background with little education, and the Bothwell family appears to have taken a dim view of this marriage. George and Ella had three children: William Alexander (1911–1984); Lois Helen (1912–1992); and Frederick Henry (1914–1974). The 1911 census records George, his wife, and their three-month-old son living with his parents, but within a couple of years they were renting a house of their own.

George Selkirk Bothwell enlisted on October 21, 1915, in the 8th Brigade, Canadian Field Artillery. He was five feet six inches tall, with medium complexion, grey eyes, and brown hair. Today, we might wonder why a married man with three small children (the youngest a toddler) and a steady job would have signed up for what was, by then, well known to be a very dangerous

Figure 7.5. George S. Bothwell.
Source: University of Toronto Archives, Robert Bothwell Fonds, B89-0044, file 11, photo 24.

enterprise. But Ella's father was a Boer War veteran, two of her brothers were at the front, and two cousins had already been killed. And George's younger brother, John Robert Bothwell, had enlisted in September 1914 with the Canadian Army Medical Corps and was already in the Ypres Salient as a sergeant with the medical services of the First Canadian Division. George assigned $20 (later $25) a month of his pay to his wife, and she received a separation allowance of $20 a month.

After training in England, George Bothwell was sent to France in early March 1916, where he was assigned to the First Division Ammunition Column and attached to a trench mortar battery. Later that month, the column was sent to what its war diary described as "our old hunting ground near Ypres." Bothwell's unit was responsible for moving supplies and ammunition from supply depots to trench mortar batteries at the front lines. Since the men were often in the open, they were favourite targets of enemy artillery, including shrapnel shells that exploded just above the ground for maximum anti-personnel effect. The Canadian front was almost continuously bombarded during April 4–5, 1916. The ammunition column's war diary recorded on April 26 that a battle had begun and there was a heavy demand for ammunition.[8] On May 3, Bothwell wrote his wife that he was fine, though with a slight cold, and was hoping to come home and see his children soon.[9]

Figure 7.6. Canadian Ammunition Column passing 6" naval guns, July 1918. This panorama shows some of the people and equipment involved in an ammunition column that kept the front-line guns supplied with ammunition, food, and materiel.
Source: Library and Archives Canada PA-040166.

On May 21, 1916, according to the Circumstances of Death Register, George Bothwell "was hit by an enemy high explosive shell and died six hours later."[10] There were no further details as to the place or circumstances. The Bothwell family register says that it happened at Hill 60, a slag heap held by the Germans between St. Eloi and Mount Sorrel. We learn more about what the soldiers had gone through from a letter, published in an Ottawa newspaper, from Ronin Morel, a soldier who also served in the ammunition column. Morel described an eight-day battle in which the men had been required to bring supplies up during the daytime in full view of the Germans, under heavy fire:

> There were about 30 of us and the Germans saw us. They put over about 30 big shells and we had to take cover as quick as we could—some in a culvert that ran under a railroad track and some in shell holes. It started to get too hot, so we had to make a run for it, one at a time, out into the open fields and away from their shell bursts. They certainly

tore things up pretty badly. Some of us got hit. [...] Jack Arnoldi, who lived at Rockcliffe, got killed, and Art Bray from New Edinburgh got wounded, also George Bothwell.[11]

Morel's letter was not entirely accurate, which was hardly surprising given the fear and adrenaline of war. Arnoldi was killed and Bray was wounded on June 9, according to their service records. Bothwell had been killed more than two weeks earlier, but very likely under similar circumstances to the action described in this letter.

The authorities were not much more accurate in providing information to the family. Bothwell's service file contains an untitled draft cable dated June 7, 1916, reporting his death, with no particulars as to date, place, or circumstances. Only on June 19 is there a draft of an official cable to the family reporting his death from wounds on May 21. George Bothwell had given his father's name, rather than his wife's or mother's, as next of kin to be notified, perhaps to spare the latter the initial pain—especially if (as happened with a report the family received in December 1914 that John Bothwell had been killed on Salisbury Plain) the report was in error. By the time the authorities got round to officially notifying the family, they already knew, because John Bothwell had sent them a cable four days after George's death.[12] Ella received the news from her brother-in-law John, and then from her father-in-law.

It fell to the chaplain of the trench mortar company to provide details (with the usual euphemisms to comfort a bereaved family) of George's "heroic death." George had died shortly after being hit by a German shell, he reported. "He seemed to suffer little pain. Death was largely due to shock." Normally, his body would have been buried just behind the lines in a temporary graveyard. But his brother John, who was serving at the No. 1 Canadian Field Ambulance at Poperinghe—an important staging and administrative centre about 10.5 kilometres west of Ypres—arranged to have George's body brought to the field ambulance, where he was given a "beautiful" casket, wreaths of flowers from the officers and staff of the field hospital, and a well-attended funeral. "The members of the trench mortar battery marched first," reported the chaplain, "then came the ambulance wagon bearing the casket, followed by the members of the field ambulance. [...] It would have done your heart good to hear the way the officer in charge of the party on Sunday spoke of your son who is gone. He said he never knew a braver man and that there was no one in the company whose loss would be more keenly felt."[13]

The cemetery near the field ambulance was converted in 1920 into the Poperinghe New Military Cemetery, designed by noted British architect Sir Reginald Blomfield. It is located just off a ring road around the town of

Poperinghe, surrounded by houses and across the road from a convenience store. At one end are Belgian and French graves and there is also a separate French military cemetery adjoining the site. The Great Cross is on a raised stone platform mid-way along the long axis, open on one side to the street, with gates on either side of it and low stone walls between the gates, and a pair of stone shelters on either side. From the inside, the Great Cross with wall and shelters forms the focal point of the cemetery, with the Stone of Remembrance at the opposite end. A hedge on a wire fence separates the cemetery from the street, while a low stone wall separates it from the back yards of the surrounding houses, most of which also have high hedges or fences of their own. Of the 951 men buried there, 55 are Canadians.

Sometime after 1921, Ella provided the following inscription for George's headstone: "In loving memory of my dear husband, who bravely gave his life for his country's sake (wife)." The inscription is significant in light of what had happened after his death.

While George was away, Ella Bothwell, like many other war wives, had experienced rapidly rising living costs. Initially, her assigned pay and separation allowance (with possibly some support from the Patriotic Fund) would have about equalled George's prewar income; but by 1916 this was no longer enough to support three small children. Unlike many other wives of absent soldiers, however, she had not moved in with her parents or in-laws but, according to notes on his service file, moved from one small house to another. When George was killed she was living in a small frame house in a narrow street off Montreal Road in a poor area of Eastview. Now, in her early twenties, she was a widow. She was awarded a small pension and an allowance for each child. She would be eligible for George Bothwell's war gratuity and other payments, but not until sometime later. At some point her children were sent to live with their grandparents, William and Adelia Bothwell. Then, on April 14, 1917, less than a year after George's death, Ella Bothwell married again.

Her new husband was George Earl Marion, 24, a returned soldier. On the marriage affidavit she declared her age as 22 (she was 24), and though the marriage was an Anglican ceremony, both gave their religion as Roman Catholic.[14] Earl Marion was a trainman who had enlisted in August 1915 in the 77th Battalion. Sent to England in the first reinforcing draft in October, he was assigned in December to the 2nd Reserve Battery of the Canadian Field Artillery. His disciplinary record was poor—he was twice fined three days' pay for being AWOL, and he was treated several times for venereal disease (VD) and urinary tract infections. From April to September 1916, he served as a driver in the First Division Ammunition Column. By July 1916 he was suffering serious shortness of breath and a high pulse rate, and was in a highly nervous condition. He was sent to military hospitals in England in September, and in February 1917 he was invalided home.

Figure 7.7. Poperinghe New Military Cemetery.
Source: Photograph by Carolyn Bowker.

Figure 7.8. Poperinghe New Military Cemetery.
Source: Photograph by Carolyn Bowker.

It would appear that his experience of war had exacerbated his already heavy drinking. A medical examination at Quebec on February 19, 1917, concluded that he had valvular heart disease—likely a pre-existing condition from a bout of pneumonia eight years previously—and a slightly enlarged heart. "He drinks pretty hard according to his own admission." His final examination in July showed no permanent enlargement of the heart but still shortness of breath. "He is tremulous in his hands due to hard drinking," the report said, and the board recommended that he be discharged with compensation to the extent of one-eighth of a full pension.

Marion was sent to the Fleming Hospital in Ottawa—a 71-bed convalescent home, formerly the mansion of Sir Sandford Fleming at the corner of Chapel and Daly Streets—where wounded soldiers in the final stages of recovery could come and go in the daytime but were required to return at night. Here he was docked three days' pay in March for being AWOL and in May he was "declared a deserter," likely because he did not return at night. Earl was at the Fleming for less than two months before his marriage to Ella Bothwell, and he was finally discharged on July 11, 1917.

We can well understand the surprise and consternation of William and Adelia Bothwell, that a mother of three children would suddenly marry someone she appears to have known for a matter of weeks, less than a year after the loss of her first husband. The Bothwells took permanent custody of their grandchildren and received the pensions for their support. The story that passed down in the Bothwell family was that Ella was read out of the family after deserting her children. On the page of a book in which William Bothwell recorded the family history, George's birth and death are recorded, as well as the names of his children, but no mention is made of her.[15]

Earl and Ella Marion soon had two children of their own: Marguerite (Margaret) in 1919 and William in 1920. The family changed addresses frequently over the next few years. Now that she had remarried, Ella was no longer entitled to a widow's allowance (though a small dowry was usually paid to a widow upon remarriage). The War Service Gratuity due to her as a soldier's widow was not paid until 1920 and amounted to only some $180. Earl Marion got a job as a clerk in the records branch of the Department of the Interior—though he had only a few years' education, he spoke English and French—and he seems to have been popular there. The 1921 census showed Earl and Ella, and their two small children, living in a rented house with her parents. Earl was the head of the household with a yearly income of $600.[16]

By the following year things seem to have slid downhill. Earl continued to suffer from his disabilities and he was devastated when his twin brother—who had also been in the artillery, had been gassed, and had been in and out of hospitals before being discharged with a similar heart condition—died on May 5, 1919 of bronchial pneumonia. With Earl probably drinking, and with

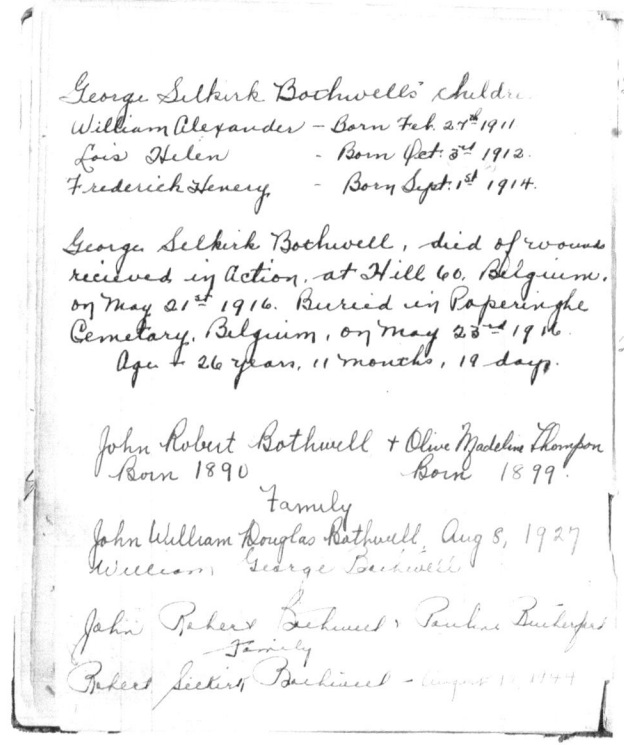

Figure 7.9. Page from William Bothwell Family History; George Bothwell and his children are listed, but Ella's name is missing.
Source: University of Toronto Archives, Robert Bothwell Fonds, Box 004, File 01, notebook with hydraulic notes, and other information.

pensions and other payments slow to arrive, the family began to have a hard time making ends meet. In 1922, now living in Eastview, Ella was writing lengthy letters to her former mother-in-law, Adelia Bothwell, pleading for help. "Dear Friend Mrs. Bothwell," she wrote in September 1922, "I am writing you a few lines to see if you will do me a favour. You see I wanted to get some Bed clothing and I can't get it without any thing Down. But I know you could always get what you wanted from freedman [Frieman's Department Store] with out any thing Down." She offered to pay when her cheque arrived. In December she again wrote: "I am right up against it. Well you see Earls clothes are off his Back another Week and he wont be able to go to Work till after Pay Day and then I cant afford to get them with out leaving some thing else go." Her letter was fulsome in its praise of how good the Bothwells (unlike the Marions) had been to her, and she requested that some of the money being kept by the Bothwells for their grandchildren be loaned to her. She asked that Mr. Bothwell co-sign a loan from the bank against the bonus (probably the remainder of the War Service Gratuity she said she was due to receive). "I sold my insurance and here after Being away for 10 days only a letter came Back stating that they had to investigate and see if I really needed the money because its paid up. But only payable at Death so they are writing about it Back to their home office that I needed it and I suppose it will be the end of the month before it comes Back. So you see I am right stuck if you will oblige me I will be very glad because I will have a very poor Christmas with out it."[17] It is not clear what the result of these letters was, but there survives a power of attorney dated 1923 giving William Bothwell power to collect all sums due to George Marion from the Government of Canada, including his salary for 1924.[18]

On April 29, 1924, while Ella and her daughter Margaret were visiting one of Ella's sisters in Germantown, Pennsylvania (a suburb of Philadelphia), Earl Marion left home to walk to the office and did not return. "The mysterious disappearance of George E. Marion, war veteran and civil servant," reported the Ottawa *Journal* in May, "has caused his wife much anxiety."[19] In early June his body was discovered in the Ottawa River in Hull. After hearing evidence from his wife, his father, and a sympathetic supervisor at the Department of the Interior, a coroner's jury concluded that he had "committed suicide by drowning, while in a fit of despondency."[20] An official Note on the Circumstances of Casualty Register says "Death Related to Service Duty" and there is a similar note on his service file.[21] His funeral mass "which was of a private nature" was at Our Lady of Lourdes Church in Eastview, attended by his widow, his father, two brothers, and four people from the Department of Interior including his supervisor, who also sent a floral tribute.[22]

The war had claimed another life and destroyed another family.

George Earl Marion is buried in the war graves section of Notre Dame Cemetery, Ottawa. On his headstone, which follows the pattern of those in Commonwealth war cemeteries, the inscription reads: "He died so that his country might live. Wife and children." Ella received Earl's victory medal and service cross. Marion had not been a model soldier but the fact that the authorities were willing to recognize his death as service-related and to bury him in a military cemetery suggests an understanding of his condition that was not always the rule. Ella decided to stay in the United States with her daughter but left her son with members of the Marion family until she sent for him two years later.[23]

The surviving Bothwell brother, John Robert, continued to serve with the medical corps. In March 1917 he was commissioned as a lieutenant and for the remainder of the war was attached to various Canadian medical units in England. Lt. Bothwell appears to have returned to Canada before the Armistice to a base hospital in Fredericton, perhaps accompanying wounded soldiers— his son has a picture of him as a member of a hockey team there in 1918–1919.

In October 1918 he was treated for influenza, and he was discharged in Fredericton in April 1919.

Figure 7.10. John Robert Bothwell.
Source: University of Toronto Archives, Robert Bothwell Fonds, Box 006, file 16, photo 20.

Captain William Bothwell retired in 1920 when the W. C. Edwards business was sold. He died in 1928 and his funeral was attended by a "who's who" of prominent figures in New Edinburgh, MacKay United Church, and the local business community.[24] His wife, Adelia Bothwell, was an important figure during the 1920s and the early 1930s in the MacKay Presbyterian Ladies' Aid and its United Church successor. She died in 1939.

On his return to Ottawa, John Bothwell rejoined the civil service as a lithographer and lived with his family at 61 MacKay Street. He continued his athletic pursuits, playing for local lacrosse and hockey teams well into his thirties. About 1923 he was posted to London, England, by the Department of Trade and Commerce.[25] There in 1924 he married and had two children. When London was threatened with the blitz in 1940, the family was evacuated back to Canada and returned to 61 MacKay Street, as John resumed his work with Trade and Commerce. After his first wife died in 1943, John married Mary Pauline Rutherford, and they had a son, Robert Bothwell. John died in 1977.[26]

The three sisters of George and John Bothwell remained active in the social and musical life of New Edinburgh. In 1916 Agnes Bothwell married a contractor of Bohemian origin; this marriage appears to have been short-lived as she almost immediately began to work in what became the Department of National Defence, where she was employed for 39 years before her death in 1955. Emma Bothwell did not marry and was a pianist and singer, an active participant in the MacKay Young Woman's Missionary Society, and a member of Hazel Rebekah Lodge No. 40 (eventually president). In 1922 Katie married Dr. David B. Allman who later became the president of the American Medical Association; they lived in Atlantic City, in New Jersey.[27] Agnes and Emma continued to live with their mother and the three are frequently reported as participating in church activities including Sunday School teaching, fundraising, and teas. They inherited the house at 61 MacKay Street, where members of their family lived until 1976.

They also helped raise George Bothwell's three children, William, Fred, and Lois Bothwell. The three attended Crichton Street School, participated in MacKay church activities, and had many friends among the young people in New Edinburgh. Fred played hockey, football, and basketball for local and school teams—at 14, he was described as "aggressive in all these sports and is a particularly dangerous puck carrier."[28] Lois took piano lessons and sang in school and church musicals, often with her aunt Emma as accompanist, and she also became involved in church activities. In 1941 she married, moved to British Columbia, and had four children. William was active in youth, church, and community affairs. In 1927 he proposed a toast to "Our Dads" at the MacKay Men's Association annual father and son banquet—he had known his father only as a very small child—and the following year he was elected proctor of the MacKay Nedimac Tuxis Group, a church organization for young men.[29] He became an accountant and joined the RCAF during the Second World War, rising to the rank of wing commander. He married in 1940 and had three children.[30] Fred Bothwell served in the army during the Second World War and afterwards worked for the Post Office. He never married and occupied 61 MacKay Street with his aunts until his death in 1974.[31]

As for Ella Robinson Bothwell Marion, information received from a descendant is that after moving to Philadelphia she continued to have a difficult and chequered life. She had another child, and then married for a third time. She had two more children by her third husband—one died young and the other was killed in Korea. Her son William Marion, who had been left with members of his father's family as a toddler and was then taken to Philadelphia as a small child, had a troubled youth, married, and had three sons and four daughters, six of whom are still living. Her daughter Margaret Marion married and had 11 children.[32] Their stories lie outside the scope of this book. But they, along with the other stories told in this chapter, bear sombre witness to how a single shell on a far-off battlefield not only ended a soldier's young life, but also changed forever the lives of his family—those living and those yet to come. This is the true measure of the cost of war, and the real meaning of the word "sacrifice."

8

CHARLES EDWARD TROTTER AND THE JACKSON FAMILY
"Lovable Disposition and Fine Character"

Charles Edward Trotter was an English immigrant with no apparent family ties in Canada, who was welcomed into the home of Thomas Isaac Jackson, who regarded him as an adopted son. Not only did Trotter enlist in the CEF and perish in a major battle, but Jackson also signed up for overseas service in middle age, and one of his sons served at the front as well. Thomas Isaac Jackson never fully recovered his health after the war. The First World War exacted a heavy price on the extended Jackson family, but Thomas Jackson and his wife preserved the memory of Charles Trotter by naming their youngest son after him.

Trotter's past is something of a mystery. Attestation papers, census documents, and his obituary give various dates of birth between 1879 and 1883. It is most likely that he was born in York, England, in 1879 as the fifth child of William Trotter, an iron fitter, and his wife, Elizabeth.[1] There is scant reference to his family in his service file, but a newspaper obituary reported that he had four brothers fighting in the Imperial army during the First World War. Trotter became a bricklayer, then served four years in the British Royal Engineers, after which he seems to have immigrated to Canada about 1907.[2] In Ottawa he joined the contracting business of Thomas Isaac Jackson, a carpenter, together with Jackson's two oldest sons: Thomas Nicholas, a steamfitter, and Manfred, a plumber. Trotter soon became a partner in the business, moved in with the Jacksons and became part of their family. He was, said a newspaper obituary, "a man of lovable disposition and fine character."[3]

Thomas Isaac Jackson and his wife, Henrietta Schayltz Jackson, came to Ottawa, also about 1907, from the Eastern Townships of Quebec. They bought a rambling wood-frame house at 212 Springfield Road, just inside the boundary of Rockcliffe (built in 1899, it was one of the earliest in the village).[4] In 1911, Jackson was appointed as the first Constable of Rockcliffe Park Village, at $2 a day, "for duty on Sundays and statutory holidays in the months of August, September, and October," responsible not so much for law enforcement as for public works and general maintenance.[5] By 1914 the

Figure 8.1. Charles Edward Trotter.
Source: 77th Battalion 1926, 70.

Figure 8.2. Jackson house in Rockcliffe c. 1912.
Source: Private collection.

Jacksons had nine surviving children. Mr. and Mrs. Jackson and son Manfred joined MacKay Presbyterian Church by Profession of Faith in 1910 and the whole family was active in the church for many years. Trotter does not appear on any MacKay church records, but in 1915 and 1916 he was on several lists of men from the church who had enlisted in the war.

Figure 8.3. The Jackson family, c. 1912; the Jackson house in Rockcliffe (detail). *Source:* Private collection.

Charles Edward Trotter enlisted in the 77th Battalion on September 8, 1915. He was five feet eleven inches tall, with ruddy complexion, gray eyes, and brown hair. He assigned $10 a month of his pay to Mrs. Jackson, but he also assigned another $10 a month to one R. Hooper, a well-to-do stone contractor—why he did so remains a mystery. Though he listed the Jacksons as his next of kin, Trotter specified that if he became a casualty, "Next of Kin is not to be notified—all correspondence to be addressed to Miss Marjorie Jackson, Record Office Staff." Trotter was part of a draft of 250 men plus officers from the 77th that was sent to England in October 1915 to provide reinforcements for CEF battalions already in the field. He was made lance corporal, then promoted to corporal, and was assigned to the 60th Battalion in the Third Canadian Division.[6] He arrived at the front at the end of April 1916.

The Canadians were holding a crucial sector in the Ypres Salient, between Hooge and Mount Sorrel, in a curve of the line where the Germans held most of the high ground and the Canadians were exposed to constant fire. Two weeks after his arrival, Trotter wrote the Jacksons that he had been in the front lines but would soon be coming out for a few days' rest. It was tiring, he wrote, to keep one's full kit on for the whole period a soldier was in the trenches, and "two weeks without a fellow taking his boots off or even getting a wash is no joke." "I am still keeping fine," he added, "so must be thankful," and he concluded: "We are having a few days [sic] rest, but by the

Figure 8.4. Charles Trotter in uniform.
Source: De Wolfe 1919, 295.

time you get this we shall be in [the trenches] again for a few weeks."[7] The 60th Battalion was indeed rotated back into the front line on May 15, then to a brigade reserve position on May 23, and then on June 1 it was moved further back, to divisional reserve. That is where it was when the Germans launched a ferocious barrage along a narrow front on June 2, 1916, and what came to be known as the Battle of Mount Sorrel began.

"The Battle of Mount Sorrel," writes military historian Norm Christie, "was in many ways the true face of the First World War. It had horror, slaughter, mass destruction and the futility of having no effect on the outcome of the war."[8] The Canadians held a few elevated positions, the loss of which would be catastrophic to the British position in the salient. Their commanders had every reason to expect an attack and yet were surprisingly unprepared when one came. The bombardment of June 2 decimated the Third Division's front-line troops and killed its commanding general. The front line dissolved and the Germans poured through, destroying the 4th Canadian Mounted Rifles and forcing its survivors, including Alfred Philp of MacKay, to surrender. The German attack was slowed down by courageous artillerymen firing over open sights, and by a stiffening resistance from the soldiers in the second line of trenches and the Princess Patricia's Canadian Light Infantry on the left flank. But the Germans had captured Mount

Sorrel, Hill 61, Hill 62, and part of Observatory Ridge, and they proceeded to dig in. It was a disaster and it threatened to become worse if the Germans pushed further forward.

The new commander of the Canadian Corps, General Julian Byng, ordered a counterattack the next day to retake the lost positions, or at least to prevent a further German advance. At midnight on June 3, the 60th Battalion was ordered to move up from its reserve position to support two other battalions which would lead the attack. But planning was rushed and organization was chaotic. The Germans rained shells on the Canadians as they attempted to organize their forces, and at one point the Canadians fell victim to friendly fire. Communications trenches that had been caved in by rain and destroyed by shell fire became clogged with men. As a result, the 60th Battalion arrived at the front before the battalion they were supposed to follow in the attack. They were then ordered to attack at once, into heavy fire through gas, smoking craters, and mutilated Canadian corpses—an experience that forever haunted Group of Seven painter A.Y. Jackson, who was with the 60th Battalion and was wounded in this engagement—until its commanding officer refused to order his men to advance further.[9] The German advance had been stopped, but Canadian losses were heavy. The 60th Battalion withdrew to support positions.

Four days later, on June 6, the Germans attacked with heavy shelling in the morning and a more intense bombardment in the afternoon, the explosion of mines, and the first German use of flame throwers. The 60th Battalion in its support position was shredded by artillery fire. Half the battalion was pulled out overnight and the other half stayed in the support position until it too could be pulled back on June 7 to "lick its wounds." During the six days from June 2 to June 7 it had suffered 345 casualties, and many of these were due to "shell shock"—men whose nerves had collapsed under the intense strain.[10] Probably during the heavy shelling on June 6, Trotter suffered a very serious wound to the right thigh. He was moved through the chain of field hospitals and casualty clearing stations and endured what A.Y. Jackson would later describe as a "long, miserable journey" to Étaples on the Channel coast, where on June 7 he was admitted to the No. 6 British Red Cross Hospital.

Étaples, about 27 kilometres south of Boulogne, was the port through which more than a million British and Commonwealth troops, as well as untold munitions and supplies, passed on their way to or from the front during the course of the war. It also contained twenty British, Canadian, and Australian base hospitals which could handle up to 22,000 wounded or sick men at a time. There they could be treated, operated on if necessary, and sent on to England for further treatment and recovery. But Trotter did not make it that far. He died at 3:30 a.m. on June 10, 1916, and was buried at the cemetery attached to the hospital complex.

Back in Canada, the Thomas Isaac Jackson family carried on with contracting, church activities, and increasingly, war work. Manfred was married during the war and continued to work as a plumber, and he became the head of the family when, as we shall see, his father and his older brother went away to war. Like some of the younger women in New Edinburgh, the oldest girl Marjorie (1892) took war work as a clerk in the Records Section of the Department of Militia and Defence. The two teenage boys, Ryland (1898) and Joseph (1899), joined MacKay Presbyterian Church in 1917, and the four Jackson daughters were also active in the church and its many activities. The youngest boy, Gordon (1904), and the younger girls, Henrietta (1901), Betty (1908), and Mary (1911), were all attending school.

The three youngest boys were still too young to enlist at the start of the war, but Thomas Nicholas Jackson, a 19-year-old who had served four years in the militia, signed up on December 1, 1915, with the 10th company of the 3rd Division Canadian Engineers. Then in February 1916, the father of the family, Thomas Isaac Jackson, enlisted in the 156th Battalion, a recruiting battalion drawing on Eastern Ontario. By this time the army was taking men it would earlier have rejected, but even so, allowing a 45-year-old man with nine children to join the infantry seems a bit much—especially since in late 1916 his wife, Henrietta, gave birth to a son, Charles Edward Jackson, presumably named after Charles Edward Trotter.[11]

Thomas Nicholas Jackson arrived in England in March 1916, and after a period of training he embarked for France in July 1916, to join the 1st Tunnelling Company. This was the first of three Canadian tunnelling companies formed in response to a British appeal for specialist units to counteract the German superiority in mining and tunnelling. At Hill 62 and St. Eloi it constructed the largest and deepest tunnels undertaken to that point. While some digging, especially near the front lines, was done by hand, much was done by machine in the soft Belgian clay, and there would have been plenty of work for a steamfitter. The work was not without danger; Jackson suffered a shrapnel wound in the hand in August of 1916 and was treated during a month-long stay in hospital. The work of tunnelling companies culminated on June 7, 1917, when tunnels packed with explosives were detonated under the German lines at Messines, in one of the largest non-nuclear explosions in history. The following month, Jackson was treated for scabies, and he was again treated for the same condition in February 1918.

Thomas Isaac Jackson was still training in Ottawa when Charles Edward Jackson was born, but in October 1916 he was sent to England. When the 156th was broken up he was (probably due to his age) assigned to a pioneer (labour/engineering) battalion in England. However, in June 1917 he was sent to France and became a corporal with the 10th Canadian Railway Troops.

Figure 8.5. Thomas Isaac Jackson, 1916.
Source: Private collection.

The railway troops built and maintained not only the main railways behind the lines but also light-gauge railways which transported shells, supplies, and men right up to the front lines. Jackson stood up under some "pretty hard service" (according to a newspaper report) until November 1917, when he reported to hospital with dyspnea (shortness of breath). In January 1918 he was gassed, and later that month he was sent to the hospital with myalgia. He was invalided to England suffering from lumbar myalgia as well as abnormal shortness of breath, cough, heart palpitations, and tachycardia especially after exercise. After passing through no fewer than nine British hospitals he was invalided home to Canada in May 1918.

His war was over. But in late September 1918, his son, Thomas Nicholas Jackson, was transferred from tunneling work to the 6th Battalion of Canadian Engineers, where he was promoted to corporal. In the swift advances and set-piece battles that marked the Hundred Days campaign (see Chapter 18), the Canadian engineers played a crucial role, keeping roads open, filling shell-holes, and building and maintaining supply lines, bases, sanitary and water systems, trenches and fortifications, often under fire. After the Armistice,

Figure 8.6. Thomas Nicholas Jackson.
Source: Private collection.

Jackson and his engineering battalion maintained camps, facilities, roads, and supply lines as the Canadians prepared for a winter in Belgium and the Rhineland. Early the following year he was sent to camp in England and returned to Canada for discharge on May 22, 1919.

Thomas Isaac Jackson arrived in Ottawa on June 7, 1918. He was sent for further convalescence to the Queen's Military Hospital in Kingston, and then on July 6 he was transferred to the Fleming Hospital in Ottawa. He was assigned light duties and recommended for discharge, but he was kept on for further service at military headquarters. When he was finally discharged on May 1, 1919, his medical report showed that while he was generally fit, he had bronchial and cardiac issues that appeared to result from his military service. He told the medical board that he could practice his former trade, "with limitations," but these proved limiting indeed. He never resumed his contracting business but instead became a carpenter with the Department of Mines. The 1921 census estimated his income at only $200–500 a year. Jackson died at age 62 in 1931 and his funeral at MacKay United Church was attended by many of those with whom he had worked as a contractor, both in Rockcliffe and in the Department of Mines. The Beechwood Cemetery register recorded his cause of death as streptococcic septicaemia. This is undoubtedly true, but the entry in the MacKay United Church Burial Register expressed a different opinion: "Cause of death—results of the Great War."[12]

Figure 8.7. Thomas Isaac Jackson during his rehabilitation. This photograph was likely taken in Ottawa shortly following his return.
Source: Private collection.

The Jackson family continued as active members of MacKay church. Their daughters were married at the church—Henrietta in 1921 and Marjorie the following year—and both left home to live with their husbands. Thomas Nicholas Jackson joined the Department of Public Works as a foreman plumber/steamfitter and worked there for 32 years. He was on the Executive Committee of the Public Works Association and was president of the Steamfitters' and Plumbers' Benefit Association.[13] He also served with the reserves for 20 years and was a piper with the Cameron Highlanders. He married and had two daughters. The family moved into the newly opened suburb of Lindenlea during the 1920s but afterward moved to Aylmer, Quebec, where he died at age 58 in 1955.[14] Manfred Jackson built a house on Springfield Road across the street from his father, and he continued in his trade as a plumber. The other Jackson children continued to live in the family home, supporting their widowed mother after Thomas's death. The youngest son, Charles Edward

Figure 8.8. Étaples Military Cemetery.
Source: Photograph by Carolyn Bowker.

Jackson, joined the RCAF (he is on MacKay's Honour Roll for the Second World War) and continued with the air force after the war. Some members of the Jackson family remained in the area until the 1970s. There was a great outcry from community and heritage groups when this house was torn down in 2008 to make room for a residence for Ashbury College.

Charles Edward Trotter rests in the Étaples Military Cemetery, which was designed by Sir Edwin Lutyens and inaugurated on May 12, 1922, by King George V and Field Marshal Sir Douglas Haig. The largest of the Commonwealth war cemeteries in France, it contains 8,817 British soldiers, 1,145 Canadians, 464 Australians, 261 New Zealanders, 68 South Africans, 17 Indians, 1 Chinese labourer, and 658 German prisoners, as well as 20 nursing sisters (four of whom were killed by a German air raid). It is breathtaking in its size and grandeur. You enter through a set of pillars and walk along a

Figure 8.9. Étaples Military Cemetery.
Source: Photograph by Carolyn Bowker.

Figure 8.10. Étaples Military Cemetery.
Source: Photograph by Carolyn Bowker.

grassy path past the Great Cross to the Stone of Remembrance on a raised platform, from which you look out on what seems an endless sea of headstones. Covered porches on the left and right provide a view of further fields of headstones on either side. But once you are down among the thousands of headstones, with green grass, carefully tended flowers, trees, and landscaping, the entrance and monument that seemed so impressive from above shrink into insignificance.

Indeed, so awe-inspiring is this cemetery that you almost forget that under each of the thousands of identical headstones, all in ordered arrangement, lies a soldier with a life story. One of these is Charles Edward Trotter, immigrant bricklayer, business partner, and adopted son of Thomas and Henrietta Jackson—whose name at least lived on in the person of Charles Edward Jackson, WO, RCAF.

Figure 8.11. Étaples Military Cemetery. Trotter's headstone is three-quarters of the way along the row running directly along the centre.
Source: Photograph by Carolyn Bowker.

9 THE ROBERTSON FAMILY
"There Is no Other Woman in Ottawa Who Has Given so Gloriously to the Cause"

The Robertsons were a Scottish family, newly arrived in Canada. Their story exemplifies not only the Scottish military tradition of service to King and Country, but also the devotion of strong women to duty and the resilience of family in the face of tragedy. Three sons in the family enlisted in the CEF, and another back in Scotland joined the Imperial forces. One son was killed, one was wounded, and a third was deeply marked by the war. Then their father signed up, and he also was killed. The Robertsons' connection to New Edinburgh and MacKay Presbyterian Church began only in 1916. But they were welcomed into the congregation, and their experience and sacrifice made a deep impression.

The father of the family, Daniel Robertson Sr. was born on February 23, 1868, in Stirlingshire, Scotland, near the battlefield of Bannockburn—he grew up, it was said, in the shadow of Stirling Castle. He was the eldest son of Daniel Robertson, who was a slater (a skilled trade working with slate for floors and roofing, which also seems to have included plastering). In 1887, now himself a journeyman slater in Glasgow, he married Mary Price (then spelled Pryce, b. 1865), a domestic servant. Over the next 15 years they had eight children. In 1901, according to the Scottish census, the family was living in the "railway cottages, Fort William" where Daniel was a "slater and plasterer." By 1911 they had moved to Shettleston, a suburb of Glasgow, where Daniel Sr. was a foreman slater employed by a railway company. Four of his sons were by then working: Daniel Jr. as an apprentice slater, James as a railway porter, George as an apprentice bookseller and stationer, and William as a 15-year-old telegraph boy for the railway.[1]

In 1913, the eldest son, Daniel Robertson Jr., decided to emigrate to Canada, and Daniel Sr. accompanied him. Father and son arrived in Quebec on the *Letitia* out of Glasgow on May 18, 1913. They were bound for Saskatoon

Figure 9.1. Daniel Robertson Sr. before the war.
Source: Private collection.

Figure 9.2. Daniel Robertson Jr. as a boy.
Source: Private collection.

where they were to be employed as plasterers for the Grand Trunk Pacific Railway.[2] But if Daniel Sr. went to Saskatoon, he was soon transferred to Ottawa, and early in 1914 he sent a telegram to another son, George, asking him to escort "mother and the children" to Canada.[3] Not all the children came—James and a married daughter stayed behind in Scotland. On May 11, 1914, Mary Robertson, 49, with children George, 20 (a "stationer"), William, 17 (a "clerk"), Jeannie, 15 (a "clerkess"), Annie, 11, and Peter, 9, arrived in Quebec, also on the *Letitia*, and from there they travelled to Ottawa.[4] Once in Ottawa, the Robertson family changed addresses several times as they settled in, while Daniel Jr. remained in Saskatoon.

Then, in the early days of August, the outbreak of war turned their lives upside down. Daniel Jr. enlisted in Saskatoon in August 1914, William and George followed in Ottawa in 1915, and then in April 1916, Daniel Sr. himself enlisted in the CEF. Mary Robertson moved to New Edinburgh, with her youngest son and two daughters, to live with the family of William Gaitens in a small, attached frame house at 54 Crichton Street. Gaitens, a baker born in Glasgow who had emigrated in 1911, had seven children ranging from 17 years to 2 years. The Gaitens family were all members of MacKay church, and Mary Robertson, a staunch Presbyterian, joined MacKay by Certificate on December 15, 1916, together with her husband *in absentia* (Daniel Sr. was already dead, though she did not know that at the time), and settled into the church and community.[5]

The families may have been related—the youngest Gaitens child was named Daniel Robertson Gaitens—and there may have been some arrangement for the two families to share accommodation since, in May 1916, William Gaitens also enlisted, as a baker in the Army Service Corps. With him gone, the only sources of income for the 12 women and children living in cramped quarters would have been from assigned army pay, plus any savings, possibly assistance from the Patriotic Fund, and any income the girls might have earned.[6] Mary Robertson received $15 a month assigned pay from her husband and two of her sons (Daniel Jr. assigned no pay), and $20 a month separation allowance, while the Gaitens family had separation allowance and William's assigned pay.

As we have said, Daniel Robertson Jr. (born in Laurieston, Scotland, on June 1, 1890)[7] had enlisted on August 26, 1914, with the 105th Saskatoon Fusiliers. He had arrived with them at Valcartier on September 2 and had been formally attested on September 23, 1914, into the 11th Battalion, CEF. He was five feet eight inches tall, with fair complexion, blue eyes, and brown hair. On October 3, 1914, his ship departed from Quebec City and and by the end of the month the regiment had settled in for the winter at the training camp on Salisbury Plain.

Figure 9.3. Daniel Robertson Jr. as a soldier, 1914.
Source: De Wolfe 1919, 259.

Here some of the men displayed the indiscipline that led the British to consider the Canadians poor soldiers; in December 1914, Daniel Robertson Jr. was docked five days' pay for some unnamed offense.[8] Besides making soldiers of the Canadians, the British had to cope with a major organizational problem. Because Sam Hughes had insisted that all the men who had gathered at Valcartier had to be sent overseas, the British had to select the 12 battalions which would form the First Canadian Division that would be sent to the front. The other four, including the 11th Battalion, would be kept in England to form the core of a Second Division. But in January 1915, the War Office decided instead to use these men to reinforce existing battalions in the First Division,[9] and in February Robertson was assigned to the 8th Battalion from Manitoba, which became known as the "Little Black Devils." The 8th went to France with the First Division on April 3, 1915, and took over a sector of the line in the Ypres Salient near St. Julien. Within two weeks it found itself in the thick of the Battle of Second Ypres.

The 8th Battalion was not part of the initial fighting when the Germans attacked using chlorine gas on April 22. But at 4:00 a.m. on April 24, it was directly attacked with gas, combined with an intense artillery bombardment. "It is impossible for me to give a real idea of the terror and horror spread among us by this filthy loathsome presence," recalled a major in the 8th Battalion.[10]

Many Canadians were wounded and some killed, but the survivors fought back, pouring a steady fire with their unreliable Ross rifles into the advancing enemy. The 8th Battalion found itself fighting desperately to avoid being surrounded when the Germans broke through the battalion to its left. Several platoons were wiped out or taken prisoner. But the 8th Battalion held, and when it was finally forced to retreat, it did so in disciplined fashion.[11] Daniel, in a letter home, described the carnage of this battle and the horror of gas (see Chapter 3). He was treated for the effects of gas fumes between May 27 and the end of June 1915, and was then assigned light work until he rejoined the battalion in August. He had a short leave in December 1915. Meanwhile the 8th Battalion was being completely rebuilt and it did not return to the Ypres Salient until early 1916.

The 8th Battalion was less engaged in the Battle of Mount Sorrel, in which Charles Trotter fell, though it was subject to shelling and rifle fire, and after the battle it was sent back to brigade reserve. But when it returned to the front line on June 13 to complete the retaking of positions that had been lost to the Germans, it was subjected to intense enemy artillery fire which cut companies off from each other, destroyed communications and supply trenches, and prevented evacuation of the wounded. The next day the battalion was shelled even more heavily. "Our own shells falling short combined with the almost contnuous enemy shelling made conditions very trying indeed," says its war diary. The men had gone 3 days without sleep and 24 hours without rations when, during the night of June 14–15, they were relieved, under heavy shelling and having to take circuitous routes. "The officers, NCOs, and men who arrived in camp," says the war diary, "were completely used up and totally incapable of further effort at the time." Nonetheless 3 officers and 75 men volunteered to go back to the front to carry out the wounded. When the final tally was completed, out of 20 officers and 550 men who had gone into action, 1 officer had been killed and 5 wounded, and 64 other ranks had been killed, 195 were wounded, and 2 were missing.[12]

Robertson was among those initially reported missing and his body was never found. His family was not formally notified until February of the following year that he had in fact been killed on June 14. It is not clear when, or on what evidence, the final entry was made for him in the Circumstances of Death Register: "'Previously reported as missing, now Killed in Action.' While on duty in the front line trenches at MOUNT SORREL, he was instantly killed by an enemy shell which exploded in the trench a few feet in front of him."[13] He was 26.

Meanwhile, on June 26, 1915, Daniel's younger brother George Robertson (b. 1894) had enlisted in the 59th Battalion. George was the smallest of the brothers at five feet three and a half inches tall and 120 pounds. He was also the best shot. When the 59th Battalion went to Barriefield Camp in Kingston in July, he managed to get into the Provincial School of Infantry for training as a scout and sniper. On completing this course in November he was assigned to the 80th Battalion, CEF, for overseas service. Once in England, in May 1916, George was given further rifle training, and when his battalion was broken up, he was assigned to the 75th Battalion, which sailed for France on August 11, 1916.

Figure 9.4. George Robertson, 1915.
Source: De Wolfe 1919, 260.

George's role as a sniper was dangerous and taxing. He particularly relished the day when his Ross rifle was replaced with a Lee Enfield. As he recalled many years later:

> Oh my, that was a rifle. It was my happy rifle. Could hit anything with it. Of course, I was a good shot. But the Lee Enfield was perfect. The Ross rifle, when it got a bit of dust or something in the breech, you never handled your shot properly. But, with the Lee Enfield, you could hit anything. I could anyways. I was trained as a sniper. Some said I was one of the best shots in my unit. Used to go out when we'd be up at the front. I'd survey the surrounding territory, pick a spot, and once it got dark enough, crawl up to it. Sometimes it would be between the two lines in no man's land. When it got dark, I'd move out and shoot there until morning.

Being a sniper probably took more of a toll than was reflected in his recollections at a late stage in a very long life. His service record shows that he spent substantial periods of time in 1917 and 1918 as a batman (personal servant to an officer) in the Fourth Division headquarters, and as an instructor at the Canadian Corps Reinforcement Camp in France. Although he survived the war without major wounds, his "32 months floating around in the mud and water of the trenches" had left him with bad legs that would get worse as time went on.[14]

Meanwhile the youngest (18 years old) and tallest (five feet eight and a half inches) of the brothers eligible for military service, William Price Robertson, a clerk for the Great North Western Telegraph Company, had signed up on August 16, 1915, in the 77th Battalion, citing three years' previous experience in the "Boys' Brigade" (presumably in Scotland). William trained throughout the fall and winter with the battalion, the only glitch being an attack of acute bronchitis during the fall of 1915.

Then on April 8, 1916, their father, Daniel Robertson Sr., enlisted as a late addition to the 77th Battalion. One wonders why. He was very fit at five feet six and a half inches tall, with medium complexion and blue eyes, and he had served for one year in the 43rd Duke of Cornwall's Own Rifles, the militia regiment that fed the 77th Battalion. But even though he lied about his age, his grey hair showed clearly that he was not a young man. The 77th Battalion was not desperate for men, as recruiters would be later in the year, and as a late recruit he would be going overseas with little training. In any case, the fact was that Daniel Sr., with a wife and three children at home and four sons already in uniform, was now a soldier, and his wife and remaining children were sharing a house wth the family of another absent middle-aged soldier.

When the 77th Battalion was broken up in England in July 1916, William and his father were assigned to the 87th Battalion, a Montreal-based regiment with a strong Eastern Ontario contingent, which was part of the 11th Brigade of the newly formed Fourth Canadian Division. (The 75th Battalion, in which George Robertson was serving, was also part of the 11th Brigade.) In August 1916, the Fourth Division was sent to a "quiet" sector in the Ypres Salient. But in September it began its move to the Somme, to play its part in a titanic struggle which had been ongoing since July 1 and had cost the British armies over 100,000 killed. The Fourth Division was still serving as part of a British Corps (all four Canadian divisions would not be united under a single command until the Battle of Vimy Ridge in April 1917). When the Fourth Division arrived, the first three divisions of the Canadian Corps had won a major victory at Courcelette but had failed to take the further objective of Regina Trench. Exhausted and depleted, they had been withdrawn from the line to regroup.

By the time the Fourth Division came into the line in October 1916, "incessant rains had turned the whole Somme area, lying between the Ancre and the Somme rivers and the Canal du Nord into a quagmire," in the words of

Figure 9.5. Daniel Robertson Sr. as a soldier, 1916. Source: De Wolfe 1919, 259.

Victor Wheeler of a sister battalion. "The heavy guns thundered continuously. The earth convulsed as land mines, planted thirty to fifty feet underground spawned, then exploded, shattering every living and inanimate thing. Madness and misery were everywhere."[15] "The mud – and rain – has been our most disagreeable enemy," wrote another man who was there. "Mud, mud, mud, ankle deep, hip deep, mud. Mud to walk in, to sit in, sleep in; mud on our clothes, on our equipment, on our rations – mud everywhere. I never knew that mud could make itself so abominably beyond the power of words to describe."[16]

George Robertson, who (as we have seen) was serving in the same brigade as Daniel Sr., many years later recalled a brief opportunity he had during this period to talk with his father, "soldier to soldier, man to man"—a talk that speaks volumes about how life in the trenches had changed profoundly the outlook of an overaged soldier whose patriotism had led him to enlist. The Robertson family were devout Presbyterians who had been scrupulous teetotallers before the war. Several Canadian generals, including the commander of the 11th Brigade, Victor Odlum, were also abstainers and tried to keep their soldiers "dry." But they were overruled by higher authority and by 1916 it was standard practice to issue front-line soldiers with a daily dram of strong Demerara rum—both to raise their spirits (and when necessary their courage) and to combat the deadening chill and damp of winter in the trenches.[17] George was thus surprised when his father asked whether he was taking his daily ration of rum and George replied that he was not. "George, drink it," said Daniel. "It's the only thing that keeps me going over here." After that talk, George drank his rum.[18]

On October 21, 1916, elements of two battalions of the Fourth Division, including the 87th Battalion, took a section of Regina Trench, and withstood fierce counterattacks and shelling by the Germans. The 87th Battalion lost 114 killed and 169 wounded in this action. What role Daniel Sr. and William played in this attack is not known—William was wounded on November 4 but returned to duty November 7. Regina Trench, or what was left of it, was not finally taken until November 11.

The Fourth Division was then tasked with capturing the next line of German trenches, Desire Trench—just one more objective, demanded British Supreme Commander Sir Douglas Haig, to push the Germans back a little further before the fighting season ended. The attack began on November 18, 1916, in sleety snow and continued in driving rain. Cold weather had hardened the ground and frozen water in shell holes provided a macabre fate for those who cracked through the ice. Desire Trench was captured with "moderate losses" and elements of the 87th and the 38th Battalions proceeded beyond it to a further objective of Grandcourt Trench. One hundred and eleven Germans were captured and sent back to the lines under escort of wounded men. But pressing forward to Grandcourt Trench had been a last-minute addition to the battle plan, and the unsupported Canadians were shredded by artillery and machine gun fire while other units made futile and costly attempts to relieve them. At dusk the survivors were pulled back. The Fourth Division had captured 700 metres of ruined trenches whose name, Desire Trench, had now become a cruel irony. On November 19, when heavy rain reduced the battlefield to a quagmire, further attacks were called off and the long Battle of the Somme was over.[19]

The war diary of the 87th Battalion grimly records the names of officers killed and wounded and then tersely adds: "Casualties among other ranks were 26 killed, 50 missing, 148 wounded."[20] Daniel Robertson Sr. was one of those "missing." It is not known how far he got in the attack or where he fell. Only in January 1917 was a final determination made that he had indeed been killed in action. His body was "not recovered for burial."[21] It seems that he simply disappeared, blown up by shellfire or buried in the ooze.

Another casualty of Desire Trench was Daniel's son William Robertson, who suffered several shrapnel and bullet wounds, the most serious being a bullet that passed through his chest and exited not far from his spine. By early December he was in hospital at Étaples and in late December he was sent back to England, where he passed through a chain of acute care and convalescent hospitals. His lung had collapsed and his heart had been displaced. It took many weeks to recover from these wounds, and after three months William was still suffering from a cough, shortness of breath, and difficulty sleeping.

Back in New Edinburgh, Mary Robertson learned in December 1916 that her husband was missing. She apparently still believed that her son Daniel Jr. was a prisoner in Germany, and while she knew that William had been wounded she did not know how serious this was.[22] All this changed in early 1917 when, as the MacKay Register of Deaths reported, "official notice reached Mrs. Robertson on January 10th that her husband was killed 'Somewhere in France' on Nov. 18th 1916." Then in February it was reported that Daniel Jr. had been killed on June 14 of the previous year. Mary also learned that her son William had been more badly wounded than previously reported. The plight of "Mary Robertson, patriot" became a news item in the local press. "As far as is known, there is no other woman in Ottawa who has given so gloriously to the cause," wrote a reporter for the Ottawa *Journal*. "Her husband and four sons she sent to the front, and now that her eldest son, for some time reported missing, has been officially declared dead, she waits resignedly in the little home at 54 Creighton Street, which will never again shelter her family, hoping and praying that her other boys will be returned to her."[23]

In March 1917, William Robertson was sent back to Canada, first to the Queen's Military Hospital and then to a convalescent facility on Fettercairn Island near Chaffey's Locks in the Rideau Canal waterway. This 45-bed house, purchased and fitted out by the sister of a soldier who fell in the Ypres Salient (and, like Charles Wendt, is buried at Bailleul), operated between 1916 and 1918. In this sylvan lakeside setting, severely wounded soldiers could regain their physical and, in some cases, their mental health.

One important aspect of Fettercairn was that families of wounded soldiers were encouraged to have lengthy visits to improve their morale and thus contribute to their physical recovery and restore their mental balance. Mary Robertson visited William frequently, perhaps in some measure subsuming her grief and worry in her devotion to the recovery of her surviving son.

On July 4, William was transferred to the Fleming Hospital in Ottawa, where a medical board judged him unfit for further service, and he was discharged at age 21 on November 30, 1917. He rented an apartment above a store on Bank Street and Mary went to live with him while he recovered. But she continued to attend MacKay Presbyterian Church and her children appear to have remained with the Gaitens family. She now received a widow's pension, as well as an advance on her husband's $180 War Service Gratuity. William had stated on an official form that his income as a clerk before the war had been $50 a month, and the medical board on discharge estimated that his earning capacity would be diminished by 25 percent for the first year. He was accordingly given a small pension as well as his War Service Gratuity, back pay, and other benefits. He became a clerk in the new Department of National Defence and married in 1920.

Figure 9.6. Soldiers and staff at Fettercairn Island; soldiers could enjoy golf, fishing, boating, and swimming while they convalesced.
Source: Chaffey's Lockmaster's House Museum.

Figure 9.7. William Robertson and his mother, Mary, at Fettercairn Island, 1917.
Source: Chaffey's Lockmaster's House Museum.

George Robertson, after his return in 1919, lived for a time with his mother and brother, and then got an apartment of his own. He also worked as a clerk in the war service records branch of the Department of National Defence, married, and had two children. In 1920 he joined the militia: first the Cameron Highlanders, then the 4th Battalion Canadian Machine Gun Corps. When the Second World War broke out he served first as a lieutenant, then as a captain. As a chief casualty officer in the Canadian Army, he was responsible for notifying loved ones of the deaths or injury of soldiers. In particular his job involved correcting errors—a difficult job but one he felt needed to be done well. "He knew exactly what his mother went through when she was advised," said a close friend after Robertson died, aged 102, in the Rideau-Perley Veterans' Home—a man who never showed much emotion but was deeply loyal to his friends and to his duty.[24]

The two Robertson daughters, who have been almost invisible in our story, remained for a time in New Edinburgh but moved elsewhere in the early 1920s, though they retained ties with the community and the Gaitens family (Agnes Gaitens was a witness at the wedding of Annie Robertson in 1921). Gaitens returned after the war, suffering from a hernia and defective vision—both pre-existing conditions—and the family left New Edinburgh in 1922. Both Robertson daughters married—Jean in 1920 and Annie in 1921—and left New Edinburgh to start families. We have no information on what happened to the youngest son, Peter.[25]

As for Mary Robertson, in December 1919 she was disjoined from MacKay (i.e., struck off the rolls and given a certificate), bringing to an end her brief association with this church. She appears to have attended Knox Presbyterian Church in downtown Ottawa, but where she lived after George married, or what she lived on, is not clear. She died in 1952 at age 87, in Toronto, where she may have gone to live with one of her daughters. She had, however, according to her obituary, lived for "many years" in Ottawa, and was a member of the Eastern Star, the Ladies' Orange Association, and a Life Member of the Clan Cameron Ladies' Auxiliary of Ottawa.[26]

She would never know any burial place for her husband or her son, because the two Daniel Robertsons, like almost half the Canadian soldiers who died in the First World War, have no known graves. They are remembered, however, on two of the iconic monuments of that war.

Daniel Robertson Jr.'s name is inscribed at the Menin Gate in Ypres. Designed by Sir Reginald Blomfield, one of Britain's leading architects, and opened in 1927, this monument stands at the ancient entrance to Ypres by the rampart on the Yser Canal. Its interior, through which a road passes, is a "hall of memory" 36.6 m (long) x 20.1 m (wide), suggestive in its design (and

Figure 9.8. Menin Gate, Ypres.
Source: Photograph by Carolyn Bowker.

acoustics) of a large church. In its centre there are arched doorways on either side which lead to broad staircases going up to the ramparts and to the outside of the structure, with its pillared loggias. Over these arches are inscribed the following words:

> HERE ARE RECORDED NAMES OF OFFICERS AND MEN WHO FELL IN YPRES SALIENT BUT TO WHOM THE FORTUNE OF WAR DENIED THE KNOWN AND HONOURED BURIAL GIVEN TO THEIR COMRADES IN DEATH.

Since the 1920s the citizens of Ypres have organized a Last Post ceremony to express their gratitude for the sacrifice made for their freedom. Every evening at 8:00 p.m., except from 1940 to 1944, when Belgium was again occupied, this ceremony has taken place regardless of weather, with two to four buglers playing the Last Post at the east side of the gate, the road on which soldiers marched forth to battle.

Figure 9.9. Interior of Menin Gate, Ypres.
Source: Photograph by Carolyn Bowker.

Nothing could more starkly express the terrible cost of war than the 55,000 names carved on the inner walls of the hall, on the arches and stairways, and on the outer walls under the loggias. The list of almost 7,000 Canadian names begins on the panel of the south inner wall next to the archway, turns the corner to continue along the inside of the arch, then turns again to fill the walls beside the steps outside, along the landing, and down the other set of steps back to the arch. The 8th Battalion is listed on the wall beside the steps, and Daniel Robertson's name is found there, with his service number to distinguish him from another D. Robertson.

Daniel Robertson Sr. is memorialized, along with more than 11,000 other Canadians who died in France with no known graves, on the Vimy Memorial. Unlike the Menin Gate, where names are grouped by unit and listed by rank, the Canadian names on the Vimy Memorial are simply inscribed one after the other, in alphabetical order. They run in a horizontal line, across the seams between stones. The overall effect is to enhance the beauty and sadness of the memorial as a whole, with its allegorical figures and soaring pillars. Daniel Robertson Sr.'s name is on the right of the monument as you approach from the upper entrance, in the third row of stones from the top, third block to the right of the mourning man.

On the other side of the monument, looking out over the Douai Plan and down at the cenotaph of a fallen soldier, Mother Canada weeps over her lost children, personifying in her bereavement not only the nation but the wives and mothers, the Mary Robertsons, of Canada.

Figure 9.10. Stairway at Menin Gate; this stairway, leading out from the barrel-vaulted main structure, is covered with the names of fallen soldiers. Robertson's name is on the wall to the left. *Source*: Photograph by Carolyn Bowker.

Figure 9.11. Vimy Memorial.
Source: Photograph by Carolyn Bowker.

Figure 9.12. Vimy Memorial.
Source: Photograph by Carolyn Bowker.

Figure 9.13. Mother Canada.
Source: Photograph by Carolyn Bowker.

10

GORDON MAYNARD PORTEOUS
"Quite a Few Homes … Will be Sad After This"

Like Daniel Robertson Sr., Gordon Porteous perished at the battle of Desire Trench and has no known grave. Gordon was an only son and his parents felt the anguish of his loss for the rest of their lives. The Porteous family moved to New Edinburgh during the war and, like the Robertsons, became active members of MacKay Presbyterian Church.

Gordon Porteous was born on January 8, 1895, in Ottawa, the only surviving son of David Porteous (1857–1923) and Sarah Jane "Jennie" Miller (1860–1941). The family had roots in Ottawa and New Brunswick, but in 1914 it was well established in Buckingham, Quebec, a thriving mill town with close links to the factories in New Edinburgh.[1] David Porteous, a carpenter at the McLaren sawmill, was a Baptist, but his wife and all the children attended St. Andrew's Presbyterian Church in Buckingham, where Gordon was a member of the Sunday School and Bible-study group. The picture below, probably taken about 1905, shows the four Porteous children including Gordon, at the centre, who was about 10.[2] In 1908 Ethel May (at the left), married William Henry Forse, an accountant, at age 18; they had a son the following year and shortly before the war moved to Moncton, New Brunswick.[3] The eldest daughter Lillian (at right), worked as a telephone operator until 1912 when she enrolled at age 24 as a nurse in training in the Lady Stanley Institute, attached to the Protestant Hospital on Rideau Street; she graduated in May 1915.[4] The third sister, Laura (top centre), was living at home when the war broke out.

Gordon Porteous studied at the Buckingham Academy but left school by age 16 to work in the McLaren mill. He was a labourer at the E. B. Eddy plant in Hull when he joined the Duke of Cornwall's Own Rifles militia regiment, and on July 19, 1915, he was formally attested into the 38th Battalion, CEF. He was five feet seven and a quarter inches tall, with fair complexion, grey eyes, and brown hair.

Following initial training in Ottawa, the 38th Battalion (after a couple of false starts due to German submarine activity) sailed for Bermuda in August to relieve the Royal Canadian Regiment. The RCR, which had been the only

Figure 10.1. The Porteous Children, c. 1905: clockwise from left: Lillie (Sarah), Laura, Ethel (Mae), and Gordon. *Source:* Private collection.

regular militia battalion when war broke out, had been sent to Bermuda rather than sailing with the First Canadian Contingent, because Minister of Militia Sam Hughes despised the regular soldiers and chose this way of showing his contempt for them. But now the RCR was going to the front as part of the Third Canadian Division, and the 38th Battalion would not only replace them as garrison soldiers but would also undergo rigorous training by British professionals—in fact, better training, in better weather, than they could have got in Ottawa.[5] Porteous proudly reported in a letter to his mother that he had received high scores for marksmanship, but that he and his comrades also had time to collect shells and enjoy the sun and sand. "I am feeling fine," he added, "and have gained thirteen pounds since I left Buckingham." On February 8, 1916, the 38th Battalion was inspected by the Governor and Commander-in-Chief of Bermuda and declared fully up to British standards—"as good as any he had inspected before they left for the front," reported Gordon.[6] On May 31, the battalion sailed for England aboard the *Grampian*.

In June 1916 the 38th Battalion was directly incorporated into the 12th Brigade of the newly formed Fourth Canadian Division, and after inspection by the King it crossed the channel in mid-August to take up a position in the Ypres Salient. On July 24 Gordon filled out the printed will in his pay book leaving all his property and effects to his mother. The 38th Battalion was rotated in and out of the front lines in a "quiet" sector of the Ypres Salient to gain experience—though as we have seen, "quiet" was term of art there.

Then in September, the Fourth Division left the salient to begin its long journey to the Somme. A jaunty report by a correspondent for the Ottawa *Journal* described this march in idyllic terms. "The experience of practically two weeks of trekking, with billets in farm buildings of French peasants every night, was distinctly novel to the Canadians and genuinely enjoyed after two weeks of trench life in Belgium," wrote the correspondent. "The march was through a rural section of unsurpassed beauty and prosperity, and the whole country side proved hospitable."[7] The reality was somewhat different: a 45-mile march to a railhead; then days in box-cars marked "eight horses, forty men," so full of men that the stench was stomach-churning and fresh air was fought for; then two days of training and a two-day, 25-mile march to their base camp at Canaas near the front—marching, with 10-minute rests every hour, in lice-infested clothes with 50-pound packs that got heavier and heavier as the rain soaked through them, while the road turned to mud that stuck to boots and caked uniforms.

When they finally arrived on October 9, their lives became a round of work parties, periods in the front line with the usual artillery and machine gun duels, and occasional rest behind the lines where they underwent intensive training.[8] The war diary of the 38th Battalion recorded "wet weather," "bad weather," "cold weather," day after day as October turned into November.[9] Readers of the Ottawa *Journal* were told that the battalion, "fully seasoned and representative of the finest type, physically and intellectually, of Canada's manhood," was joyously reuniting with Ottawa men in other battalions, with every man "entering on the task set for him here with unbounded enthusiasm and confidence, and most optimistic in the outcome for other historical achievements, supplementing the list of Canada's success in the area."[10] The grim reality for Porteous and the 38th Battalion, which was temporarily attached for the purpose to the 11th Brigade, would be the battle for Desire Trench.

As we have seen, on November 18, 1916, the 11th Brigade spearheaded the Canadian attack. The 38th Battalion was on the left and the 87th Battalion—including Daniel Robertson Sr. and his son William—was on the right. Before they even got started, a number of men in the 38th Battalion were killed or wounded by a direct hit from an enemy gun. The battalion slogged forward in the sticky mud of a battlefield torn by shells and obscured by smoke and rain. The terse language of the 12th Brigade War Diary is eloquent in its very dryness in describing the horror of what happened. It reads that the 38th Battalion:

> attacked with the greatest determination, gained their objective and consolidated it. In addition, pushing out Battle Patrols, which entered GRANDCOURT TRENCH and cleared a considerable portion of it in conjunction with the 87th Battalion on their Right. 38th Battalion established a Machine Gun Post in GRANDCOURT TRENCH which remained until ordered by II Corps to retire. This ~~retreat~~ retirement took place that evening.

By the end of the day only one officer was left in the front line. The 38th had lost 4 officers killed, 11 wounded, 1 missing in action; along with 43 "other ranks" killed, 153 wounded, and 74 "missing."[11] Gordon Maynard Porteous was among the "missing." "Killed in Action," reads the Circumstances of Death Register, "in an attack at Desire Trench, Courcelette." It gives no further details.[12] He was 21.

"There will be quite a few homes that will be sad after this," wrote a soldier in the 38th Battalion.[13] The dreaded telegrams poured into the homes of Ottawa families. Luckier ones received messages from their sons that they were safe. But unlike previous engagements involving Canadian soldiers, there was surprisingly little reportage in the Ottawa press—least of all from the Ottawa *Journal*, whose correspondent had been so upbeat just days before. There were vague reports of a great battle in which Ottawa regiments had covered themselves in glory. Lengthy casualty lists over the next few weeks, obituaries for some individual soldiers, and a story about a decoration given to one commanding officer, indicated that something big had taken place. But perhaps the authorities were leery of providing any more information about how two Ottawa regiments had been effectively destroyed in this useless coda to the profligate squandering of life on the Somme. A short obituary for Porteous in the local Buckingham paper noted that the flags of the village would fly at half-mast in his honour, and that a memorial service would be held at St. Andrew's.

In the year following Gordon Porteous's death, his family—father David (listed in the 1918 city directory as a millwright), mother Jennie, and sisters Lillian, a nurse at the Protestant Hospital, and Laura, a saleslady at the Charles Ogilvy department store—moved into a small house in New Edinburgh at 3 Vaughan Street. David Porteous may have found work at the Edwards factories or other workshops, and Lillian and Laura would have found this location convenient to their places of work on Rideau Street. In June 1918, Jennie and Laura joined MacKay church by Certificate from a church in

Figure 10.2. Canadian troops returning from the trenches, Battle of the Somme, November 1916. The anguish of the soldiers after the battles of Regina and Desire Trenches is clearly etched on the faces of these exhausted troops.
Source: Library and Archives Canada PA-000839.

Moncton. Laura immediately became a "trainer" in a Bible-study class conducted in 1918,[14] and Lillian joined the church in October by Profession of Faith (as a Baptist, David did not join MacKay). In 1920, the family moved to 35 Vaughan Street, half of a new double house. All three women were in regular attendance until the end of 1921, when the two daughters married and left to live with their husbands in Sudbury and Moncton respectively.[15] Jennie and David then moved to Hull. It was there that he received Gordon's plaque and scroll, and she the Silver Cross.

David Porteous died in 1923. Two years later, Jennie began attending MacKay United Church once again, even though she was no longer living in New Edinburgh. Perhaps one reason was that her son's name on the In Memoriam plaque was the only tangible memorial to him that she could visit. She continued to be an active member until early 1932 when she moved to New Brunswick to live with her daughter.

In 1936 King Edward VIII (who as Prince of Wales unveiled the memorial plaques at MacKay in 1919) inaugurated the Vimy Memorial, where Gordon Porteous's name, like that of Daniel Robertson Sr., is carved in stone. Thousands of Canadian veterans and their families made the pilgrimage to

Vimy for the unveiling, but Jenny Porteous was not among them. She died in Moncton in July 1941. Her funeral in Ottawa was attended by many old friends from Ottawa and Buckingham, and she was buried in St. James Cemetery, Hull, beside her husband and their infant son who had died in 1888. Along with her name, that of Gordon Porteous was carved into the family headstone.[16]

Figure 10.3. Vimy Memorial showing the location of Gordon Porteous's name, second row of stones from the top, first full stone to the left of the mourning woman.
Source: Photograph by Carolyn Bowker.

11

HENRY JAMES MAYO
A "Home Boy" Serves His Country

Henry Mayo was a "home boy," sent out from Britain and raised in a Boys' Home in Ottawa, who became a man of unusual leadership skills and took on family responsibilities at a very young age. When, like so many "home boys," Henry signed up to fight for King and Country, his wife and children went to Glasgow to live with his father. When he was killed, the loss of such a promising young man, who had achieved so much from such humble beginnings, was keenly felt at St. Bartholomew's Anglican Church as well as at MacKay Presbyterian. His young widow now had to face the challenge of raising two young boys on her own, working in menial jobs to give them a good home and a proper upbringing.

Henry Mayo was born on September 18, 1896, in Chaubattia, India, within sight of the western peaks of the Himalayas. His father, Frank Mayo, had enlisted in the Scottish Rifles in 1884 at the age of 14 as a bugler and had been posted to India. He had married Margaret Georgina Murphy and they had had three sons: Percy (1889), Frank Jr. (1895), and Henry James.[1] Frank was honorably discharged in Glasgow in 1909, probably with a meagre pension. His marriage had by then broken up. The two older boys joined the British Army, but Henry was only 12 and his father could not look after him. An arrangement was made, possibly through a Glasgow organization, for Henry to go to the Liverpool Sheltering Home and from there to be sent to Canada as one of the 100,000 British "home children" transported to Canada between 1870 and 1930. Henry arrived in Liverpool on May 19, 1909, and the following day he boarded the SS *Corsican* for Quebec.

The Liverpool Sheltering Home was founded in 1872 by Louisa Birt under the auspices of her sister Annie Macpherson (1833–1904), a Scottish evangelical Christian who dedicated her life to helping poor children in the urban slums of Victorian England. Macpherson and others, most notably Dr. Thomas Barnardo, founded shelters in London that provided some semblance of home life and prepared the children for life as domestic workers or tradesmen. But because there were far more such children than British society could absorb, these organizations began in the 1870s to send children to Canada and Australia. Macpherson established homes run

Figure 11.1. Henry James Mayo.
Source: 77th Battalion 1926, 70.

by trusted friends in Canada, from which home children were sent out to farms across Ontario, Quebec, and the Atlantic provinces. Inspectors were to regularly visit the children, respond to their needs, report on their condition, and ensure they were well treated and fitting into their new roles. Some home children found at least some of the home life and healthy surroundings the program advertised, but many others were treated as little more than slaves. Regardless of how they were treated, the strongest memory most of them had was the sense of being an outsider without a real home or family. Nonetheless, the majority of them went on to marry and raise families, serve in the military during the First and Second World Wars, and become successful citizens of their adopted country.[2]

Louisa Birt began in the mid-1870s to make yearly visits to Canada accompanying groups of children. She took over the Distributing Home in Knowlton, Quebec, as a receiving centre, and by 1912 almost 5,000 children, including orphans brought out for adoption, had been placed from there.[3] Mayo was one of 300 children ranging in age from 7 to 16 who disembarked from the *Corsican* at Quebec on May 29, 1909, on one of Louisa Birt's last journeys to Canada.[4]

Figure 11.2. Knowlton Distributing Home c. 1890.
Source: Brome County Historical Society BCHS4093_S2_D1_P01.

Figure 11.3. Knowlton Distributing Home, side view, c. 1905.
Source: Brome County Historical Society. BCHS4093_S2_D1_P02.

Mayo was unusual among the children on the ship, in that he had not spent the normal six months in the Liverpool Sheltering Home, nor did he go to a farm. Instead, after a month at Knowlton, he was sent to the Ottawa Boys' Home, which had been founded about 1908 as an "incorporated organization which provides a home for poor working boys of any denomination who have no homes of their own."[5]

In Ottawa, as in all Canadian cities, teenage boys without families were struggling to make a living and find shelter. The Ottawa Boys' Home, located at 161 George Street in the ByWard Market, was described in a newspaper article in 1913 as "doing good work in this city in a quiet way." Under the guidance of a superintendent and matron, the boys were not only "given good food and comfortable beds but they are made to feel that this is indeed a home for them." They received instruction three nights a week from the principal of the George Street Public School next door, and from the Boy Scouts. They had access to a large reading room furnished with books, to a piano (chorus singing was encouraged), and to a gymnasium. They were allowed to go out at night but had to be back before 10. The superintendent (sometimes called the manager) was to find work for the boys and to ensure that they were fairly treated by their employers, as well as to "keep a fatherly eye" on them. The boys paid their board and lodging according to their wages. "The Home has sent a lot of useful young men forth into the world and boasts of 57 men wearing khaki," wrote a newspaper article in January 1917. "One of these, Corporal Mayo, has recently been killed in action."[6]

Mayo was one of the first boys at the Home, and it is unclear why this fledging Home would have taken in a 13-year-old "home child" when there were teenage working boys in Ottawa needing assistance. But for Henry, an intelligent, personable, and hard-working lad with a maturity far beyond his years, the Home provided a real opportunity. The Macpherson inspector reported that he began work at the Baker Laundry on Wellington Street and was so "well-liked by his employers" that they raised his wages to $3.25 per week and thought that he "would soon be manager of one of the branches." By 1912 Henry was working at the American Bank Note Co. as an apprentice lithographer and printer. By 1913 he was working at the Bank Note Engraving Co. at a salary of $5 per week, and by 1915 he appears to have become a full-fledged lithographer.[7] He attended St. Bartholomew's Anglican Church in New Edinburgh, where he was well known and sang in the choir. (A newspaper report says that he lived on MacKay Street but there is no record of this, nor of his working at Rideau Hall, as the article suggests.)[8] He also found time to do some militia service with the Canadian Engineers, according to his attestation papers, though it is not clear what or when this was. This is a remarkable record of achievement for a young man who had come to Canada without family and was still only 17 when the war broke out. And by August 1914 he had also taken on family responsibilities.

On August 2, 1913, the Macpherson inspector reported that Henry was no longer at the Ottawa Boys' Home but was "living with Mr. Welford on Lyon St. Ottawa. Miss Welford is the attraction."[9] Mary Elizabeth (May)

Welford, born April 6, 1893, in Kill, County Kildare, Ireland,[10] was the 20-year-old daughter of the Manager of the Boys' Home, William Welford, and his wife, Mary Jane (Beck), the matron, who held these posts for parts of 1912 and 1913. Welford, born in Tuam, County Galway, had been a Church of Ireland School Headmaster and church organist in Kill, and later schoolmaster and organist at St. John's Cathedral, Cashel, Tipperary.[11] In the 1911 Irish census the family was recorded as living in Drumrush, County Fermanagh, where he was also a teacher.[12] William, Mary, and May arrived in Montreal aboard the *Scandinavian* from Glasgow on September 1, 1912.[13] They may have answered an ad for a "Married Couple to take charge of the Ottawa Boys' Home. Husband as Manager, Wife as Matron. Salary with Board and Lodging."[14] They both had relatives in Canada—in particular William Welford's sister was the wife of Joshua Tobin, who at this time was president of W. J. Tobin Ltd., an Ottawa business that sold tents, awnings, and other canvas goods.[15] But by mid-1913 the couple and their daughter had moved to 257 Lyon Street, and later in 1913 a new manager and matron were in place at the Ottawa Boys' Home—a couple described in a newspaper article as "the right sort of people" for the place.[16]

On January 1, 1914, a son, William Henry, was born to Henry Mayo and May Welford.[17] On January 14, they were married at the home of Mr. Welford at 257 Lyon Street, with an Anglican priest from Christ Church Cathedral presiding, witnessed by Mr. and Mrs. Welford. The marriage certificate gives Mayo's age as 21; in fact, he was not yet 18.[18] The couple and their child lived with the Welfords for a time, but very soon tragedy struck. On March 18, 1914, William Welford, now a "labourer," died of septicemia, at age 54.[19] The Mayos had to leave the Lyon Street house, and the 1914 city directory shows Henry and his family living at 223 Kent Street. His attestation papers in July 1915 give his wife's address as 41 Ivy Avenue in New Edinburgh, but in his service file this is changed to a new apartment building at 135 King Edward Avenue, just across the Rideau River.

Though Henry and May were Anglicans, he must also have attended MacKay or belonged to one of its organizations such as the Young People's Association. His name is included in a list of men from the church who enlisted before June 1916, and his death was recorded in MacKay's Death Register in January 1917. His widowed mother-in-law, Mrs. Mary Jane Welford, was a Presbyterian and the city directory for 1915 shows her residing living at 37 Noel Street in a newly developing part of New Edinburgh.[20] In any case, she did not stay long in New Edinburgh, and she died of acute dysentery in 1919 at age 49.[21]

Henry Mayo enlisted at Ottawa on July 26, 1915, in the 77th Battalion. His service record shows that he was five feet five and a half inches tall, with medium complexion, blue eyes, and brown hair. He again concealed his true age, claiming to be 21 instead of barely 18. But he clearly had the bearing of one much older, because he was quickly promoted to corporal, then to sergeant. This meant that while he could live at home with his wife and young family, he could also dine in the sergeant's mess. Mayo was among the members of the 77th Battalion called out to help firemen and provide security and crowd control when the Parliament Buildings burnt down on February 3, 1916. Some soldiers helped evacuate people from the building, at great risk to themselves, and others rescued valuable portraits, including one of Queen Victoria, from the Senate Chamber. Family lore has it that he risked his life during the fire.[22] On March 31, 1916, a second son, Percy Welford Mayo, was born to the young couple.[23]

In June 1916, the 77th Battalion crossed to England and were put under canvas at the Canadian training camp at Bramshott on June 29. Mayo had barely arrived when he was admitted to the Connaught Military Hospital on July 4, 1916, for treatment of gonorrhea. By that time, the presence of VD among new recruits was no longer shocking to doctors, who had come to realize its prevalence in the overall Canadian population. In spite of all attempts to curb it, VD continued to be a scourge in the Canadian Corps—at some 66,000 cases it would be the largest single reason for hospitalization for disease, with influenza a distant second.[24] The good news was that, while antibiotics were still a thing of the future, recent medical advances meant that VD could be successfully—if sometimes painfully—treated and, by the end of the war, its incidence among soldiers would be lower than in the general population back home. What is puzzling about Henry Mayo's case was that treatment took only three days, which may suggest a misdiagnosis. Nor does there appear to have been any penalty or stigma attached to his record.

Indeed, when the 77th Battalion was broken up, Mayo was one of the first to be assigned, with 38 other men, to the 50th Battalion, an Alberta regiment being formed as part of the 10th Brigade in the new Fourth Canadian Division. Although he lost his sergeant's rank in the transfer, he was appointed lance corporal in "D" Company of the 50th. On August 11, the 50th disembarked at Le Havre in France and was sent to a "quiet" portion of the Ypres Sector for the usual acclimatization to life in the trenches. Then in September, as part of the Fourth Division, the 50th moved to the Somme, where it was engaged, with heavy losses, in the battle for Desire Trench. Mayo does not appear to have participated in this battle, because from November 1 to December 12 he was assigned to "Copse Dump," a reserve position (he may have been part of the 10 percent of each battalion that, by 1916, was being held back from major battles so that when the battalion had to be rebuilt, there would be a core of experienced soldiers to build around).

When he rejoined his battalion, it had already moved north to the Arras Sector to prepare for the Battle of Vimy Ridge. The Fourth Division took up positions on the northern end of the ridge, with the Germans holding the high ground to their front and left, observing their movements and inflicting steady casualties with machine gun and artillery fire. The 50th Battalion set about restoring their camps to living order, rebuilding roads and railways, and training for the battle to come. As usual, the men were rotated in and out of the front lines—six days in the forward trenches, six in reserve just behind them, and six in reserve further back. As it happened, the 50th went into the front lines on Christmas Day, 1916. Soldiers with the opportunity to celebrate in relative peace would have enjoyed bully beef, or a turkey if one could be got to them, and a plum pudding, plus whatever sweets and delicacies the men might have got in parcels from home and shared out. Those like Mayo's company in the forward trenches would have had to continue their normal rounds of vigilance and work parties, under fire, while breaking off as best they could for Christmas dinner, and perhaps, an opportunity to read mail from home (which the supply chain made a special effort to get to the front for Christmas).[25] For Henry Mayo this would have included news from his wife.

In July 1916, when Mayo's battalion was dispatched to England, May Mayo went back to Britain, with her two-year-old and three-month-old children, on the *Pretorian*, a CP liner, from Montreal to Glasgow. Third-class passage at $100 or so for a family would have been a major investment for a working-class woman. It may be that she got help from the Patriotic Fund, which in some provinces was helping wives of soldiers who had recently immigrated and did not have the means to live in Canada to return to the Old Country;[26] or perhaps her uncle Joshua Tobin helped out. Twenty dollars a month in assigned pay (later $25) and $20 in separation allowance went a lot further in Scotland than in Canada and she probably also hoped that he would be able to visit them when on leave. May and the children appear to have visited friends or relatives in County Fermanagh, Ireland (where the family had lived before coming to Canada). But their final destination was the home in Glasgow of Frank Mayo, who had shipped Henry off to Canada seven years before.[27] Frank's other two sons were already at the front. (Percy was serving with the 2nd Battalion of Cameronian Scottish Rifles, had won the Distinguished Conduct Medal, and would be killed on the Somme just two months before Henry's death. Frank Jr. would be wounded and after the war would live with his father for many years.)

By Christmas 1916, the storied Christmas Truce of 1914 was a distant memory. "In 1915," wrote Victor Wheeler of the 50th Battalion,

> orders had been issued that holiday rapprochement with *les Allemands* was strictly *verboten* because of the enemy's use of poison gas and his reported cruel treatment and bayoneting of prisoners of war, but there had been a brief pause in the year's bitter and costly fighting. On this Christmas Day 1916, there was a relentless exchange of lethal greetings. Peace reigned not amongst men.[28]

The war diary of the 50th Battalion records a constant stream of casualties due to shelling, raiding, and sniping. On Christmas Day it records "1 OR [Other Ranks] killed, 6 OR wounded." The following day the war diary recorded "4 OR wounded," which presumably included Henry Mayo. "While in charge of a party working in a trench North of Souchez on the morning of December 26th 1916," recorded the official Circumstances of Death Register, "he was hit in the head and rendered unconscious by an enemy rifle bullet. He received first aid and was taken to a dressing station and later evacuated to No. 12 Canadian Field Ambulance where he died."[29]

May and the children remained in Scotland until 1919. She continued to receive a separation allowance until a pension was granted in April 1917. It is not clear what May Mayo's circumstances were in Glasgow, or whether she had found work. By 1917 the Canadian government was putting pressure on the wives of Canadian soldiers in Britain to return to Canada, but the cost and the dangers of German submarines were an impediment for many. However, in 1919 the government offered assistance for them to return, and many chose to take this last opportunity to come back to Canada rather than face the uncertain prospects of life in postwar Britain. Together with some 50,000 wives and dependents of Canadian soldiers, May and her sons crossed the Atlantic in the first months of 1919.[30] Initially they stayed with her uncle Joshua Tobin, by now possibly her only living relative in Ottawa.[31] In 1921, she and her children moved into a new home at 27 Bertrand Street, one of a row of attached houses in a part of New Edinburgh that was just beginning to be developed.[32] She became a close friend of the occupant of a neighbouring house in the row, a young widow with two small children whose husband had died in the 1918 influenza epidemic. In 1920 and 1921 she received Henry's effects and awards, including a plaque and scroll (memorial) and a Certificate of Service, and on July 8, 1920, a cheque for $116 (being his $180 war gratuity, less $64 special pension bonus already paid to her).

With this money, the small pensions for her and the sons, and what she could earn, she raised her two boys. According to her family, she worked in the early 1920s as a charwoman in the Parliament Buildings, walking to work in the small hours of the morning and returning home in time to prepare the boys' breakfast and get them off to school. The boys grew up in New Edinburgh, attended Crichton Street School, and fished and swam in the Rideau River with the other boys in the neighbourhood. But during the Depression they had to work to augment the family income—for example, by picking wild mushrooms which they sold to the chef at the Chateau Laurier—and they left school as soon as they could to find employment. William ("Bill") Mayo served in the Second World War and took advantage of a veterans' program to get a degree from Carleton College. Percy ("Bud") Mayo served in the circulation department of the Ottawa *Citizen* and later worked at Morgan's department store. He was active in boys' work and was an avid hunter and fisherman. May Mayo later worked at the Civic Hospital; in the late 1930s she moved to Connecticut, then returned to Ottawa in the 1960s and died in 1975. She never remarried.[33]

Henry James Mayo is buried in the Villers Station Cemetery near Arras, about 2 kilometres northwest of the small village of Villers-au-Bois (which is about 11 kilometres northwest of Arras). Villers Station was used mostly for Canadian burials from late 1916 to the middle of 1917, with a few in 1918. It contains 1,009 Canadians, 179 British, 205 Australians, and 32 Germans (who are unidentified and buried in a row marked with a single headstone). Several rows of headstones mark the graves of men killed in the Battle of Vimy Ridge (April 9–11, 1917) or in subsequent battles later that summer. But the majority of the headstones attest to the steady stream of casualties, usually three or four a day, throughout the last months of 1916 and the first half of 1917. The 19 men buried in the same row as Mayo are mostly Canadians from various battalions who were killed between December 11 and 31, 1916.

The cemetery is laid out with the gravestones at an angle to the main axis and the Great Cross. There are large Canadian maple trees around the perimeter, and plants including a number of roses decorate the rows of stones. The cemetery is some 300 metres off the main road, separated by a low brick wall from the open fields. When we visited in October 2015, the ploughed fields were shrouded in fog and the maples were just beginning to change colour. Henry Mayo's grave lies under a maple tree toward the side of the cemetery. On his headstone, his age is given as 24. In fact he was just 20. The inscription, presumably provided by May Mayo, reads: "Until the day break."

In memory of his life, his four grandchildren and one of his six great-grandchildren paid tribute to him in March 2005 at the Peace Tower of the Parliament Buildings in Ottawa, when the Book of Remembrance was opened at the page showing his name. Then, on May 16, 2009, one hundred years after Henry James Mayo landed in Canada, a great-great grandson was named Henry in his memory.[34]

Figure 11.4. Villers Station Cemetery.
Source: Photograph by Carolyn Bowker.

Figure 11.5. Villers Station Cemetery.
Source: Photograph by Carolyn Bowker.

12

A CHURCH AT WAR
1917

At the Annual General Meeting of MacKay Presbyterian Church in January 1917, the minister read out the report of the Session, which outlined the many activities of the church during the previous year, as well as its membership and financial position. The first two sentences of the summary of this report in the minutes of the AGM reveal how central the war had now become to the life of MacKay church: "It noted the fact that over 112 men had responded to the call of King and Country. The past year being the most eventful in the history of the world." In fact, 119 men whose names would appear on the church Honour Roll had enlisted in Canadian or Imperial forces, including some whose families would later join MacKay church.

The year began with news of the deaths of Henry Mayo and of Daniel Robertson, Sr and Jr. Spring brought great victories for the Canadian Corps—the capture of Vimy Ridge on Easter weekend, the advance through Fresnoy in May, and the capture of Hill 70 in August. Many MacKay men were engaged in these battles, in the infantry, artillery, machine gun batteries, service corps, and medical services. Their families and friends could be justifiably proud, even if these victories were only a small part of a much less successful British offensive in the Arras Sector.

But they had also come to know that even victories came at a terrible cost. At its April meeting the Ladies' Aid agreed "that a letter of sympathy be sent Mrs. Stalker on the death of her son who was killed in action in France [at Vimy Ridge]." Jack Ryan died on May 2 after a month of carnage in the air services that the British pilots would call Bloody April—he was the second Ryan brother to die. Reginald Brunel perished on May 3 in an artillery duel in the aftermath of Vimy Ridge. And then the Death Register recorded the death that same day of Leslie Watters Tubman, M.C. "decorated April 1917 'for conspicuous gallantry and devotion to duty.'" Four men in less than a month, and three in two days! And the names of the wounded rolled in: Ray Tubman and George Cruikshank, seriously wounded in April at Vimy; Andrew Jardine, shot in the foot in May at Fresnoy; Albert Kendall, injured in a motorcycle accident in July; and in August, George Powers, shot through the arm at Hill 70, and Gordon Clark, wounded in the chest at Lens. All these men were seriously injured and required lengthy convalescence in England. None of them would return to the front.

Nor, as the Death Register makes clear, was tragedy confined to the battlefield. At home there were the usual and expected deaths, including long-time Elders in the church and members of pioneer families in the community. But there were also deaths of children and young people, and two babies who died within days of birth. Especially sad was the death in December 1917 of Elizabeth Edwardson Lamb at age 26 from pneumonia following the birth of her fourth child, who also died within three days of its birth. The daughter of a Scottish Hudson's Bay Company factor and an Indigenous Canadian mother, Elizabeth had come from Oskélanéo in the remote interior of Quebec to work as a domestic in the home of Peter and Clara Anderson. In 1912 she had married a Scottish immigrant, James Lamb, who lived with his brother and sister-in-law on Noel Street and worked for the Ottawa Gas Company. All the Lamb family attended MacKay church, and the "very pretty house wedding," in the words of the Ottawa *Journal*, had been conducted by Rev. Anderson at the home of James Lamb's brother on MacKay Street.[1] Also living with the Lamb family was Elizabeth's brother Angus Edwardson, who had come from the North to learn the gas trade; he had enlisted in the infantry and was training in England when Elizabeth died. After a funeral service conducted by Rev. Peter Anderson, mother and baby were buried together in Beechwood Cemetery.[2] It is often asked how the people of the time could have accepted the appalling losses of the war. One answer, besides their religious faith, is that premature death and tragic loss were no less frequent visitors at home.

By 1917 the trickle of wounded men returning to New Edinburgh had become a steady stream. Joseph Munro had been wounded in 1916 at St. Eloi but had gone back into the line, only to suffer shrapnel wounds in both legs in June from a mortar bomb. He underwent operations in hospitals in England and France to remove pieces of metal, and endured weeks of convalescence while the wounds drained, before being sent back to Canada. Discharged with a 25 percent disability pension in May 1917, he resumed his job in the civil service while he continued his recovery. John Powers had suffered several wounds to his leg at St. Eloi and had also had a series of operations to remove metal and to repair his Achilles tendon and the external peroneal nerve. He was evacuated to Canada in June 1917 and after several months at the Queen's Military Hospital, Kingston, he came home to the Fleming Hospital as he sought to regain the use of his legs. Ray Tubman, who had lost parts of fingers on his right hand in the Battle of Vimy Ridge (and had lost his brother a month later), sailed for Canada in September 1917 and resumed his old job as a clerk in the Department of Militia and Defence, as well as his athletic career.

Others had suffered wounds of a different sort. Russell White was diagnosed as suffering from "Stress of Campaign" and was sent home in February to a convalescent home in Toronto. He was discharged with a disability pension and settled in New Edinburgh, boarding with Christina Munro, adoptive mother of Joseph Munro; though a Baptist, he began to attend MacKay. Robert Smith, who had enlisted at age 50 and endured months of hard service in the artillery until his health collapsed in May, returned in November, racked with pains in his legs and hips, which made ordinary exercise impossible, as well as hardened arteries and a somewhat enlarged heart. Oscar May underwent lengthy treatment in November for "pyrexia of unknown origin," a persistent fever whose cause was difficult to determine, which may have been a sign of battle fatigue; he was transferred to the 3rd Canadian Field Ambulance where he served out the remainder of the war. Dr. Neil MacLeod was still recovering from battle fatigue when he married in February 1917; the following month he was named president of the Standing Medical Board at the Base Recruiting Office with the rank of major.

Some men had become ill. Emil May was serving at the front when he suffered an inguinal hernia and later an edema on his leg. Others never got to the front: Frank Miles and Abraham Ferguson had heart problems; F. S. Wright was discharged from training camp with rheumatism; William Finter, after being rejected because of varicose veins, had had an operation to correct them and had been sent overseas, only to have them flare up again due to hard labour in a forestry battalion. These men had volunteered to serve their country but should not have been accepted. They were now back home with their families.

At the same time, the people of MacKay Presbyterian Church were facing shortages, rationing, and a skyrocketing cost of living. Young women were finding work as government clerks, but war wives were finding the going increasingly hard, since there had been no increase either in separation allowances or soldiers' pay, and there were no allowances for children. America's entry into the war precipitated a shortage of anthracite coal from Pennsylvania—no minor inconvenience in an Ottawa winter, as the number of infant and adult deaths during the cold winter months attested. The church managers frantically searched for, and finally found, a supply of coal to heat the building. Even more disturbing was the news that Rev. Peter Anderson had received a call to return to his old congregation at Shelburne. The Session informed the minister in no uncertain terms he was still needed at MacKay and sweetened the deal with a raise and a garage for his new car.

The war undoubtedly strained traditional conventions and beliefs, at home as well as among the soldiers at the front. But there is no evidence that MacKay church had anything to rival the doings of, for example, the "Naughty Nine" young ladies whose behaviour scandalized the more staid elements of Ottawa society, as described by Madge MacBeth and Sandra Gwyn.[3] Nor is there evidence that the relatively small number of returned men altered in any substantial way the values or perspectives of the church. Rather, they seemed determined, with the help of their families, to pick up, as best they could, the threads of their lives. For some, like John Powers and Russell White, the church was an essential part of this healing experience. Indeed, the church redoubled its commitment to combatting the sin that it believed had afflicted Canadian society before the war and threatened its effective action during it. As the temperance movement evolved into a crusade for total prohibition, MacKay church supported Ontario's decision to go "dry" and the federal government's banning of the manufacture, import, and sale of all alcoholic beverages. The Session also devoted considerable time to the management of a newly established Boy Scout troop, appointing the Scoutmaster and, it would appear, regarding this troop as an integral part of church activities. The role of a Boy Scout troop in the moral training and physical development of boys had become vitally important now that many of the young men who would have been their role models were instead fighting in Europe.

Figure 12.1. Prohibition parade, 1916. MacKay Presbyterian Church and its minister had always supported temperance, including restrictions on saloons and public drinking. By 1916 prohibition of the manufacture and sale of alcohol had become a wartime crusade. Over the next few years Prohibition laws would be enacted by the federal and provincial governments but would be gradually repealed in most jurisdictions in the early 1920s.
Source: John Boyd. Library and Archives Canada PA072527.

MacKay Presbyterian Church remained steadfast in its support for the war and the soldiers. On the seventh anniversary of the opening of its new Sanctuary, Major the Reverend B. W. Thompson "preached an evening sermon on The Call of the Hour to the Church."[4] In June, the Session resolved "that we procure two flags 'Union Jacks' and have them put up in the end of the church behind the pulpit." The Ladies' Aid continued its Red Cross work, conducted a supper and a lecture on the work of the Hospitals Commission, and raised money with bazaars, garden parties, and dinners. "Everyone was unanimous that our boys should be remembered whatever else was allowed to go," read the minutes of one of its meetings. In September the Ladies' Aid held a "sock and money shower" for the soldiers at which "Rev. Captain Horsey gave a very entertaining account of life in the trenches." (One must assume that this account left out a good deal of his wartime experience. Horsey, minister of First Congregational Church and a veteran of the 1885 North West campaign, was chaplain to the 38th Battalion during its training but was declared surplus to requirements when the battalion went overseas. He reverted to a combat officer's role so that he could go to the front with his men, and was present at the attack on Desire Trench, where he saw many horrors.) At Christmas the Ladies' Aid sent 84 parcels to soldiers and formed a committee to consult with the Red Cross on getting a parcel to Alfred Philp, who was a prisoner in Germany.[5]

The Presbyterian Church, like all churches, was wrestling with the issues of the meaning of the war, of faith and, increasingly, of grief and loss, as most poignantly expressed in a 1916 editorial in the *Presbyterian Record*:

> How little those can realize who have not paid that price! The price of victory? What is it? Go ask the wife whose husband's homecoming when his work was done made bright the day with hope and the evening with that hope fulfilled; but whose days and evenings alike are shadowed now, for that strong step will be heard no more. Ask the children who wonder why daddy does not come, and who are beginning to realize with a nameless dread that he will not come again. Ask the father and mother whose son, perhaps an only one, in whom centred the love and hopes of the home, lies "somewhere" in an unkown grave. All these know something of the price. They may be told of the heroism that like a halo surrounds that grave, of the glory of a life given for freedom's sacred cause, of the results beyond measure to the world; but the sore heart feels as yet only the price paid, the loneliness and pain. Time, the great healer, will gradually make it less hard to bear; but in the meantime it is to those who are paying, at such cost, the great price, that the sympathy of a nation should go out, and for them a nation's prayers ascend.[6]

In press editorials and at its General Assembly, Presbyterian leaders stressed the need to keep faith, to persevere in the cause of righteousness, and to endure pain and privation. They rejected categorically all peace overtures, including those by Woodrow Wilson and the Pope, not only because premature peace would negate their sacrifice and lead to more war, but because to abandon a just war before victory had been achieved would be a sin against God. Indeed, by 1917 the just war had become a holy crusade, an elemental struggle of good against evil.[7]

In the summer of 1917, the General Assembly established a Commission on the War, led by Dr. Thomas Kilpatrick, a leading Presbyterian theologian whose son was a senior military chaplain in France. Its report asserted that the war, "with its manifold losses, and indescribable sorrows [was] the consequence, the exposure and the judgement of human sin." The Germans had "take[n] up arms against the Kingdom of God," "organize[d] civilization in the service of the Kingdom of Evil" and thus had committed a "sin against mankind, which God has given mankind the right to arrest and judge." God would "not allow Satan, or the Kaiser, to overthrow His Kingdom." The Germans would lose, and they would pay a heavy price, but defeat would redeem them. There was also, however, a sin that was more general in the modern world, one which affected Canada deeply, namely the prevalance of secularism, materialism, and selfishness. The report scolded the Canadian clergy for their conservatism, uninspiring preaching, flaccid theology, and declared that the church's religious formalism, "natural religion," and smug complacency had contributed to this sin. The message of the war was that the church needed to reaffirm its commitment to evangelism, which "must centre in the Cross. Any other Gospel is no Gospel, a mere imagination of man, vapid, flaccid, useless." It must proclaim "the facts of Salvation, as these are set forth in the Word of God, and sincerely grounded in God's redeeming deeds." But this did not mean abandoning the church's mission of social reform; quite the contrary:

> Everything which stands between man and the fulness of his humanity, in body, mind, soul and spirit, is the enemy of God and is to be fought as such by every servant of God, till it be replaced by such conditions as shall further the realization of all that God meant man to be. Sin and disease, ignorance and poverty, stand out conspicuously as such enemies of God, and against them the Church must wage unending war. The battlefront is far extended and includes Parliament House, and Court [sic] of law, street and market, villa and slum. There can be no rest for the church so long as any part of the territory of human life remains in the hands of the enemy.[8]

This report was undoubtedly food for thought for MacKay Presbyterian Church and its minister. Its strong reiteration that the war was a just war to be fought to the finish, and its reaffirmation of the need for social and moral reform, reinforced their already deep convictions. They would have heartily agreed with its strong emphasis on the need for the church to remain true to its faith in Christ, individual salvation, and evangelism. But they might have found more troubling its apparent conflict with the belief, which was often expressed by military chaplains, that in putting their lives on the line the soldiers were emulating the example of Christ, whether or not they adhered to strict religious doctrines or standards of behaviour.[9] In their eulogies of their fallen men, and in memorials that would be established later, the people of MacKay church expressed the conviction that by their sacrifice the men had redeemed themselves and their society.

Enlistment in 1917

Only 13 men from MacKay enlisted in 1917, mostly in specialist services including the developing Signals branch. Some of these men had been too young to enlist earlier; others had previously been turned down. Most of them would not see front-line duty. But by 1917 recruitment standards for front-line service had been considerably relaxed—infantrymen could now be five feet tall, and support services could take men even shorter and older, or with dentures, glasses, or mild health issues—and it was recognized that even those who were less than able-bodied could still contribute, in Canada, England or behind the lines.[10]

The continuing desire of some men to enlist, and the willingness of the CEF to recruit men with less than stellar health, was shown by the ongoing story of **Robert Finter**, who signed up for the third time in January 1917, in the 3rd Division Ammunition Column (he is the only MacKay soldier with four different service numbers). Finter had joined the artillery at Valcartier in 1914, in spite of a weak heart caused by an attack of rheumatic fever in 1911. He had gone to England with the First Contingent, only to land in hospital with an enlarged heart, systolic murmur, and a faint, rapid pulse, "emaciated, anemic, unable to walk very far." He had been sent back to Canada for medical discharge. He had then enlisted in July 1915 in the 77th Battalion, only to have an appendectomy at training camp reveal the extent of his other medical problems, and he had been again discharged as medically unfit, but he had remained in the active militia. His service after his third enlistment lasted until May 16, 1917, when he suffered an attack of epilepsy at Kingston and a renewal of his valvular heart condition.

Three men enlisted in the infantry:

- **Jason Davidson**, 24, a street railway conductor whose father was an Ottawa policeman, was a late addition to the 207th Battalion in January. In England, he suffered an injury which required several operations including the removal of a tumour, and he spent the year in a series of hospitals.

- **Percival Lister**, 26, who owned a butcher shop in New Edinburgh, enlisted in July in the 5th Princess Louise Dragoons reinforcing draft. A medical exam revealed a systolic heart murmur, and he was not sent overseas.
- **Angus Edwardson**, 21, the only First Nations soldier from MacKay (and the brother of Elizabeth Lamb), enlisted in February in the 253rd Battalion at Haileybury, Ontario, a battalion that was broken up in England. Edwardson was the only MacKay man who enlisted in the infantry in 1917 and actually got to the front.

Two men joined the artillery:

- **George Bruce English**, 21, a civil servant whose father was also a civil servant as well as a mining entrepreneur, enlisted in May. His journey to England was interrupted by the Halifax Explosion of December 6, 1917, as soldiers were required to keep order and help with relief and clean-up. There, he contracted severe bronchitis, which turned into pneumonia, and he was sent back to hospitals in Kingston and Ottawa.
- **Levi Boston**, 24, who had been appointed as Scoutmaster in the troop connected with MacKay, enlisted in December in the 74th Battery CFA. He had previously tried to enlist in 1914 but had been turned down because of heart issues. He would reach the front in the last months of the war.

Four men enlisted in medical and service corps:

- **Dr. Malcolm David Graham**, 26, enlisted in October as a captain in the Canadian Army Medical Corps. A 1914 Queen's medicine graduate and a Rhodes Scholar, he had opened a practice on Crichton Street and in May 1917 he had joined the Petawawa Military Hospital as a staff physician. He served on the medical staff of Military District 3 in Kingston and would receive the Canadian Efficiency Decoration. In 1918 he would marry Olive Marie Brunel, a nurse who was the sister of Reginald Brunel (see Chapter 15).
- **George Silsby**, 29, and **William Silsby**, 27, carpenters who had come from England in 1911 and 1912 respectively, enlisted in July in the No. 2 Overseas Army Service Corps Training Depot and would serve in England with the Canadian Army Service Corps.
- **Clifford Earl**, 27, a steamfitter working as foreman of maintenance with the Ottawa School Board, enlisted in August in the CASC. His file was marked "Service in Canada Only," and he served in Toronto with No. 2 Special Service Co., Canadian Engineers.

Four men, all of whom had health issues, joined the expanding signals corps:

- **Charles William Powers**, 25, enlisted as a Signals instructor in Ottawa. Undersized and nearly blind in one eye, he had twice attempted unsuccessfully to enlist.
- **Gerald McLatchie**, 26, a clerk in the Bureau of Statistics, **Percy Thomas Mansell**, 24, and **John Regan**, 31, a civil servant in the correspondence branch of the Secretary of State, enlisted and were sent to England in late fall.

Autumn: Hope Turns to Deeper Despair

Whatever hope had been aroused by the victories of the Canadian Corps in the spring and summer of 1917 was snuffed out by war news from elsewhere. In April, the French army, strained beyond endurance by the endless slaughter at Verdun, mutinied, or more accurately, went on strike. Although discipline was restored by July, the French army remained fragile. In October, the Italian army collapsed under an attack by the Germans and Austrians at Caporetto, and though it stabilized its defensive line by the end of the year, it would not be an effective fighting force for many months. The Bolshevik Revolution in early November ended any hope that a democratic Russia would remain in the war. The new Soviet government withdrew from the conflict and, in March 1918, preoccupied by civil war, it would sign a humiliating peace treaty. Germany was now free to transfer hundreds of thousands of troops to the Western Front. Germany's unrestricted submarine warfare was sinking thousands of tons of Allied shipping and was threatening to starve Britain of food and supplies. Although this had led to the entry of the United States into the war, it would be many months before enough American troops could be raised, trained, and transported to make a difference on the Western Front. Throughout the summer and fall, the British Army was bogged down in costly campaigns at Passchendaele and Cambrai. The only good news was in the Middle East where British troops captured Jerusalem on December 11, 1917 so that, symbolically for Christians, they would mark Christmas in the city.

For the Canadian Corps, the fall of 1917 would bring its grimmest battle, for which the name—Passchendaele—would ever afterward encompass all the horror and futility of the war. This strategic ridge in the Ypres Sector had for many months resisted all attempts by the British, Australians, and French to take it, at a cost of hundreds of thousands of casualties. Now the Canadians were sent in. It was late fall, and months of shelling and heavy rain had churned the battlefield into a porridge of mud through which men could hardly move. The unburied bodies on the battlefield could be smelled miles away. German defenders were dug into a checkerboard of pillboxes and bunkers. The Canadians began the attack on October 26 and took Passchendaele three weeks later, at a cost of 17,000 casualties. All the MacKay men who were at the front were engaged in this battle and some, like Homère Joliat, won medals for their courage. But Fred Stalker was badly wounded, and the memory of this traumatic experience would haunt the survivors for the rest of their lives.

Figure 12.2. Stretcher-bearers bringing wounded through mud. This picture shows the appalling conditions in which this battle was fought.
Source: Library and Archives Canada PA-002229.

Recruitment had stalled. But men were still needed to replace the severe losses at the front. In August, the Canadian Parliament passed the Military Service Act, which required some 400,000 men of military age to register for service. Prime Minister Borden tried to entice Opposition Leader Sir Wilfrid Laurier into a coalition; when that failed he began putting together a Union government committed to conscription and to winning the war, composed of Conservatives, conscriptionist Liberals, and a few labour and farmers' representatives. The Wartime Elections Act disenfranchised Canadian citizens who had entered Canada from enemy countries after 1902. At the same time it gave the vote to mothers, wives, widows, and sisters of serving soldiers. Many of the women in MacKay Presbyterian Church would now be able to cast their first vote.

The issue of conscription dominated life in New Edinburgh in November and December 1917, even as long lists of casualties from Passchendaele poured in. We have no evidence about what the minister or congregation of MacKay thought about conscription. It is likely that most, especially those with sons and husbands abroad, would have agreed with a General Assembly resolution approving "every legitimate effort to rouse the laggards among the youth of Canada to a consciousness of duty and to enroll those who are available as soldiers in a great crusade for the world's freedom"[11]—though perhaps with less animus toward French Canadians than some Presbyterian journals were expressing, and with little desire to see their own younger sons called up.[12] In the early fall of 1917, single men of military age were ordered to report for medical examinations and potentially for service, but provision was also made for them to appeal for exemption to a series of tribunals which were set up across the country. It quickly became clear that all but a small minority of the men being called up would apply for exemption and that the tribunals would be very busy.[13]

In November 1917, Tribunal No. 238, which served the Rideau Ward, held hearings at the New Edinburgh fire station. Only two identifiable men from MacKay made appeals for exemption. George Esdale, 29, son of a prominent member of the church, whose brother-in-law Sidney Mansell was serving with the Borden Motor Machine Gun Battery, appealed on the grounds of ill health, as did Arthur Stalker, who had three brothers overseas (see Chapter 13). Both appeals were granted.[14] Though most people of German extraction supported the war, a few, like Charles Wendt's cousin Archie Wendt, applied for exemption on the grounds of holding an essential job (the Tribunal ruled that his application was premature because his category had not yet been called).[15] Herbert Boehmer, on the other hand, claimed that he should not have to fight Germans. He then refused to report to a medical board and was ultimately ordered to report for duty—but in the end he never served. Some other German claimants were treated more harshly by the board. One was forced to apologize for a letter in which he claimed he had been discriminated against because of his German accent and did not "believe in fighting for crooks and grafters"; two were told that "if the country was good enough to live in it was good enough to fight for."[16] But Tribunal No. 238 was able to wrap up its work early, because it had many fewer cases to hear than others around the city.

In November and December, a tense and bitter federal election was fought on the issue of conscription. On December 17, Prime Minister Robert Borden's Union government racked up an overwhelming majority. A French-speaking Catholic, Dr. John Leo Chabot, a lieutenant colonel in the 5th Louise Dragoon Guards and commander of the Ottawa Military Base Hospital, was elected as a Unionist MP for the riding of Ottawa Centre. Chabot was married to the elder sister of Reginald Isambard Brunel, who had been killed earlier in the year (see Chapter 15). But although New Edinburgh and Rockcliffe had probably voted overwhelmingly for the Union government, they were part of the heavily francophone riding of Russell, which elected an Irish-Canadian Liberal, Charles Murphy.

In the end, there does not appear to have been any lingering animosity against the German or French Canadian communities in New Edinburgh, many of whose members had in fact supported the war or enlisted. After the war, Herbert Boehmer played on a number of sports teams in New Edinburgh with the Tubman brothers and Doug Stalker. Whichever way they had voted, the people of MacKay Presbyterian were left to contemplate another dark winter of war, and of looming shortages and hardship. What horrors would the new year of 1918 bring, when the weather warmed and the armies moved again?

13 THE STALKER FAMILY AND THE MANY FACES OF COURAGE

Courage has many faces and takes many forms. There is the courage that led Robert Stalker, a 37-year-old businessman with four small children to go off to war and die at Vimy Ridge; his elder brother, Fred Stalker, to be badly wounded at Passchendaele; and their youngest brother Doug, to win distinction in the battles of the Hundred Days. There is the courage that allowed their mother, Clarinda Stalker, to continue steadfast in her faith and devotion to duty after the untimely deaths of her husband and her four daughters, as well as the loss of her son. And there is the courage and resourcefulness of Robert Stalker's mother-in-law, who fought to raise his orphaned children in the aftermath of tragedy.

The father of the family, George Frederick Stalker, was a rising young architect in London, England, when he married Clarinda Bell, a draper's daughter, about 1875. Both had Scottish roots. In 1883 the Stalkers, with four young children, immigrated to Canada, where they would have five more children.[1] George Stalker designed some important Ottawa buildings and, as a founder of the Ottawa Architectural Institute and Headmaster of Drawing at the Ottawa School of Art, he influenced a generation of architects in the national capital.[2] But in 1895, at age 50, he suffered a stroke, collapsed on the steps of the Rideau Club, and died in a cab on the way home.[3] His 45-year-old widow, Clarinda, was left with nine children ranging in age from 18 years to a newborn: George Frederick Jr. ("Fred," 1877), Robert (1879), Moray (1880), Violet (1882), Clara ("Daisy," 1884), Jean Belle ("Queenie," 1888), Arthur (1889), Andrew Douglas ("Doug," 1892), and Ivy Emeline (1895).

After her husband's death, Clarinda and her children moved to 37 Charles Street in New Edinburgh, a large brick attached house where she would live for the rest of her life. In her early widowhood she had to collect debts owed her dead husband, and although she appears to have had enough to live on, the family circumstances must have been challenging. In 1897 her oldest son, Fred, left to seek work in British Columbia, and her second son, Robert, followed in early 1899.[4] But tragedy continued to haunt her family. One by one her daughters died: Violet of tuberculosis at age 15 in 1897;[5] Ivy of pneumonia at age 4 in 1899;[6] Daisy of tuberculosis at age 19 in 1904; and Queenie of tuberculosis at age 19 in 1908. We can only imagine the depth of her sorrow as loss piled upon loss:

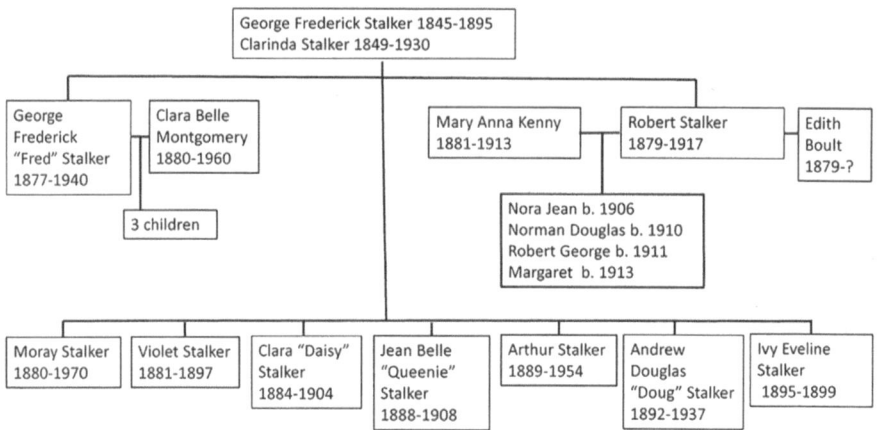

Figure 13.1. Stalker family tree.
Source: Created by the author.

a happy, healthy little girl dead within four hours of falling ill; a teenager now lost to history; two bright, popular young women, of whom we now catch only fleeting glimpses—Queenie, active in her church; Daisy, with "a bright and cheerful disposition," who had been "ailing from consumption for several months, all hope of her ultimate recovery being given up some time ago."[7]

Out in British Columbia, the two oldest boys quickly put down roots. Fred, an accountant for a lumber business, married Clara Belle Montgomery, had three children, and settled in the Kootenay region.[8] Robert, a general store clerk in Golden, married Mary Anna Kenny, a Catholic, in 1904. In 1909 he moved his family to Prince Rupert, which appeared poised to become a major seaport as the western terminus of the Grand Trunk Pacific Railway. With a partner he started a store, Stalker and Wells, and did well enough that he could build his own house and buy a $5,000 life insurance policy. But in 1913, Anna Stalker died of a perforated ulcer, leaving Robert a widower with four young children.[9] His mother-in-law, Martha Kenny, who had raised eight children of her own, took them to her home in Golden. But in 1914 Robert brought Martha, her youngest daughter, and his four children to live with him in Prince Rupert.[10]

Meanwhile back in New Edinburgh, Clarinda's remaining children attended Creighton Street Public School and became young adults active in the life of the community. The family had some ties with MacKay Presbyterian Church—Robert was treasurer of its Young People's Association before his departure for British Columbia, and Doug attended its Sunday School as a small boy.[11] But they were most deeply involved in St. David's Reformed Episcopal

Figure 13.2. Robert Stalker in the early 1900s.
Source: Private collection.

Figure 13.3. Robert Stalker c. 1914.
Source: Private collection.

Church, where Clarinda was on the Executive Committee of the Women's Guild, Moray was active in the young peoples' groups, Daisy was on the visiting committee for the hospital, and Queenie was president of St. Hilda's guild, a young women's association.[12] Then in 1909, along with several other families from St. David's, Clarinda, Arthur, and Moray formally transferred to MacKay, and Doug joined by Profession of Faith the following year. Clarinda at once became active in the MacKay Ladies' Aid and by 1917 she was on the executive committee. In 1918 she was named MacKay's visitor to the Protestant Hospital, an important position for a woman in the church community.

When it came time for the younger boys to find work, Moray became a clerk with the city and was so successful that in 1910 he was promoted to a second-class clerkship, and in 1912 his salary was raised to $1,500 as a first-class clerk. Arthur became a carpenter. Doug began work in 1911 as a rodman and draughtsman in the sewers branch of the city engineering department, did survey and other field work, and completed his high school matriculation by private tuition. In 1913 he entered Queen's University as an undergraduate in applied science.[13] Arthur and Doug were noted athletes in rowing, swimming, and football. Both were members of the New Edinburgh football team that won the city championship in 1911, and they were on championship rowing teams with the Ottawa New Edinburgh Canoe Club.

The two oldest brothers in British Columbia had both been active in militia regiments. Fred had served for two years with the 43rd Ottawa and Carlton Rifles, and in British Columbia he had been a captain with the 107th (East Kootenay) Regiment. Robert had served for three years in the Duke of Connaught's Own Rifles, an elite Vancouver regiment, and on his arrival in Prince Rupert he had joined the 68th regiment, Earl Grey's Own Rifles.[14]

In 1916 Robert's regiment was converted into the 102nd Battalion of Northern British Columbia (nicknamed the "Buck Twos") for overseas service with the CEF. Stalker and the other men from Prince Rupert arrived at the 102nd Battalion's training camp at Comox in late April, and on May 1, 1916, he was formally attested as a lieutenant.[15] Not for the first time, our eyebrows go up. Robert was 37, a widower with four small children and a successful business.[16] But he had a tradition of military service and a strong sense of duty, and he was a fit man at five feet eight inches tall. Nor was he the only member of the 102nd who joined at an advanced age; the battalion attracted rough and ready lumbermen from the northern interior of British Columbia, and people like Frank Gott, a member of the T'it'q'et Nation, who dyed his hair to hide his 65 years and served as a sniper. Robert's children would be cared for by his mother-in-law and her daughter, who would receive $40 a month deducted from his pay and a $30 a month separation allowance. Mrs. Kenny was listed in his service file as the guardian of the children, but this was never legally formalized—with serious consequences, as we shall see.

On June 10, 1916, the 102nd Battalion boarded trains in Vancouver. As they travelled east, the men were feted at every stop and were reviewed in Ottawa by the Duke of Connaught and the Minister of Militia, Sir Sam Hughes. On June 18, they boarded the CPR's *Empress of Britain* at Halifax for England, where they encamped at Bramshott. "[W]hen the authorities found out that we were the tallest, the heaviest, and the most maturely aged of any unit that had reached England," boasted its early historian, the 102nd Battalion was incorporated directly into the 11th Brigade of the newly formed Fourth Canadian Division. There followed six weeks of rigorous training, with only two weekends' leave, one of which was cut short so that Sam Hughes could inspect the division. ("We surely did love our Minister of Militia when this news came through.") On a sweltering hot August 11, the 102nd Battalion departed for France and the long train trip to Belgium.[17]

But Robert Stalker was not with them, for on August 14, 1916, he was married again—this time to Edith Boult, a 36-year-old Englishwoman, at Marylebone in London.[18] There is a mystery surrounding this marriage. Edith is mentioned only once in Stalker's service record, as a person to be notified in case of casualty; even after the marriage the names that more frequently appear are (at home) his mother or his brother Moray, (in London) a Mrs. Gordon Melville in Hurlingham whose relation to him is not known, or (in Prince Rupert) Mrs. Kenny, to whom money was being sent.

Edith had, one might say, an interesting background. Her father, Peter Rawlinson (Rollo) Boult, had spent much of the 1880s and 1890s in prison, and Edith and her brother were raised by her mother and grandmother.[19] Rollo Boult appears to have been sentenced once again to prison for forgery in 1897, and when released in 1898 he declared his intention to travel to the United States to join his son in New York; but he was apparently again sentenced in 1902 to a year in prison in Nottingham. That same year Edith travelled to the United States, where in 1904 she married one Ernest Bordat, a French national, in Fall River, Massachusetts.[20] By 1911 she was back in England, living in Islington with her father.[21] Then in 1914, for reasons unknown, she and Rollo travelled to Prince Rupert, where they lived for two years. It is possible that she met Stalker there and travelled to Britain about the same time as the 102nd Battalion shipped overseas—but all this is conjecture.[22]

After a few days' special leave to be married, Stalker joined his company in the St. Eloi Sector of the Ypres Salient, where, as usual, it was paired with a more experienced unit to gain experience of trench warfare. "Wastage" during this "quiet" time included a company major and several sergeants and NCOs, as well as six men killed in an artillery barrage,[23] and on September 7, Stalker joined the list of casualties with a bullet wound to his left arm. The bullet passed through the upper third of the left forearm, without breaking bones or leaving any foreign matter. He was sent to field hospitals and then to a general hospital in Boulogne, and finally to England where he was admitted on September 9 to "Mrs. Pollock's Hospital," London, for convalescence. Although the wound was not serious, it proved slow to heal, and Stalker went through two monthly medical boards before he was cleared to return to duty on November 16. All this time Edith was living in Liverpool. Whether she travelled to London to be with him is not clear; he does not appear to have gone there. Stalker finally rejoined his unit, which had now moved to Vimy in the Arras Sector, on December 30, 1916.

At Vimy the 102nd settled into a cold and snowy winter. In February, Stalker was dispatched for a week's training as a platoon commander, and in March he was sent for training in preparation for the coming attack on Vimy Ridge. "By the time that the Battalion was ordered into the trenches," says its historian, "not only the commissioned and non-commissioned officers, but every individual man, knew what he had to do and when he had to do it."[24] The Fourth Canadian Division occupied the northern sector of the battlefield and was given the unenviable task of attacking Hill 145 (where the Vimy Memorial now stands), the highest point of the battlefield and the most heavily defended. The 102nd and another battalion of the 11th Brigade were to advance to a position in front of Hill 145, then dig in and hold while two other battalions passed through them to capture the objective. The men would be subject to heavy fire not only from the front, but a hill to the left of their position called "The Pimple."

On April 9, 1917, the 102nd began its attack in a blinding snowstorm. Its war diary reflects the confusion in its headquarters as it lost touch with the battle and relied on reports from runners. Initially these reports were good, but within a couple of hours it was clear that "things were not going well." The brigade on their left, coping with muddy terrain and deep shell holes into which men fell and drowned, and facing withering fire from the front and enfilade fire from The Pimple, had bogged down, leaving the 11th Brigade's flank unsupported. Furthermore, the 11th Brigade had fallen behind its artillery barrage and the 102nd Battalion was exposed to murderous machine gun and artillery fire. Members of the German regiment defending Hill 145 later recalled Canadian corpses forming "small hills of khaki" in front of the slopes. When the Canadians finally reached their objective, most of the officers of the 102nd had been killed or wounded; for an intense hour, while it desperately held onto its position against repeated counterattacks, command devolved for a time to a seriously wounded company sergeant major.

Stalker was killed early in the battle, and all the other officers in his company were killed or missing. According to the battalion war diary, his death was confirmed by a runner at 8:10 a.m.[25]

Other battalions completed the task of capturing Hill 145, the Pimple, and the rest of Vimy Ridge, but the 102nd was no longer an effective fighting unit.

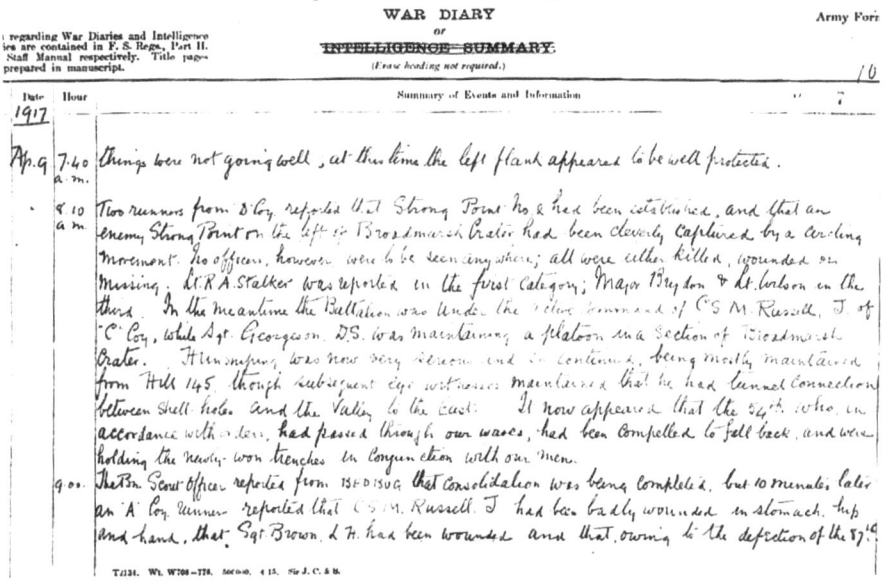

Figure 13.4. Page from the war diary of the 102nd Battalion, which records the death of Robert Stalker. Source: LAC, War Diaries of the 102nd Canadian Infantry Battalion, 1916/08/12–1917/09/30.

It took days to remove the wounded and recover the bodies. Robert Stalker's body was taken to the Villers au Bois Cemetery near Arras, about 10 kilometres from the battlefield, where Henry James Mayo (see Chapter 11) was also buried. After the war this cemetery was redesigned by Sir Reginald Blomfield as Villers Station Cemetery. Stalker's headstone is closer to the centre of the cemetery than Mayo's, among a few rows of other men who also fell at Vimy; in one of the pictures below it is in the foreground in front of the Great Cross.

Meanwhile, Robert's older brother, Fred, had also enlisted for overseas service. He had served with his militia regiment as a guard at an internment camp from July to September, and then during the first five months of 1916 he had attended the Royal School of Infantry in Victoria. Then on May 19, 1916, while Robert was settling into training with the 102nd Battalion in Comox, Fred Stalker resigned his commission and enlisted with the 196th Western Universities Overseas Battalion. He was five feet ten and a half inches tall, with ruddy complexion, blue eyes, and iron-grey hair. The battalion arrived in England aboard the SS *Southland* on November 11, 1916, and was encamped at Seaford a week later. At this time Robert was in convalescent hospitals recovering from his wound suffered at St. Eloi.

Once again we have some cause for surprise—here is a man pushing 40 with a wife, Clara, children aged 6, 4, and 2, no business or substantial property, and now no income except the military pay of a private. Twenty dollars

Figure 13.5. Villers Station Cemetery.
Source: Photograph by Carolyn Bowker.

Figure 13.6. Villers Station Cemetery.
Source: Photograph by Carolyn Bowker.

a month from his pay and a $20 separation allowance, even if supplemented with support from the Patriotic Fund, would not have been enough for Clara and the children to remain in British Columbia. They moved first to Winnipeg where her family lived, and then, about December 1916, they moved to live with Fred's mother Clarinda Stalker at 37 Charles Street in New Edinburgh. They would reside there until Fred's return in 1919.

The 196th Battalion was broken up in England, and after service in a reserve battalion as a lance corporal, Fred went to the front with the 46th Battalion (South Saskatchewan) in the Fourth Division on April 25, 1917, a little over two weeks after his brother's death. He had reverted to private to go to the front, but he was promoted to corporal and then lance sergeant in August. He may have seen some action in the summer, but his big test was to be at Passchendaele.

The 46th Battalion had one of the toughest assignments on the first day of the assault on Passchendaele. On October 26, 1917, it attacked Decline Copse, a section of ground protected by trees and at least 10 pillboxes, along a narrow front with mud and water on each side. Before long the men, slowed down by the mud, became easy targets for the enemy, and at times for its own artillery which fired short as its guns sank into the mud. Only incredible heroism by some of the survivors enabled the 46th Battalion to take its objective, and more heroism was required to hold the position while waiting for reinforcements before it could retire to a defensible line. At some point Fred Stalker sustained shrapnel wounds to his arm, shoulder, and back, the most serious of which shattered bones in his right hand.[26]

Fred was evacuated to a field hospital and then to the No. 3 General Hospital in Le Tréport, where the shrapnel was surgically removed. His hand swelled up and for about a week he ran a temperature, but there was no serious infection. He was then evacuated to England where on November 6 he was admitted to Bath War Hospital. He needed nearly a year of convalescence to regain the use of his right arm. In October 1918 he sailed for Canada, to recover further at the Fleming Hospital in Ottawa. There he also received dental treatment including new plates, which appear to have been sorely needed.

On April 16, 1916, their much younger brother, Andrew Douglas Stalker, had enlisted in Ottawa as a lieutenant in the 207th Battalion. The battalion was nicknamed "MacLean's athletes," and at 23 years old and five feet ten inches tall Doug was one of the best, leading its football team in games against Queen's. But the 207th Battalion never reached full strength and was broken up in England. As an officer, Doug had to wait in a reserve battalion until he was assigned in October 1917 as a lieutenant in the 38th Battalion, which had been raised in Ottawa, and despite having been rebuilt several times after heavy losses, still had a preponderance of Ottawa men.

Figure 13.7. Andrew Douglas Stalker.
Source: Gould 1919, 285.

The 38th Battalion reached Passchendaele on October 28, two days after Fred Stalker was wounded. It was held in brigade reserve as the Canadians continued their attack on October 30, but it was nonetheless shelled heavily, and early in the afternoon three of its companies were sent up to reinforce the forward battalions. Doug's company was used for carrying parties and the war diary is full of praise for the transport section. On November 5, the 38th Battalion was pulled back for a month's rest, having suffered some 400 casualties.[27] In December 1917, the battalion returned to the Arras Sector and spent a relatively calm winter (with the usual work parties, raids, snipers, gassing, and shelling). With his engineering experience, Stalker was appointed works officer for the 12th Brigade, which involved dangerous forays into no man's land. Near Lens on June 9, 1918, Doug was slightly wounded by a gunshot to the face. He was treated at the 12th Field Ambulance and returned to duty. On July 22 he was given 14 days' leave in England and when he returned in early August, the 38th Battalion was moving into position for the Amiens offensive, which began the final Hundred Days of the war and would lead to victory.[28]

The first wave of the offensive on August 8, 1918, pushed the German line back eight miles in the biggest advance thus far in the war. After this initial success, it was the 12th Brigade's turn to take over the lead by attacking the village of Rosières. The 38th Battalion was initially in a supporting role, but when the two lead battalions bogged down, with their flank exposed under heavy fire, the 38th pressed forward to support them. It too became bogged down, and, in the words of its war diary, "orders were issued to the various Companies of the 38th to reorganize as quickly as possible and continue to push forward [...] Owing to severe officer casualties this proved difficult indeed." However, during the night they achieved their objective and were now exposed to heavy counterattack. "About 8.30 a.m. on [August 11] the enemy placed a very heavy concentration of artillery on our right Companies. 'A' [Stalker's] and 'B' Companies withstood this attack gallantly, but suffered many casualties, especially from the left flank where the enemy worked in behind them."[29] These companies held their positions until evening when they were withdrawn, after a day without food and water. The Canadians had won another great victory, advancing almost 12 miles, capturing hundreds of guns and taking over 22,000 prisoners.

Instead of resting and refitting, the Canadians were moved to the Arras Sector to exploit Allied success and keep the Germans on the run. The 38th Battalion saw some action on August 30 and September 1, but its biggest challenge came on September 2, in the battle to break the Drocourt-Quéant Line—in the words of historian Tim Cook, "the hardest single battle of the war for the Canadian Corps."[30] On the left flank of this attack, the 10th Brigade took the town of Dury against heavy resistance. The 12th Brigade then passed through them to take on the toughest portion of the German line, with little artillery support. The 38th Battalion was in the centre of this attack and "A" Company was one of two in the lead; when its senior commanders were wounded, Stalker took charge of the company until it took its objective. The other two companies then passed through them until they too encountered stiff resistance. Then "A" and "B" companies reorganized and pressed the attack until they were all forced to dig in. The 38th Battalion had captured 325 prisoners, four trench mortars, and 40 machine guns. During this battle, sergeant "Red" Nunney won the Victoria Cross and when he was wounded, Doug Stalker and another lieutenant carried him to battalion headquarters.[31] The battalion's casualties were relatively light for such a desperate battle, but they were sobering nonetheless: three officers and 57 other ranks killed, 7 officers and 176 other ranks wounded, and 57 missing, for a total of 300.[32]

Doug Stalker had fought through some intense days of battle and served with distinction in his last one. Although he did not know it, his war was over. On September 29 he proceeded on course to the 1st Army Infantry School and did not return until November 4, 1918, seven days before the Armistice.

Back in Prince Rupert, Robert Stalker's 54-year-old mother-in-law, Martha Kenny, was dealing with the fact that he had left no will, nor had she been legally named the guardian of his children. For a man heading into what

Figure 13.8. Doug Stalker.
Source: Private collection.

he knew would be a risky situation, Robert had been surprisingly cavalier in his personal arrangements, but he did at least leave a $5,000 life insurance policy with his eldest daughter as beneficiary.

And that turned out to be an attractive prize. Within a month of his death, in May 1917, his widow, Edith, and her father, Rollo Boult, landed in Halifax on their way to Prince Rupert.[33] She and her father took the children away from Martha Kenny and she declared that as Stalker's lawful wife she was the administrator of his estate—a claim that was approved by the probate court in August 1917. The final amount of his estate (which did not include the life insurance policy) was some $200 with no debts, and no real property, investments, or securities of any kind. This was divided among Mrs. Edith Stalker, who got $66.66, and the four children who got $33.33 each.[34]

This was small potatoes; the real prize was Stalker's life insurance, along with his final military payments and the pensions and benefits for the children. Custody of the children thus became crucial. In May 1918 an application was made to the British Columbia Supreme Court on behalf of the four children, "by their next friend Martha Kenny." According to a Prince Rupert newspaper—the case appears to have had some notoriety in that city—Martha claimed that "Edith Stalker is not a fit woman to have charge of the young people." Edith and Rollo were forced to "produce" the four children before the court.[35] On September 12, Mr. Justice W. A. Macdonald heard the case in chambers with affidavits by Mrs. Kenny, Nora Kenny (her daughter), and witnesses who knew the family, as well as Edith Stalker and Rollo Boult, with lawyers for both parties and for the province's Official Guardian. The court ordered "that Martha Kenny, of Prince Rupert, British Columbia, widow, be and she is hereby appointed guardian of persons of the said infants Nora Jean Stalker, Norman Douglas Stalker, Robert Fred Stalker and Margaret Stalker during their respective minorities until other order shall be made to the contrary," and that the costs of the Official Guardian would be paid out of the estate.[36] The children returned to live with their grandmother in Prince Rupert.

Edith Stalker did not take long to recover from her defeat. On January 5, 1918, now resident in Victoria, British Columbia, she married a 33-year-old returned soldier, an artillery lieutenant who had been discharged with injuries. Edith declared herself a widow, occupation housekeeper, age 30 (she was actually in her 39th year).[37] This union did not last, but Edith was not yet finished. On June 13, 1921, declaring her age as 35, she married a bachelor farmer from Manitoba, in Toronto.[38] They may have moved to England, and what happened after that we do not know.

After fighting in the courts to gain custody of her grandchildren—an expensive process and difficult terrain for a woman at that time—Mrs. Martha Kenny then raised them in what must have been challenging circumstances. She had the pensions for the children and other amounts owing to Stalker (his medals and decorations were sent to his son Norman c/o Mrs. Kenny in 1920), and the $5,000 life insurance policy was doled out to her by the Official Guardian in instalments of $458 per annum, except for an amount of $244.13 that was retained to pay the government's commission under the Official Guardian's Act. In 1927, Mrs. Kenny successfully petitioned the government to pay her this money as well, since she, "being a widow, is having difficulty in meeting expenses in connection with the maintenance of the children."[39]

Martha Kenny died at age 76 in 1937 and is buried with her daughter, Anna Stalker, in Fairview Cemetery, Prince Rupert—an example of quiet courage in the face of great odds, who saved and raised her four grandchildren.

Back in Ottawa, Clarinda Stalker continued to work tirelessly with what the Ladies' Aid minutes described as the "little band of faithful" in the wartime activities of MacKay.[40] Moray, in his mid-thirties, was managing the family's affairs and Arthur was working as a carpenter and active in sports. Both were living at home and, as we have seen, by December 1916, her

Entered Vol. 37 fo. [illegible]
Date 20/9/17
By 15. 1917 [illegible]

IN THE SUPREME COURT OF BRITISH COLUMBIA.

669

IN THE MATTER OF NORA JEAN STALKER, NORMAN DOUGLAS STALKER, ROBERT GEORGE STALKER, and MARGARET STALKER, INFANTS.

BEFORE THE HONOURABLE MR. JUSTICE MACDONALD,
IN CHAMBERS,
WEDNESDAY THE 12TH. DAY OF SEPTEMBER, 1917.

UPON the application of the above-named infants by their next friend Martha Kenny; UPON READING the several affidavits of Martha Kenny sworn the 18th day of May 1917 and the 4th and 10th days of September 1917, and the exhibits thereto filed herein and the affidavit of Nora Florence Kenny sworn and filed herein the 4th day of September 1917; the declaration of Edward C. Gibbons and Michael P. McCaffery declared the 31st day of August, 1917, and filed herein the 4th day of September 1917; the affidavits of E. M. Bunos and John Hugh McMullin sworn the 18th day of May 1917 and filed herein the 10th day of September 1917, and the affidavits of Edith Lilian Stalker and the exhibits thereto and Peter Rolla Boult both sworn and filed herein the 6th day of September 1917: AND UPON HEARING Mr. W. H. Bullock-Webster of Counsel for the above-named infants, Mr. E. C. Mayers and Mr. A.D. Macfarlane of Counsel for Edith Lilian Stalker and Peter Rolla Boult, and Mr. C. Dubois Mason of Counsel for the Official Guardian:

IT IS ORDERED that Martha Kenny, of Prince Rupert, British Columbia, widow, be and she is hereby appointed guardian of persons of the said infants Nora Jean Stalker, Norman Douglas Stalker, Robert George Stalker and Margaret Stalker during their respective minorities until other order shall be made to the contrary.

AND IT IS FURTHER ORDERED that the costs of the Official Guardian (if not agreed) be taxed and paid out of the said infants' estate.

Approved,
E. C. M.
A. D. M.
C. D. M.

W. A. Macdonald J.

C.B.

Figure 13.9. Judgement in favour of Martha Kenny and custody of Stalker children.
Source: Provincial Archives of British Columbia, Victoria Supreme Court Judgements, vol. 34, fl. 428.

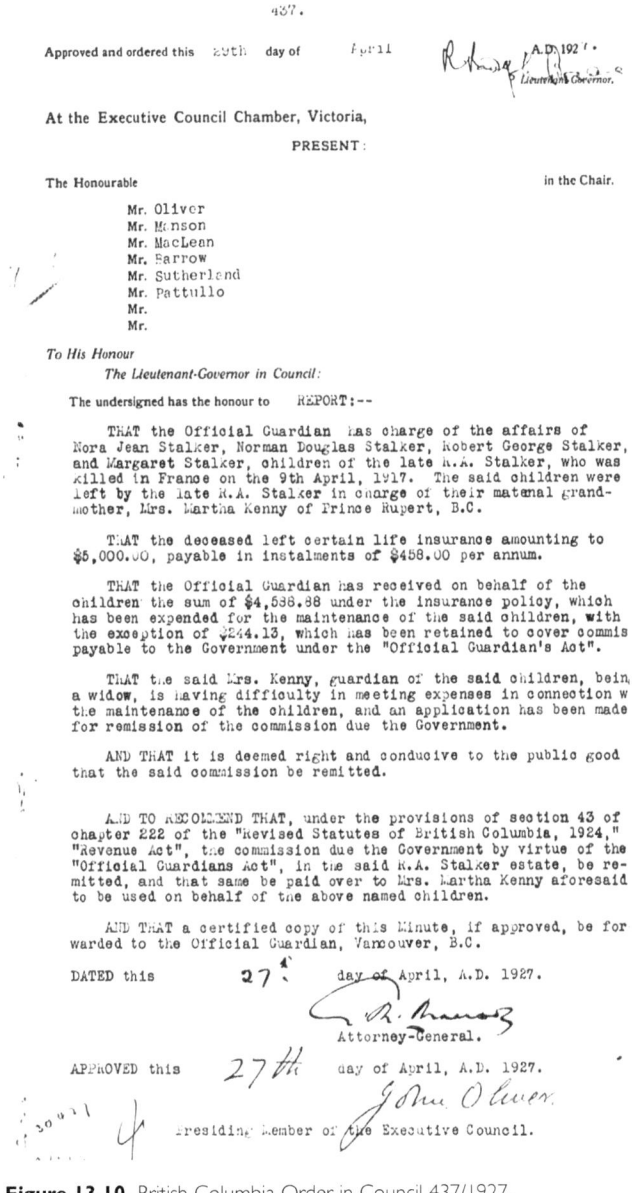

Figure 13.10. British Columbia Order in Council 437/1927.
Source: Provincial Archives of British Columbia.

daughter-in-law Clara and three grandchildren had also moved in with her. Clara was receiving assigned pay from Fred, and Doug was also contributing $30 a month to his mother. In April 1917 she received the tragic news of Robert's death; then in October came news of Fred's wound. In June 1918 she was told of Doug's wound, which was fortunately not serious, but it must have added to her already considerable anxiety. In November 1917, her son Arthur was granted exemption from conscription as medically unfit. Although an athlete, he had recently suffered injuries and he may have had other limiting conditions—and the tribunal noted that he had three brothers in the service, one of whom had been killed and another wounded.[41]

By October 1918, Fred, who was at the Fleming Hospital, could now visit his family during the day. Following his discharge on February 5, 1919, he stayed for a short time with his mother and family at 37 Charles Street, then moved his family to a house on Crichton Street. He was taken on strength as staff sergeant (later quartermaster sergeant) at the Corps of Military Staff Clerks at Militia HQ in Ottawa, in a records section dealing with pay, rations, discipline, and clothing. He was finally discharged from the military on January 31, 1920.

Doug Stalker had emerged unscathed from the war, but in November 1918 he was treated in field hospitals for scabies and gonorrhea, and he did not return to duty until January 12, 1919. His place in the 38th Battalion had been taken by another officer, so he proceeded to England and ended up as an officer in District Department 3 at the holding camp at Kinmel, Wales, near Liverpool, where, on March 4, 1919, Canadian soldiers, fed up with the long wait and terrible conditions, rioted for two days until troops fired on them, killing five. On April 3, 1919, Douglas Stalker sailed on the SS *Lapland* from Liverpool. He was discharged in Ottawa on April 14, 1919, with no disabilities, healthy and fit.

He once again became a leading athlete, including playing football for the Ottawa Rough Riders from 1919 to 1921. He joined the city engineer's office of the City of Ottawa, managed a number of important projects including the water filtration plant on Lemieux Island—which finally ended the scourge of water-borne diseases which had been disgracefully present in the city for decades—and rose to be Deputy Waterworks Engineer for Ottawa. On April 14, 1923, still residing at 37 Charles Street, he married Annie Isobel Naismith, a 28-year-old civil servant, at MacKay Presbyterian Church. They had one daughter.

Fred was not so lucky. In his medical history it was noted that he had a shrapnel scar about one inch long across on the right side of his thorax, a shrapnel scar on his back, and a two-inch scar on his right hand. The report further noted:

> Restricted movement of (the) right hand – flexion off all fingers impaired – 3rd finger worse – extension of first finger impaired. Extension of the wrist beyond a straight line impossible. Flexion of the wrist to a radius of 30 degrees from a straight line with arm. Grip of thumb and index finger fair, remainder poor, impossible to close hand beyond ¼ of normal. Can use pen with restrictions.

Figure 13.11. Doug Stalker and the 1919 Ottawa Rough Riders.
Source: Newspaper clipping, paper and date unknown, private collection.

But more than his physical wounds, Fred Stalker had trouble sleeping, and his medical report on discharge describes his state of mind: "Complains of inability to concentrate [...] Memory poor – pain in forearm when he tries to grip an object tightly. General condition otherwise good, other systems normal." His family, which had moved from British Columbia to live with his mother during the war, would have to nurse this wounded soldier back to mental, as well as physical, health.

After his discharge, Fred joined the forerunner of the Department of Veterans' Affairs to continue the work he had been doing at Militia HQ, and he later served for 20 years in the records branch of the Department of National Defence. About 1921 he and his family moved to a modest house near where Carleton University is today. He became a prominent member of the St. Andrew's Society and became an active member of an Anglican church. Now approaching 50, he went back into the militia in the 1920s, joining the Cameron Highlanders as a captain and rising to the rank of major until he retired in 1933 at the mandatory age limit. In 1940 he suddenly took ill and died at the age of 63. He was buried with semi-military honours in Beechwood Cemetery, with a number of military and ex-military men in attendance. "Of a friendly and likeable personality," read his obituary, "he enjoyed the respect and admiration of his associates, in the Government service and in military circles generally."[42]

Doug Stalker also left New Edinburgh and died tragically at age 44, in 1937. He had only a few months earlier survived an explosion, but in June he had had an operation from which he never recovered. The Ottawa *Journal*

Figure 13.12. Fred Stalker in his military uniform in the 1920s.
Source: Private collection.

reported: "His passing has greatly saddened all officials and employees of the Corporation for he was a man of cheery disposition, exceedingly well-liked" with "broad, technical knowledge of water purification systems."[43]

Moray Stalker was appointed Assistant City Clerk in 1936 and retired in 1946 after almost 48 years' service.[44]

Arthur Stalker worked as a carpenter, taking small jobs and contracts in the New Edinburgh area, serving on athletic boards as a referee and organizer, and as a member of the Horticultural Society. He continued to live at 37 Charles Street and attended MacKay. He died in 1954, leaving a wife and one child.[45]

As her surviving sons rebuilt their lives, married, and pursued their careers, Clarinda Stalker continued to attend MacKay Presbyterian Church and to be active in its work. She remained one of the Church's Visitors to the Protestant Hospital and was on the the Executive Committee of the Ladies' Aid until 1924. In 1930 she died at home and was buried at Beechwood cemetery—in the words of the MacKay Death Register, "an old and honoured member of MacKay church."

Figure 13.13. Moray Stalker.
Source: Private collection.

Figure 13.14. Arthur Stalker.
Source: Private collection.

14

THE RYAN FAMILY
"Who Played the Game Through"

John Henry "Jack" Ryan was one of the greatest athletes of his day, and when he died in the air battles of Bloody April 1917 in the Arras Sector, the sports community in Ottawa and other cities mourned his loss. But the story of the Ryan family is also that of his more unassuming older brother, Mathew William ("Billy"), who was killed a year earlier, and of their sister Mabel, whose death after childbirth was another reminder that tragedy at home, was as common during the war as losses in battle. It is also the story of Mabel's husband, John McElroy, and the faith and fortitude that allowed him and the surviving Ryan sister and her husband to carry on after so much loss.

The four Ryan children—Mabel (1880), Mathew William (1882),[1] John Henry (1885), and Margaret Lena (1886)—grew up in an ample two-story frame house at 39 Crichton Street. Their father, John Ryan, a contractor working from this house, was a Catholic, while their mother Susanah was a Presbyterian and a member of MacKay church.[2] The children attended Sunday School at MacKay and joined the church as adults. In 1903, 16-year-old Lena served as one of the MacKay delegates to the Ottawa Presbyterial Women's Missionary Society, and she displayed musical talent in Sunday School and other productions.[3] Jack participated in at least one of Mrs. Anderson's plays before the war (see Figure 2.9). The boys went to work at an early age: Billy as a conductor for the Ottawa Electric Railway, and Jack as a clerk with the Department of the Interior, each making $800 a year according to the 1911 census.[4] Their mother died about 1906, and their father some three years later.[5]

In 1910 Lena Ryan married William Crowe, who had grown up in Lowertown and competed with and against the Ryan brothers at the New Edinburgh Canoe Club.[6] He had started out as an electrician with the Ahearn and Soper Company, which owned the street railway and pioneered electrical development in Ottawa; in 1907 he and a partner had started Costello and Crowe, which had quickly become a leading electrical supply, repair, and contracting firm.[7] Lena continued to attend MacKay Presbyterian Church when their first children were born in 1912 and 1913, but the following year the family moved to a more prestigious house in a newer part of the city.

Figure 14.1. John T. McElroy served as team manager for many New Edinburgh and MacKay sports teams; team picture (detail) of the Ottawa Seconds in 1908 as city league champions.
Source: City of Ottawa Archives, MG 101 Ernest Stitt Fonds, Box #A2012-0381.

Then in 1911, Mabel Ryan married John T. McElroy, the youngest child of John McElroy Sr., a carpenter who had built houses in New Edinburgh (including his own family home at 68 Crichton Street) and was a founder of MacKay Presbyterian Church. But John Sr. had died at age 41, when John Jr. was still a boy, and his widow had found work as a practical nurse. John Jr. had worked part-time while attending school and at age 13 had become a mill hand. He had then gone to work in the Post Office Department, where he had risen to oversee equipment and supplies. He was well connected in the New Edinburgh community and was prominent in the athletic world as a manager and organizer. He was also beginning to play an important role in the church as a member of its Board of Managers. John and Mabel McElroy had a son in 1912 and a daughter in 1913, and when his mother died they inherited the McElroy family home. With their sisters now married, the Ryan brothers moved away to separate apartments. In 1915 Jack Ryan returned to New Edinburgh to board with his brother-in-law John McElroy, and Mabel McElroy was the family member both her brothers gave as their next of kin when they enlisted.

The Ryan brothers were very athletic and played on a variety of New Edinburgh sports teams. Billy Ryan appears to have been, as described in the eulogy given by Rev. Peter Anderson, "a big-hearted, unassuming, hard-working man" whose death caused "great regret throughout the congregation."[8] Jack Ryan was a much more outsized personality, whose adventurous nature was revealed in April 1902 when at age 16 he enlisted to fight in the Boer War with the 3rd Canadian Mounted Rifles, which was being recruited as part of the Fourth Canadian Contingent for service in South Africa. (In the event, Ryan did not go to South Africa and he served only until August 1902.)[9] Then, during the decade before the First World War, Jack Ryan blossomed into one of the greatest all-round athletes of his era in Ottawa. He played for New Edinburgh hockey teams—the Ottawa Seconds won the Ottawa championship in 1908 with Ryan as a star player and John McElroy one of the team's managers. He rowed on several championship teams with the New Edinburgh Canoe Club. He became one of the finest ski jumpers in the city, who gave "some of the greatest foreign jumpers right royal runs for their laurels, and became a big favourite with those who patronized the competitions at Rockcliffe in 1913 and 1914." In 1914 he set a record for distance on a ski jump established beside the Chateau Laurier hotel. "No man learned the difficult points of ski jumping quicker than Jack Ryan," wrote a member of the Ottawa Ski Club in a eulogy. "Jack was a daredevil of the nerviest type."[10]

But Jack's greatest fame was achieved as a football player. "Rufus" Ryan (so named because of his auburn hair) was repeatedly described in newspaper reports as "peerless," a "star," "incomparable," "the greatest outside wing ever to play the game in Canada." When the Ottawa Football Club joined the Interprovincial Rugby Football Union (IRFU)—a forerunner of the CFL, which included the Toronto Argonauts, Hamilton Tigers, and a Montreal team—Ryan was a fixture on the Ottawa squad. Year after year, sports reporters for the two Ottawa newspapers rejoiced that Ryan was turning out for football, and when Ryan was in the lineup, the team won. In 1908, Ottawa beat its arch-rival Hamilton in a hard-fought contest to claim the IRFU championship but lost to the University of Toronto in a game for the newly established Grey Cup. In 1911, the Ottawa *Journal* reported that in one match against the Toronto Argonauts, "Rufus Ryan was undoubtedly the star. He tackled like a fiend, but what is best of all, he was clean."[11] Hockey and football were often marred by lax officiating, dirty play, and sometimes serious brawls. On several occasions in various sports Ryan was often injured, but he always came back for more.

Ryan was repeatedly dogged by questions regarding his amateur status, because he had played for the Ottawa Victoria senior hockey team against the Montreal Wanderers and a Renfrew team that included some professionals.

Figure 14.2. Jack Ryan; team picture (detail) of the Ottawa Seconds in 1908 as city league champions. *Source:* City of Ottawa Archives. MG 101 Ernest Stitt Fonds, Box #A2012-0381.

In 1908, a special meeting of the IRFU Board of Governors met for a whole day to consider his case. The board made it clear that it took any violation of amateur status seriously but that these were "special circumstances." In view of the fact that he had not received any remuneration, his own explanation, and the "testimony they have received as to the excellent character of the applicant," it confirmed Ryan's amateur status.[12] Nonetheless, almost every year after that, questions continued to be raised—prompted, as the Ottawa *Journal* darkly suggested, by the desire of rivals Toronto and Hamilton to keep him off the field (the Montreal governor supported him, likely because Montreal was trying to pry him away from Ottawa).[13] But by 1914 injuries had taken their toll and Ryan's career, at least as a top-level athlete, was winding down.

With the outbreak of war, both brothers turned their thoughts to enlistment.

Mathew William Ryan enlisted on July 1, 1915, in the 59th Battalion, based at Barriefield camp in Kingston (now CFB Kingston). He was a stocky man at five feet eight inches tall, with medium complexion, blue eyes, and brown hair. Billy Ryan's service record is, like his personality, very "quiet"—no illnesses, wounds or hospitalization, no discipline problems. And unfortunately, it is very short.

Figure 14.3. Mathew William Ryan.
Source: From De Wolfe 1919, 267.

The 59th Battalion did not sail for England until April 1916, and it was then broken up to provide reinforcements for battalions at the front. Ryan was sent to join the 24th Battalion in June 1916, giving up his rank of lance corporal in the process. This battalion, built around the Victoria Rifles of Montreal, was part of the Second Canadian Division, which was based at Dickebusch, a small, agricultural village in the Ypres Salient, whose buildings had been destroyed by shellfire and whose surrounding farms had been turned into a sea of mud. The Canadians, who were holding the Hooge-St. Eloi sector, fought no major battles after Mount Sorrel in early June; nonetheless, during the following three months a thousand soldiers were killed in the usual "wastage." A dramatic example of this occurred on August 19, 1916. The men had been enjoying a "quiet" period of training, route marches, and work parties, with only the occasional disturbance by shells and sniper fire. Then, at 1:00 p.m., suddenly and for no apparent reason, the Germans launched a heavy artillery barrage that lasted five hours. Forward positions of the 24th and 102nd Battalions were flattened. Twelve men were wounded and three killed, including Mathew William Ryan. The MacKay Death Register described his passing in heroic terms. But the laconic entry for Ryan in the Circumstances of Death Register—"Killed in Action in the trenches South East of St. Eloi"—was a truer account of the sudden death of a soldier in a meaningless bombardment. The next day was again "quiet," and the battalion regrouped and began its march to the Somme.[14]

Billy's brother Jack Ryan had enlisted in the militia even earlier, though it is not clear in what capacity.[15] But his real desire, according to one account, was "to get into an aeroplane, so that he could fly to the clouds."[16] Until 1918 there was no Canadian air force, not even a Canadian wing of the British air services, as the Australians had. Instead, more than 22,000 Canadians served with the Royal Flying Corps and the Royal Naval Air Service (merged in 1918 into the Royal Air Force). To get into the RFC in 1915, candidates had to have first served in the militia.

Figure 14.4. Jack Ryan, 1916.
Source: From De Wolfe 1919, 267.

The first batch of Canadians from Ottawa for the RFC was recruited in 1915 through the Governor General's office. It included young men like John Booth, grandson of a lumber baron, Eddy Soper, son of the co-owner of the Ottawa Electric Railway, and Don Brophy, a star athlete well known in Ottawa society.[17] It is a testament to the stature Ryan had achieved that despite his mundane job he mixed easily with these well-connected men. It is also a testament to his desire to fly that he made an important investment in getting the pilot's license these early recruits were required to have. Lessons in the only Canadian school cost as much as $400 for 500 *minutes* of flying plus ground instruction. This was half a year's salary for Ryan. He may have had a small inheritance, and for his (non-)service in the Boer War he had received a land grant which was turned into cash. He could also recoup his outlay if he was accepted into the RFC as his costs would be reimbursed. One account says that Ryan attended a flying school in the United States, a cheaper option which a number of Canadian pilots took.[18] But a newspaper article reported in late October 1915 that he was taking a flying course in Toronto, and that he would be going to Bermuda "in the winter" to complete it.[19] He may not have done so, since he was accepted by the RFC in late 1915. Whichever path he took, his flight training was probably minimal.

On January 1, 1916, Jack Ryan was gazetted as a 2nd Lieutenant in the RFC and at the age of 30 left for the RFC flying school in Reading, England. The Head of the registration branch of the Interior Department presented him with the gift of a meerschaum pipe on behalf of the staff. "He had a great record in football," wrote a reporter, "and will take with him the best wishes of a very wide circle of friends."[20] Ryan mingled with other Canadians flying in England, enjoyed some club and restaurant life, and was probably taught to fly all over again. Instruction was slowed by bad weather, scarce equipment, and a shortage of trainers (the British had sent their best pilots to France in 1914 where most had been killed). Aircraft design was evolving and student pilots often discovered things about new aircraft that even their instructors did not know—that is, if they survived.[21] On July 20, 1916, Ryan was gazetted as 2nd Lieutenant Flying Officer (confirmed on August 17) and was sent to France to join 21 Squadron, Royal Flying Corps.

Pilots were a special breed. They needed daring to go aloft in what were still, despite the incredible pace of innovation during the war, flimsy crates built of canvas, metal, wood, and wire, difficult to manoeuvre, cold, noisy, and with balky engines. They had to be physically fit with good eyesight and reflexes. They needed to have good judgement, self-confidence, adaptability, the kind of courage that was cool under fire, a sixth sense for danger, a killer instinct, and above all the fortitude to withstand adverse conditions and prolonged stress. They had to be intelligent but not burdened with the excessive imagination that might induce doubt, hesitation, or fear. Athletes and students made the best candidates, and the British also believed that Canadians were especially well suited, being (as they thought) rugged frontiersmen who could nonetheless fit easily into an elite service still regarded as the preserve of "gentlemen."[22] Ryan fit the profile to a T.

Flying officers lived in air bases well behind the lines, had servants, wore stylish uniforms, slept between clean sheets, ate four-course meals with wines in an officers' mess, and had trained mechanics to service their machines. But their comforts on the ground belied the stark reality that, in the words of historian Ian Mackersey, "several times a day, the pilots and observers were ordered into the air to attack fellow human beings."[23] They flew missions over enemy territory, searching the skies for the plane that would dive from behind and riddle them with machine gun bullets before they could react. Aerial combat meant twisting and turning, two miles above the ground, trying to keep the engine from cutting out, firing a Vickers machine gun or a Lewis gun as best they could, relying on luck as well as skill. A newly arrived pilot might have as little as 15 hours of solo flying in England, and by early 1917 his life expectancy at the front was 11 days. Major-General Trenchard, head of the RFC, instructed that new pilots should be forwarded to the front as fast as possible to replace those killed so there would be "no empty chairs" at the breakfast table.

Aircraft had by 1916 demonstrated their strategic value in support of infantry operations. Trenchard's doctrine was to assert air superiority by sending patrols 15 miles deep into German territory to perform aerial reconnaissance and to bomb and strafe enemy artillery, aerodromes, and transport and communications networks. Like the infantry generals, Trenchard was prepared to sustain heavy losses in pursuit of this objective.[24] The 21 Squadron was part of a special wing attached to General Headquarters for strategic reconnaissance and bombing operations.

When Ryan joined the squadron it was being refitted with a new aircraft, the Royal Aircraft Factory B.E.12—a noisy, clumsy, single-seater that could fly 95 miles per hour in straight flight but could not climb or manoeuvre easily. It had a primitive mechanism to allow the pilot to fire a belt-fed Vickers machine gun through the propeller (perhaps), and another Vickers on the wing that required the pilot to make an awkward movement to sight—jammed guns and shot propellers were a constant problem. That it could be a difficult plane to fly was shown by several training accidents, including one involving the commanding officer. On August 8 Ryan crashed into an adjoining field on takeoff on a practice run; fortunately, he was unhurt.[25] When 21 Squadron went to the front in late August 1916, the B.E.12 proved wholly inadequate to the tasks assigned to it.

That summer the Germans deployed the Albatross, a single-seater with a big Mercedes engine with a top speed of 109 miles per hour, which could climb to 3,000 feet in 5 minutes and fire a machine gun through the propeller with devastating accuracy. The German pilots were well-trained and supremely confident, and their leader was the "Red Baron," Manfred von Richthofen, so named because the colour of his squadron's planes struck fear into the hearts of British pilots. Outnumbered, the Germans grouped fighters into "wolf packs" that attacked patrols, inflicting heavy damage on the British planes, and then running for cover. In September the British lost over 100 planes as against one-quarter that many lost by the Germans; in October it was over 80 as against 12. The 21 Squadron lost 19 airmen killed or wounded, and 6 whose nerves were so shattered they had to be taken out of the line.[26]

Jack Ryan had suffered a blow with the death of his brother in August, and by late October he was reported to be "suffering from shell shock."[27] In December, a few days before his own death, his friend Don Brophy wrote in a last letter home that after some "hot old times on the Somme, Jack Ryan was pretty badly used up, and is in England now."[28]

As the Somme campaign drew to a close in November, the remaining pilots of 21 Squadron were sent on leave to England. The RFC had succeeded in its strategic objective and kept the Germans on the defensive, but at a terrible cost. It now underwent a reorganization, increasing the size of squadrons, recruiting many more pilots, and increasing the number of training hours required before pilots could be sent to the front.[29] Ryan, probably still recovering, was assigned to lead a training squad in England. But like many pilots who chafed at being away from the action, he wanted back in the fray. In early 1917, he joined 57 Squadron based in Fienvillers, France.[30]

But even as it reorganized, the RFC still faced one formidable challenge. New and improved aircraft were being produced but were not yet available in sufficient numbers; until they were, the RFC would have to reply on obsolescent planes as it performed its crucial role of observation and reconnaissance. The 57 Squadron was equipped with the Royal Aircraft Factory F.E.2d, an updated version of the F.E.2b, which had been the mainstay of the British forces in the Somme battles. The F.E.2d was a two-seater push-plane (that is, the engine was mounted behind the body) with the pilot sitting above and behind the Observer. The pilot could fire one Lewis gun while the Observer (who had to stand up in the nacelle, exposed to the elements from the knees up) had two others on swivel mounts that he could fire in all directions. Unlike belt-fed machine guns, the ammunition drums of Lewis guns had to be changed frequently as the aircraft shuddered, turned, and dived.[31] The F.E.2d was faster than the F.E.2b, with an upgraded, 250-horsepower Rolls-Royce engine. It was vulnerable to attack from the rear but if pilots kept their nerve and flew in a circle formation so that each observer could cover the blind spot in another plane, it could (just) hold its own against the smaller, faster, better armed German planes.

Throughout the winter of 1917, the RFC did the aerial reconnaissance that would be crucial in planning the coming Arras offensive, in particular providing information on the new German strategy of defense-in-depth, locating enemy artillery and machine gun positions, and preventing the Germans from observing British preparations. When the British offensive began with the Canadian assault on Vimy Ridge on April 9, aircraft played an essential support role, including spotting German artillery and reporting on troop and supply movements. But the Germans, greatly outnumbered but with even better aircraft and wolf-pack tactics than the year before, exacted a horrific toll—during Bloody April the British flying services lost 400 pilots.

Figure 14.5. Royal Aircraft Factory F.E.2b.
This photograph depicts an air-worthy replica of an F.E.2b aircraft. The F.E.2d had a similar design but a bigger engine. Note the exposed position of the observer in the nacelle, the pilot above and behind him, and the engine at the rear of the body of the aircraft.
Source: Created by Philip Capper.

The 57 Squadron, part of 9th (HQ) wing, was a reserve squadron used where needed for "line patrol," strategic reconnaissance, and bombing, always operating in German air space, engaging in desperate combat, and sustaining heavy losses which mounted by the day.[32] Toward the end of April the Germans upped the ante by forming a super wolf pack, combining all the fighters in a sector into a single group. On April 30, 1917, in the words of the official historian of the RAF:

> The new group numbering twenty single-seaters, in two formations, set out from the Douai aerodrome on the morning of the 30th. Their first encounter was with seven F.E.2ds of a line patrol of No. 57 Squadron and three Sopwith triplanes of No. 8 (Naval) Squadron. Two of the F.E.s were shot down in the German lines and a third, with a wounded pilot and a dying observer, crashed in the British area.[33]

This wounded pilot would appear to have been Jack Ryan. According to his service file, on April 30, 1917, Ryan was wounded in combat while on patrol at Miramont in the Lievin-Noreuil Sector. His observer was also wounded. Ryan was taken to 45 Casualty Clearing Station in Achiet-le-Grand, a large village 19 kilometres south of Arras along the Arras-Bapaume Road, where he died of wounds on May 2. He was buried, alongside others who died at the hospital that day, in the extension to the Achiet-le-Grand communal cemetery.[34]

The death of "one of the most popular athletes that ever lined up with an Ottawa team" hit the sports community like a bombshell. Tributes poured in from cities whose teams Ryan had played against—tributes not only to a great athlete, but to "one who had always played the game fairly and squarely."[35]

On May 5, the Ottawa *Journal* devoted an editorial to him:

Thousands of Ottawa people have cheered Jack Ryan, brilliant rugby player. These same thousands feel the loss of Flight-Lieutenant Jack Ryan of the Royal Flying Corps, dead of wounds in France.

Of all games for boys, none is better than rugby football. It teaches the player to keep going, to stay in the game, despite hard knocks. Rugby is a school of experience for the youth who stands on the threshold of life. The habit of setting the teeth and plunging ahead in spite of hard knocks is useful. Those who do not possess it are the better of [sic] acquiring it.

Not many years ago, Ottawa had a famous rugby team. The strong combination of that team was Ryan and Stronach, outside wings, who were always "on the ball." Many will recall how these two stalwart athletes used to dash down the field, through a maze of opponents.

And now Ryan is dead at the front, where Stronach is fighting as an officer in the infantry. The old combination of speed and pluck that brought Ottawa some of her proudest athletic triumphs is broken in the terrible game of war. Ottawa will not soon forget Jack Ryan, who played the game through.[36]

Mabel McElroy, now with a young family of her own, had to settle the effects of her two brothers killed in the war. Jack Ryan left no will and the British War Office generated a huge paper trail collecting a mess debt of a little over three pounds, calculating the amounts due his estate, and itemizing his personal effects—a watch, a cigarette case, and a case for goggles, as well as his discs, buttons, and shoulder badges. They misspelled Mabel's name and at first erroneously informed her that he had died in a flying accident. Then, because his estate was a little over 100 pounds—a substantial sum at the time—it had to be collected from the militia department in Ottawa and Mabel McElroy needed a letter signed by her husband certifying that she was indeed the person entitled to claim it.[37]

Then Mabel McElroy herself died, at home, on July 24, 1918, at the age of 38. The MacKay Death Register attributed her death to heart trouble and pleurisy; the Beechwood Cemetery Register gave her cause of death as Graves' disease, an autoimmune disease of the thyroid.[38] Her death came only a few

JACK RYAN PAYS SUPREME SACRIFICE

Best Outside Wing Player in Canada Dies of Wounds Received in France.

Still another is added to the long list of famous Ottawa athletes who have paid the supreme sacrifice for the Empire. While it was generally known that Flight Lieut. Jack Ryan was dangerously ill from wounds received in the great conflict in France, hardly anyone was prepared for the news received yesterday by his brother-in-law and sister, Mr. and Mrs. T. J. McElroy, 68 Creighton street in a cable from the War Office that the great football player, hockeyist and paddler had passed away. The news of Jack Ryan's death spread quickly throughout the city and profound sorrow was expressed on all sides for Rufus Ryan was one of the most popular athletes that ever lined up with an Ottawa team.

Was Well Known.

Perhaps no Ottawa athlete was better known than Jack Ryan. Playing on the Ottawa Football team he was one of the best outside wings that ever played the game and his name went down in history along with Lieut. MacMurray, Frank Knight, Lieut. Bert Stronach, and Liz Marriot as the best five outside wings that ever put on a football uniform. They were in a class by themselves. Jack Ryan was also a fine paddler and distinguished himself in this sport and hockey with the New Edinburgh Club.

On Championship Team.

The late Flight Lieut. Ryan was with the Ottawa football team the year Tigers were beaten at Rosedale in the play off for the championship of the Big Four and his great tackling had much to do with Ottawa winning. He also did some running and could play a real good game at cricket. He was employed in the Interior department and was unmarried. Two sisters survive him, Mrs. J. T. McElroy and Mrs. Crow both of Ottawa. A brother, Private Billy Ryan, was killed in action last year. Lieut. Ryan joined the Royal Flying Corp in December 1915, training at Toronto and in the United States.

Figure 14.6. Jack Ryan's obituary.
Source: Ottawa Journal, May 4, 1917.

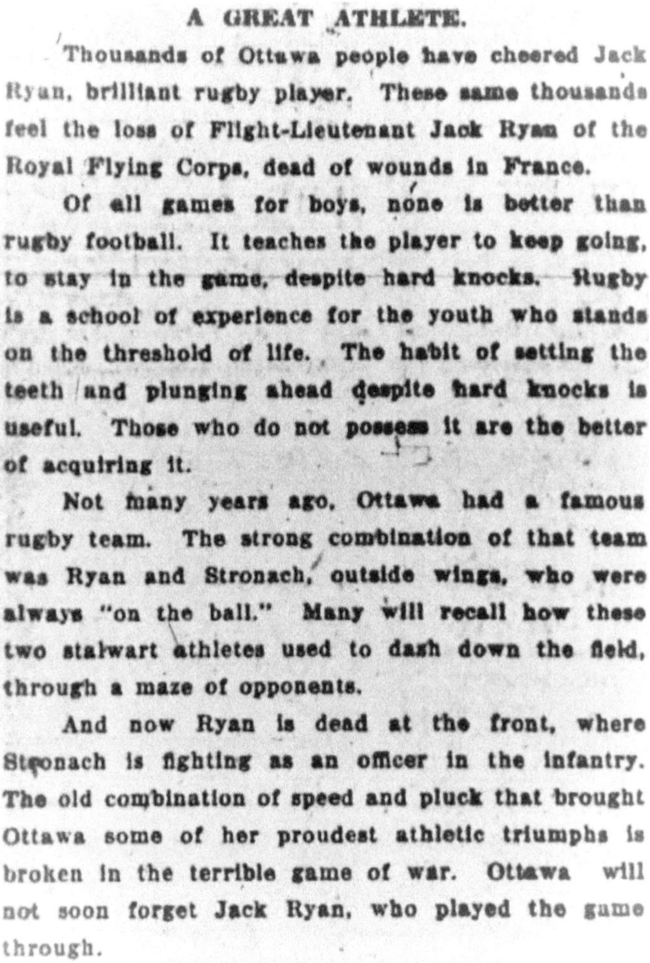

A GREAT ATHLETE.

Thousands of Ottawa people have cheered Jack Ryan, brilliant rugby player. These same thousands feel the loss of Flight-Lieutenant Jack Ryan of the Royal Flying Corps, dead of wounds in France.

Of all games for boys, none is better than rugby football. It teaches the player to keep going, to stay in the game, despite hard knocks. Rugby is a school of experience for the youth who stands on the threshold of life. The habit of setting the teeth and plunging ahead despite hard knocks is useful. Those who do not possess it are the better of acquiring it.

Not many years ago, Ottawa had a famous rugby team. The strong combination of that team was Ryan and Stronach, outside wings, who were always "on the ball." Many will recall how these two stalwart athletes used to dash down the field, through a maze of opponents.

And now Ryan is dead at the front, where Stronach is fighting as an officer in the infantry. The old combination of speed and pluck that brought Ottawa some of her proudest athletic triumphs is broken in the terrible game of war. Ottawa will not soon forget Jack Ryan, who played the game through.

Figure 14.7. Editorial honouring Jack Ryan.
Source: Ottawa *Journal*, May 5, 1917.

weeks after the birth of a daughter. And there was probably an element of truth in the suggestion in the Ottawa *Journal* that "her death was hastened by grief caused by the loss of her two brothers, John Ryan and William Ryan, both well-known Ottawa athletes, who were killed in action."[39] To fill to the brim the cup of tragedy, her infant daughter then died at age five months. John McElroy had lost two brothers-in-law and was now the widowed father of a five-year-old boy and a three-year-old girl. Lena Crowe, as the sole survivor of the four Ryan children, would receive the medals and honours awarded to her brothers.

Mathew William "Billy" Ryan is buried in the Dickebusch New Military Cemetery, located on the Kerkstraat, which is a small street leading out of the town of Dikkebus (modern Flemish spelling) past the village church. Some 200 metres from town the road divides a substantial cemetery in two, with the larger part, where Ryan is buried, on one side and the extension with the Cross of Remembrance on the other. Around the cemetery are small suburban houses and some open areas for playing fields and storage buildings, with a corn field at the back, and a low hedge on one side separating it from a house which is literally next door. It has minimal landscaping but there are a few large trees and there are flowers among the headstones. Ryan is surrounded by several rows of Canadians, interspersed with British soldiers, who perished in this "quiet" time in the Ypres Sector.

Figure 14.8. Dickebusch New Military Cemetery.
Source: Photograph by Carolyn Bowker.

Jack Ryan rests in the Achiet-le-Grand Military Cemetery, at the northwest side of the village of Achiet, alongside a communal cemetery that serves the town. It lies amid open, gently rolling terrain where wind turbines now turn lazily in fields of sugar beets and canola. It is a large cemetery, containing 1,424 Commonwealth and 42 German graves. It is well laid out with trees around the perimeter and neat rows of headstones with flowers planted among them, with a stone wall surrounding it and the Stone of Remembrance

Figure 14.9. Dickebusch New Military Cemetery.
Source: Photograph by Carolyn Bowker.

and cross in the middle. Many of the soldiers buried here are "known unto God," especially a long row from the 1916 Battle of the Somme. Ryan, whose headstone is in the foreground in front of the Great Cross in Figure 14.10, is one of a very few Canadians buried there.

Mabel McElroy is buried in Beechwood Cemetery, together with her husband, the infant daughter who died so soon after her, and her other two children—John M. ("Jack") McElroy, who served and was wounded in the Second World War; and Margaret Mabel (1913–2002), who had a long career in the public service. In 1929, John T. McElroy, now a middle manager in the Post Office, married again and he and his wife had seven children. As chair of MacKay's Building Committee, he spearheaded the campaign to pay off the debt for the new Sanctuary the church had built in 1910. He opposed Church Union in 1925, but when MacKay Presbyterian voted to become MacKay United Church, he stayed with the congregation and at his death in 1965 he was the church's senior Elder.

Lena's husband, William Crowe, was prospering as Costello and Crowe joined with a third partner, Joseph William Bellamy, to form CCB Electric Works. This company quickly developed into one of the best equipped and most advanced supply, repair, and contracting firms in Ottawa. William and Lena had two more children during the war and in all had nine children

Figure 14.10. Achiet-le-Grand Military Cemetery.
Source: Photograph by Carolyn Bowker.

Figure 14.11. Achiet-le-Grand Military Cemetery.
Source: Photograph by Carolyn Bowker.

between 1912 and 1927, eight of whom would survive them. She continued to arrange entertainments for various organizations to which she and her husband belonged. When she died in 1947, her funeral was attended by the mayor and prominent civic officials and business people, as well as many old friends from MacKay and New Edinburgh; she was remembered in an obituary as "highly regarded for her fine gifts of heart and mind."[40] William Crowe was still president of CCB at his death in 1958 at age 80.[41] They are buried in Beechwood Cemetery.

Billy Ryan is now remembered only as a name on a memorial plaque. And despite the belief of the Ottawa *Journal* editorialist that Jack Ryan would not be soon forgotten, his name was overshadowed within a few years by other famous athletes from Ottawa and from MacKay church. But in their day, and in the great trial of war, all the Ryan siblings "played the game through."

15 REGINALD ISAMBARD BRUNEL
Engineer and Artilleryman

Reginald Isambard Brunel came from a long line of distinguished Canadian civil engineers and was training for that profession when he enlisted in the artillery in 1915. He seems to have been named after Isambard Kingdom Brunel, the great Victorian British engineer, though we cannot identify any direct family connection. His stepmother, Frances Brunel, was a talented pianist, accompanist, music teacher, and church organist with a studio in downtown Ottawa who established a reputation as a choral director capable of staging major productions such as Mendelsohn's *Elijah* with church choirs. His father, Henry Brunel, was by 1914 well established as an engineer in the naval service of the Department of Marine and Fisheries, and the Brunel family lived in a comfortable brick house at 95 Victoria (now Queen Victoria) Street in New Edinburgh.[1]

Henry Brunel's grandfather was Alfred Brunel, a leading Canadian engineer of the mid-nineteenth century who worked with T. C. Keefer on the Victoria Bridge in Montreal, was superintendent of the Ontario, Simcoe and Huron Railroad Union Company, and was a Toronto alderman and city engineer. To round out his career, Alfred Brunel was appointed inspector of customs, excise, and canals for the Province of Canada, and later became the first Commissioner of Inland Revenue for the Dominion of Canada. His son Troilus Brunel also became an engineer and was employed by the federal government as late as the early 1870s. Henry Brunel was Troilus's son, but it is not clear who his mother was—he was raised by his aunt Helen and his uncle Alex Goforth, a lawyer. By 1891, 24-year-old Henry Brunel had also come to Ottawa to work as an engineer, and he had also joined the public service.[2]

In 1892 Henry Brunel married Gertrude Finley, a Catholic. Henry had to affirm "that after being duly instructed, I have been conditionally baptised and received in the faith of the R. C. Church in which it is my firm and sincere determination to persevere unto death."[3] Five children followed: Hope (1893), Olive (1895), Joseph Reginald Isambard (March 28, 1897), William Troyless (1901, died 1902), and Ivan (1902). All were baptised Catholics at St. Joseph's Church. However, in 1906 Gertrude died of tuberculosis,[4] and a year later Henry Brunel married Frances Maud Gaynor, who at 26 now had four stepchildren, the eldest a teenager.[5]

Frances was a Presbyterian and the marriage affidavit in 1907 described Henry as Anglican (which he had been before his first marriage). In the 1911 census the whole family was listed as "1st Congregational," which probably reflects the fact that Frances was employed as an organist at the First Congregational Church. But Henry's two daughters would remain Catholics all their lives. Reginald's attestation papers list his religion as Anglican, but he appears to have had a strong connection with MacKay Presbyterian Church, where his mother, whom the Session had tried to hire in 1912, had special permission to practice on the organ one hour each day. His death in 1917 was recorded in MacKay's Death Register.

Reginald Brunel attended Creighton Street Public School and in 1912 he entered Ottawa Collegiate Institute. While his entrance marks show that he was intelligent, he left after first form in 1913 with less than stellar grades.[6] He took a job as a clerk in the City Engineer's Department and on his attestation papers he described himself as an engineer-in-training. At that time engineering could be learned on the job, in the same way that lawyers could still be trained by articling in a law office.

Brunel enlisted at age 18 on July 5, 1915, in the 25th Battery of Canadian Field Artillery. He was five feet seven and a half inches tall, with fair complexion, grey eyes, and light-brown hair. Artillery would have been attractive to someone with a scientific and technical background. It involved a degree of education and practical skill as well as courage, physical strength, and for some, the ability to handle horses. Brunel spent most of his service as part of a gun crew in the 25th Battery, which, soon after his enlistment, moved to Valcartier to join the other batteries that would make up the 7th Brigade CFA in the Second Canadian Division. The 25th Battery consisted of four 18-pounders, field guns that were more mobile than the heavy siege guns, but which, given in the static conditions of trench warfare, were usually dug in. Each gun was crewed by six gunners commanded by a sergeant.

The batteries were only able to begin training with qualified instructors in August 1915, when they arrived at the training camp in Shorncliffe, England; even then, they had to use obsolete weapons. "When will they have up-to-date guns?" King George V asked British Defence Minister Lord Kitchener when he inspected the Canadian artillery brigade. "Next year, sir," was the reply.[7] As a result, the artillery brigades did not go to France with the Second Division in August 1915, but had to wait until January 1916.

Then began the arduous process of moving to the front. Forty trains were needed for each artillery brigade, with guns and equipment on flatcars, horses in special cars, and the men in "side-door Pullmans," using circuitous routes to conceal movements and requiring frequent stops to feed, water, and calm horses. Then followed a long route march with guns, ammunitions and supplies hauled by horses and wagons—each battery made a column a

Figure 15.1. An 18-pounder and its crew; this artillery piece was the mainstay of the British field artillery, and each gun required a six-man crew, with different roles assigned to each man. *Source:* Library and Archives Canada PA-022712.

quarter of a mile long. Finally, the 7th Brigade CFA settled into its quarters southeast of Ypres.

Then in early February 1916, the 25th Battery moved to the front and began "registering" its guns—that is, firing repeatedly at an enemy target to calibrate their range. This provided the gunners with their first real experience of trench warfare, as periodic shelling on both sides, despite bad weather and poor visibility, disrupted operations and caused casualties and frayed nerves. But by 1916 the Canadian artillery were beginning to emerge as an effective force. Problems with the manufacturing and supply chain of artillery shells had been overcome and there was now a plentiful supply available. Field gun batteries were now firing, often for days at a stretch, 4 shells a minute and in extreme cases up to 15. And of course, the enemy duly retaliated. From March to May 1916, the war diary of the 7th Brigade CFA records constant artillery duels as well as bombardments to support trench raids and attacks.[8]

In an artillery duel the most accurate artillery won and discipline and teamwork were essential. As it gained experience, the battery learned to function efficiently as a team, each member of the six-man gun crew knowing the work of the others so he could step in if someone was killed or wounded.

Gunners had to know how to load, fire, and care for their weapons, read maps and aim their shots. The many horses that were essential to the operation had to be managed, fed, watered, and cared for by skilled drivers. Though located to the rear of the front-line trenches, gunners were nonetheless exposed to enemy fire, and they might have to move in a hurry if the enemy zeroed in on their position. Artillery batteries were constantly on duty, firing in the nighttime as well as the day, and gunners had to be ready at any time to stand to their guns. Combined with physical exhaustion was the constant din that could fray a gunner's nerves and destroy his hearing.[9]

In April and early May, Brunel spent six days in the hospital being treated for dermatitis—eczema of the leg. This was a common condition in the wet and cold of the front, and it was potentially serious since it could easily become infected and lead to sepsis and death. He rejoined his unit in early May and remained at Dickebusch through July and August. During this time the 7th Brigade was engaged in constant firing, but it was not subjected to serious counter-fire. In late August, the 7th Brigade moved to the Somme, where it established a base at Pozières (opposite Regina Trench). On September 28, the 25th Battery sustained a direct hit: one man was killed, three wounded, and a gun was badly damaged, but Brunel seems to have escaped unharmed. Throughout October, the batteries were heavily engaged in support of the attack on Regina Trench. They stayed in place when the first three Canadian Divisions were withdrawn, in order to support the Fourth Division's attack on Regina and Desire Trenches. When they were finally relieved on November 27, the men were exhausted, having fought continuously for three months. The mud and snow made it impossible to move the guns—they were simply left behind for their replacements.[10]

After a few days' rest in good billets the 7th Brigade CFA moved to new positions in the British line to the north and west of Vimy. There, in December and January, they engaged in the usual fire and counter-fire on the enemy positions opposite. Then they were moved back to billets some 30–40 kilometres northwest of Arras, for a program of lectures and training, integrating new men, recovering their strength and fitness, and above all, learning the new artillery techniques that would be utilized at Vimy Ridge. Chief among these was the creeping barrage, in which an infantry attack was supported by waves of artillery fire which moved forward 100 metres every 3 minutes—an operation that required careful map-reading and calibrations, correction for the condition of the guns, wind, temperature and barometric pressure, precise timing, and accurate firing. The artillery was also reorganized, with fewer batteries, each having six guns instead of four. The 7th Brigade was abolished, and Brunel's 25th Battery, with two more guns added to it, joined the 6th Brigade CFA. About 30 men at a time were sent on leave, so it is likely Brunel had some break from his routine, perhaps in England. By the end of February, the 25th Battery was back in the line preparing for the major assault to come.[11]

The artillery barrage that preceded and accompanied the attack on Vimy Ridge was unprecedented—the Canadians poured a million shells into the German lines, knocked out 80 percent of the enemy's artillery, and inflicted on the Germans what they called the Week of Suffering.[12] But once Vimy was taken and the Canadians pressed their attack forward, the artillery could no longer remain dug in and static. The guns and their supply trains now had to move forward, in sleet and rain, under conditions so arduous that according to one witness, many horses "quietly laid down and died." Even worse, they were now out in the open and the Germans could exact their revenge. The Canadian batteries were shelled for days on end and on May 2 the commanding officer of the 5th Brigade CFA was killed by a direct hit on his HQ. "No one," recalled Bert Sargent, a gunner in a sister battery, "will forget the heavy shelling sustained in this position, especially with gas shell." Resupply could only be done at night and the area was drenched in gas and churned up by shells.[13] During this intense duel, sometime on May 3, Brunel was "killed in action." The Circumstances of Death Register gives no other details.[14] He was one of many casualties in a desperate fight. He was 20 years old.

Back in Ottawa, on June 28, 1916, Reginald's younger brother Ivan A. Brunel had been formally attested into the 207th Battalion, as a 13-year-old student who was "[t]aken on for Band purposes by Special Order of Col. MacLean." He was discharged in August, "[b]eing under-age for service." On January 7, 1916, his eldest sister, Hope Brunel, at age 23, had married Dr. John Léo Chabot, a physician, soldier, and Conservative MP, in a Catholic marriage performed by the Archbishop of Ottawa.[15] Two years later, Hope's 22-year-old sister Olive married Dr. Malcolm Graham, 26, a physician with the Canadian Army Medical Corps, at a Catholic church in Kingston, with the Chabots as witnesses.[16] Dr. Graham was a Presbyterian and would remain a member of MacKay all his life; his wife, Olive (née Brunel), would remain a Catholic.

After the war, Henry and Frances Brunel had their own child, John Erskine Brunel, in 1919. On February 9, 1921, the Session was informed that (following yet another round of dissatisfaction with its organist and choir director) Mrs. Brunel had been appointed, as from December 1, 1920, at a salary of $575 per annum, with one month vacation in July or August.[17] She remained at this post for a several years in the 1920s, then resigned. She returned for a second stint from 1936 until about 1956. During her first tenure as organist and choir leader the choir won the J. R. Booth Challenge Shields at the music festival then known as the Eisteddfod.[18]

Figure 15.2. MacKay United Church Choir, c. 1930.
This picture also shows the original front of the Sanctuary built in 1910, with organ and choir along a flat front, and the pulpit at the centre, all on a raised platform—all similar to the original church. In the 1950s this would be replaced by a recessed chancel extended into the old Sunday School hall.
Source: MacKay United Church.

In the 1920s the Brunels moved to the newly opened development of Lindenlea, where Henry died at age 68 on October 30, 1945. Frances then lived in the newly opened suburb of Manor Park where she taught piano privately at her home; she died in 1966. Léo Chabot did not run for parliament in the 1921 election, in which the Conservative Party was decimated, but he was elected in 1925, only to be defeated in the 1926 "King-Byng" election. He and Hope had no children and he died in 1928. Malcolm and Olive Graham had a house built at 251 Crichton Street where Dr. Graham settled into half a century of general practice. "It is estimated," said an article written about him late in his life, "that he has brought four or five generations of babies into the world." His waiting room was noted for its organization and Olive filled the home with antique furniture and prints. He remained a staunch member of MacKay Presbyterian/United Church and a close friend of its minister. In 1972 he was named a Member of the Order of Canada.[19] Olive died in 1974 and Malcolm in 1977. Ivan Brunel became a public servant, but remained a musician and was a life member of the Ottawa-Hull Federation of Musicians. He married, had one daughter, and died in 1986. Erskine Brunel also became a civil servant and left New Edinburgh; he married in 1952, had two children, and died in 1988.

Figure 15.3. Écoivres Military Cemetery.
Source: Photograph by Carolyn Bowker.

Figure 15.4. Écoivres Military Cemetery.
Source: Photograph by Carolyn Bowker.

Figure 15.5. Écoivres Military Cemetery, showing Brunel's headstone.
Source: Photograph by Carolyn Bowker.

Reginald Isambard Brunel is buried in Écoivres Military Cemetery near the town of Mont-Saint-Éloi. The cemetery was taken over from the French in 1915 and incorporates a French military cemetery that includes many North Africans whose headstones are in Arabic. It was used by the British during the fighting around Vimy from late 1916 into the summer of 1917, and in 1918. It is large, with 391 British, 830 Canadians, 787 French, a few other Commonwealth countries, and 4 Germans. Designed by Sir Reginald Blomfield, it is reached by a paved secondary road and is surrounded by maize fields and small farmhouses. Above it on a hill stands the towers of a ruined abbey, which was used as an observation post to study German gun positions as they prepared the attack on Vimy Ridge. When we visited on a foggy day in October 2015, the abbey seemed to watch over the cemetery like a ghostly presence. There are trees of different kinds around the perimeter, and flowers along the row of headstones, with neatly trimmed cone-shaped bushes at the end of every other row making a central pathway to the Great Cross. The row in which Brunel's headstone is found contains Canadians killed on May 3, 4, and 5, and one British Field Artillery gunner who fell about the same time, perhaps in the same artillery duel. At the bottom of Brunel's headstone, almost obscured by vegetation, is the inscription "Of Ottawa."

16

THE TUBMAN FAMILIES
"Conspicuous Gallantry and Devotion to Duty"

All the Tubman boys were athletes. Before the war, Reed, Leslie, and Ray Tubman were stars on New Edinburgh and Ottawa city teams in just about every sport there was, and their younger brothers Harry and Arnold would follow in their footsteps after the war. Ray was the person who got the young athletes of New Edinburgh up at six in the morning to go running in the grounds of Rideau Hall.[1] Their first cousin and next-door neighbour Elmer ("Joe") Tubman would lead the Ottawa Rough Riders to two Grey Cups in the 1920s. That the Tubmans should also be warriors seemed almost self-evident. Five of them would serve in the First World War. Leslie, "the indomitable ... hero of many hazardous enterprises," "the idol of his men,"[2] would die in battle. Ray would be wounded at Vimy Ridge and would later sign up for the Canadian Expeditionary Force to Siberia. Harry would fight, suffer a prolonged illness, and recover to fight again in the Hundred Days campaign. Their families would bear the strain and grief of war along with the glory of their sons' military and athletic achievements.

The two families that produced these soldiers were part of a large extended Tubman clan that had lived in New Edinburgh for many years. Thomas Tubman (1834–1895), a teacher, and his wife, Mary, had built a house at 53 Crichton Street in the 1880s and were well respected in New Edinburgh—Mary was especially renowned for always being ready to help others in times of sickness and trouble.[3] Their two sons, William John Tubman and Robert James Tubman, grew up in New Edinburgh and were both athletes and strong supporters of sports in the village.[4] The younger son, Robert Tubman, a painter or "finisher," for W. C. Edwards, built a house next door to his parents at 51 Crichton Street. There, he and his wife, Rebecca, had two children: Edith Mary (1895) and R. Elmer ("Joe," 1897). The elder son, William Tubman, a bookkeeper, moved in the 1880s to Chicago, where he met and married Jennie Watters (1867-1935). They had three children in Chicago: William Reed (1889), Leslie Watters (1891), and Thomas Raymond (1895). In 1896, after the death of his father, William Tubman moved his family back to New Edinburgh to live with his widowed mother at 53 Crichton Street. There they had three more children: Norman Harry (1897), Jean (1899), and Russell

Arnold (1904).[5] The two Tubman families living side by side thus had between them six boys and two girls.

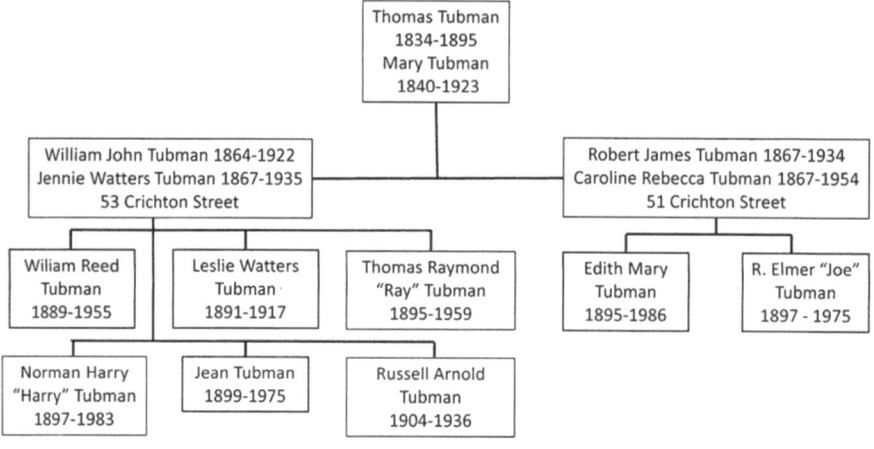

Tubman Family Tree

Figure 16.1. Tubman family tree.
Source: Created by the author.

Most of the extended Tubman family were Anglicans who attended St. Bartholomew's. Robert Tubman's family for a time attended St. David's Reformed Episcopal Church, and Joe Tubman is on that church's Honour Roll.[6] But William Tubman's wife, Jennie, was a member of MacKay Presbyterian Church and her husband attended as well. Three of their sons formally joined MacKay church before the war—Reed in 1907, Leslie in 1910, and Raymond in 1914—and the younger boys attended Sunday School. They were joined about 1909 by Robert Tubman's family, including Joe, who were among a number of families that moved from St. David's to MacKay. Rebecca Tubman became very active in the work of her new church.[7]

As befits the son of a schoolteacher, William Tubman ensured that all his children received an education. All attended Ottawa Collegiate Institute for at least a couple of years, including the only daughter, Jean, who graduated. High school fees ($30 per year in 1911) must have been a major strain on his modest income as a bookkeeper, first for the Ottawa *Free Press* and later for the Municipal Electric Department. After they left school, his older sons found work while they continued to excel at athletics.

Reed Tubman, the eldest, went to work as a salesman for the W. C. Edwards Company and was employed by this company and its successors in the lumber industry for over two decades. He was a renowned multi-sport athlete, a constant fixture on Ottawa, New Edinburgh, and other teams in hockey, lacrosse, rowing, and football. He was good enough to play with his neighbour Jack Ryan on the Ottawa Football Club, and he was especially gifted as a middle-distance runner—a newspaper article in 1912 wondered why he had not been selected for the Olympic team.[8]

The second son, Leslie Watters Tubman, was an honour student at OCI from 1906 to 1908. At five feet nine inches tall, he was "one of the most prominent athletes in the city, a crack middle-distance runner, and lacrosse and football player."[9] But after two years of high school, Leslie left to work in the Bank of Ottawa and was posted to its branch in Porcupine, Ontario, where in 1911 he suffered slight burns to his face when a fire consumed the town.[10] He returned to Ottawa and in 1913 joined the civil service as a clerk in the refunds branch of the Customs Department.

Ray Tubman, taller than his brothers at five feet ten inches, was "one of the best all-round athletes developed in Ottawa in years."[11] He, too, played for the Ottawa Football Club, as well as for New Edinburgh and YMCA teams, and was a distance runner, lacrosse, hockey and basketball player, and a paddler with the Ottawa New Edinburgh Canoe Club. After attending OCI, he joined the civil service as a clerk in the printing, stationery, and contingencies branch of the Department of Militia and Defence.

"Harry" Tubman was 17 when the war broke out, attending OCI and beginning to excel at athletics, even though he was smaller than his brothers, at five feet seven inches and 125 pounds. Jean, along with the youngest brother, Arnold, was a student at Creighton Street Public School in 1914; she would begin attendance at OCI the following year.

Their first cousin and next-door neighbour, Robert's son "Joe" Tubman, had taken work as a railway clerk with the Grand Trunk Railway after public school, and with the outbreak of war he became a clerk with the Imperial Munitions Board. He was beginning to make his mark in athletics in spite of his short (five feet five inches) but stocky build. His sister Edith Mary ("May") took the commercial course at OCI and won that school's prize for stenography in 1912. In 1913 she passed the civil service exam and became a stenographer with the immigration branch of the Department of the Interior.

Leslie Watters Tubman was the first of his family to enlist when war broke out. In August 1914, at age 22, he joined an Ottawa militia regiment that went to Valcartier to become the 2nd Battalion in the Canadian Expeditionary Force. After weeks of chaos—in a single day the battalion had five commanding officers—Tubman was formally attested on September 22, 1914.[12] On October 3, the 2nd Battalion sailed for England aboard the SS *Cassandra* and proceeded to Salisbury Plain for a miserable winter of training. In February 1915, as part of the First Canadian Division, the battalion crossed the channel and took up a front-line position in the Ypres Salient. In April, Tubman was promoted to lance corporal, just in time for the Battle of Second Ypres, which began on April 22. The 2nd Battalion was in reserve when the Germans made their initial gas attack, and it was sent in to relieve the front-line battalions that had borne the brunt of the assault. It was then engaged for a full week in almost continuous firefights. Whole companies were virtually wiped out and by the end of April, in the words of its historian, "[t]he battalion that had come into being at Valcartier, that had griped impatiently over disembarkation delays in Plymouth Sound, that had for months endured the exposures and privations of Salisbury plain, was now destroyed. [...] Only a small nucleus survived."[13]

Figure 16.2. Sam Hughes reviews 2nd Canadian Infantry Battalion, August 1916. By then, the 2nd had fought many battles and had been rebuilt several times.
Source: Library and Archives Canada PA-000716.

As part of this nucleus, Leslie Tubman was promoted to corporal on June 22. The 2nd Battalion was rebuilt and saw more action in 1915 and 1916 at St. Julien, Gravenstafel, Festubert, and Mount Sorrel. Tubman fought in every one of these battles and at the end of December 1915 he was promoted to sergeant. The steep price in lives is shown in a picture taken at Ploegsteert in

1915 and kept by family friend William Bothwell, on which is written, verso: "left to right. RG Haley killed in action, Les Tubman MC, killed in action; Sgt Maxwell RCM, wounded, Herb Michael, wounded."

Figure 16.3. Photograph of four soldiers at Ploegsteert; Tubman is second from left. *Source:* University of Toronto Archives, Robert Bothwell Fonds, Box 005 file 06.

In August 1916, the First Canadian Division moved to the Somme where, on September 9, it was ordered to attack German positions at Moquet Farm near Courcelette. Several companies of the 2nd Battalion took heavy losses capturing German positions, and then found themselves having to withstand counterattacks without reinforcements and running low on food, supplies, and ammunition. When the commanding officer of his company was wounded, Tubman was effectively in command under heavy fire until another officer was sent up to relieve him. "Sergeant Leslie Tubman did yeoman service," recounted the official history of the battalion, "practically directing all the efforts of No. 2 Company. [Captain] Chrysler had been borne back to the dressing station, but having complete confidence in Tubman, whose front-line experience was lengthier than that of the two subaltern officers who were left, the Company Commander had ensured that Tubman had been given complete knowledge of all that had to be done."[14] The battalion covered itself in glory, winning one Victoria Cross, but at a heavy price. When the survivors were relieved on September 10, it had lost over 200 men—one man killed or wounded for every metre it had advanced.[15]

In October 1916, the 2nd Battalion moved to the Vimy area, where it spent the following months absorbing reinforcements and replacing its lost officers. On November 12, 1916, sergeant Leslie Tubman was given a field promotion to lieutenant—a practice that was becoming increasingly common as the Canadian Corps evolved into a more professional force. He was then given a leave of absence and sent to England on a grenade course.

In February 1917, the Canadian Corps staged a number of trench raids on German positions at Vimy Ridge, designed to disrupt the enemy and capture prisoners to gain intelligence for the attack that was being planned. The 2nd Battalion staged such a raid on March 3, composed of two parties, one of which was commanded by Lt. Tubman. The men, their faces blackened and with no identification, crept across no-man's land into the German trench, supported by an artillery barrage. "They bombed to the right and left," says the battalion historian, "causing considerable damage and for 20 minutes remained in undisputed occupancy of the German line." The success of the operation was limited by the fact that no prisoners were taken.[16] As the date for the attack on Vimy Ridge approached, staff planners demanded more such raids. "The intrepid Leslie Tubman … never unresponsive to the call of hazardous duty … led bands of adventurers, not once but many times, through the fires of No Man's Land, raising havoc with enemy posts, penetrating into their trenches, and retaining possession until it suited the raiders to return in their own good time."[17]

Especially daring was a daylight raid organized by Lt. Tubman and an NCO on April 6. An account by one of the men, quoted in the official history, speaks for itself:

> At about 2:30 p.m. we assembled in an outpost of the front line and, after giving us some brief advice, Tubbie led us into No Man's Land, to a large mine crater. The far edge was some 50 yards from the German front line.
>
> Leaving the remainder of the squad there, he and Joe Simons crawled forward to the enemy trench. In a few minutes we heard a couple of shots, and Tubbie waved for us to come on. We did so, and found the German soldier whom Tubbie had disposed of, lying in the bottom of a trench, which was very deep. Jack Arnold extracted his papers, buttons, and shoulder straps for identification.
>
> We were supposed to have had a box barrage from the artillery, but it failed to materialize. Unfortunately for us a second man who had been in the German post had escaped and he obviously turned in the alarm, for within a few minutes we were attacked from each side of us simultaneously. Bombs exploded all around us, and to these we responded with heavy Mills No. 5s. Eventually we exhausted our supply, but Fritz had quite a store of 'potato-mashers' on the post, and these we used liberally.

Despite a machine-gun barrage from our front line, the Boches attacked overland from their support trench, as well as from the trench on either side. A bomb exploded at Pat Malone's feet, breaking both his legs, while Scotty McIntosh was also badly wounded. Tubbie ordered us to get out as quickly as possible. There were several steps leading up to a sniping post, and the boys scrambled up and over. Joe Simon, Gyp Doane, and Jim Campbell attempted to carry Pat and Scotty out, but Pat resisted:

"Get to hell out of here," he shouted.

Reluctantly we had to leave him, and we were able to reach the mine crater where we turned and sniped the Germans who had tried to follow us. Tubbie's "got that one!" "missed that guy" will never be forgotten. In the gathering darkness we succeeded in getting back to our own lines. The required information was obtained and the Battalion was relieved that night.[18]

This raid earned two of the survivors a commendation and a personal interview with General Currie, who outlined the plans for the great battle that would commence three days later. It also won Tubman a Military Cross "For conspicuous gallantry and devotion to duty." "On several occasions," read the citation, "he led patrols in the most gallant manner, and succeeded in obtaining most valuable information. He has on many occasions done fine work."[19]

As a reward for his bravery, Tubman was selected to sit out the attack on Vimy Ridge. The 2nd Battalion was not engaged in the initial attack but was scheduled to perform a mop-up role later in the morning of April 9. As the battalion began its assignment, Tubman was seen going into action with his platoon. When his major reprimanded him for disobeying orders, Tubman replied that he was not leading his platoon but was only there in an advisory capacity. In a letter to his father he said that he had not been in the battle but was looking forward to seeing action in a few days' time.[20] "No braver man had ever come to the western front," reported a fellow officer, Lieutenant Fred James.[21] But it is also difficult to avoid the conclusion that his long months at the front, and his survival against all odds, had bred in Tubman an addiction to derring-do and a killer instinct that made him an outstanding battlefield leader, but a very different person from the athletic young man who had left New Edinburgh to serve King and Country in the autumn of 1914.

After Vimy Ridge, the Canadians regrouped and pressed forward as part of the British Arras offensive. They took the village of Arleux, and then on May 3, 1917, the 2nd Battalion was given the task of spearheading the attack on Fresnoy, a few kilometres east of Vimy. In spite of careful planning and rehearsal, the Canadians would have to advance across open ground against heavily defended positions. A moon that set just before the jumping-off time allowed the Germans to see the assembling Canadians and disrupt

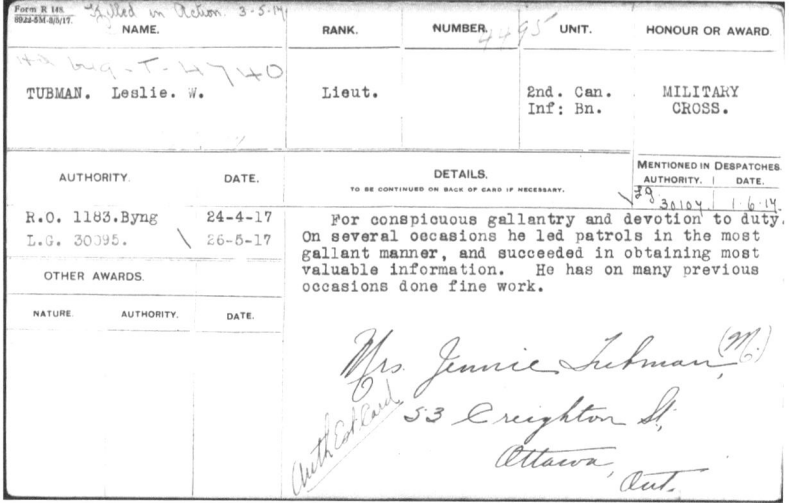

Figure 16.4. Leslie Tubman's Military Cross citation.
Source: Canada, Military Honours and Awards Citation Cards, 1900-1961 (file Toole, A. M. – Vail, William James).

their movements with shellfire. The Canadians' creeping barrage helped their attacking battalions to attain their early objectives, but a German counter-barrage then cut them off from reinforcements and forced them to fight it out all day without support. As Lieutenant James recounted: "Within an hour after we had gone over the Second Battalion had rounded up 300 prisoners, six machine guns and a considerable quantity of material. Poor 'Tubby' was hit with a machine gun bullet as we entered the village, but was not wounded badly, though it was too serious for him to continue. He was ordered back to one of the dressing stations and he started to go back alone. Just outside the village towards our lines he was hit by shrapnel and killed."[22] He was 25.

"To old members of the 2nd Battalion," says its official history, "the unit without 'Tubbie' was simply not the 2nd Battalion. More than anyone he was the symbol of that daring and hearty spirit which, spread widely through the ranks, gave the Battalion its character. There were still others of the Old Originals remaining … all of them belonging to that sphere which held up Tubbie as a shining example and acknowledged him as a moving spirit in the life of the Second."[23] The recovery of his body was recorded in the battalion's war diary. His friend Lieutenant James recounted this event to an Ottawa newspaper in terms that were presumably intended to be comforting and inspiring to the folks back home, even as late as 1917: "One of our men found him lying under the shade of some trees with a smile on his face, looking just as natural and happy as in life."[24]

The MacKay Register of Deaths mingled pride with sorrow: "Lieut. Leslie Watters Tubman, M.C. Killed in action May 3rd 1917, decorated April 1917 'for conspicuous gallantry and devotion to duty.'" Tubman was awarded the Military Cross, the 1914-15 Star, and the British War and Victory Medals with "Mentioned in Dispatches" emblem—the latter awarded posthumously for his gallantry in the battle in which he was killed.[25]

Figure 16.5. Leslie Tubman's medals, the Military Cross, British War Medal and Victory Medal, Victory Medal with Mentioned-in-Dispatches Oak Leaf.
Source: Private collection.

Leslie Tubman was buried with many other Canadians in a small cemetery near the battlefield, marked by a wooden cross. "All the officers of the 2nd Battalion and some from other units, as well as hundreds of the men, attended his funeral," wrote his friend Lieutenant James. "To do any service for Tubby's relatives and friends, any officer or man of the Second Battalion or among those who knew him, would be counted a privilege for he was one of the bravest and most courageous men, who has come to France. Few officers in this war have to their credit such a record of fine service as 'Tubby' as he was affectionately called by everybody."[26]

Meanwhile, Leslie's younger brother, Thomas Raymond Tubman, had enlisted on September 23, 1916, after serving for some months in the Duke of Cornwall's Own militia regiment. He qualified as an officer in the 139th Battalion, but resigned his commission to go overseas with a draft of the Cobourg Heavy Battery which was feeding replacements to artillery units in the Canadian Corps. He sailed for England in September and assigned $15 a month of his pay to the family. He was posted to the No. 1 Siege Battery, CFA, but on December 11, 1916, he transferred back to the infantry. In March

1917, he joined the 4th Battalion, as a lieutenant, at Vimy. His time at the front would last less than a month.

Figure 16.6. Ray Tubman.
Source: Canadian War Museum, Thomas Tubman Photo Album, Box 6. image cwm_tubman_20050110-009_portrait. ID 759, George Metcalfe Archival Collection.

In the Battle of Vimy Ridge on April 9, the 4th Battalion was assigned to the second wave of attack in the southern sector of the Ridge. It would advance over ground captured by the first wave—littered with the mangled bodies of Germans torn open by the barrage—and then attack in its turn.[27] By the end of the day, the 4th Battalion had attained all its objectives, but with heavy losses. Ray Tubman was wounded in the right hand. He was admitted to the No. 32 Stationary Hospital Wimereux, where he was probably operated on, losing his little finger and part of two other fingers. He was then sent to hospital in Norwich, England, and completed his recovery at the Canadian Convalescent Hospital in Woodcote, Epsom. On September 15, 1917, he sailed for Canada on the same ship he had arrived in a year earlier. There are two references in his service file to "special case" authorization for his being sent home but it is not clear what this refers to.

The third brother, Norman Harry Tubman, had enlisted as an 18-year-old student in the 50th (Queen's) Battery, Canadian Field Artillery in March 1916. After training in Kingston, the battery was sent to England in September 1916, where it was broken up. In January 1917, Harry was assigned to the 52nd Battery in the 13th Artillery Brigade, which was sent to France in August. He was a driver, in charge of a team of horses pulling guns or supply wagons. He assigned $20 of his overseas pay to his mother.

The 13th Brigade was assigned to support other artillery brigades as required, so Harry would have participated in the bombardments that preceded, accompanied, and followed the attack on Hill 70 in August 1917. At Passchendaele in October and November 1917, moving supplies, guns, and millions of shells in the thick mud, he would have experienced the horror recalled by a survivor, of facing an enemy "barrage that was constantly and accurately placed on the one main road, a road with deep sucking mud on either side, which formed a death trap for the animal that got into it." The Canadian artillery performed magnificently but the men grew so exhausted that they had to be rotated every 48 hours.[28]

On November 14, 1917, Harry Tubman reported to the 34th Field Ambulance with pains in his back, legs, and head, and "pyrexia of unknown origin," a lingering fever whose cause could not be determined. He was sent through a series of hospitals in France and England, and then to the Canadian Convalescent Hospital in Woodcote, England, where his brother Ray had also been. For over two months, no doctors could figure out what was wrong. He was a fit man who had withstood a punishing physical ordeal and his two or three pipes and 10 cigarettes daily were moderate for soldiers in the line. But doctors were detecting a tachycardia and what was described as "disordered action of the heart." He was clearly exhausted and perhaps suffering from battle fatigue.

Harry slowly recovered and by March 1918 he was fit enough to be discharged from hospital. On April 2 he resumed his duties as a driver with the 52nd Battery. With the rest of the artillery he went into training in the new techniques that would mark the Canadian advance in the Hundred Days. At Amiens, the Drocourt-Quéant Line, the Canal du Nord, Cambrai, Valenciennes, and Mons, the pattern was the same—massive firepower for days to soften up the enemy, a creeping barrage to support the infantry advance, directed counter-fire against enemy guns, firepower to break up counterattacks; move forward, repeat. The demand for ammunition and supplies, and the need to move the guns forward quickly, were intense, as was the risk from enemy fire. Harry Tubman went through all this for the remainder of the war, only to be hospitalized with a serious case of the Spanish Flu from November 1918 to January 1919.

Figure 16.7. Elmer "Joe" Tubman.
Source: De Wolfe 1919, 303.

Their first cousin and next-door neighbour, Elmer Tubman, known as "Joe," was working as a clerk with the Imperial Munitions Board when he enlisted at age 19 in the 72nd Battery CFA in September 1916. The battery trained at Petawawa and proceeded to England in April 1917, where it was broken up. Joe Tubman was then assigned to a series of clerical positions with artillery units in England, including orderly room clerk for the HQ Commander Royal Artillery at Witley, and clerk at the HQ of the 3rd Artillery Brigade. In that capacity he went to France in March of 1918 and remained there until the end of the war. He appears to have had an exemplary service record.

The war was hard on William and Jennie Tubman, with one son killed, one wounded, and one temporarily disabled by illness. Their oldest son, Reed, had attempted to enlist but had been turned down—in spite of his athletic ability he had problems with toes on both feet and needed glasses—and he was also exempted from conscription.[29] Reed managed the family's affairs and did what he could to spare his mother from anxiety until his brother Ray returned in September 1917 (a note on Harry's service file says that Ray, not his mother, was to be informed in case of casualty). Robert and Rebecca Tubman had an easier time of it—Joe was serving in England, and later in France at an assignment that was behind the lines, and May Tubman was well established as a public servant.

Figure 16.8. Reed Tubman; Ottawa Seconds Football Club (detail), QRFU Champions, 1912. *Source:* City of Ottawa Archives CA 002053.

Despite being turned down for military service, Reed Tubman continued his stellar athletic career. His brother Ray had resumed athletics even while convalescing in England, and once back and working at his old job, he plunged into sports with almost manic intensity. In late October 1917, playing for the civil service football team against the Ottawa Rough Riders, "Ray Tubman, still carrying a bandage around his right hand, which was wounded in France, showed brilliant form on the wing line, going down under Gerard's punts with remarkable speed." (Reed Tubman was playing the same position for the Rough Riders.)[30] John McElroy was also organizing a New Edinburgh team to compete in the same league, which would have included both Tubman brothers and Eddie Gerard, a MacKay man who would later be a Hall of Fame hockey player. And so it continued throughout the war, with Reed and Ray starring for hockey and football teams, paddling, and in track meets.

Then, in September 1918, with the war almost over, Reed Tubman was finally allowed to enlist as a lieutenant in the Canadian Engineers and was posted to St. Jean, Quebec, probably as a training officer (he was demobilized before the end of the year). The following month, Ray, who had sufficiently recovered from his wounds to seek further action, enlisted as a lieutenant in the Canadian Expeditionary Force (Siberia) and was sent for six months to Vladivostok. (This story is told in Chapter 24.)

After the war, as their surviving children resumed or established their careers, the older generation of Tubmans, who had played such a leading role in New Edinburgh, began to pass from the scene. William John Tubman's health declined, he left his home at 53 Crichton Street, and he died in 1922 at age 58 at the home of his son Reed.[31] Jenny left New Edinburgh and was "disjoined" from MacKay. In 1923 the matriarch of the family, Mary Tubman, died at 51 Crichton Street, aged 79. Robert Tubman died at age 66 in 1934. His wife Rebecca lived on at 51 Crichton Street with her unmarried daughter May; she died in 1954 and May retired the following year after 42 years in the public service.[32]

Reed Tubman continued to win athletic competitions well into his thirties. In 1919 he married, bought a house on Putman Avenue (a newly opened street in New Edinburgh), and had two sons and a daughter. After a variety of jobs, he spent the last 18 years of his career in the City Engineer's Department. He continued to be an active member of MacKay and was an active supporter of the YMCA, especially boys' camps; when he died at 65 in 1955 he was honoured by leading civic and sports personalities.[33]

Ray Tubman returned from Siberia in the spring of 1919, resumed his football career with the Ottawa Rough Riders, won a 15-mile canoe race with the Ottawa New Edinburgh Canoe Club, became Canadian champion in the half-mile run, and tried out for the Olympic team. Ever restless, he pulled up stakes in April 1920 and moved to a farm near Red Deer, Alberta, with two friends and his brother Harry.[34] The venture failed, and he moved to Calgary where he again played football, married, and had a daughter, and got a job in the theatre business. In 1925 he was hired by Famous Players, and after managing cinemas in several cities he returned to Ottawa in 1926 to become manager of the Regent theatre, and later the Imperial and Capitol theatres—then doing vaudeville as well as showing movies. He oversaw the transition from silent movies to sound—he is credited with showing the first "talkie" in Ottawa in 1928—and later to colour and wide screen. A dapper man with a perennial cigar, he had a capacity for making friends and helping people. He was noted for opening his theatres to local charities for fundraisers, setting up a disabled watchmaker in business in a theatre, and supporting down-and-out veterans. In 1936, he was appointed District Manager for Famous Players in Winnipeg, but he returned to Ottawa the following year to manage all its theatres in the region. He tried unsuccessfully to enlist in the Second World War and headed up a Victory Loan campaign. He was widely mourned when he died of a heart attack at 63 in 1959.[35]

Harry Tubman did not stay long in the west. He returned to Ottawa (but not to New Edinburgh), married, had a lengthy career in the public service, and died in 1983. The youngest brother, Arnold, went to Calgary in 1922, where he finished high school and was a star athlete in several sports. He too went into the theatre business but a serious illness—sarcoma of the spine—forced him to retire in 1932 at age 27. He returned to Ottawa and died at age 31 at the home of his brother Reed.[36] Jean Tubman completed high school and left for Toronto in 1919 to enter the Toronto General Hospital nursing training program. She too went west for a time, then settled in Kirkland Lake where she married and had two children.

Their cousin Joe Tubman returned to work for the Canadian National Railways, as chief clerk in the supervisor's office, until his retirement in 1962. In 1922, he was caught up in a small scandal regarding conversion by soldiers of military pay from British pounds to Canadian dollars but although there was a judgment against him, this affair did not appear to affect his reputation or standing in the community.[37] Joe had played many sports in New Edinburgh and overseas, but he came into his own as a star football player for the Ottawa Rough Riders for 13 seasons, as a halfback, fullback, and especially as a "brilliant kicker," leading the team to the Grey Cup in 1925 and 1926. After retiring as a player, he was a referee for 15 years and in 1970 he was inducted into the Canadian Football Hall of Fame, the Canadian Sport Hall of Fame, and the Ottawa Sports Hall of Fame. He married in 1921 and had a daughter. He died in 1975.[38]

After the war, Leslie Tubman's body was moved into the Ste. Catherine British Cemetery, designed, like so many others, by Sir Reginald Blomfield. It is located just behind what is now a housing subdivision in a suburb of Arras—in fact the cemetery is today reached by a laneway between two houses and a grass path behind back yards to the cemetery gate. It is small, with 339 graves including 314 British and 32 Canadians. A low stone wall marks it off from the houses at one end but on the other three sides it is surrounded by fields and trees. It descends in steps from the gate at the top to the Great Cross, which is on an elevated grass platform bordered by stone. There are a number of tall trees, well-kept grass, and rows of flowers in front of the headstones. Tubman is just in front and to the right of the Great Cross (fourth from the right in the first row in Figure 16.11), flanked on one side by a "Soldier of the Great War Known Unto God" and on the other by a British Seaforth Highlander, with several other Canadians in the same row. It is a quiet and secluded resting place for a man whose military career was so full of action, and whose family excelled on the playing field as on the battlefield.

Figure 16.9. Ste. Catherine British Cemetery.
Source: Photograph by Carolyn Bowker.

Figure 16.10. Ste. Catherine British Cemetery.
Source: Photograph by Carolyn Bowker.

Figure 16.11. Ste. Catherine British Cemetery.
Source: Photograph by Carolyn Bowker.

17 ERLAND DAURIA PERNEY
"Sorrow Which Is Almost Intolerable"

Erland Perney's father, Frank Perney, was a central figure in several of the institutions that gave New Edinburgh its cohesiveness and character: Creighton Street Public School, where he was principal from 1904 to 1912; the New Edinburgh Canoe Club, of which he was a founding member; and MacKay Presbyterian Church, where he was an Elder. Growing up in New Edinburgh, Erland Perney was an athlete like the Tubman brothers, with a bright future in front of him. Like Jack Ryan, he sought excitement, adventure, and danger in the air, and he paid the ultimate price. His family's ineffable grief at the loss of their only son was an experience shared by thousands of others.

Erland Perney was born on May 11, 1895, in Norwood, Ontario, where his father was a teacher. Three years later the family moved to Ottawa and Frank became principal of the Mutchmor Street Public School. In 1902 Frank earned his BA, and in 1904 he became principal of Creighton Street Public School, which had recently been enlarged and was soon to be enlarged again. There Frank Perney continued and enhanced the high degree of scholarship (as well as athletic prowess) for which the school was known. "Anyone can learn under Mr. Perney," a scholarship winner told a reporter in 1909.[1] In 1910 he received his Bachelor of Pedagogy degree from Queen's University.

Even before his appointment to Creighton Street Public School, Frank Perney had bought a house at 190 Rideau Terrace. There in 1902 a second child, Margaret, was born.[2] Frank's wife, also named Margaret, was a talented singer who appeared in many concerts and recitals at MacKay, and in 1915 she was a member of the Ottawa Select Choir. Perney's salary of $2,000 a year in 1911 gave him a certain social standing (and the ability to hire a maid), and his neighbours on Rideau Terrace included several prominent members of the community. Living in the house next door was fellow teacher (Dr.) J. H. Putman, who in 1910 was appointed Chief Inspector of Ottawa Public Schools. From then until his retirement in 1936, Putman would be the prime creator of what was widely considered one of the best public school systems in Canada.[3]

Frank Perney was a leading advocate for parks and other public improvements, and in 1912 he served for a year on the city council as alderman for

Figure 17.1. Erland Dauria Perney.
Source: Ottawa *Citizen*, March 10, 1919.

Rideau Ward. That same year he left Creighton Street Public School to become principal of Glashan Public School, one of the premier schools in Ottawa. He continued to reside on Rideau Terrace and remained an Elder at MacKay church, but his attendance became less regular and his wife was "disjoined" in 1909. (She may have attended St. Andrew's Presbyterian Church in downtown Ottawa, since E. D. Perney is also on the memorial plaque at that church.) In 1917 Frank Perney was an unsuccessful candidate for school inspector of Wentworth County near Hamilton. A "strong fight" was made for him, according to an Ottawa newspaper, "some of the controllers claiming that his familiarity with bilingualism would help him to handle any attempt at French propaganda here"—a reference to the school language issue that was then roiling Ontario politics.[4] Later that year he was appointed to the staff of the Normal School in Hamilton, and the family left Ottawa.

Erland Perney attended Creighton Street Public School, and then in 1908 he entered Ottawa Collegiate Institute. He was clearly intelligent, but although he got honours in his first year at OCI, his marks declined to Pass in the later forms.[5] He completed Grade 12 and went to work as a clerk with the health of animals branch of the Department of Agriculture. He continued to live at the family home on Rideau Terrace. Erland Perney was a star athlete—a fine football player, the winner of the first long-distance ski race organized by the Ottawa Ski Club in 1912, and a member of the Ottawa New Edinburgh Canoe Club. In 1915 he paddled stroke for the ONECC war canoe when it won the half-mile championship of Canada, and later that year he participated in a 200-mile race from Prescott to Kingston and then to Ottawa.[6]

On January 10, 1916, Erland Perney joined a militia artillery battery and from March to May he attended the Royal School of Artillery at Kingston, learning the rudiments of gunnery, horsemanship, and above all, discipline and the ability to command. He then went to Petawawa for further training. In July he was among a group of officers selected to proceed to England in response to a British request, and on August 30 he was attested as a 2nd Lieutenant in the 72nd Battery CFA.[7] Instead, however, on October 12, 1916, he was accepted as a candidate pilot in the Royal Flying Corps.[8]

Following heavy losses on the Somme, the RFC had broadened its recruiting efforts in Canada and was now laying the groundwork for the training camps that would, by the end of the war, produce thousands of Canadian and American pilots. Candidates were no longer required to have a pilot's license; instead, they would take a four-month training course at the flying school in Reading, England, to be commissioned if they were successful as 2nd Lieutenant Flying Officers. The RFC took 12 or 14 recruits from Canada in late September, 32 more in mid-October (which included Perney), and additional groups through the remainder of the year.[9]

Perney reached England on November 11, 1916, and arrived at Reading two days later. Although the RFC had recently made substantial improvements, pilot training was still far below any acceptable standard today.[10] On June 4, 1917, Perney was gazetted as a flying officer in the RFC Special Reserve (confirmed July 12). In September he was assigned to 11 Squadron, based at Bellevue, France, in the Arras Sector.

The 11 Squadron was flying the Bristol, a two-seat biplane fighter and reconnaissance aircraft. Its powerful engine (up to 200 horsepower in some models), which was located at the front of the plane, allowed it to fly faster and higher than its predecessors and carry a larger payload. Its stronger fuselage could take more punishment and its sleeker design permitted greater manoeuvrability and provided a better field of fire for the observer, who sat behind the pilot. It was armed with a Vickers machine gun synchronized with the propeller and a Lewis gun with a flexible swivel mount in the observer's cockpit. The first version of the Bristol had an inauspicious beginning when introduced in mid-1916, but once pilots and strategists understood how to use it, this aircraft became a mainstay of the RFC in the second half of 1917, and it was a big improvement over the planes that Jack Ryan had flown.

Figure 17.2. Bristol F2B Fighter aircraft of the Royal Flying Corps.
Source: Library and Archives Canada PA-006422.

The 11 Squadron was part of III Brigade Royal Flying Corps, whose assignment was to support the operations of the British Third Army. Through September and October 1917, 11 Squadron flew reconnaissance missions preparing for the Battle of Cambrai. The British commanding general, Sir Julian Byng (who had been promoted from commanding the Canadian Corps), applied some innovative approaches in this battle, including the use of massed tanks, hurricane bombardment without warning, and coordinated air support to report troop movements and disrupt the enemy by bombing and strafing assembly points, artillery, reinforcements, and trenches. The 11 Squadron's reconnaissance role required virtually continuous flying as long as weather permitted.

The battle began on November 20, 1917. Perney had a narrow escape when his plane was shot up after he lost his way returning from a reconnaissance mission. He and his observer landed safely, but the engine and much of the gear was a write-off and the air frame had to be sent back for rebuilding.[11] The battle went well for the British at first. But by November 23, the attack had stalled and the Germans had brought up extensive reinforcements. At Bourlon Wood, a German strong point bristling with interlocking defences and fortifications, attacking British troops were pinned down by artillery and machine gun fire. Between morning and dusk, four

British squadrons totalling over 50 aircraft flew in relays over the German lines, attacking as many low-level targets as they could find in support of the British infantry.

But the Germans had also reinforced their air defences in the sector. Von Richthofen had taken personal charge, and his "flying circus" and other squadrons of single-seat aircraft began to take a heavy toll on British planes. On November 23 alone, III Brigade lost 26 air crew, wounded or missing.[12] Perney and his British observer, Lieutenant Ewan Blackledge, were among them. They were dropping propaganda leaflets—a strange occupation in the midst of a serious battle, but one that may have had serious consequences, as we shall see—when their squadron was attacked by German aircraft. "With other aviators," read the official report, "[Perney] flew over the German lines at Arras on Nov. 23, 1917 and 'failed to return' – he was last seen over Cambrai."[13] He was 22.

Perney and Blackledge were reported missing, but initially there was hope. Witnesses on the ground and fellow pilots insisted that Perney's plane had gone down under control behind the German lines and that they would therefore probably have been taken prisoner. In May 1918, a Canadian officer in 11 Squadron reported, apparently to the Perney family, that a German airplane had dropped a message that Perney and Blackledge were prisoners, and in August it was rumoured that the Germans had included Perney and Blackledge in their monthly bulletin of prisoners. Later in the fall, Perney's flight commander, Captain McKeever (a flying ace from Listowel, Ontario, who had notched 31 victories in the Bristol), visited the Perneys when on leave in Canada, and he also called on the Deputy Minister of Militia and Defence, urging them not to give up hope. He suggested that the Germans might have decided to punish the two men for dropping propaganda by locking them away and denying all access to outside communication. Frank Perney wrote to Ottawa in November repeating this theory, and his letter was duly passed to the British.[14] The Deputy Minister weighed in with a request to the British authorities for investigation.[15]

McKeever knew whereof he spoke. In the autumn of 1917, as heavy losses and hardships began to erode morale in the German army, British aviators were dropping thousands of leaflets showing German prisoners of war being well treated in England, in contrast to what the soldiers had been told would be their fate if they surrendered. This appears to have had some success, and it certainly got under the Germans' skin, as the German High Command proclaimed that they would shoot or hang any aviator caught carrying propaganda. On October 17, two flyers from Perney's squadron were shot down near Cambrai dropping leaflets. They were tried by a German civilian court, found "guilty of treason," and sentenced to 10 years' hard labour in the ordinary German prisons. When the British threatened reprisal, the Germans relented and sent the men back to their prisoner of war camp. Perney and Blackledge were thus taking a great risk, whether they knew it or not, and within months the British had curtailed this practice—many British flyers were reluctant to perform what they considered a non-essential and demeaning, as well as dangerous, task.[16]

By the fall of 1918, all the rumours that Perney and Blackledge were prisoners had been disproven and the British War Office concluded, based on past experience, that they should be declared dead. As a first step, they asked Mrs. Perney to confirm that Erland had not been in contact with the family. But she refused to entertain the possibility that he might not be still alive. "I fully understand owing to the long length of time," she wrote the War Office on September 7, 1918, "that something must be done officially, but I know positively of six officers at least who were missing longer than my son, & were found to be alive in Germany. [...] I also know of two others (Canadians) who were missing 7 months. [...] I have letters from five of the six who were with my son on his last flight, & they all think he landed safely & is alive." A week later she asked the British not to send his effects to Canada but to keep them for him in England, as he would need his clothing when, as she was confident, he turned up as a POW.[17]

The War Office was undoubtedly sensitive to pressure from Canada, and there was also pressure from a British source: the father of Ewan Blackledge. The Blackledge family were prominent bakers and confectioners in the small town of Bootle, near Liverpool. After public school education and officer training, Blackledge had been sent to the front with the King's Liverpool Regiment and in 1917 had transferred to the Royal Flying Corps. His father was determined to get information, and he was not a man to be put off.[18]

On October 4, the War Office replied to Mrs. Perney that "there is no desire to proceed to official acceptance of an officer's death on the ground of length of time contrary to the wishes of his relatives. While [...] there can, it is feared, be no hope that he is still alive, an enquiry is now being sent through diplomatic channels to the German government in order to see if any information concerning him can be obtained."[19] The same promise was made to Ewan Blackledge's father. A memo was dispatched to the Prisoners of War Department, which sent a message to the British Legation in The Hague, which contacted the Netherlands Legation (British Section) at Berlin, which sent a note to the Prussian Ministry of War. The war had ended when the report came back through the embassy and the POW Department that there was no information on the two airmen, and the British authorities so informed both sets of parents.[20]

Meanwhile, Blackledge had grasped at another possibility. On November 23, 1918, a note appeared in the "In Memoriam" section of the London Times: "To an UNKNOWN AIRMAN, shot down 23rd November 1917, whilst attacking a German strongpoint south-west of Bourlon Wood, in an effort to help out a company of the Royal Irish Rifles, when other help had failed." During this furious day of battle, when a unit of the 10th Royal Irish Rifles had become trapped in an exposed position under heavy German fire, a British plane had repeatedly strafed German troops and saved many British lives. The officer who posted the note wanted to thank the airman for his sacrifice and to ensure it was not forgotten. Blackledge contacted this officer who provided more details, including that the pilot had crashed and was probably killed instantly. Undaunted, Blackledge wrote the War Office asking for information on all the planes missing on that day. Unfortunately, there were quite a few.

In January 1919, the War Office responded that the plane referred to in *The Times* note was a single-seater and that official reports showed that the Perney-Blackledge plane had gone down under control. But Blackledge persisted. The officer, he said, only *thought* the plane was a single-seater; he also thought it might have been a Bristol, so there was room for further investigation. "It would not only relieve me," he wrote, "but might enable someone else to identify the airman referred to." In April 1919, the War Office reported that the only two planes lost on November 23 which could not be accounted for by the repatriation of personnel were one single-seater and Perney's plane, which was a two-seater.[21] But if Perney's and Blackledge's plane had crashed they were certainly dead. (It was later established that the plane in question was a DH.5 from 68 [Australian] Squadron, piloted by an American.)[22] Blackledge therefore accepted that the plane referred to was not his son's and reverted to hoping that Ewan would turn up as a prisoner in Germany. In the meantime, however, Blackledge had written Frank Perney with his account of the "heroic death" of the two airmen, and Perney had written to his friend John McElroy (brother-in-law of Jack Ryan) with this account. McElroy provided this letter to the Ottawa *Citizen,* which published it on March 10, 1919, with the comment from Perney that although his wife would likely disagree, such a death was better than languishing in a Hun prison. This report was widely circulated in Ottawa.[23]

By the time this letter appeared in the press, however, the Perneys had come to accept that their son was dead and that "there is no longer any need of asking you [the War Office] to withhold the official announcement to that effect."[24] In order to settle his son's insurance, Frank asked the War Office to secure from McKeever (now a major) a statement that Perney had been unmarried.[25] This request was complied with and Frank also wrote McKeever directly to ask whether his son had left a will.[26] The Department of Militia and Defence in Ottawa asked the British War Office to issue a certificate of death.[27] The Air Ministry offered the family its condolences and began the process of treating Perney as killed in action (including the marginal notation "King" to trigger the appropriate certificate signed by King George, a copy of which is posted in Perney's entry in the Canadian Virtual War Memorial). But it also assured the families that Perney's and Blackledge's names would be kept on a special list of missing airmen about whom continuing enquiries would be made.[28] With the war over and peace negotiations under way, perhaps the Germans would now be more forthcoming. In addition to diplomatic channels, parallel enquiries were made in Berlin involving the German Society of the Red Cross. However, on June 10, 1919, the Netherlands Legation (there were still no formal diplomatic relations between Britain and Germany) reported that "although thorough inquiries have been made, nothing has become known regarding the fate of Lieutenant E. J. Blackledge and Lieutenant E. D. Perney, Royal Flying Corps."[29]

Now began for the Perneys the further ordeal of winding up Erland's affairs, in which Frank Perney's respectful and even-tempered correspondence with the War Office nonetheless reflected his frustration. The War Office had concluded that Erland Perney was dead. But his body had not been recovered, nor had his death been certified by British military authorities in the field, nor had the Germans provided any official information as to his fate. Therefore, no official death certificate could be issued. Instead, the War Office provided to Militia and Defence in Ottawa a formal statement that there was no chance that Erland Perney was alive and that it was acting on this presumption. Not good enough, said a Canadian probate judge when Perney presented this letter; an official certificate was needed. Perney pleaded with the War Office: "Now that there is no chance whatever that he is alive, the sooner we can make a complete separation of the past from the future, the sooner will my wife's sorrow begin to become alleviated."[30] A flurry of memos ensued within the War Office, and a letter was dispatched to Militia and Defence in Ottawa on July 11, 1919 that repeated the formal statement that for official purposes Perney was dead. But the judge still refused to settle Perney's insurance claim without an official certificate.[31]

In August, Frank Perney once again addressed the War Office: "My son declared that his mother Mrs. F. E. Perney should be the beneficiary of his insurance. The delay and the technical obstructions to carrying out his wishes only add to her sorrow which is already almost intolerable. Therefore I am asking you to furnish me with a statement or certificate of death in such a form as will satisfy the Judge and enable him to issue the necessary Letters of Administration." "The loss of our only son, as you are doubtless aware," he continued, "has been a terribly hard one to bear; more especially so from the uncertainty of this kind of casualty. You are buoyed up with hope and alternately cast down with despair until you feel that the strength to suffer such unspeakable anxiety is completely exhausted."[32]

In September 1919, the War Office responded with an assurance that a letter to his mother from Erland Perney, as a soldier going to the front, stating that he intended to leave all his effects to her, was accepted as the equivalent to a will. It then advised Perney that in 1916 the High Court of Justice in England had ruled "that when it is certified by the War Office that a soldier, previously reported missing, is considered for official purposes dead" the appropriate court should accept this as sufficient to settle an estate. "It is possible that the refusal of the Canadian Legal authorities to accept the letter may have been due to their lack of knowledge of the procedure adopted in the United Kingdom and of the general acceptance of letters such as those addressed to you and to the Canadian Department of Militia and Defence."[33]

This appears to have broken the logjam, as there is no further correspondence about the insurance. Erland Perney's accounts were duly tallied up in London, and Margaret Perney received his estate of a little over a hundred pounds from Militia and Defence in Ottawa. She also received his personal effects: a log book, two boxes of correspondence, a notebook, a wallet, a safety razor with case, a pipe with case, a charm, a knife, and a chequebook. In 1921, Mrs. Perney would receive his Memorial Cross for service in the RAF, as well as the certificates from the King.[34] A year after the war ended, two years after Erland disappeared, the Perneys could at last begin to heal.

Not so Blackledge, who continued to resist all attempts to declare his son dead.[35] Finally, on November 29, 1919, the War Office pulled the plug. "A long period of time has elapsed since the conclusion of hostilities," it informed Blackledge, "and experience has shown that no Officer, who has been missing for so long, (and of whom no news has been received), can have survived." The Army Council was thus "regretfully constrained to conclude that Second Lieutenant Blackledge died on or since 23rd November, 1917, and I am to express their sympathy with you in your bereavement."[36]

Perney and Blackledge were never found or traced. What had happened to them? There are many possibilities, but it is not improbable that the Germans carried out their threat to execute captured aviators who were carrying propaganda, on the spot or later following a trial, and the matter was then hushed up. We will likely never know.

Erland Perney is memorialized on the Flying Services Memorial in the Faubourg d'Amiens Cemetery, in Arras. This large cemetery, situated just off a ring road on the outskirts of Arras, was designed by Sir Edwin Lutyens. A wall closes off the cemetery from the busy road. The Cross of Remembrance actually sits outside the wall on the street, and behind it an open arch invites visitors into the carefully tended cemetery with its thousands of headstones.

Figure 17.3. Faubourg d'Amiens Cemetery, Arras, France, showing the Arras Memorial and the Flying Services Memorial, to the right.
Source: Photograph by Carolyn Bowker.

But the main feature is the Arras Memorial, a cloister built upon Doric columns, which faces west. On its wall are carved the names of almost 36,000 British and Commonwealth soldiers who fell in the Arras Sector between mid-1916 and August 1918 with no known graves. In the broader part of the site the colonnade turns to form a U-shaped recessed court, with the Stone of Remembrance forming its fourth side.

In the centre of this court is the Memorial to the Flying Services, also designed by Lutyens. This monument consists of a square pedestal and obelisk, at the top of which are badges of the Royal Naval Air Service, the Royal Flying Corps, and the Royal Air Force, as well as the combined badges of Canada, Australia, New Zealand, and South Africa. Atop the obelisk is a four-and-a-half foot, three-tonne sculpture by Sir William Reif Dick depicting a globe surrounded by wings. This globe, said Air Marshall Lord Trenchard in dedicating the memorial in 1932, "stands exactly, with its North and South points, as our globe hung in space on the morning of Armistice Day 1918. On every anniversary of that morning it will recall the sacrifice that these kinsmen of ours made, winning infinite peace for themselves in the struggle to win peace for their country, and it will catch, however faintly, the warmth of the sun that shone down that day on the trenches of the Arras Front,

Figure 17.4. Flying Services Memorial courtyard.
Source: Photograph by Carolyn Bowker.

when at last no longer on the airman's wings."[37] On the sides of the pillar are the names of 934 British, 47 Canadian, 10 Australian, 2 New Zealander, 1 South African, and 6 Indian airmen in the flying services who have no known graves—including Perney and Blackledge. The majority of those on the monument (more than 500) were lost in the final year of the conflict.

Frank Perney continued as a lecturer at the Normal School in Hamilton and then became a school inspector. He retired in 1935 and died in 1947. He had remained an Elder at MacKay after his departure from Ottawa, but as he was no longer attending the church, the Session wrote him in January 1921 to ask whether he wished to be removed from the roll or receive a certificate of disjunction. Perney responded expressing his kind wishes to the minister, Session, and congregation, and was duly issued a certificate of disjunction.

The Perneys' daughter, Margaret, who had attended Ottawa Collegiate until 1917, completed high school in Hamilton, attended Osgoode Hall, and became a lawyer in 1927—one of a very small number of women lawyers in the 1920s. After articling in Hamilton, she moved to Toronto where she was employed by the Ontario Farm Development Board. In 1931–1932 she served as president of the Women Lawyers Association of Ontario

Figure 17.5. Flying Services Memorial; Perney's name is in the left-hand column about one-third of the way from the bottom. *Source*: Photograph by Carolyn Bowker.

(WLAO), formed in 1921 to further the interests of women lawyers and secure equal treatment in the Law Society of Upper Canada. In the 1930s the WLAO went to bat for three women lawyers who were laid off by the Ontario government because their income was deemed non-essential to their families, and in 1940 she went into practice on her own. She served again as president of the WLAO in 1939–1940. In 1950 she was appointed King's Counsel, the only woman among 39 nominees that year. She lived in Toronto, sharing apartments and houses with her mother after her father's death, and she never married.[38]

In 1919, Frank Perney and William Tubman, who had been pioneers in the New Edinburgh Canoe Club, donated the Perney-Tubman Challenge Trophy, for the half-mile war canoe championship of the northern division, Canadian Canoe Association. The trophy was to commemorate the lives of their sons, Erland Perney and Leslie Tubman, who had competed many times for the club and had won prizes in this race; they had last paddled together in 1914, just before Tubman went off to the war that would claim his life.

Figure 17.6. 1924 ONECC War Canoe team. Many of the young athletes who served in the First World War, including Perney and the Tubman brothers, competed for the Ottawa New Edinburgh Canoe Club in teams like the one shown here.
Source: City of Ottawa Archives CA1226.

The cup was to be open for competition for 10 years, at which time it would become the property of the club that had won it most frequently during that time.[39] Perney was a teacher and Tubman a teacher's son. In honouring their sons in this way, they may well have had in mind a poem that was widely known in their day, A. E. Housman's "To An Athlete Dying Young":

> Now you will not swell the rout
> Of lads that wore their honours out,
> Runners whom renown outran
> And the name died before the man.
>
> So set, before its echoes fade,
> The fleet foot on the sill of shade,
> And hold to the low lintel up
> The still-defended challenge-cup.

In 1929 the Ottawa New Edinburgh Canoe Club was permanently awarded the trophy and it is now in their possession.

Figure 17.7. Perney-Tubman Trophy.
Source: Ottawa New Edinburgh Canoe Club.

18   A CHURCH AT WAR
1918

The winter of 1918 was a dark time for the people of MacKay Presbyterian Church. The war had dragged on for three and a half years, with frightful losses. Passchendaele had strained morale among the British and Canadian forces, and now the Germans were moving hundreds of thousands of troops from the east to the Western Front. At home the conscription crisis had divided Canadian society. There was rationing, scarcity, and a shortage of coal to heat their homes. The cost of living was skyrocketing. Despite the fact that separation allowances were raised to $25 a month in December 1917 (and would be raised to $30 in September 1918), numerous studies were showing that women with children now needed far more than their husbands had made before the war just to survive.[1] Would the hardship and sacrifice never end?

The Presbyterian Church in its press editorials and General Assembly resolutions continued to affirm that this war must be seen to the finish, and that the church must continue with equal zeal its mission of evangelism and social reform. Increasingly it stressed the need to combat war-weariness and despair through prayer, and to maintain a constant faith that victory would bring Christian regeneration to a suffering country and peace to a broken world. Some Protestant churches and clergy translated this vision of a nation redeemed and purified by the sacrifice of war into utopian pronouncements and radical politics. But there is no evidence that such beliefs took hold to any great degree at MacKay church. The emphasis remained, as it had been throughout the war, on ensuring the victory of righteousness, in the name of God, King, and Country, keeping faith with the God who, steadfast and sure, was "keeping watch over Israel."

That religion was still central to the lives of many recruits was shown when the chaplain at the Rockcliffe military base informed Rev. Anderson that several soldiers in training, probably conscripts, "desired to become members of the Presbyterian Church before going overseas and there was no time for them to go home." Anderson consulted some members of the Session and asked that the soldiers come to MacKay on July 18, 1918, when they were received into full communion in the Presbyterian Church, with some Elders and the chaplain present. They were not enrolled as members of MacKay church, but their names were sent to the churches they had attended in their hometowns. This extraordinary procedure (at least for the Presbyterian Church) reflected the continuing need of many soldiers to affirm their religious faith as they prepared to journey overseas to risk death on the battlefield.[2]

In February 1918, the Ladies' Aid provided supper and a program of music to the soldiers who were still in barracks. "Patriotic work undertaken this year," read their Annual Report, "consisted of taking the tea every second Wednesday during the winter at the Women's Canadian Club, making forty-two suits of pyjamas and knitting 15 pairs of socks." In April, Mrs. Anderson's character sketch "Aunt Susan's Visit" was performed with great success. But other events the Ladies had planned for the spring had to be cancelled—there was too much to do. Meanwhile the Managers and Elders were busy conducting the routine business of the church: discussing a new constitution for the church; managing yet another upheaval in the choir and appointing a new music director; making plans to retire the debt; and most urgently, securing a supply of coal. The Session paid special attention to re-constituting the Boy Scout troop so that it would no longer be directly controlled by the church but would continue its close association with it.

But in March, urgent news from Europe once again intruded. In late March, the Germans launched a great offensive and, in a repetition of 1914, swept past British forces and threatened once again to push on to Paris. Canadian mobile machine gun and cavalry brigades helped to slow down this assault and gave the British time to regroup, but this heroism cost the life of another MacKay soldier. "Lance Corp. Homer [sic] Joliat," recorded the Death Register, "died of wounds in No 2 Hospital Amiens in France, March 24th, 1918. A brave soldier, having won the Military Medal." Another MacKay man, Sidney Mansell, was among a handful of survivors in the battle in which Joliat was killed. A week earlier the Death Register had recorded that John Marshall, "a brave soldier" who had left Ottawa in 1915 to join the British Army Service Corps as a driver/mechanic, and had served in Egypt, had died in a hospital in Scotland. A "certificate of disjunction" was granted to his widow living in Perth—neither of them would be back again.

Only nine men from MacKay church enlisted in 1918. Three were volunteers, three were conscripts, and three signed up in the last days of the war for the Canadian Expeditionary Force (Siberia) (see Chapter 24). This number does not include **Robert Finter**, who enlisted, for the fourth time, in the Canadian Ordnance Corps HQ detachment, on July 18. This time he suffered intestinal problems, Spanish Flu, and more endocarditis, which required a stay in the Fleming Hospital. After an uncharacteristically generous assessment by a medical board that his disabilities were caused by overseas service, he was discharged with a pension in November.

Of the three volunteers, **Henry Warren Ferguson**, a clerk six months shy of his eighteenth birthday, whose father was a druggist, enlisted in March and served in Canada in a railway construction unit, and other special services; **William Harold Milne**, 20, who had come to Canada from England in 1916 with (in spite of his young age) extensive experience in British shipbuilding, and was working in the marine department of the Imperial Munitions Board, enlisted in April in the 74th battery of Canadian Field Artillery and went to Kingston for training; and **William Reed Tubman**, 31, who had been earlier turned down, enlisted in September 1918 as a lieutenant in the Canadian Engineers and was posted to St. Jean, Quebec.

Of the three conscripts, **John Gordon Hughes**, 30, a carpenter, and **James Wallace McPhail**, 26, a resident of Eastview, were conscripted into the 1st Depot Eastern Ontario Regiment; and **Frederick Munro**, 34, a junior civil servant with militia experience who had probably been the primary support for his mother and aunt (and had a systolic heart murmur), was conscripted for the new 2nd Tank Battalion. Hughes was discharged in November 1918 after training in Kingston; McPhail and Munro fell victim to the Spanish Flu on their troopships to England (McPhail was "dangerously ill") and both took months to recover.

The German offensive in March and April pushed the British back but it did not break through. The Germans then attacked the French, who, stiffened by growing numbers of American troops, also bent but did not break. Though they made one last, futile attempt at a breakthrough in July, it was clear the German army was exhausted. It was now the Allies' turn. After a few months of regrouping, re-equipping, training, and planning, they launched an offensive on a broad front. On August 8 at Amiens, Canadian troops pushed the German line back eight miles in what General Ludendorff later called "The Black Day of the German Army." Thus began the Hundred Days of rapid Allied advance toward victory, during which the Canadians relentlessly pressed forward on the Arras front, fighting battle after battle, with less and less of the meticulous preparation and planning, or the "bite and hold" tactics, that had marked their previous campaigns. In a series of battles in late August and early September, they broke the formidable Drocourt-Quéant defensive line, crossed the Canal du Nord on September 26–27 in a brilliant tactical feat, and pushed on to take Cambrai, which the British had failed to capture the previous autumn. From there they pursued the retreating Germans to Mons in Belgium, where the British had suffered their first defeat in 1914. The Canadians had just taken the city when the Armistice was declared on November 11.

As many as 34 MacKay men were likely involved in the Hundred Days. Only nine of these were in infantry (including motor machine gun) battalions, while 19 were in the artillery—a fact that illustrates the attrition and declining recruitment in infantry battalions and the greater popularity (at least among MacKay men) of the artillery in 1916 and 1917. The remainder were in cavalry or horse artillery units serving with the British Army, in Signals, and in Engineering.

The Canadians had won great victories, a lasting reputation as soldiers, and a place for their country in the world. But, once again, this came at a frightful cost, as chronicled in the MacKay Death Register. "Pte. Irwin Kelly killed in action in France Aug 31st 1918. Word received by his parents Sep 15th, 1918." "Sgt A. MacKenzie [sic] – killed in action in France, Aug [actually September] 27th 1918. Son of Mr A. MacKenzie [sic], Victoria St. Ottawa."[3] Clifford Erskine's lungs were destroyed by a phosgene and mustard gas shell in September in the attack on the Drocourt-Quéant Line. John Askwith was wounded at Amiens; Archie Jardine at the Canal du Nord; Angus Edwardson and Arthur Henry Sproule at the Drocourt-Quéant Line. Archibald McLaurin and James Cairncross were injured in October while serving with the cavalry. With the war about to end, Gordon Munro was wounded in the hand by a shell explosion.

Wounded soldiers continued to return throughout the year. Some, like George English, had never made it overseas: he had contracted pneumonia in Halifax while helping with relief and clean-up after the 1917 explosion, and had returned to Ottawa where he was discharged in June after months of convalescence. John Powers arrived home in March after almost two years of hospital treatment in England for severe wounds suffered at St. Eloi in April 1916. Norman Willson had undergone a year's convalescence after his hip had been severely injured by a blow from a shell casing in October 1916. John Simpson was shipped home after a year of hospitalization for double pneumonia contracted at the front. Thomas Isaac Jackson arrived in May after his health collapsed in France (see Chapter 8). George Sayles, an overage soldier who had been assigned to the railway troops, had suffered acute nephritis from heavy labour in damp conditions. By the end of the war, about one-third of the men on MacKay's Honour Roll were in Canada, of whom 21 had returned to New Edinburgh. This included five men still recovering in the Fleming Hospital. They, and their families, community, and church now had to adjust to each other.

By this time New Edinburgh and MacKay Presbyterian were facing their own immediate ordeal. For six terrifying weeks, from late September to early November, the Spanish Flu held Ottawa in its thrall. The virus had come into Canada from Boston, and it spread rapidly across the country, especially on troop trains, as the medical science of the time had little idea how to cure or contain it. Most people suffered only mild illness, or perhaps a high fever and severe debilitation for a week or two. But for some, death came within hours from suffocation or cyanosis. Many more contracted pneumonia and died within 10 days or 2 weeks. The Spanish Flu did not kill only the very young and the elderly, or those with respiratory diseases like tuberculosis. It claimed its greatest number of victims among healthy people between ages 18 and 45.

The Flu was especially deadly to people in the poorer districts in Ottawa like Lowertown, where people lived in crowded conditions, suffered from poor ventilation and air pollution, worked long hours, and in many cases already had chronic illnesses. New Edinburgh was not as bad, but the presence of many people in small houses, and air pollution from the railways and sawmills, had already produced a high incidence of tuberculosis and respiratory disease. But the Flu also reached into middle-class homes, leaving no one unscathed.[4] In the register of Beechwood Cemetery (which drew from a much wider area than New Edinburgh), out of about 200 entries between the middle of September and the end of November 1918, at least 105 are of people in their 20s and 30s who died of influenza or pneumonia; of the 55 deaths recorded on a single page between October 5 and October 15, 48 were from influenza or pneumonia. Some people stayed in their houses, avoided crowds, prayed; others plunged into nursing family members, volunteering to help others, bringing comfort where they could. Women were encouraged to take up caring for the sick as they would war work. "Knitting socks for soldiers is very useful work," said Mayor Harold Fisher, "but we are now asking the women of Ottawa to get into the trenches themselves."[5]

MacKay Presbyterian Church was closed for five weeks as part of the city's plan to prevent the spread of disease. The minutes of the Session record only that this closure made normal church work impossible. There is no mention of the tragic deaths in the community, or to the visits to stricken homes that Rev. Anderson and the physicians in the congregation must have frequently made. There seem to have been only two deaths from influenza during these months among the MacKay congregation, but these included a soldier whose name would appear on the Honour Roll. On October 26, 1918, the Death Register recorded that "Pte. A.F. Hawke died in hospital at Kingston was buried in Beechwood on October 28th by Rev. P. W. Anderson." His story is told in Chapter 23.

Two weeks after Reverend Anderson buried Arthur Hawke, the war that only a few months before had been predicted to last until at least 1920, suddenly ended. In the wee hours of the morning, on November 11, 1918, church bells rang out all over Ottawa and people spilled into the streets in the middle of the night in an outburst of spontaneous joy.[6] On the following Sunday the congregation of MacKay Presbyterian gave thanks in a church newly reopened after the Spanish Flu epidemic. "Now that the black cloud of war hanging over us so long, has disappeared," wrote Margaret Askwith in the Ladies' Aid annual report for 1918, "might we not go forward with

258 A Church at War

Figure 18.1. "The Morning of Armistice Day, The Plazza [sic], Ottawa, 1918"; silver gelatin photograph. *Source:* Bytown Museum, P2041.

greater confidence to bigger and better things."⁷ Time would tell. For the moment, the people of MacKay Presbyterian Church, like all Ottawa, were content to rejoice, to listen to speeches at the Parliament Buildings, to extoll the heroism of their men, to thank God for their deliverance, and to sing hymns of praise and thanksgiving.

19

JOHN MARSHALL
A Chauffeur in Egypt

The first of the MacKay soldiers to die in 1918 was John Marshall, not on a battlefield in France or Belgium but in a hospital in Scotland, as a result of a sunstroke he suffered while serving in Egypt with the British Army Service Corps. When he had gone overseas in 1915, his wife and children had moved to Scotland, but they had remained members of MacKay church and probably intended to return after the war. Instead, Marshall was buried in a public cemetery in Perth, Scotland, his widow remarried and stayed in Scotland, and the family disappeared from the history of MacKay church and New Edinburgh.

John Marshall was born in Monifieth, Forfarshire, near Dundee, in 1875 or 1876, the son of Archibald and Margaret Marshall. His father was a coachman, as was his elder brother. John was listed in the 1891 Scottish census as a law clerk at age 15, but 10 years later he was living in Perth and was, like his father, listed as a "coachman domestic" or "cabman," reflecting the transition being made by coachmen from being drivers of horse-drawn carriages to driving taxicabs, trucks, or automobiles as chauffeurs.[1] On December 6, 1901, he married Catherine Nicol Birss, who had come to find work in Perth from her tiny village near Balmoral where her family were crofters.[2] The couple had a daughter, Margaret, in 1905, and in 1910 they immigrated to Canada on board the *Dominion* out of Liverpool. According to the passenger manifest, John Marshall intended to work as a chauffeur in Ottawa. He may have done so, though the 1911 census shows him employed as a chauffeur in Whitby, Ontario, earning $360 a year.[3] We do know that sometime in 1913, the Marshall family took up residence on Vaughan Street in a newly developed part of New Edinburgh. A second child, John Roy, was born early the following year.[4] John and Catherine Marshall joined MacKay Presbyterian Church by Certificate on June 26, 1914.

Marshall was not merely a chauffeur as we would understand the term, but was, according to an obituary, "well known as an automobile engineer."[5] At a time when there were many types of cars and few repair shops, chauffeurs had to have the mechanical skills to ensure reliable operation of their employers' automobiles, and in the years before the war they were in high demand and well paid—a newspaper article in 1916 stated that an owner could not expect to get "an experienced driver and mechanic, the latter point being the more important, for anything less than $30 a week."[6] We do not know what kind of work Marshall did or for whom, or whether he made that kind of money, but he had developed a reputation in the city.

In the fall of 1915, Marshall enlisted, in Ottawa, in the British Army Service Corps (BASC). Why the Imperial army and not the Canadian Army Service Corps? The British were the most mechanized of the armies on the Western Front and, according to Richard Holt, early in the war they were in desperate need of "skilled driver-mechanics, wheelers, fitters, electricians, or blacksmiths" for the Mechanical Transport Section of the British Army Service Corps. The Canadan government gave the BASC permission to recruit in Canada, as the Royal Flying Corps was also doing. An elaborate system was set up to test trade proficiency, and although the British had hoped for 2,740 men, only 1,100 enlisted—possibly because British Army pay was much below what they would have been earning in civilian life or could have got in the Canadian Army. Marshall was qualified and willing to serve with the British. His British service number, M2/152731, indicates that he was in the Mechanical Transport Company and had not previously served in the British or Canadian forces.[7]

When John Marshall went overseas in the late fall, Catherine Marshall decided to follow him to the old country. His British Army pay would not have been enough to meet the rising cost of living in Ottawa. Living in Britain was cheaper, she could be with relatives, and she might be able to see her husband during training and on leave. Thus in January 1916, she and their children travelled second class to Glasgow on the *Cameronian* out of New York, giving as their destination 28 Balfour Street, Dundee—the address of John's father, Archibald Marshall.[8]

But Marshall was not to serve in France or Belgium. Instead, following his basic training, he was sent in early 1916 to Egypt. Though it was nominally ruled by a khedive, Egypt had been for many years under *de facto* British control, and with the coming of war the British had placed it under virtual military rule. The Suez Canal was the British lifeline to India and two divisions of Indian troops had been brought in to protect the canal against attack by the Ottoman Empire, which was allied with Germany. In 1916 Egypt's strategic importance was greatly increased when the British suffered defeats in campaigns against the Ottomans in Mesopotamia and Gallipoli, and when the attempt to open a southern front in Europe based on Salonika collapsed into stalemate. Egypt now became not only an important rear base for the eastern Mediterranean, and a staging area for Australian and Indian troops headed for the Western Front, but also the front line for campaigns against the Ottomans to the west in the Libyan desert and to the east in the Sinai Peninsula. In Libya, Senussi rebels in Cyrenaica were induced by the Ottomans and Germans to attack Egypt, and the fight against them became a testing ground for the use of motor transport in desert warfare.[9] This campaign was largely over by 1917. In Sinai, the Ottomans had attacked the Suez Canal in 1915 and, after being driven back, had built a railway to Beersheba in Palestine as a supply base for further operations against the British. In 1916 the British, having decided that the best way to defend Egypt and the canal was to carry the war to the Ottomans, were preparing to advance on Palestine through the Sinai desert.

By 1916 there were over 100,000 British Empire troops in Egypt. They required logistical support, including motorized transport. The Mechanical Transport Section of the BASC operated supply depots and mechanical facilities at the main bases in Cairo and Alexandria. In the field, a wide variety of motor transport companies provided ambulance, courier, and messenger services to infantry battalions and forward HQs, and convoyed supplies and ammunition to forward positions. They needed more trained mechanics and skilled drivers. So it was that early in the year John Marshall found himself on a troopship working its way carefully around the coast of France and through the Mediterranean, always alert to the threat of German submarines. We do not have Marshall's service record, which was likely destroyed in a bombing raid in the Second World War, so we can only surmise what role he played from the scraps of available information. At first, he was probably engaged in the effort to establish an effective motor transport network, with depots and supply lines, and to ensure quality maintenance of vehicles and equipment. Given his background and the important role played in Egypt by all kinds of automobiles and light trucks, it is a safe bet that he was driving and/or servicing them.

In August 1916, the British repulsed an Ottoman attack on the Suez Canal at Romani, and then began moving forward, following the ancient caravan route through the Sinai toward Palestine, building as they went a water pipeline and railway. By March 1917, a large British force under General Edmund Allenby was encamped before Gaza. After taking this city and Beersheba, they advanced into Palestine and took Jerusalem before Christmas 1917.[10]

In this campaign, supplies, food, ammunition, and above all, water—1.2 million gallons were required each day—had to be kept flowing to the front over longer and longer supply lines. In the deep sand of the Sinai desert, the predominant method of transport in the early stages was by camel, but this was costly and inefficient and mechanical transport increasingly took over. "Only two types of mechanical transport were possible in the desert," writes

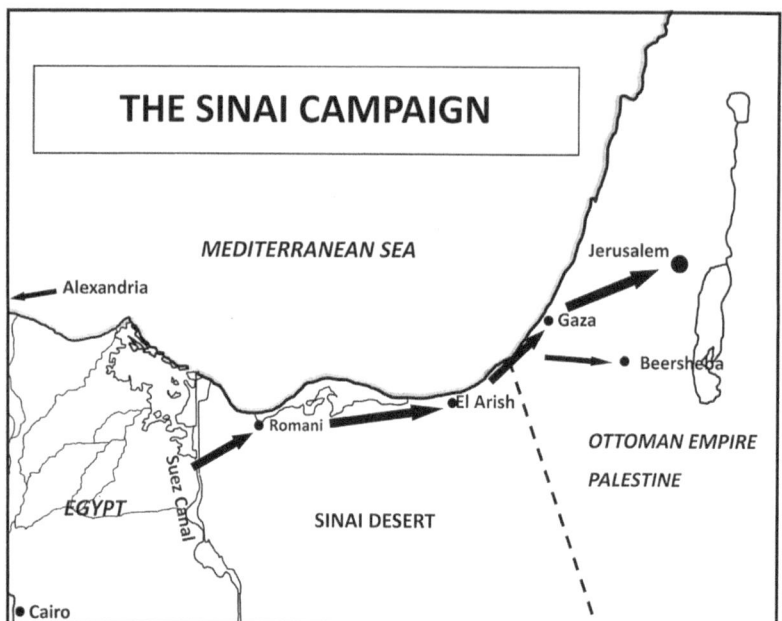

Figure 19.1. The Sinai campaign.
Source: Created by the author.

the historian of the transport services in this theatre: "Holt trucks and Ford cars."[11] New roads were laid down using wire mesh to hold the sand in place and allow light vehicles to operate as long as they carefully disciplined their speed. By early 1917 light cars, armoured cars, and field guns were also part of the order or battle, and as the campaign wore on and supply lines lengthened, trucks became essential.

It would be difficult to imagine worse conditions for a military campaign than the Sinai. Daytime temperatures go as high as 50°C. "[I]t was almost too hot to breathe," recalled one solder, "and we used to strip naked and lay [*sic*] in the tent, trying to keep cool, but even then we simply poured out sweat and our skin blistered, yes it was hot, enough for fowls to lay hard boiled eggs all day long."[12] There was little shade, except when frequent sandstorms blotted out the sun for days. Histories of the campaign contain numerous stories of men found unconscious after a day in the open, sometimes recovering, often dead or dying; of water being guarded by men with guns and doled out by the pint after a long day; of men so parched that their tongues swelled and they became delirious. At night the desert could become bitterly cold. Operating conditions—sand in the carburetors, radiators, fans, and lubricant; breakdown of axles, wheel bearings, and steering gears; overheating; wear and tear on engines and transmissions—required constant attention to maintenance and the ability to make repairs on the fly. Drivers and mechanics were at great risk. If a vehicle got lost or broke down in the desert, the driver was doomed.[13]

We do not know what role Marshall played in all this, or even if he was involved in the Sinai campaign. What we do know is that, probably in late 1917, he suffered sunstroke, which appears to have caused such a severe brain injury that he was evacuated to Scotland where he died in March 1918, at age 42. Sunstroke, now referred to as heatstroke, occurs when the body's heat-regulating system fails due to prolonged exposure to the sun or intense heat; the blood and circulatory system cannot dissipate the heat, sweating deprives the body of essential minerals; then the patient stops sweating and his internal temperature rises. If the victim receives hydration and salts he will usually recover fully. If not, heatstroke can be fatal, sometimes within 30 minutes, often within 24 hours. Even if the patient does not die at once, damage to the kidneys, internal organs, and brain may lead to prolonged suffering and eventual death from organ and heart failure. It is unlikely that Marshall would have suffered such severe sunstroke in Cairo or Alexandria. It is more likely that heatstroke so severe that it required treatment in Scotland rather than in the extensive medical facilities available in Egypt, would have occurred in the fall of 1917 in the Sinai campaign, when heatstroke was the main cause of admission to hospital.[14]

John Marshall was taken to the Dykebar Military Hospital in Paisley, near Glasgow—a "lunatic asylum" that had been opened in 1909 and had then been taken over in 1916 as a war hospital.[15] Given its origins, it was the ideal place to send soldiers who had suffered brain injuries. At some point Catherine Marshall and the children had left what would have been cramped quarters with her father-in-law in Dundee to take up residence in a flat above a store in Perth, the city where the Marshalls had lived before emigrating to Canada. She would presumably have been able to visit him in the hospital—for how long we do not know.[16] On the MacKay church Communion Roll beside his name is the note: "killed in action in France, March 1918." The MacKay Death Register equally erroneously records that he "died of 'Gas' in hospital in Perth Scotland." These errors indicate that there had not been detailed communication between MacKay church people and Mrs. Marshall, though his obituary in the newspaper indicates that he had other friends in the city who knew, generally, what had happened. But the church had at least kept in touch, and they did know her address in Perth. And it was in Perth, at Wellshill Cemetery, that John Marshall is buried, with a granite headstone similar in design to those in Commonwealth war cemeteries.

Figure 19.2. Wellshill Cemetery, Perth, Scotland.
Source: Photograph by Carolyn Bowker.

Wellshill is the main cemetery for Perth and it is very large indeed. It is also a Commonwealth War Graves site with over 80 soldiers from the First World War who died at the Perth Royal Infirmary, whose graves are scattered throughout the cemetery. (During the Second World War when the Perth Royal Infirmary was also used as a military hospital, more war graves were added, and there is also a Polish war cemetery.) In the corner of the cemetery with the highest concentration of soldiers' burials, a granite Great Cross was erected after the war which, as its inscription states, is "one in design and intention with those which have been set up in France and Beligum and in other places throughout the world where our dead of the Great War are laid to rest." The headstones are similar in design to those in Commonwealth cemeteries, with the name and rank of the soldier, sometimes a cross, and the badge of his regiment, with a small inscription provided by the family; but they are of grey granite rather than cream-coloured limestone, and the lettering is outlined in black. Marshall is not located with the majority of the Commonwealth soldiers, and is far away from the Great Cross, in the 'Parochial" section. This is because he did not die at the local hospital but was brought to Perth for burial by his wife. There is no cross on his headstone, but there is an inscription: "He died that we might live."

Figure 19.3. Wellshill Cemetery, Perth, Scotland.
Source: Photograph by Carolyn Bowker.

On July 7, 1918 Catherine Marshall received John's personal effects and back pay of a little under 26 pounds and on February 22, 1919, his War Service Gratuity of ten pounds, in addition to whatever pensions she was entitled to as a widow and for the children. She also received his war and victory medals.[17] On April 30, 1918, only a few weeks after John's death, MacKay Presbyterian Church granted her a certificate of disjunction to Perth, Scotland. On July 18, 1919, at the age of 45, she remarried, to James Clark, 42, of Canal Street, Perth.[18] They moved to Glasgow and lived there through the 1920s. We are unable to trace their movements after this, or what happened to the children. She and her family fade out of MacKay's story, of which they had been a part for less than two years.

Figure 19.4. Area of Wellshill Cemetery where Marshall is buried; his headstone is in the centre of the frame.
Source: Photograph by Carolyn Bowker.

20

HOMÈRE JOLIAT
"A Brave Soldier, Having Won the Military Medal"

The Joliats were a well-established New Edinburgh family which was held in high regard in the community. Émile Joliat, a policeman noted for his great physical strength, empathy, and intelligence, would rise to be Police Chief of the City of Ottawa. His wife, Azilda, was widely known for her charity and leadership. Their sons were great athletes: Homère (1894) was described as "one of the finest football players in the city";[1] René (1899) was a football player, a paddler, one of the city's best wrestlers, and a star hockey centre; Aurèle[2] (1902), also a star at rowing, played football for the Ottawa Rough Riders, and went on to excel in the National Hockey League. Their daughters Alice (1898) and Jeanne (1910) were artistic and musical. The Joliats were staunch members of MacKay Presbyterian Church. The children attended Sunday School and joined the church. Alice sang for many years in the choir and Jeanne would be married at MacKay United Church.[3] All these things made the Joliats typical of many MacKay families, but in one important respect they were unique. Émile, a Swiss Protestant, and Azilda, a French Canadian Catholic who had converted to Presbyterianism, were francophones in an anglophone community, and the family was proud of its heritage.

Émile Joliat was born in 1868 in Reconvilier, Bern canton, Switzerland, and grew up speaking French and German. Apprenticed as a butcher's boy, he left home at 17 to come to Buckingham, Quebec, to join his cousin Félix Cornu (1866–1934), a medical doctor who had come to Canada at a young age, had studied at McGill and Toronto and then in Paris under Pasteur, and had also developed an active interest in the mining industry.[4] Quickly learning English, Émile found work in the MacLaren-Buckingham phosphate mines, which at the time were some of the richest deposits in Canada. In 1888 he left for the United States to work on a dairy farm in Illinois and at a department store in Nebraska, but he returned to Canada in 1890 to work in the mine and then on a farm.[5] His older brother and his nephew Henri were also working in the mines.[6] Henri went on to study theology in Montreal and would become minister of the Presbyterian Église-St.-Jean in Montreal (after Church Union in 1925 it became the Église Unie St.-Jean), the largest French-speaking Protestant church in North America.[7]

In 1892 Émile married Azilda Lavictoire (1873–1924) of Hull. A special dispensation was required for this marriage in the Église Notre Dame de Grace between a Catholic and a Protestant (described in the church records as a Presbyterian).[8] After a short period in the meat business, Joliat was accepted in 1895 into the Ottawa Police as a beat cop in the ByWard Market area. A great athlete who excelled at bicycle racing, sprinting, and hammer and caber throwing, he needed all his strength and courage to face down a mob of 500 shantymen out for a night on the town, or, in middle age, to chase a much larger fugitive from downtown to Sandy Hill and subdue him with his fists. But he was also a kindly, intelligent man with great leadership and interpersonal skills who quickly rose to sergeant and then to detective with a salary of a little over $1,000 a year in 1910. "Considered one of the finest members of the force," a newspaper noted at the time, "he is of exceptionally fine physique and thoroughly reliable."[9]

Figure 20.1. Émile Joliat as Ottawa Police Chief, 1932. Photograph (detail) of the Ottawa Police Department, May 23, 1932.
Source: City of Ottawa Archives, Police Service Fonds: CA001245.

About 1902 the family moved from Lower Town to a house Émile had purchased at 101 Stanley Avenue in New Edinburgh. The children quickly integrated into the New Edinburgh community. The oldest boy, Homère, went to Creighton Street Public School, and then to a francophone academy in Pointe-aux-Trembles, Montreal. After courses at the Gowling Business College in Ottawa, he took a position as a clerk in the municipal waterworks department. A newspaper obituary described him as "a fine, well-set-up youth of just over 20 years, when he left Canada for the front. He was popular with all who knew him and he was held in high esteem by those under whose authority he worked and was schooled."[10] His younger brother René, after attending Creighton Street Public School, joined the Royal Canadian Mint as a craftsman. Aurèle and Alice were in Creighton Street Public School when the war broke out, and Jeanne was just starting school. Alice was already becoming a gifted singer.

Homère Joliat (Homer on his attestation papers) enlisted on January 14, 1915, in the 8th Canadian Mounted Rifles. When 8 CMR was broken up in England in October, most of its men were dispersed among other regiments in the Canadian Corps. But Joliat wanted something more adventurous than just being a foot soldier, and while awaiting re-assignment he took extra training to join the Canadian Machine Gun Corps. Then in February 1916 came an even better opportunity: along with two other MacKay men in 8 CMR—Sidney Mansell and Albert Kendall—Joliat was transferred to the Borden Motor Machine Gun Battery and the following month he was sent to the front.

Motor machine gun batteries were the brainchild of Brigadier Raymond Brutinel, a wealthy expatriate French officer who believed that a mobile force able to provide concentrated firepower at any point on the front would be the key to modern warfare. When the war broke out, he offered to raise two batteries, which became the 1st Canadian Motor Machine Gun Brigade (1CMMGB). These improvised mobile gun platforms consisted of Colt machine guns mounted on truck chassis with armour plates, supported by the trucks and men needed to transport supplies and ammunition and assist the gunners. But the British were skeptical of the whole idea, in part because mobile batteries would have limited usefulness in the static conditions of trench warfare. The 1CMMGB was accordingly left out of the First Contingent and it did not get to France until September 1915.

In the early days of the war, 1CMMGB was deployed to reinforce regular stationary machine gun units when they needed extra firepower. But it still kept its vehicles and its mandate as a mobile force, and in 1915 three new motor machine gun batteries were formed as a result of private initiatives. The Eaton Battery was funded by the department store family; the Yukon Battery was paid for by Klondike gold magnate Joe Boyle; and the Borden Battery, named after the prime minister, drew from mining towns in the Porcupine district of northern Ontario. Unlike the two Brutinel batteries in 1CMMGB, these three new batteries did not have their guns mounted on armoured vehicles; the men and their guns were carried in trucks and dismounted for

Figure 20.2. Original Brutinel armoured machine gun batteries, which became Batteries A and B of 1st Canadian Motor Machine Gun Brigade in 1916.
Source: Canadian War Museum, Canadian Official War Photograph O.2595.

action. The 1CMMGB and the three new Batteries were each assigned to one of the four Canadian Divisions in the Ypres Salient.[11] The Borden Battery was attached to the Second Division.

Within days of his arrival at the front, Joliat was engaged in serious action. On April 6, 1916, the Germans directed heavy artillery fire on a section of the Canadian trenches in the Ypres Salient to cover an attempt to occupy several shell craters. The Borden Battery set up a machine gun to direct fire on the advancing Germans, but this was put out of action for a time by a concerted artillery barrage. A second machine gun was then rushed into position and the two guns directed heavy fire at the enemy, which allowed the Canadian 29th Battalion to retreat from its exposed position without serious loss. The war diary of the Borden Battery recorded the thanks of the officer commanding the 29th Battalion and noted that several members of the battery, including Joliat, "came in for very favourable comment."[12]

In a letter to his father after this battle, Joliat gave an upbeat description of this battle and the heavy bombardment they had endured, the fact that three men had been wounded, and that for 24 hours they had had no sleep and nothing to eat but a little rum. He was modest in describing the praise they had received: "Our section made a very good name for itself and it is talked about all over." And he expressed a feeling widespread among young soldiers writing home: "I wish I could describe the sights that were to be seen in the trenches but it is impossible. You people cannot imagine what it is like." Joliat said that the beautiful weather helped their spirits and that he was all right except for a headache, which he attributed in part to wearing a steel helmet which had saved his life once or twice. "These helmets are pretty heavy and between that and the bursting of shells, which is deafening. I am not surprised at having a headache. However, I guess it will pass off."[13] He had probably suffered a concussion.

Throughout the following summer, including the battles of St. Eloi and Mount Sorrel, the Borden Battery was in the thick of the action, inflicting heavy damage but also becoming prime targets for enemy counter-fire. From June 16 to July 1, Joliat was treated in a field hospital for a contusion of the hip—whether this was a battle wound or an injury is not clear. A week later he was sent for a week to a machine gun school at Camiers to learn how to use the new Vickers machine guns which were replacing the unreliable Colts.

During these battles the value of the machine gun was increasingly recognized, not only for close support to infantry but as an adjunct to artillery, firing thousands of rounds into enemy positions, breaking up attacks and harassing supply and communications.[14] The extra value of mobile batteries was also becoming apparent and in July 1916 the existing batteries were grouped into a new 1st Canadian Motor Machine Gun Brigade. The two original Brutinel batteries became Batteries A and B, Borden became Battery C, and Eaton and Yukon became Batteries D and E respectively. The newly created 1CMMGB was not attached to any of the four Canadian Divisions but was now a separate unit serving the Canadian Corps as a whole. It brought together all the array of motor vehicles, motorcyclists, specialized services, and supply chains needed to support and transport the five mobile machine gun batteries.

The Borden Battery, now part of 1CMMGB, moved to the Somme in September 1916 to support the Canadian assault on Courcelette. On September 26, its devastating fire annihilated a German counterattack on a Canadian battalion. The battery's war diary recorded that the Germans retaliated with an artillery barrage "all afternoon and during the night. Some [German] Batteries made [the Borden Battery] their target and searched the areas which we occupied." In all the battery suffered 23 casualties, including Joliat, who suffered a serious wound to his right arm.[15] After passing through a chain of field and base hospitals in France and England, Joliat spent four months at Epsom in treatment and convalescence. He then spent a further four months in a reserve pool in France.

It was not until April 22, 1917, that he rejoined the Borden Motor Machine Gun Battery, which had suffered losses at Vimy Ridge. From June 17 to July 29, he was attached to Second Division HQ, perhaps in preparation for Hill 70, where, from mid-July to early August, moving up and down the First and

Second Divisions' rear areas, the mobile machine guns fired an astonishing 2,694,700 rounds.[16] The "well-set-up" 22-year-old who had left Canada in 1915 had experienced things that no one of his background could possibly have been prepared for, and the stress was beginning to tell. In September, Joliat forfeited three days' pay for being absent from his billet after curfew, and that same month he was sent to the First Army Rest Camp, a haven of peace behind the lines where soldiers could recover from battle exhaustion. There he was court-martialled for being found drunk and was sentenced to 14 days of Field Punishment (FP) Number 1.

This punishment is difficult to understand or justify today. It involved being lashed to a fixed object such as a wagon wheel for two hours a day, three days out of four, with food limited to bully beef, biscuits, and unsweetened tea. FP No. 1 was banned in Canada and would be abolished in the British Army in 1923, but Imperial officers at the front considered it essential to maintaining discipline.[17] To apply it in this case seems excessive to say the least. Perhaps being drunk was a more serious offense at a rest camp where men needed peace, quiet, and order in their lives. Perhaps British officers resented the free-wheeling Canadian motor machine gunners who saw themselves, in the words of historian Alex Lynch, as "an élite force in an élite army," and were by late 1917 being commanded by officers risen from the ranks who were more tolerant of lax discipline off the battlefield.[18] In fact, it does not appear that Joliat served all his punishment, for he was soon back at the front at Passchendaele, where he would win the Military Medal.

Mobility was out of the question in the churned-up mud of Passchendaele; the men carried machine guns, equipment, and supplies into battle by hand. During weeks of intense struggle, 1CMMGB was constantly engaged, moving forward with advancing troops and facing hostile fire. A surviving member of the Borden Battery recalled it as "the worst and most horrible experience imaginable. ... When you consider the liquid mud and water-filled shell-holes which we had to go round or through with our heavy equipment; and sometimes 100 pounds of ammunition on our backs, it is almost indescribable for if one fell down or got mired to the waist it was impossible to get up without help."[19] Thirteen men in 1CMMGB were awarded the Military Medal, six got the Distinguished Conduct Medal, and six officers received the Military Cross—all this in a brigade of fewer than 300 men. Joliat was one of four men in the Borden Battery who got the MM.[20] But the cost was horrendous. Ninety-five men were killed or wounded. "By the time the five batteries were withdrawn into reserve on 18 November," says historian Michael Holden, "they had been reduced to the fighting equivalent of three."[21] A newspaper account reported that "in one engagement in which [Joliat] distinguished himself, he was the only member of a gun crew who came through the engagement alive."[22] In December he was promoted to lance corporal.

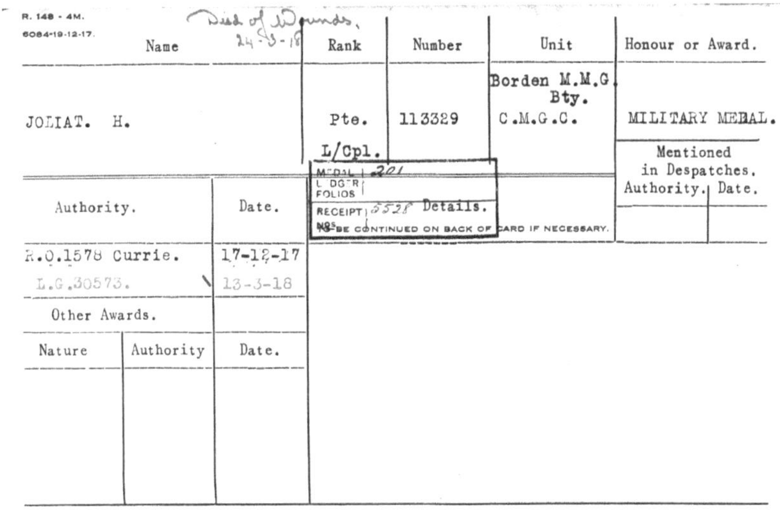

		Name	Died of Wounds, 24-3-18	Rank	Number	Unit	Honour or Award.
		JOLIAT. H.		Pte. L/Cpl.	113329	Borden M.M.G Bty. C.M.G.C.	MILITARY MEDAL.
				MEDAL 201 L. DG'R FOLIOS RECEIPT 3538 Details. NB BE CONTINUED ON BACK OF CARD IF NECESSARY.			Mentioned in Despatches.
Authority.			Date.				Authority. Date.
R.O.1578 Currie.			17-12-17				
L.G.30573.			13-3-18				
Other Awards.							
Nature	Authority		Date.				

Figure 20.3. Military medal citation for Homer Joliat, December 1917.
Source: Canada, Military Honours and Awards Citation Cards, 1900-1961, file Johnston, G. H. – Kelsey, H. G.

No one could question the bravery and skill of the men in the mobile machine gun brigade. But as Joliat's experience showed, their disrespect for traditional military discipline was a matter of concern, not only for British officers but for the Canadian commander, General Currie, who inspected 1CMMGB at Vimy on March 11, 1918. The men were in a testy mood after a cold, wet February and one sergeant had clearly been drinking. As fate would have it, this was the very soldier Currie decided to question. "Sergeant, what do your men do?" he asked. The sergeant kept quiet, trying to hide his condition. Currie repeated the question. "They do what I bloody well tell them to do!" was the slurred reply.[23] Currie appointed Major "Tiny" Walker, a disciplinarian, to whip the brigade into shape. Joliat likely missed this inspection, because after being given two weeks' leave in Paris in January—and telling his brother in a letter that in spite of the horrors of recent months he was in excellent health—he reported on January 29 to a field ambulance unit for treatment of gonorrhea. In February and March he reported to two other field ambulances for further treatment, the last requiring a week in hospital. He returned to duty on March 23 and was promoted to acting corporal. Walker would have no chance to impose discipline on the brigade, for once again, they would be called upon to display their courage, and this time it would cost Joliat his life.

On March 21, 1918, the Germans launched "Operation Michael" against the British Fifth Army in a last, desperate attempt to win victory on the Western Front. After a hurricane bombardment of 3.2 million shells, elite

German troops punched through the British lines, took thousands of prisoners, and sliced whole divisions into pockets of men fighting for their lives. By the third day, the Germans had driven the British 20 kilometres behind the Somme. The front was collapsing and if it broke nothing stood between the Germans and Paris. "There was panic in the British High Command," says Tim Cook: "the Germans had scored an impressive victory."[24]

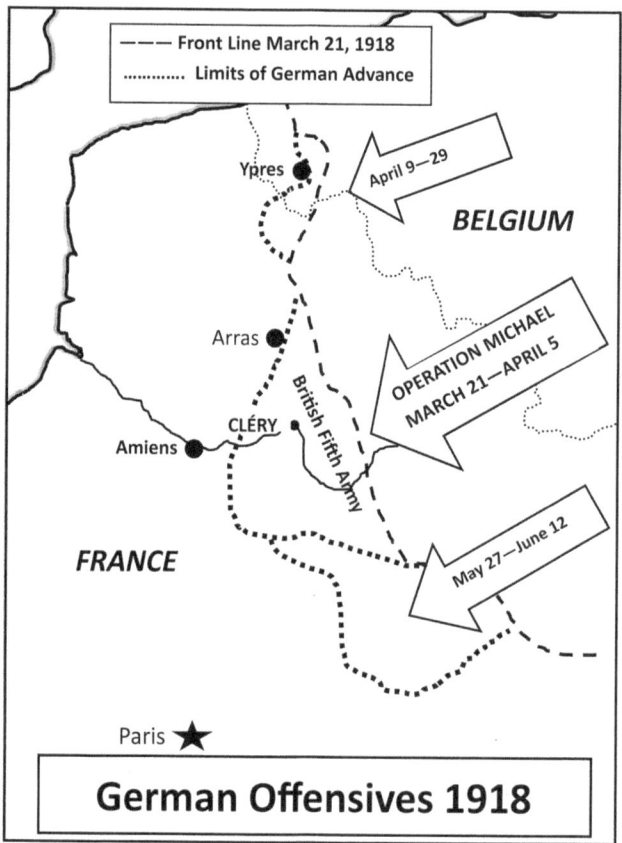

Figure 20.4. German offensives, 1918.
Source: Created by the author.

General Gough of the British Fifth Army made an urgent request to the Canadian Corps. He had heard of the Canadian mobile machine gun batteries and he hoped that their mobility and firepower could help slow the German advance, stabilize the situation, and buy the time needed to regroup. On a few hours' notice, 1CMMGB left Vimy in the early morning of March 23. The armoured trucks of A and B Batteries, trucks carrying the guns of the other three batteries, trucks with supplies and ammunition, trucks with men swaying and rocking as they sat upright on benches, cars carrying the officers, and 65 motorcyclists who were scouts and messengers—in all about 330 officers and men—took 9 hours to cover the 70 miles to Amiens, on roads choked with traffic. General Currie sent them the kind of message that in war is an encoded death sentence: "The Corps Commander wishes you the best of luck and has every confidence that you will do more than well."[25]

In the disarray of Gough's headquarters they got their battle orders: divide into groups, head for points of the front that were near collapse, try to slow down or stem the German tide.[26] For the next two weeks batteries of 1CMMGB, in the words of Tim Cook, "raced across the front, providing much-needed firepower and shoring up desperate situations. [They] covered British withdrawal and punished German units with raking fire." "Everywhere they went," wrote *The Times*, "they steadied the line."[27] But while machine gun crews could deploy tremendous firepower, in the open and without infantry cover they were sitting ducks for artillery and rifle counter-fire.

The Borden Battery, together with "B" Battery, were sent to the village of Cléry on the Somme, where they were ordered to "hold at all costs." They drove all night to cover the 15 miles to the village—their second day with little or no sleep—and set up in the early morning of March 24, 1918. Time and again throughout the day and into the evening, the Borden Battery took up a position, rallied retreating British troops to establish a temporary defensive line, fired devastating volleys into the advancing Germans, suffered heavy losses in their turn, covered the British retreat, and retreated themselves just before the Germans reached their position. Much of the time their guns were not even taken off the trucks but fired into the enemy from this highly exposed position until the barrels literally melted down. At 2:00 p.m. the sole remaining officer sent a desperate message to HQ asking for reinforcements and supplies; the message was kicked from HQ to HQ until it was too late, but in fact there was no real help to give. "Too much cannot be said of the heroic stands made by the [Borden] battery," wrote an after-battle report. "They saved our exhausted infantry over and over again." They fought for a day and a night and "blocked the advance of a German division," until a tattered remnant retreated to Maricourt. Fifty-two of the battery's 56 men were dead or wounded.[28]

Sidney Mansell, also from MacKay church, was one of the survivors (he would also win a Military Medal and would return to the front with a reorganized Canadian Motor Machine Gun Brigade for the Hundred Days). But Joliat was wounded in the "right chest" and evacuated to No. 42 Stationary Hospital at Amiens, where he died the same day.[29] He was 23—"a brave soldier," said the MacKay Register of Deaths, "having won the Military

Figure 20.5. Canadian Motor Machine Gun Brigade waiting alongside the Arras-Cambrai Road, August 1918; this picture shows the motor machine gun batteries which, like the Borden Battery, did not use armoured vehicles but carried men, guns, and supplies on trucks. The Borden Battery might have looked like this as it went into action in March 1918.
Source: Canadian War Museum CCO-CWM-FWWWP-168-EO-3363.

Medal." Furious when the British high command—largely to cover their own inadequate preparations for the German offensive—failed to recognize the heroic role the motor machine gun batteries had played, General Currie ensured that the men got the decorations they deserved. Joliat was posthumously awarded a bar (i.e., the equivalent of a second Military Medal).[30]

The Joliat family was undoubtedly heartbroken at the tragic loss of their eldest son, however heroic may have been his sacrifice. But life went on. At Christmas 1918, eight-year-old Jeanne Joliat wrote a letter to Santa Claus, which was printed in the Ottawa *Journal*, asking for "a toboggan, and a little watch, one box of chocolates, one picture book, a pair of skates. That will be all for this time."[31] Émile Joliat continued to rise steadily in the police service and his work in solving several major crimes was widely publicized. In 1931 he was appointed chief of police, a position he held with distinction until retiring in 1937. But in 1924, at age 51, Azilda Joliat suddenly died of an embolism after an operation for phlebitis. "[E]steemed as a loving mother and a staunch friend," her funeral was attended by many prominent citizens of Ottawa. The service was conducted by Rev. Anderson of MacKay and by Rev. Henri Joliat of Montreal.[32]

Alice Joliat joined the public service and continued for many years as an amateur singer and sang in the choir at MacKay.[33] In 1934 she married Jules Cornu (1901–1990) of Buckingham, Quebec, one of several children of her father's cousin Dr. Félix Cornu. The couple lived in the big house in Buckingham once occupied by his father, and then had a house in Sandy Hill, where Émile also spent the last years before his death in 1953. In 1936 Jeanne married William Allan Ralph, an accountant.

René Robert ("Bobby") Joliat had a tryout with the Montreal Canadiens and played one NHL game in 1924. He played senior hockey for the Royal Canadian Mint, and as late as 1931 he was playing for a senior team which competed for the Allen Cup. He continued to live in New Edinburgh with his wife and family and died in 1953.

Aurèle Joliat became the star athlete of the family. After playing hockey as a teenager, he went west to play until the owner of the Montreal Canadiens traded "Newsy" Lalonde, the star player of the day, to get him. Aurèle went on to star for 16 years as a speedy, versatile, smart two-way forward for Montreal, centring a line with Howie Morenz and Billy Boucher (who had also grown up in New Edinburgh and played on local teams with his brothers and the Joliats). Called "The Little Giant"—he was five feet seven inches and his playing weight was never over 135 pounds—he could nonetheless look after himself in the corners and in a fight. He scored 270 goals, won the Hart Trophy and three Stanley Cups, and in 1945 was inducted into the Hockey Hall of Fame.

Homère Joliat is buried in St. Pierre Cemetery, Amiens. Situated on the northeastern outskirts of the city, on the northern side of the main road to Albert, it is an extension of the large Amiens Communal Cemetery. To reach it, you pass along a tree-lined lane by the communal cemetery with its elaborate monuments dating back into the nineteenth century. At the end of the lane there is a French military cemetery on the right, and the Commonwealth cemetery on the left. Designed by Sir Edwin Lutyens, the cemetery is bordered by large trees and there are plants and flowers along the rows of headstones. There are 676 burials from the First World War, of whom only 16 are Canadians. There are also 82 burials from the Second World War, including 12 Canadians, all pilots and air crew.

In 1928, Émile Joliat travelled to Europe to visit his Swiss birthplace and his extended family in France, but mostly to see the burial place of his son.[34] He is thus the only parent or spouse of any of the MacKay fallen that we know for certain visited their lost soldier's grave in France or Belgium. The simple inscription placed on Homère's stone, now only visible when the sand was brushed away from the bottom of the stone, well expresses his family's heartbreak as well as their pride in his heroism: "Here reposes our beloved son, who gave his life for his country."

Figure 20.6. Aurèle Joliat.
Source: James Rice/Hockey Hall of Fame.

Figure 20.7. St. Pierre Cemetery, Amiens.
Source: Photograph by Carolyn Bowker.

Homère Joliat 279

Figure 20.8. St. Pierre Cemetery, Amiens.
Source: Photograph by Carolyn Bowker.

Figure 20.9. St. Pierre Cemetery, Amiens.
Source: Photograph by Carolyn Bowker.

280 A Church at War

Figure 20.10. St. Pierre Cemetery, Amiens; Joliat's headstone is in the centre of the frame, with the bottom inscription obscured by earth.
Source: Photograph by Carolyn Bowker.

21

IRWIN KELLY
"Blessed Are Those that Have Not Seen, and Yet Have Believed"

Irwin Kelly's family exemplified the religious eclecticism of a surprising number of people in New Edinburgh at the time. Irwin's father Samuel John Kelly (1860–1924) was raised Methodist, but at the time of his marriage he gave his religion as Presbyterian, while his mother, Olivia Irwin Kelly (1862–1931), declared her religion to be "Episcopal"—and the wedding took place in the First Congregational Church in Kingston![1]

The family attended an Anglican church for some years after coming to Ottawa, and the 1891 and 1901 censuses listed the religion of all members of the family as "Church of England." After the family moved to New Edinburgh, Olivia and her two daughters continued to be Anglicans (one of the daughters was married in their old church after the war), and "I. Kelly" appears on the memorial plaque at St. Bartholomew's Church.[2] But Samuel Kelly was a regular attendee at MacKay church and Irwin and his younger brother Samuel Jr. declared their religion as Presbyterian on their attestation papers. To top things off, Samuel Kelly Sr.'s sister Catherine, who lived for many years with the family, was a staunch member of the Catholic Apostolic Church (CAC). The CAC, founded in England in the early nineteenth century and brought to Canada in the 1850s, believed that the Second Coming was imminent. The returning Christ could only be received by a universal church, led by twelve men designated as Apostles and receiving the Holy Spirit. But when the Apostles began to die off and the Second Coming had still not arrived, the CAC had to revise its raison d'être: it would now be a band of the faithful whose duty was to watch, pray, live in holiness, and prepare. For a time Samuel Kelly Sr. himself professed adherence to this sect.[3] The religious atmosphere in the Kelly home must have been interesting.

Samuel Kelly was a housepainter, or home decorator, who took his profession seriously. He was well known in Ottawa and in 1906 he is reported as speaking at a public meeting in favour of forming a union of painters and other decorating trades.[4] Originally from the Kingston area, the family had come to Ottawa about 1900 after a sojourn in the Canadian West. About 1909

GUNNER IRWIN KELLY.
Had Been Previously Wounded at the Somme.

Figure 21.1. Irwin Kelly.
Source: Ottawa *Citizen*, September 18, 1918.

they moved to New Edinburgh where they occupied a series of rented houses.[5] They had four surviving children: Sarah (1891), Lillian (1895), Irwin (1897), and Samuel Jr. (1900). In 1914 Sarah Kelly married Percy Lister, a butcher, who had come to New Edinburgh from England in 1910 to join his cousins who were staunch members of MacKay. Lillian found work as a bookkeeper. Irwin and Samuel Jr. likely attended Creighton Street Public School. In 1912, at age 15, Irwin passed the civil service exams and went to work as a clerk with the Royal Mint. A promising athlete and member of the Ottawa New Edinburgh Canoe Club and the YMCA, he was also a cadet and a volunteer in shooting competitions.[6]

In the spring of 1915, Irwin Kelly joined a militia unit of field artillery, and on July 30, 1915, two weeks past his eighteenth birthday, he was formally attested into the 32nd Battery in the 8th Brigade of the Canadian Field Artillery. He was five feet five and a half inches tall, with fair complexion, blue eyes, and brown hair. During training in Kingston, Kelly transferred to the 9th Brigade, CFA, and then managed to sail for England in the fall of 1915 (five months before either the 8th or the 9th Brigades). After service in a reserve battery (where he assigned $15 per month of his pay to his mother) he was sent, likely as a driver or in the ammunition column, to the 7th Brigade, CFA, in the Second Canadian Division, and reached the front at Dickebusch in the Ypres Salient in January 1916.

From February to August 1916, the 7th Brigade fought almost continuous artillery duels and delivered bombardments to support attacks and trench raids.[7] Then in September it moved to the Somme and took up positions near Pozières, where for the next three months it was engaged in constant fire and counter-fire in support of the Canadian attacks on Regina Trench and Desire Trench.[8] On November 18, 1916, during the battle of Desire Trench, Kelly was wounded by shrapnel in three places in the shoulder.[9] After treatment in the field he was sent to the No. 1 Australian General Hospital in Rouen, and three weeks later he was transferred to the War Hospital in Reading. On December 7 he was sent to a Canadian Casualty Assembly Centre in Hastings, where he was deemed to be progressing satisfactorily with no permanent disability. In January 1917, he went to a convalescent hospital and then to a series of reserve brigades and base depots in England.

According to a newspaper report, Kelly was offered an assignment in England but refused, insisting that his place was at the front.[10] After temporary postings in France, he returned to the front in April 1917 to join the 18th Battery of the 5th Brigade CFA.[11] Kelly had missed the Battle of Vimy Ridge, but he arrived just in time for Fresnoy on May 3—"a very lively affair," in the words of its official history, in which the 18th Battery, now in an exposed position, "suffered many casualties, but the guns were kept in action in spite of almost insurmountable difficulties."[12] In June, the battery took part in an attack on La Coulette, again with little cover and sustaining a number of casualties, and then the battle for Hill 70.

In October 1917, the 18th Battery returned to the Ypres Sector to take part in the Battle of Passchendaele. On October 30, an airplane attacked the battery, killing 3 men, wounding 7 (of whom 4 later died), and killing 30 horses. With no cover, more and more guns were put out of action and a steady toll of men were killed, wounded, and gassed. In the words of the official history, "too much praise cannot be given to the NCOs and men who so diligently and courageously carried out this important work." In 30 days of fighting at Passchendaele, the 18th Battery suffered 99 casualties and had over 30 guns put out of action. But in the jaunty language of its official history, "after getting rid of the Passchendaele mud, men and horses alike regained their old-time vigour and appearance. On Christmas Eve, 1917, the Battery settled in at Ames [northwest of Arras] for a well-earned rest."[13]

In February 1918, Kelly was granted two weeks' leave in England. In April, he was felled by a sudden serious attack of tonsillitis which took him out of action for two weeks. In July, the 18th Battery began its march south to rest, refit, and train in the new barrage techniques and in the mobile warfare that would make possible the great victories of the Hundred Days.

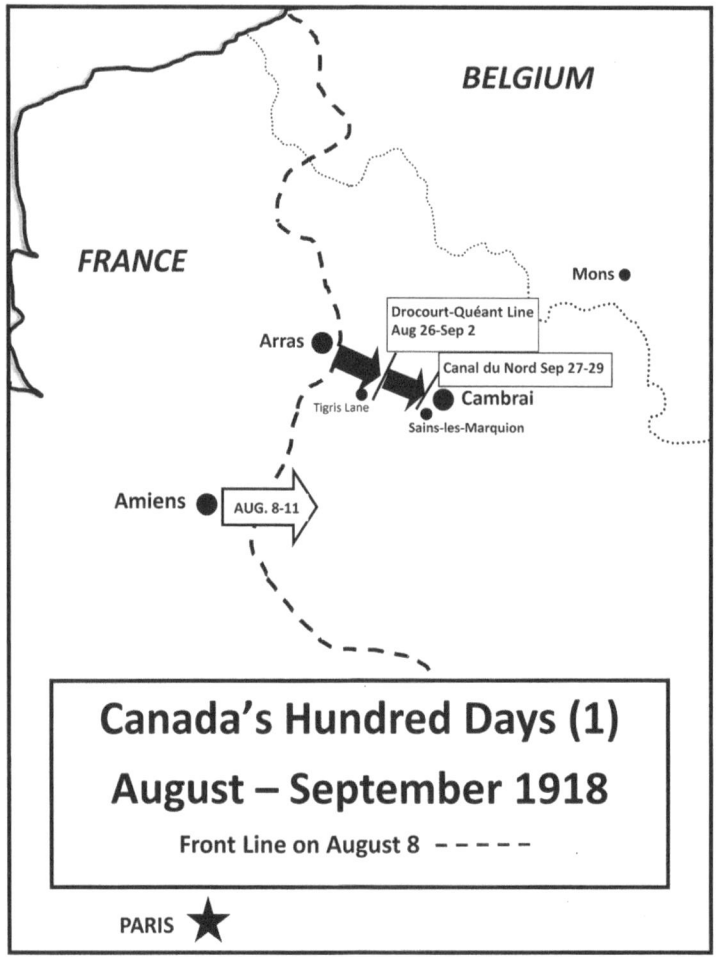

Figure 21.2. Canada's Hundred Days, Phase I (August–September 1918). *Source:* Created by the author.

At the very start of the attack at Amiens on August 8, 1918—the battle that began the Hundred Days—the 18th Battery got caught in an enemy barrage, but it still managed to advance. As the Canadians pushed the Germans back, "trench warfare tactics were pushed aside," and the 18th Battery, in the words of its official history, "'jumped the bags' with the infantry." The advance was so rapid and unexpected "that one did not get the opportunity to get a fair idea of what was actually happening." Now the field artillery batteries were performing as they had been intended to do, moving forward with the infantry, clearing the way with bombardment and counter-fire, supporting their advance with rolling barrages—often on an hour's notice—and then picking up and moving forward again. The 18th Battery took 10 days to rest and refit after Amiens and then moved to the Arras front for the campaign to take Cambrai. The way forward was blocked by the heavily fortified German Hindenburg line, which was based on the concept of "defence in depth"—a series of trenches which allowed the defenders to give ground and draw attackers into a killing zone. Within that line was a series of trenches called the Drocourt-Quéant Line, a hinge in the German position which, if taken, would open the way for the Canadians to press forward all along the line.

On August 26, 1918, the Canadian Corps began a series of set-piece battles which, mile by mile and objective by objective, pushed the Germans back and took possession of stretches of the Hindenburg line.[14] For each attack, the artillery laid down a barrage, silenced enemy guns, and then prepared to advance as each objective was taken. The risks involved, and the logistics of constant movement, were immense, and men and horses were worked to exhaustion. On August 28, the 18th Battery was subjected to a "nasty little barrage" when it had to advance along the only road available in full view of the enemy, but it pushed forward and continued to support the attack. By August 30 it had taken up a position between Cherisy and Hendercourt and had, "in spite of heavy fire, put all our guns in action and prepared for the barrage that was to be fired on the following morning."[15] On August 31, the 18th Battery opened its creeping barrage in support of this ongoing attack. "[O]ur guns were serving the usual four rounds per minute when the Hun, aggravated beyond endurance, commenced to retaliate, and for a short space of time ma[d]e things very disagreeable and inflicted a few casualties."[16] During this battle, in the words of the Circumstances of Death Register, Kelly was "returning from a forward position with a working party, that had taken up ammunition" when "he was struck in the back by a piece of shrapnel, that penetrated to the heart, and caused death instantly."[17] He was 21.

The Kelly family in Ottawa had read with trepidation the news from the front from early 1916 on, and had received the news of Irwin's wound in November 1916 with relief that he was at least still alive. In 1917, Sarah's husband, Percy Lister, who had opened a butcher shop in New Edinburgh, had enlisted in the 5th Princess Louisa Dragoons reinforcing draft. He was posted to Belleville, transferred to other regiments, and became a sergeant, but he was never sent overseas, probably due to a systolic heart murmur. Lillian was working as a bookkeeper, and the Kellys' youngest son, Samuel, a rower, and hockey and lacrosse player, had left school to become a clerk.[18] The devastating news of Irwin's death did not deter Samuel Jr. from enlisting two months later (lying about his age) in the Canadian Expeditionary Force for the Siberian Campaign (this story is told in Chapter 24).

In the early 1920s, Olivia Kelly received a small amount of money, Irwin's medals, and his personal effects. His name was carved on the family monument in Beechwood Cemetery and each year on the anniversary of his death an "In Memoriam" notice was placed in the local papers (as was also the case with some other MacKay soldiers). Then on January 13, 1924, Samuel Kelly Sr. died suddenly at age 63 from pneumonia.[19] The family then left New Edinburgh.

Samuel Jr. departed for Montreal in 1925 to work as a bookkeeper for the Consolidated Mining and Smelting Company. There he married in 1931 and had three children. He later moved to Toronto where he worked as a bookkeeper, then chief statistician, for the Ontario Department of Municipal Affairs, and at his death in 1970 he was in public relations with Ryerson Press.[20] He also continued his involvement with the military and served as sergeant major in home service during the Second World War.

Sarah's husband, Percy Lister, opened a butcher shop in Ottawa's Glebe neighbourhood, which became very successful. The Listers had three children and became very active in community work and Progressive Conservative politics.[21] Olivia Kelly went to live with her oldest daughter, Lillian, until her death in 1931, and Lillian in turn went later in life to live with the Listers. Aunt Catherine also lived with the Listers until her death in 1946; her funeral service was held at the Catholic Apostolic Church in downtown Ottawa, of which she was now one of the last remaining members, still waiting for the Second Coming.[22]

Irwin Kelly is buried in the Tigris Lane Cemetery, about 11 kilometres southwest of Arras, along a side road about 2 kilometres south of the main road from Arras to Cambrai.

A former quarry, it was captured from the Germans by the British in April 1917, lost to the Germans in April 1918, and taken back by the Canadian Corps in August 1918; it is one of a series of small cemeteries that mark the line of advance of the Canadian Corps in August and September of 1918. Except for a little hotel nearby, it sits in sugar beet fields in low rolling country, with large windmills turning lazily in the sky, a TGV (Train à Grande Vitesse) line and the main highway not far away, and a small wooded area in the distance. The Great Cross sits on top of a set of steps which also constitutes the Stone of Remembrance and marks the entrance to the cemetery, which is elevated behind a low stone wall. The headstones are decorated by plants and small shrubs but there are no large trees. Kelly's grave is in a row of Canadians

Figure 21.3. Tigris Lane Cemetery.
Source: Photograph by Carolyn Bowker.

Figure 21.4. Tigris Lane Cemetery.
Source: Photograph by Carolyn Bowker.

killed between August 27 and September 3, 1918, in the great battle for the Drocourt-Quéant Line. His headstone bears the inscription: "Blessed are those that have not seen, and yet have believed."

Figure 21.5. Tigris Lane Cemetery. Headstone of Irwin Kelly.
Source: Photograph by Carolyn Bowker.

22

THE MCKENZIE BROTHERS
Service and Sacrifice

Alexander Lyon "Sandy" McKenzie and his younger brother John Langsdale "Jack" McKenzie were athletes who rowed for the New Edinburgh Canoe Club and played on a variety of local and church football and hockey teams. They signed up together in 1915 and went to the front with a Canadian Highland regiment. Jack was severely wounded in 1916 and served out the war in England. Sandy fought through many battles, was wounded several times, won the Military Medal and other decorations, and died in the Battle of the Canal du Nord, six weeks before the end of the war. A few days before the Armistice, their youngest brother Kenneth lied about his age to sign up for the Canadian Expeditionary Force to Siberia. The surviving brothers would build new lives after the war, but Jack would carry its scars for the rest of his life.

The McKenzie family occupied a substantial wood-frame house at 50 Victoria Street in New Edinburgh. Alexander Sr., a Scottish immigrant, had been a retail merchant in Finch, south of Ottawa, when he had married Dora Bennett, who came from nearby Spencerville, in 1887.[1] About the turn of the century he had come to Ottawa to work for the T. Lindsay Company, Ottawa's first department store, which in 1905 opened a four-storey building at Rideau Street and Sussex Drive. (Later known as the "Daly Building," its distinctive architecture and prominent location would make it a landmark to generations of Ottawans.) With an income of $725 a year in 1911 and a $2,000 life insurance policy, McKenzie was a solid though not wealthy member of the community.[2] The family attended MacKay Presbyterian Church, where Dora McKenzie was an active member of the Ladies' Aid.

The couple had eight children. The two oldest sons left New Edinburgh early in the century to seek their fortunes in North Bay. Daughter Dora ("Dollie," 1892), died tragically in 1908 of spinal meningitis.[3] When the war broke out Sandy (1893) was a brakeman, whether on a railroad or the Ottawa street railway is not clear. Jack (1896) had gone to Manitoulin Island to work for relatives as a store clerk in Gore Bay. Kenneth (1901) and the youngest daughters Jessie (1899) and Ellen (1904) were still in school. Kenneth was not an athlete like his older brothers, being afflicted on both feet with hammer toe, a condition that causes the toes to bend upward.

Figure 22.1. Alex Lyon McKenzie.
Source: Gore Bay Museum.

In the summer of 1915, Sandy was visiting Jack in Gore Bay when both young men signed up in a northern Ontario regiment, the 37th Algonquin Rifles, and they were formally attested at the Niagara Camp on September 7, 1915.[4] John Langsdale McKenzie was five feet five and a half inches tall, with dark complexion, brown eyes, and dark brown hair. Alex Lyon McKenzie was five feet six and a half inches tall, with dark complexion, hazel eyes, and black hair. When the 37th Battalion was broken up in England in December 1915, the brothers were assigned to the 13th Battalion in the First Canadian Division, which had been built around Montreal's Royal Highlanders and had suffered heavy losses at Second Ypres and in subsequent battles. On April 8, 1916, the brothers joined this battalion in the Ypres Sector.

Jack McKenzie's war lasted a matter of days. On April 15, 1916, the 13th Battalion moved forward to a line called "the bluff," formed by earth excavated in the digging of the Ypres canal, where the men were exposed to constant sniping and shelling. "During April 16th there was artillery activity on both sides," says the battalion's history. "In the morning the enemy fired about thirty rounds of high explosive into a trench on No. 3 Coy's front, smashing in the parapet, burying a machine gun and causing several casualties, while later in the day an automatic trench thrower projected a series of bombs

Figure 22.2. Jack McKenzie.
Source: Private collection.

into Hedge Row, a trench held by No. 4 Coy. Here, however, the damage was slight. Casualties for the day totalled 3 killed and 6 wounded."[5] Jack McKenzie was wounded when a piece of shrapnel tore through his face above the eye to the bridge of his nose and also entered his arm. On April 17 he was admitted to the No. 6 British Red Cross Hospital at Étaples, and on April 25 he was evacuated to England where he would spend the rest of the war.

Sandy McKenzie remained with the 13th Battalion through another week of heavy shelling and bitter skirmishing in the craters in front of Mount Sorrel, in which the battalion lost 9 officers and 164 men killed, wounded, missing, or taken prisoner, before it was relieved on April 23. Returning to the front in May, it again suffered heavy bombing, sniping, and shelling as the men worked to rebuild their damaged defences.[6] On May 28, 1916, Sandy was admitted to the 2nd Canadian Field Ambulance with an infected finger—which, as we have seen, was not a trivial matter given the filthy conditions in the trenches. He did not rejoin his unit until June 12, and he may not have participated in the Battle of Mount Sorrel. The 13th Battalion had now become a full-fledged kilted regiment with strong ties to the Black Watch in Scotland. It endured two further stints in the front line at Sanctuary Wood in June and July, where thousands of men on both sides were sacrificed for little gain.

In late August the 13th Battalion marched to the Somme. There it was immediately and prematurely thrown into battle in support of an Australian attack on Pozières Ridge. Two companies that were rushed forward to plug gaps in the line were exposed to heavy fighting and shelling in a series of desperate struggles that lasted all day, with the Germans at various times getting behind the Canadians or between them and the Australians. Groups of men were cut off and had to fight it out without food or water. Casualties were heavy, with 60 men killed, 247 wounded, and 16 missing.[7] During this battle, on September 4, Sandy suffered a severe shrapnel wound to the left buttock.

After treatment at field hospitals and then a general hospital at Camiers, France, he was evacuated to England and entered hospital on September 15. A medical admission report read: "The wound at present is a deep long wound in the buttocks drained by two large tubes that have their exit about 6" below. The wound has evidently been excised. He complains of pain in gastric region, back and legs on arrival and wound is in very septic condition." Sandy endured several weeks of painful recovery in a series of hospitals. By November 6 the wound was healing well, though still discharging, but it did not properly heal until the end of the year. On January 23, 1917, he was discharged to a Canadian Casualty Assembly Centre, then passed through convalescent units and a reserve battalion until on May 18, 1917, when he returned to the front with the 13th Battalion.

He had missed some terrible battles but he probably participated in the attack on Hill 70 in August that cost the battalion 40 percent of its strength.[8] On August 28, 1917, he was made lance corporal. In October, the 13th Battalion marched to Passchendaele where, fortunately, it played only a supporting role. Even so, the men in sodden kilts coated with layers of mud dug and repaired trenches that constantly caved in and buried the thousands of soldiers who had been killed, all in a steady rain. On November 8 the battalion was pulled back and sent to Arras for the winter, where they could at long last bathe, get new clothes, put on "trues" (trousers), and rid themselves of the mud of Flanders.[9] On December 31, Sandy McKenzie was made corporal and five weeks later he was granted 14 days' leave in England. On March 20, 1918, he had his pay stopped to make up for lost property, an offense that does not seem to have been too serious since he was appointed lance sergeant and then sergeant in May. In July 1918 he went on a musketry course as the Canadian Corps began to prepare for the attack at Amiens that began on August 8.

The 13th Battalion was at the forefront of the Canadian attack. As it moved forward under a rolling barrage, hampered by mist and smoke that made coordination with tanks difficult, it suffered casualties when shells from its own guns fell short. Hampered by a shortage of grenades, it had to take heavily entrenched machine guns. Through many acts of bravery and sacrifice (one man won a Victoria Cross), the battalion advanced the line 5,000 yards, one-quarter of the total Canadian advance in one of the great Canadian victories of the war.[10] Losses were heavy and the battalion had to retire and regroup, but this time only for weeks and not months as the Canadian pressed forward relentlessly. On September 1, the 13th Battalion attacked the Drocourt-Quéant Line, a heavily fortified entrenchment bristling with machine guns that had to be knocked out one at a time, with grenades, rifles, and bayonets. The number of officers who were killed or wounded in these battles was so great that NCOs like McKenzie played a crucial role keeping attacks together and holding off counterattacks. More Military Medals and two Victoria Crosses were added to the 43 medals awarded for Amiens.[11] Then it was on to the battle that would be the high point of the war for General Currie and the Canadian Corps—the crossing of the Canal du Nord on September 27, 1918.

The Canal du Nord was the last remaining obstacle on the road to Cambrai. The Germans had flooded the land so that it was marshy and nearly impassable. The 3rd Brigade, including the 13th Battalion, would have to cross the canal at a narrow point where it was fordable, then fan out on the other side to widen the bridgehead and allow the hundred thousand men of the Canadian Corps to pour through and engage the Germans on an ever broader and deeper front. It was a risky plan but Currie had experienced troops, coordinated artillery, air cover, machine guns, tanks, and an engineering corps ready to build bridges so that tanks and artillery could move forward to support the Canadian advance.

The 14th Battalion of the 3rd Brigade crossed the canal and then made a left hook to take the village of Sains-les-Marquion, driving forward against heavy fire from determined German machine gun crews. By 10:00 a.m. they had achieved their objective. It was then the turn of the 13th Battalion to pass through them and advance on the heavily fortified town of Marquion. Speed was of the essence. The men encountered obstacles of wire, were forced into narrow positions against heavy fire, and did not get the tank support they were promised. Company after company pressed forward and took the town before giving way to the next wave that passed through them. But casualties were severe. "Every time I look around for a familiar face," wrote one soldier two days later, "I find they are gone."[12] One of those lost was Sandy McKenzie. According to the Circumstances of Death Register: "While attacking an enemy machine gun post near Marquion he was hit by a machine gun bullet and killed."[13] He had been cited for bravery in previous battles and now he was posthumously awarded the Military Medal.[14] He was 24.

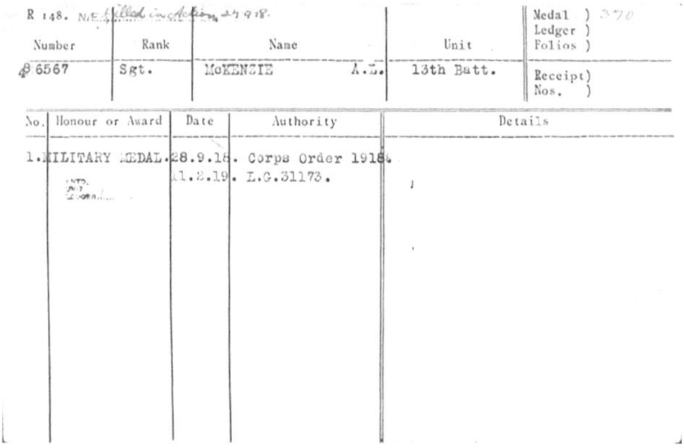

R 148. N/E. Killed in Action

Number	Rank	Name	Unit	Medal Ledger Folios 370
486567	Sgt.	McKENZIE A.L.	13th Batt.	Receipt Nos.

No.	Honour or Award	Date	Authority	Details
1.	MILITARY MEDAL.	28.9.18.	Corps Order 1918.	
		11.2.19.	L.G.31173.	

Figure 22.3. Military Medal citation for Alex Lyon McKenzie; in the last year of the war, citations for Military Medals and Military Cross often did not provide details.
Source: LAC, Canada, Military Honours and Awards Citation Cards, 1900–1961, McKaig, Albert William – McMordie, H. C., image 341: 486567 Sgt. McKenzie A. L., 13th Batt.

Meanwhile, Jack McKenzie was convalescing in England. On April 27, 1916, he was admitted to hospital in Folkestone, and on May 6 he was transferred to another centre in Epsom; then on May 30 to a long-term recovery centre, from which he was released on June 5. He had a "large scar from the outer angle of Right eye across face + over nose." There was damage to the eyeball itself and although his wounds healed within a month, he was never again able to see clearly from that eye. For the rest of the war, he served in reserve battalions and Canadian Army Service Corps units in England as a clerk with the rank of sergeant. He was also attached to the YMCA, which ran canteens, libraries, stores selling goods from Canada, and other facilities where soldiers far from home could meet, sing, and write letters home. He may well have been able to visit with his brother during Sandy's lengthy convalescence between September 1916 and May 1917. On December 17, 1918, he was moved to the base at Kinmel, Wales, and he sailed for home in January 1919. A medical board ruled that 22-year-old Jack McKenzie had a 30 percent disability and could return to his previous occupation with some limitations.

Figure 22.4. Jack McKenzie after his wound.
Source: Private collection.

The news of Sandy's death reached the McKenzie family in Ottawa on October 10. Nonetheless, only a month later, the youngest son, 17-year-old Kenneth McKenzie, lied about his age to sign up on November 9, 1918, with the Canadian Expeditionary Force (Siberia).[15] By any criterion—his age, the fact that he had just lost a brother, and his disability—he should have been disqualified for military service. The story of his experience in the Siberian campaign is told in Chapter 24. When he returned to Canada in May 1919, he moved to Hamilton to work as a clerk.

Jack McKenzie returned to Manitoulin Island, was discharged in February 1919, and on November 12 married 20-year-old Evelyn Purvis. They settled down to raise a family (they would have six children). Jack McKenzie became a prominent local businessman and he and his wife were both active in their church and in community groups. He died in 1984, "best known for his keen interest in the sport of curling and the community curling rink. His love of curling was even more obvious when he made a trip last winter at the age of 88 years to throw a curling stone in the new Gore Bay Curling Rink."[16] He is buried in Gore Bay.

On August 25, 1921, Alexander McKenzie Sr. died at age 68 of Bright's disease.[17] During the next few years daughters Ellen and Jessie left New

Edinburgh to work as a civil servant and clerk respectively, and Dora (who was on the Executive Committee of the MacKay Ladies' Aid until 1922) also left, to live with Ellen. In 1925 Ellen, aged 21, married Donald Murray Delahey, also a 21-year-old clerk.[18] Though she no longer resided in New Edinburgh, she continued to be listed on the MacKay Communion Rolls as "Mrs. Delahey" until she left Ottawa in 1928. That same year, Jessie McKenzie married George Francis Dalton, a surveyor and war veteran who was the son of the former Clerk of English Journals of the House of Commons. The Daltons were well placed in Ottawa society, and Jesse did volunteer work with women's groups in the Second World War.[19] Dora McKenzie moved to Hamilton to live with her son Kenneth, and she died there in 1939. She is buried in Spencerville near her birthplace, together with her husband and their daughter Dora, who had died so tragically in 1908. Sandy's name is also inscribed on their tombstone.

Sandy McKenzie is buried in Sains-les-Marquion British Cemetery, near where he fell taking the village that was so important in the Battle of the Canal du Nord.

Figure 22.5. Sains-les-Marquion British Cemetery.
Source: Photograph by Carolyn Bowker.

The cemetery is about 12 kilometres northwest of Cambrai and 2 kilometres south of the road leading from Arras to Cambrai, which was the main axis of the Canadian advance in the Hundred Days. Along this road are two

Figure 22.6. Sains-les-Marquion British Cemetery.
Source: Photograph by Carolyn Bowker.

major Canadian war memorials and many small cemeteries, some of which bear names like Quebec, Ontario, and Dominion. The Sains-les-Marquion cemetery is located at one corner of a crossroads about half a kilometre from the village of the same name, with a few houses and buildings along the roads on two sides. It is raised above the level of the roads with a stone wall, and it is enclosed on the other two sides by low stone walls, outside of which are large open fields. The Great Cross sits outside the cemetery at the crossroads, and the main entrance is a gate and some steps halfway along one side off the main road. There is no Stone of Remembrance. One hundred eighty-five Canadians who fell between September 27 and the middle of October 1918 are buried there, along with British and Australian bodies brought in from surrounding battlefields. Sandy McKenzie was among the first to be buried in this cemetery, along the back wall in a row of men who fell on September 27. His headstone bears the inscription "Safe in the arms of Jesus."

Figure 22.7. Sains-les-Marquion British Cemetery, headstone of Sandy McKenzie.
Source: Photograph by Carolyn Bowker.

23 ARTHUR FRANK HAWKE AND THE WAR AGAINST TB

Of the 19 men named on the In Memoriam plaque at MacKay Presbyterian Church, the last to die was, like the first, a member of the German-Canadian community in New Edinburgh. Arthur Frank Hawke was born August Frank Heinrich Haak. That he and others in his family signed up to fight in the war against Germany is one story. Why he is on the memorial plaque of MacKay Presbyterian Church is another. But the most important story is that he died not on the battlefield but in hospital, of tuberculosis, a disease that was rampant in New Edinburgh and claimed more lives during the war than did the war itself. To top it off, Hawke was probably a victim of the 1918 influenza epidemic.

The Haak family lived in a small wood-frame house at 38 Dufferin Road, just across the street from MacKay Presbyterian Church. Arthur Hawke's father, Johann Albert Haak, had come to Canada from Pomerania in the early 1880s with his parents, two brothers, and his sister Augusta and her husband, Albert Christian Schroeder.[1] In 1888 Johann married Johannah Miller, also a German immigrant, at St. Paul Lutheran Church in Sandy Hill. Haak, a motorman on the Ottawa Electric Railway, built the house on Dufferin Road in New Edinburgh and his brother-in-law, Albert Schroeder, a sawmill worker, built a house next door.[2] Johann and Johanna had three children: August (1889),[3] Elizabeth (1892), and a girl who died as an infant. Then in 1894, Johanna died at age 26 of tuberculosis.[4] The following year Johann married Matilda Bolduan, 23, a recent immigrant from Pomerania[5] and they had six children together: Richard (1896), Mary (1897), Bertha (1899), Charles (1901), Augusta (1903), and John (1904). But Johann was probably also ill as early as 1900—the 1901 census records him working as a labourer for only one month in the previous year—and in 1905 he, too, died of TB.[6] Matilda Haak was left at age 34 to raise her six children and two stepchildren in a six-room house, which, fortunately, she owned.[7]

The family remained Lutheran, attended St. Paul, and probably spoke German at home; but inevitably they became more integrated into the wider community. Johann was identified in the 1891 census as John Hawke. Three of his children would marry people of other religions, and at various times

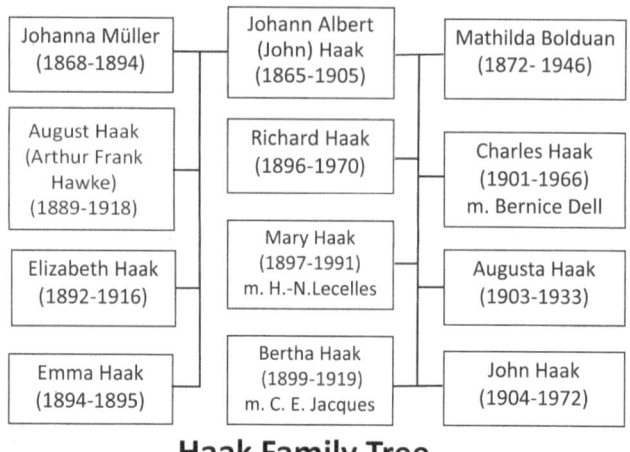

Figure 23.1. Haak family tree.
Source: Created by the author.

some of them would go by names such as Hawke, Hawk, or Hack.⁸ The family also seems to have had close ties with Rev. Peter Anderson, a neighbour and friend. We do not know whether Arthur Hawke ever attended MacKay, but when he enlisted he gave his religion as Presbyterian, and when he died it was Rev. Anderson who conducted his funeral, as he did for Hawke's half-sister Bertha (her death is also recorded in MacKay's Death Register).⁹

As a widow, Matilda had little income and was busy with small children, so the older children had to do what they could to support the family. In the 1911 census, 21-year-old August Haak (not yet Arthur Hawke) was described as a labourer for "Corporation"—probably the City of Ottawa—earning $450 a year.¹⁰ His 19-year-old sister Elizabeth was a dressmaker working at home. One of his stepsisters, Mary, 14, was working as a domestic in a private home for $60 a year. His grandmother, Carolina, now 84, who had been living with the family when Johann was alive, had now moved next door to live with the Schroeders. One of the Schroeder sons, Charles, had built a much larger house at 34 Dufferin Road where he lived with his wife and their three small children.

Still, they knew how to have fun. A brief item in the Ottawa *Journal* in 1914 described a surprise twenty-second birthday party at 38 Dufferin Street for Elizabeth Haak, the dressmaker, by "a number of her young friends."

> The entertainment of the evening consisted of games and other amusements. About midnight refreshments were served, and then Miss Rosie Schroeder with fitting words, presented Miss Haak with a beautiful pearl

sunburst pendant, the gift of the assembled guests. Miss Haak's reply indicated her appreciation not only of the gift, but also the congenial spirit manifested by her friends. The verdict from the young people was a good time.[11]

The guests—36 in all, which must have made quite a house full—included several members of the Schroeder extended family, her half-sisters Bertha and Mary, and young men and women from the German community. This glimpse into a family and a community is poignant in light of the war that would shortly break out and the fate of the young woman for whom the party was given.

Another, less happy, glimpse is offered by a report in the Ottawa *Journal* in 1913 that Richard Haak, August's 17-year-old half-brother, was one of three thieves found guilty of stealing lead pipe worth $20.[12] His partners in crime were the ringleader, Michael Sandusky, a 16-year-old labourer who had already been in trouble with the law, and Reinhold Gromoll, who was two years older than Richard and would remain a close friend for many years. (Interestingly, the investigating police officer was Detective Émile Joliat.) There is no record of what sentence they received; one would like to believe that at least for Richard and Reinhold it was light, since they do not appear to have got into any trouble after that incident. That high-spirited boys might run afoul of the law in small ways is hardly surprising, though it could hardly have been pleasing to his widowed mother with three unmarried daughters and two younger boys still at home. But when country called, each of the three miscreants enlisted in the CEF: Haak and Gromoll signed up in December 1917 in the 72nd Battery CFA; and Sandusky enlisted in the 240th Battalion in 1916.[13]

Less obvious, but a very present concern, was the fact that tuberculosis ran through the Haak family, going back to its time in Germany. As we have seen, tuberculosis was prevalent in New Edinburgh, especially among women. It is caused by a bacterium, *M. tuberculosis*, whose existence has been known since 1882, but before the discovery of antibiotics there was no cure. It is spread through the air by droplets of sputum from those with active TB (but it can also be contracted through infected milk) and thus easily infects families living together for long periods in crowded conditions. Although it can attack other parts of the body, it most commonly affects the lungs, where it destroys the cells in the alveoli and fills the sacs with bloody mucus. In 90 percent of infections, the disease never expresses itself and a person neither infects others nor suffers from the disease. Even in active cases, an otherwise healthy body might mask the disease for a long time and it would thus go undiagnosed. About 50 percent of active cases might recover or at least tolerate the infection, though damaged lungs would make the victims vulnerable to other diseases. But for the other

50 percent, the disease meant a long illness in which the sufferer would waste away (hence the name consumption), coughing blood, perhaps even improving for a time, but eventually succumbing to respiratory or organ failure. Arthur Hawke's grandfather Augustus probably died of it and his mother and father certainly did. In the next generation one of his uncles would die of it as would the wife and children of another uncle. His sister and two half-sisters would also fall victim to the disease.[14] No wonder some early students of TB believed that it was hereditary.

Arthur Frank Hawke enlisted on February 13, 1915, in the 42nd (Smiths Falls) regiment, which was quickly absorbed into the 38th Battalion in Ottawa. Hawke was five feet ten and a half inches tall, with fair complexion, grey eyes, and dark hair. He gave his occupation as grocery clerk and declared that he had served with the militia for a year in Toronto. He assigned $15 per month of his pay to his stepmother (which was raised to $20 in June 1916), and she was also given a separation allowance of $20 a month as a widow for whom he was the sole support. His will, dated July 27, 1916, left all his property and effects to his stepmother.

Hawke was not a model soldier, though he never stepped over any serious lines. While training with the 38th in Kingston, he was given 14 days' detention on July 2, 1915, and on July 22 he forfeited seven days' pay and was given 168 hours' detention. After the 38th went to Bermuda, he was fined $2 for drunkenness. He kept his record clean for the rest of his time in Bermuda, but in England, on July 2, 1916, he was sentenced to eight days of Field Punishment No. 2 for not complying with an order and bringing liquor from a canteen. This punishment involved being placed in handcuffs but still able to march with his unit, with no forfeiture of pay.

One explanation for his behaviour is that Hawke probably had some very serious things on his mind. On February 27, 1915, a cousin died of tuberculosis at age 14, and about the same time, his only full sister, Elizabeth, began showing signs that she, too, had TB. Working at home as a dressmaker, probably unable to afford the medical care and certainly not the treatment in a sanatorium that might have alleviated her condition, she steadily worsened. On February 12, 1916, she died at the age of 24, two years after her surprise birthday party.[15] On November 14, 1916, another cousin also died of the disease at age 22. It is likely that Hawke was beginning to detect signs that he, too, might fall victim to this family scourge. Within a month of the 38th Battalion's arrival in the Ypres Sector in August 1916, Hawke was transferred to the newly created 4th Division Salvage Company, whose job was to gather equipment and debris from battlefields and encampments for recycling and re-use. This was an important job given the quantity of, for example, rusted steel for salvage. But Hawke was a tall, strong man whose battalion was being marched to the Somme where it would take part in some terrible battles. His discipline record alone should not have kept him from the front.

In early February 1917, he reported sick and was given "med and duty." On March 6, he was sent to a field ambulance, and then on March 22 to a Casualty Clearing Station where he was diagnosed with pneumonia and transferred to a general hospital in Camiers (part of the complex at Étaples) on March 24. Hawke would have known this was not pneumonia. His persistent hacking cough and pain in his lungs, difficulty sleeping, night sweats, and an irregular temperature would have been symptoms he had seen before in others. He was sent to England, and on April 4 he was admitted to a hospital in Sheffield where he was definitively diagnosed as having a tubercle of the lung. He was then sent to the Ontario Military Hospital in Orpington for long-term treatment.

Tuberculosis was a problem for the military. The recruitment of hundreds of thousands of young men had shown for the first time how prevalent TB, as well as other diseases like VD, were in the Canadian population. Many men like Hawke who had enlisted with asymptomatic TB were sent to the trenches where damp and cold, overcrowding, and frequent exposure to residual poison gas allowed the disease to express itself and to spread. There were over 3,000 cases of TB in the CEF during the war and 176 deaths, and by 1917 military doctors were being told to screen recruits more carefully for it. Tuberculsosis was not a war wound, but who knew whether a soldier had had it when he joined or had contracted it in the trenches? The military had to care for them, and while Hawke's condition may have been made worse by his military service, he received a much better standard of care than did the other members of his family.[16]

In June 1917, Hawke was shipped back to Canada, and July 14 he was admitted to the Sir Oliver Mowat Memorial Hospital in Kingston. This hospital had opened in 1912 as a treatment centre for TB and was one of several institutions taken over during the war by the Department of Militia and Defence. Treatment consisted of rest, nutrition, fresh air, and control of germ-laden sputum to allow the body to fight off the infection. Patients could sit on the balconies of the stone building, or in good weather in beds or chairs on the lawn in the sun. For most patients this was palliative care, to prolong life and improve its quality; but for a few, it might lead to recovery. Though some soldiers did not adapt well to the routine of a military hospital, Hawke seems to have kept to the prescribed regimen. Indeed, his situation seems to have improved somewhat, as he was allowed to visit his family in Ottawa where on July 26, 1917, he attended the wedding of his half-sister Bertha.[17]

In May 1918, a decision was made by the Department of Militia and Defence to discharge soldiers who were long-term TB patients rather than

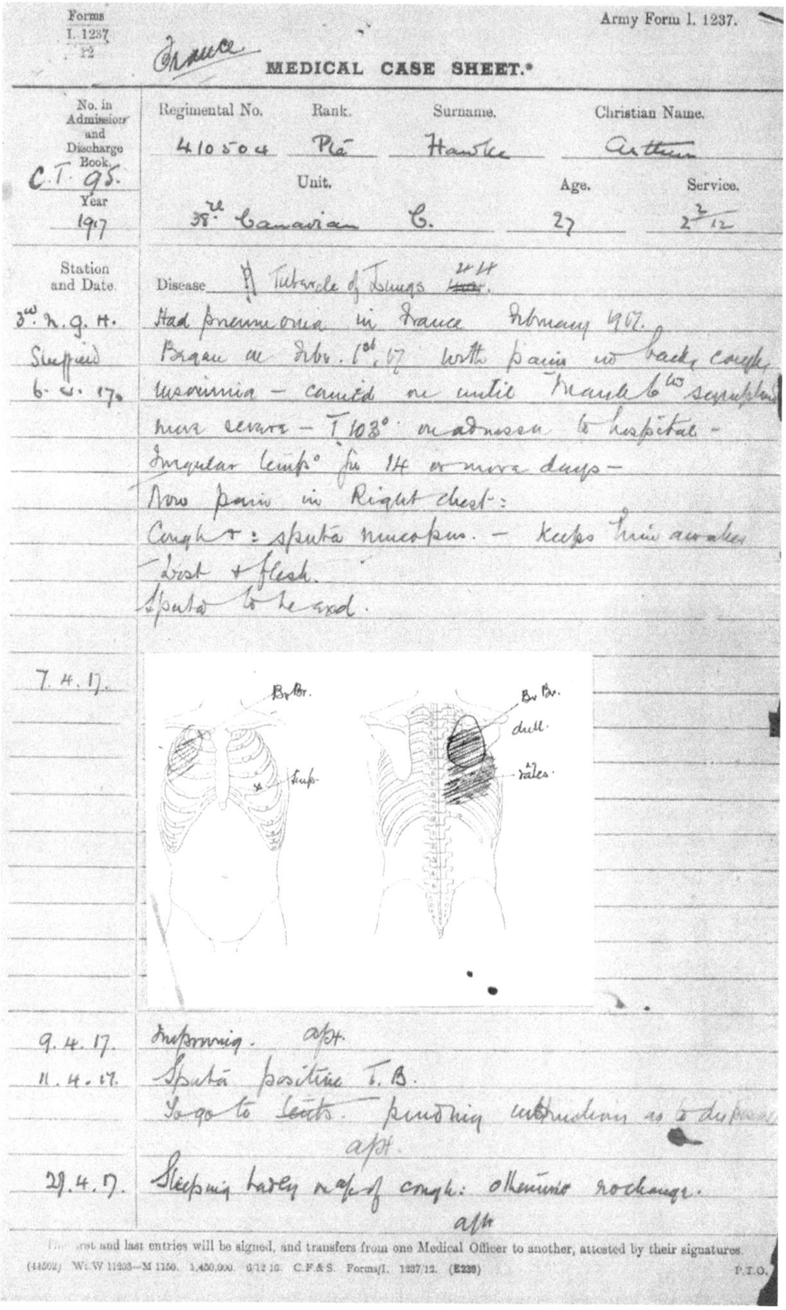

Forms I. 1237/12

France

Army Form I. 1237.

MEDICAL CASE SHEET.*

No. in Admission and Discharge Book	Regimental No.	Rank.	Surname.	Christian Name.
C.T. 95.	410504	Pte	Hawke	Arthur

Year	Unit.	Age.	Service.
1917	38th Canadian C.	27	2 2/12

Station and Date. Disease: Tubercle of Lungs

3rd N.G.H. Stepped 6.4.17. Had pneumonia in France February 1917. Began on Febr. 1st, 17 with pain in back, cough, insomnia — carried on until March 6th — symptoms more severe — T 103° on admission to hospital — Irregular temp° for 14 or more days — Now pain in Right chest: Cough +: sputa mucopus. — Keeps him awake. Lost + flesh. Sputa to be exd.

7.4.17.

9.4.17. Improving. afh

11.4.17. Sputa positive T.B. To go to Seats. pending instructions as to disposal. afh

29.4.17. Sleeping badly a/c of cough: otherwise no change. afh

The first and last entries will be signed, and transfers from one Medical Officer to another, attested by their signatures.

(44502) Wt.W 11203—M 1150. 1,450,000. 6/12 16. C.F.&S. Forms/I. 1237/12. (E239) P.T.O.

Figure 23.2. Page from Arthur Hawke's medical file.
Source: LAC RG 150, Service Files of the Canadian Expeditionary Force (CEF): Arthur Frank Hawke 410504.

keeping them in uniform. The Invalided Soldiers Commission had taken over the network of TB hospitals across the country, and patients would now be treated as disabled veterans, receiving treatment and training to start a new life if they ever left the hospital.[18] Hawke was therefore formally discharged from the CEF on July 31, 1918. His conduct and character in the service were described as "good." Instead of being paid as a soldier, he was given—in addition to the clothing allowance and payments due to all discharged soldiers—a disability allowance to enable him to continue to receive treatment at the Mowat Hospital.

Unfortunately, like other TB sufferers, Hawke was a sitting duck for the Spanish Flu which hit Kingston in October 1918. The MacKay Register of Deaths recorded that on October 26, 1918, "Pte. A. F. Hawke died in hospital in Kingston." The official cause of death was pulmonary tuberculosis, but it is a fair assumption that the proximate cause was influenza.[19] On October 28, 1918, Arthur Hawke was buried in the Haak family plot in Beechwood Cemetery, by Rev. P. W. Anderson.

Arthur Frank Hawke did not die a hero's death on the battlefield, but he was a soldier in a different war, in which eventually a more lasting victory was won than in the one fought in Europe. In 1919, Parliament created a federal Department of Health, which among other things began programs of gathering statistics, doing research in public health, and controlling TB nationwide. Provincial ministries of health were also formed, which financed schools of hygiene and public health, local health units and inspection programs, and TB education, detection, monitoring, and treatment. Volunteer organizations like the Red Cross and the Canadian Tuberculosis Association teamed up with government agencies at all levels in programs of immunization, slum clearance, sanitation, and education. In the 1920s schools began screening programs with portable X-ray machines. In 1927 the Christmas Seals campaign began to increase awareness and raise funds for research and treatment. Hospitals and sanatoriums became more accessible and new surgical procedures and treatments, including antibiotics, increased the survival rates. As the incidence of TB fell the "sans" began to close, and in 1924, the Department of National Defence divested itself of all but one of the TB hospitals it had taken over. By the 1970s the TB epidemic that had once struck fear into every heart was a distant memory.[20]

The First World War also marked a turning point for German-Canadians: in the words of a historian of the Lutheran Church, "a period of awakening out of their dream world and a coming to grips with the realities of life. It was also a period of clarification, for themselves as well as the non-German element."[21] There was healing to be done, and a new concept of citizenship to be considered, a new definition of Canada as an independent, inclusive nation. Those who served came back changed by the war—not least the three young men who only a few years before had been in trouble with the law, and who now got married and settled down to jobs and stable lives.[22] Many German-Canadians in New Edinburgh were naturalized in 1917 and in the 1921 census all listed their nationality as "Canadian." One of these was Matilda Haak, whose "nationality" was originally written as "German," then crossed out and replaced by "Canadian," and there is a note on the census record that she had had sons in the military. The presence of Charles Albert Wendt and Arthur Hawke on the memorial plaque at MacKay Presbyterian Church showed that MacKay embraced these German-Canadians as part of the church community.

Of the remaining members of the Haak family, Richard on his return from military service found work as a "lathe hand in a factory." In 1920 he married (at St. Bartholomew's Church, declaring himself Anglican) and left New Edinburgh.[23] John Haak, a clerk, became a star lacrosse player for New Edinburgh teams and a well-known figure in the village.[24] Charles Haak, a machine operator, married and occupied the house at 38 Dufferin Street (together with his mother, brother, and a sister before their deaths) until 1966. Another sister married a Franco-Ontarian and left New Edinburgh.

In 1921 Matilda Haak, working as a "charwoman" in a government building, received Arthur's Victory Medal, his British War Medal, and a Memorial Cross, as well as the plaque and scroll given to all soldiers.[25] Little could she have realized, when she left Germany and came to New Edinburgh as a 23-year-old bride, that she would lose her husband to tuberculosis, raise eight children only to see four of them die of TB, and live through two wars fought against the country of her birth, in which two of her sons and stepsons would serve and one would die. When she died, at age 76, her surviving family placed a notice in the Ottawa *Journal:* "In loving memory of a beloved mother and grandmother, Matilda Haak, who passed away March 27, 1946."

> A loving mother, so gentle and kind.
> What a wonderful memory she left behind.
> Long days, long nights she bore the pain.
> To wait for cure, but all in vain.
> 'Til God Himself knew what was best,
> He took her home and gave her rest."[26]

She was laid to rest in the family plot in Beechwood Cemetery. The only headstone in this plot is that of Arthur Hawke, placed there by the Commonwealth War Graves Commission. The inscription on it reads "In sacred peace Let him remain / Some day in heaven We shall meet again."

Figure 23.3. Haak family plot, Beechwood Cemetery, with Arthur Hawke's headstone in the Commonwealth design.
Source: Photograph by Carolyn Bowker.

24

1919
The Men Come Home

On Sunday, November 9, 1919, Edward, Prince of Wales, visited MacKay Presbyterian Church to unveil two brass plaques that honoured the men and women who had fought for King and Country in the Great War. The prince was 25, handsome and charming, not yet the man who would abdicate the throne in 1936 and live out a bitter exile as the Duke of Windsor. He had served with the British Army in France and Flanders and had even been attached to the Canadian Corps for a time (one of the last things he did during his visit to Ottawa was to visit his friend Leonard Askwith, the cousin of a MacKay veteran, who had been badly wounded at the Somme). He was staying at Rideau Hall during the Ottawa leg of a three-month tour, whose purpose was to promote the vision of a new Canadian nation born of the war that would also be a full partner in a reformed and revitalized British Empire. Everywhere he went, the prince drew enthusiastic crowds, combining the dignity of royalty with the democratic spirit and the celebration of youth and life that were emerging from the war.[1] And now the Prince of Wales, the heir to the throne, the embodiment of the Empire and all it stood for, a celebrity with movie-star looks, was coming to MacKay Presbyterian Church!

The church was splendidly decorated and people were sitting in the aisles. Arrangements had been made to ensure that all who needed them had tickets to the service and that those who could not come on their own had transport. "MacKay Street outside the church," according to the Ottawa *Citizen*, "was thronged with people, eager to catch a glimpse of the future ruler of the Empire before he goes away, and scores of cameras were waiting for him as he came along the street. His appearance was the signal for the usual loud burst of applause, a welcome which was responded to with that characteristic winning smile."[2] It was a year almost to the day since the war had ended.

On that day, crowds had thronged Parliament Hill singing hymns like "O God Our Help in Ages Past." But after that—what? As we have seen, about one-third of the soldiers from MacKay church were in Canada when the war ended, though some of them had not returned to New Edinburgh. But what of those still overseas? When would they come home? How had the war changed them? How would they adjust to a profoundly altered society, with

Figure 24.1. Edward, Prince of Wales.
Source: Canada Patent and Copyright Office, Library and Archives Canada.

families who had struggled to cope with meagre incomes and rising prices, with wives who had become independent, cast votes, experienced their own share of suffering and sacrifice? The families at MacKay who still had men overseas had settled down to another long, cold winter of waiting.

Nineteen men would not be coming home at all, and for their families the pain of the war would never really end. As the rest of the world rejoiced or turned to caring for the wounded men who had returned, families like the Perneys faced the endless reality of loss, whatever the rhetoric of heroism and martyrdom. The Bothwell, Mayo, Stalker, and youngest Robertson children (not to mention the Marshall children in Scotland) would grow up without their fathers, with their lives dislocated and their mothers or grandparents struggling to raise them. Most families would never visit their loved one's resting place in Imperial war cemeteries or see his name on a monument for those who had no known graves. They could only treasure the fading memory of a hasty embrace, or a fleeting last glimpse at a train station, months or years before.

And although most Canadians could celebrate the Armistice as marking the end of the war, in Eastern Europe and parts of Asia, warfare and ethnic cleansing would continue to rage as new nations emerging from the wreckage of the older empires sought to establish their independence and define their boundaries. In Russia, the Bolsheviks who had taken power in November 1917 were locked in a desperate civil war against the White Russians who wanted to restore the Tsar. The Allies had intervened to support the Whites and several expeditionary forces were sent to Russia to combat the communist regime.

One such force was sent to Vladivostok, Siberia. In July 1918, the Allies had decided to send an expeditionary force to secure the port and the Trans-Siberian Railway as a supply line for White Russian forces in central Asia. Prime Minister Borden had committed 4,000 Canadian troops to the British contingent, which would be commanded by a Canadian, General James Elmsley. But the war ended while the force was being assembled, and public opinion instantly turned against sending men—many of whom had been conscripted to fight in Europe—to another war half a world away. Still, Borden refused to renege on his commitment, and preparations for this campaign continued through the fall of 1918.[3]

The Canadian Expeditionary Force (Siberia)

Four men from MacKay signed up to serve in this expeditionary force. Lieutenant Ray Tubman had been invalided home after being wounded at Vimy Ridge. He was restlessly working in an office in the Department of Militia and Defence when he re-enlisted on October 19, 1918; he departed a few days later and arrived in Vladivostok on December 7. Three other young men, whose names would appear on the MacKay church Honour Roll, were conscripted less than a week before the end of the war. In fact, they were volunteers who had responded to a recruiting campaign in Ottawa for men to serve in the signals corps in the CEF Siberia. It is a mystery why they should have been conscripted rather than simply allowed to enlist. By November 1918 men were no longer being conscripted for the Western Front, and in any case two of them would never have been conscripted under normal circumstances.[4] **Samuel John Kelly Jr.** and **Kenneth McKenzie** were younger brothers of soldiers who had recently been killed; both were underage and gave false information on their attestation papers. The third, **Arthur Reginald Johnston**, 20, was the son of Lancelot Johnston, a long-time resident of New Edinburgh who had made the decorative ironwork on the fence around Parliament Hill, and who was now working as a craftsman for an Ottawa piano manufacturer.

Whatever the circumstances of their enlistment, the three young recruits began Signals training in Ottawa. This would have included everything from installing and using telephones to the rapidly developing wireless technology, to older techniques of light and flag signals. They were then sent for further training in Vancouver, where Johnston was hospitalized for a week with a relatively mild case of the Spanish Flu. Not until February 12, 1919, did the three men embark for Vladivostok to serve in the 6th Signals Company CEF Siberia. The main force, including Ray Tubman, had already been in place for two months.

During that time the situation on the ground had changed dramatically. The White Russians were divided and suffering major setbacks. The various allied nations participating in the expedition had differing objectives and there were clashes among the officers. At home, an increasingly militant labour movement was expressing vocal opposition to sending Canadian workers to fight Bolshevism. In February 1919, Prime Minister Borden told the British he intended to withdraw the Canadian contingent as soon as possible, and General Elmsley was ordered to avoid any engagement that might result in casualties. The men passed a boring winter in what Elmsley described as "this cesspool of a place." They were entertained by amateur vaudeville productions organized by Captain Raymond Massey.[5] They played sports, heard lectures, and explored the local life, such as it was. Ray Tubman has left a photo album of life in Vladivostok, which is now in the Canadian War Museum, with some gruesome pictures from the morgue, Chinese market scenes, and a French funeral parade, as well as fellow officers, sports events, horse races, and daily activities.

A poem on the front cover of Tubman's album sums up the experience of all the men:

> The Base Company, C. E. F. S.
> In Vladivostok is stationed,
> No work to do but this we guess
> Is each one's occupation.

Beginning in April 1919, the troops were brought home, having lost 19 men who had died of accident or disease, but with four Russian-speaking Canadians who had defected to the Bolsheviks. The three young conscripts from MacKay came back in May 1919. They received dental work courtesy of the military, a war gratuity, and the memory of a unique experience. Ray Tubman returned the following month.

The Men Return from Europe

Over half the MacKay men, and one woman, who had survived the war were still overseas when the war ended.[6] Twenty-two were in various front-line

Figure 24.2. Pages from Ray Tubman's album from Siberia.
Source: Canadian War Museum, photo album of Lieutenant Thomas Raymond Tubman, Canadian Siberian Expeditionary Force CWM 20050110-009_p12, George Metcalf Archival Collection.

locations, 18 were serving in France behind the lines, 14 were serving in Britain, and 12 were in hospital or recuperation centres in Britain. They had profoundly changed. Some had not been at the front but had experienced war and military life nonetheless. Others had lived in an alternate reality beyond the understanding of anyone in the peaceful community they had left. They had forged unshakeable bonds with the men they had fought beside, faced danger with, and trusted with their lives. Artilleryman Nairn Grant wrote his family in the fall of 1918 that he hated to part with the "dear old gun and team" which had "been in so many tight places together with such little chances of getting out that they seem part of myself."[7] But what they now wanted was to go home—back to the old place, and back to the old life, if it still existed—and at once.

However, the Armistice was only a truce. Who knew whether the Germans would regroup and decide to fight again? The First and Second Canadian Divisions were sent to the Rhineland in December and January as part of an Allied army of occupation. Grant proudly wrote his father that he was sending home some souvenirs, including a ring made from aluminum off a German biplane and brass from a German cartridge shell, as well as a German officer's helmet, German soldiers' song-books, declarations in French and English of Germany's offer of an armistice, and German uniform buttons and an officer's fatigue cap.[8] Repatriating 300,000 men would be a mammoth task, including assembling them in camps in England, organizing shipping, and doing the paperwork to ensure their smooth discharge and transition to Civvy Street. The men would have to wait through the winter in cold, wet, camps. A significant number of MacKay men were treated for VD in the months after the Armistice. They would not be sent home until they were completely free of the disease.

To make things worse, the Spanish Flu swept through the Canadian Corps, in France and Belgium, in its camps in England, and even in troopships carrying men from Canada. At least twelve MacKay men required hospital treatment (four serious enough to be life-threatening). Three of these men were sick in the first wave in July–August. Of the other nine who were in hospital between October 1918 and February 1919, two were conscripts who had contracted the illness on the troopship over. (Another man, John Bothwell, was being treated in Fredericton, New Brunswick.) Many others had milder cases and recovered after a few days.

Sick and wounded men were sent home in January and February 1919, and between March and June most of the rest crossed the Atlantic. Of the soldiers from MacKay, 5 came home in January and February, 10 in March, 14 in April, 19 in May, and 7 in June. There were eight others who returned to Canada between July and September—usually men who were injured or ill, who were bringing home a war bride, or who had been kept overseas longer in essential service occupations. A handful of men remained in England to help wind up the CEF administration—one stayed on into 1920 and another came back in 1921. About one-quarter of these returned men did not come back to New Edinburgh; indeed, in many cases their families had left the village during the war. Many more would leave in the following few years. But for the moment, they were home, with their families, and most would have been in attendance at MacKay Presbyterian Church for the service on November 9, 1919.

The Prince of Wales Unveils the Memorial Plaques

The prince's visit was his second that morning to a church in New Edinburgh. Earlier, at St. Bartholomew's Anglican Church, he had unveiled a magnificent stained-glass window donated by the Duke of Connaught in honour of the 10 men from the staff of Rideau Hall who had fallen in the war.

Figure 24.3. Victory parade in Ottawa: the Princess Patricia's Canadian Light Infantry make their triumphant return, March 1919.
Source: Canadian War Museum, photo album of fifties teams Post WWI CWM 19840059-223_p39a George Metcalf Archival Collection.

At MacKay he would unveil two plaques: the Honour Roll listing those who had served, and the In Memoriam plaque bearing the names of the 19 who had died.

The prince's appearance had been requested by Rev. Peter Anderson six weeks earlier. MacKay, he had written, was "situated in the parish in which Government House is located" and had "among our heroes names of those who resided at Government House."[9] The prince's chief of staff had replied that His Highness would be happy to do so but "would far prefer that the ceremony should be a small one and only include those who are relatives of the men who served and those who have subscribed to place the tablets in the Church."[10] In expressing his appreciation, Anderson added pointedly that "all the families of our Congregation have subscribed to the tablets."[11] The Session then decided that every soldier and their family, and every member and adherent, would receive a ticket to the service. They also agreed on an elaborate protocol according to which, according to seniority, some Elders would greet the prince, others would stand by the tablets, and still others would hand him the ribbons he would pull to unveil them. Then—and we can only imagine the back story—a week before the visit the Session in an "informal" meeting scrapped this protocol and decided that the Elders "would hand the ribbons to Miss E. Ralph who would then hand them to HRH the

Figure 24.4. MacKay Presbyterian Church Honour Roll plaque.
Source: MacKay United Church.

Prince of Wales" at the unveiling. And in the event it was the minister, not Elders, who met the prince at the door.

When the prince arrived at the church, accompanied by the Governor General, the Duke of Devonshire, together with the Duchess and aides from Rideau Hall, the party was escorted by Rev. Anderson to special seats at the front of the church. At the end of the service, the organist played the national anthem and the minister read an address of welcome to the prince. The address

MacKay Church

MEMORIAL SERVICE
AND
UNVEILING CEREMONY
BY
H. R. H. THE PRINCE OF WALES, K.G.

SUNDAY, NOV. 9TH, 1919 AT 11.00 A.M.

Admit *Lillian Woods*

NOT TRANSFERABLE

SEATS WILL BE RESERVED FOR CARD HOLDERS UNTIL 10.55.
NO SEATS RESERVED AFTER THAT TIME.

REV. P. W. ANDERSON, M.A., B.D.
PASTOR

Figure 24.5. Admission ticket to service of unveiling of the memorial plaques, November 10, 1919. *Source:* MacKay United Church.

expressed the loyalty of the church, its gratitude for the prince's visit, and its pride in those who had "joined the colours to do battle in defence of world righteousness and for the glory of God, among whom is the name of one nursing sister. We reverently mention that nineteen of our heroes sleep on the field of honour, buried with their faces to the foe 'where the poppies grow [in Flanders Fields].'" The prince replied to this purple—and not entirely accurate—oratory with a short, simple speech, pulled the ribbons to unveil the tablets, and the bugler sounded the Last Post.[12]

Elizabeth Ralph

Who was "Miss E. Ralph," the sole woman on the Honour Roll, who had been selected to hand the ribbons to the prince? Elizabeth Ralph was a 34-year-old nursing sister from a pioneer family in New Edinburgh, who had taught Sunday School at MacKay, had served as secretary of the Mission Band, and had attended Ottawa Ladies' College.

"Lizzie" Ralph was diminutive (a little over five feet tall, with a "slight" build), intelligent, ambitious, and motivated by deep religious beliefs and a desire to serve. She had graduated in 1910 from the nursing school at the Clifton Springs Sanitorium in upstate New York, a pioneer institution under the direction of an evangelical Methodist physician, which combined modern medicine with homeopathy and hydrotherapy, mental health treatment, patient-centred medicine, and an emphasis on spiritualism. The Clifton Springs nursing school was one of the first in the United States.[13]

The war should have opened new possibilities for service by a patriotic, religious woman with a solid professional training. However, the Canadian Army Medical Corps (CAMC) was taking only a limited number of nurses

Figure 24.6. Program of service, November 10, 1919.
Source: MacKay United Church.

early in the war—and to get in you likely had to have connections. Not so the British, and when the Queen Alexandra's Imperial Nursing Service (QAINS), which had been formed during the Boer War to recruit military nurses, sent out a call for nursing sisters from "the Dominions," some 313 Canadian nurses answered. In April 1916, Elizabeth Ralph and six other nurses from the Ottawa area boarded a ship for England. Their contract was to be for one year at 40 pounds per annum plus board and laundry, with an option to renew for the duration of the war. They were to travel to England in civilian clothes under the auspices of the CAMC, but they would then

Figure 24.7. The three Ralph sisters, Isabel (1883), Edna (1879), and Elizabeth, taken in 1896 or 1897.
Source: Private collection.

Figure 24.8. Clifton Springs Sanitorium and Clinic—School of Nursing, Graduating Class of 1910; Elizabeth Ralph is second from the left in the front row.
Source: Clifton Springs Historical Society.

Figure 24.9. Elizabeth Ralph, 1910.
Source: Private Collection.

be turned over to the QAINS with the clear stipulation that they had no connection with the CAMC.[14]

We do not know what Ralph did in the QAINS. A nurse of similar age and background who joined about the same time has left a memoir describing postings at Casualty Clearing Stations and general hospitals at the front, and supervising an ambulance train—positions of great responsibility requiring fortitude and skill. But she also recorded dissatisfaction with the competence and professionalism of some British medical personnel, arbitrary regulation and discipline, the British sense of superiority to the "rough" colonials, the abrupt movement from one assignment to another, and probably a degree of sexual harassment, among other grievances. Thus when the opportunity presented itself to join the CAMC in 1917, she jumped at it.[15]

Ralph may or may not have gone to the front, but she was just as anxious to make the jump to the CAMC when she had the chance. On October 16,

1917, lying about her age to appear four years younger, Ralph was attested as a lieutenant/nursing sister in the Canadian Army Medical Corps. This rank, equivalent to 2nd Lieutenant, allowed her to have authority at least over local hospital staff and "other ranks" patients (but not outside the hospital). She was assigned to a Canadian general hospital in Bramshott, England, which had some 600 beds, as well as a VD unit with 350 beds and a pulmonary unit with about 200 beds. Between 1916 and its closure in 1919, 33,097 patents were treated there—some 12,000 in 1918 alone—of whom 14,487 were Canadians. There were 510 deaths.[16]

With her training in hydrotherapy and restorative healing, it is possible that Ralph worked in recovery and rehabilitation wards, perhaps with "shell shock" cases—a task that would have been sensitive and difficult. The responsibility accorded nurses in military hospitals blurred traditional gender and rank relationships and gave them a respect they had not been accorded in civilian life. But she would also have shared the challenges of all thirty-something nursing sisters: navigating the military hierarchy; having any social life while maintaining the decorum due her rank; and squaring her training in restorative healing and her religious mission to care for the sick and broken soldiers with the military emphasis on getting men back to the front. She must have performed well because after she was discharged in August 1919 she was "brought to notice Secretary for War for valuable services rendered during the war"—the equivalent of "mentioned in dispatches."

As a returning veteran from a leading family in the church, she was held in great respect. But unlike her older sister Isabel, who continued to live at home, look after her widowed mother and participate in the varied activities of the church, Elizabeth had a profession and the experience of a much wider world. She seems to have gone in the early 1920s to the United States, and in 1927 she commenced (but apparently did not complete) an application for American citizenship. No longer of "slight" build (she reported her weight as 128 pounds), she was living in New York City and working as a "trained nurse."[17] Her address, 71 E 77th Street in Manhattan, was a posh apartment not far from Central Park. On February 2, 1929, at age 43, she was united in marriage by Rev. Anderson with Peter Butler Olney at her mother's home at 76 Stanley Avenue. "The bride wore a beautiful Parisian gown of beige chiffon, hand painted in a design of pink roses and combined with beige lace, and a hat of beige felt and straw, and she carried a bouquet of sunset roses and orchids," reported the Ottawa *Citizen*. She was given away by her eldest brother, Claude, and attended by her sister Isabel, and the groom's brother and two sisters-in-law travelled from New York to Ottawa for the wedding.[18]

Figure 24.10. Studio portrait of Elizabeth Ralph by J. Alex Castonguay, likely at the time of her wedding. *Source*: Private collection.

Peter Olney, 47 and a widower, was the son of a prominent New York Democrat who had played a key role in taking down the infamous Tammany Hall political machine in the 1880s. His uncle Richard Olney had been US Secretary of State in the second administration of President Grover Cleveland. Peter had graduated from Harvard Law School in 1906, had become assistant US Attorney in the Southern District of New York in 1919, and had succeeded his father in 1922 as Federal Bankruptcy Referee in New York City. Then he had lost two children who had drowned, together with his nephew, when they had pursued a toy sailboat into a deep river. He and his wife had had two more children, but she had died in 1927. It is likely that Elizabeth Ralph was providing private nursing care to Peter Olney's wife, or his mother, when they met.

Peter and Elizabeth Olney set off for a honeymoon in Quebec, after which they moved to New York. There Elizabeth would undertake a very different role than "Lizzie" Ralph had known in New Edinburgh—wife of a prominent American, stepmother to his children, and member of a well-connected family with social responsibilities. She and Peter had a close and loving relationship and her two step-children were very fond of her—one of her step-grandsons has "Ralph" as his middle name. She became an American citizen in 1936. She died in 1947 at age 62 at the Neurological Institute of the Columba Presbyterian Medical Centre, following an operation. She was buried in the Olney family plot in Long Island.[19]

Figure 24.11. The Olney family; the picture was likely taken shortly before Elizabeth's death. She is at left, holding hands with her husband; at right in foreground is her stepson Peter Butler Olney III, and at centre rear is her stepdaughter.
Source: Private collection.

25 AFTERMATH

The men had come home. The community began to heal. The church moved forward. The families got on with their lives. But nothing could be the same again. For some the adjustment to the postwar would be painful; for others it would mean the start of a new life. But the war had been a defining moment for all of them, and they would remember.

Many church leaders, of all denominations, were concerned that the war had shaken the religious convictions of some believers, and that it had failed to bring about the spiritual regeneration and the moral and social reform they had hoped for. And there was much truth to this. But when the Moderator of the Presbyterian Church assured the congregation of MacKay in March 1919, that "[t]here never was a time [...] when the church had a greater hold on its people than it has today,"[1] it is likely that most of those who attended would have shared his view. The evidence from MacKay church supports Stuart Macdonald's conclusion about the Presbyterian Church as a whole:

> The world that Canadian Presbyterians envisaged after the Great War was not markedly different from the world they had longed for prior to August 1914. The Church continued to call for the redeeming and saving of individuals, for transforming them with the saving knowledge of Christ, and then empowering them to transform society by abolishing alcohol, social vice (white slavery or prostitution), observing the Christian sabbath, and creating a more equitable economic system. The sacrifice of so many in war only emboldened Presbyterians to believe that God might profit their venture even more, if only they could improve preaching and evangelism.[2]

The continuing conviction that the war had been fought for nation and Empire, for righteousness, and for God is expressed not only in the memorial plaques but in the address Rev. Anderson had read at the service of dedication. The hymns that were sung and the passage of scripture (Psalm 46) that was read at this service all conveyed the assurance that God was ever-present, ever-faithful, watching over His people, promising salvation to those who accepted His word and followed His commandments. It appeared self-evident that those who had made the supreme sacrifice in a just war had by their actions taken the way of Christ.

In the years immediately after the war, this conviction was expressed in many ways. Church members visited soldiers in hospitals, a horticulturalist in the congregation created a war garden, a collection was taken up towards a proposed memorial church at Vimy Ridge. In 1920, a packed Sunday School attended the presentation by a military chaplain of two wooden plaques with silver maple leaves engraved with the names, respectively, of soldiers from the Sunday School and from the Young Peoples' Association who had fallen in the war. The motto on each was "Our Church, Our Country."[3] In March 1921 the church's anniversary service featured a lecture by Major General Sir Edward Morrison on "Winning of the War," and the following year this same service was attended by Lord Byng of Vimy. In 1922, Elder David Esdale presented a flag to the congregation, and the Session thanked Mrs. Graham McLaurin (née Lumsden, a wealthy widow who had recently divorced her second husband—a rare thing in those days) "for the silk flags so neatly draped over the memorial tablets." As Armistice Sunday became an annual commemoration, these flags and tablets remained a focal point in the church. Men wearing medals and walking with canes featured prominently, as did aging women wearing silver crosses honouring the sacrifice of their husbands and sons.

Between November 1919 and March 1920, the Protestant denominations conducted an Inter-Church Forward Movement with discussion groups, evangelical crusades, clubs, meetings, and outreach activities designed to stimulate spiritual awakening, attract new members, and renew their commitment to evangelism and social service. A fundraising blitz in February 1920 used wartime rhetoric to mobilize the faith: "If on the eve of our great Thank-offering," said the principal of Knox College, "our noble dead whose bodies sleep in Flanders Fields, could speak to us, would they not say, 'Give as we gave to you!' 'Give as Christ gave to the world!' What a challenge to sacrificial giving."[4] At MacKay church, the Annual Report of the Session for 1920 "expressed it[s] devout thanksgiving to God for the evidences of His guidance and blessing, the Session urging the continuation of the spirit manifested in the Forward Movement Campaign, viz. the strengthening of the character and deepening the spiritual life of those who compose the congregation."[5] The Forward Movement undoubtedly reinforced the relentless fundraising that had begun during the war to eliminate the operating deficit and pay off the building debt. In 1919, with the cost of living rising, the minister's salary was raised by $200 and he was given a bonus of the same amount. Three years later the church held a ceremony at which its mortgage was burned.

Figure 25.1. Young Peoples' Memorial plaque.
Source: MacKay United Church.

MacKay church and New Edinburgh were not unaffected by the social ferment and labour unrest that swept through Canada in 1919. A bitter strike on the Ottawa Electric Railway, which had employed many men from New Edinburgh, tied up the streetcar service between July 1 and July 19. Soldiers were called out to guard street railway property, including the car barns in Rockcliffe. The strike was broken by a combination of state intervention, "jitney" service (private motorists selling rides), and the hiring of scabs (including returned soldiers). The workers got a raise from 39 cents an hour to 45 cents rather than the 60 cents they had demanded, but 138 strikers were let go so that the company could give permanent jobs to these "replacement workers."[6]

One place where unrest might have been anticipated was the mill and factory complex at the Rideau Falls. But by the end of the war these industries were in decline. Even before the war, many of the sons and daughters of the skilled tradesmen and labourers who worked there had found that a growing civil service, retail enterprises, and diversified trades and services provided more attractive avenues of employment. And many workers in the W. C. Edwards industries had enlisted for war service and found other work when they returned. In spite of this decline in its major employer, and a country-wide recession between 1920 and 1923, New Edinburgh seems to have remained relatively prosperous, but its social makeup changed considerably.

The only prominent member of the church involved in the labour movement was A. E. Sheppard, who for some years was an important figure in the Typographical Union. But he was never a labour radical and in 1920 he partnered with another MacKay member, civil servant D. H. Macdonald, to start a business, Progressive Printers. He frequently campaigned for the public school board as "A Business Man for the People's Work." He was respected within the church and community even by those who did not share his views and was for many years an Elder of MacKay and president of the New Edinburgh Community Club. Another labour leader who was briefly a member of MacKay was Grant MacNeil, the leading force in the Great War Veterans' Association, which fought tumultuous battles on behalf of the rights and interests of returning soldiers (he would be a Co-operative Commonwealth Federation MP in the 1930s). He and his wife joined in 1920, but their stay was short—he asked to be disjoined in 1921.

All the traditional organizations of MacKay church saw rapid expansion and new energy in the early 1920s, and new ones such as the Progressive Class, the Women's New Era Class, the Men's Business Federation, Young Ladies Missionary Society, the Kings Recruiters Class, and Semper Parata reflected an increasing engagement in social issues and the pursuit of international peace, the expanded role of women, and the influence of younger people, including returned soldiers. The Ladies' Aid contributed to the "Girls Teenage Conference" and other organizations and affiliated for the first time with the local Council of Women. The church presented to the Ottawa Welfare Bureau a list of names of deserving families requiring assistance, participated in a campaign by the Ottawa health board to visit addresses in the area to get people to fill out cards aimed at improving health conditions in the city, and of course, continued to support temperance (now enshrined in law as Prohibition). In 1921 the Session finally succeeded in hiring Mrs. Frances Brunel as music director. Under her leadership in the 1920s the choir won a number of competitions, and MacKay's musicians began to rival its athletes in winning city-wide reputations.

These changes were important but they were more incremental than radical, and there were boundaries the church was not yet ready to cross. In March 1921, the Men's Federation asked permission to hold entertainments within the church that would have involved dancing and card parties, presumably with the idea of attracting and retaining younger people, especially veterans. After exhaustive discussion the Elders unanimously decided that, "after duly considering and sympathetically viewing the entire question of recreation and entertainment from the standpoint of the whole Church, and the relationship she bears to the community, and her undoubted influence on the world," they could not sanction such activity on the part of any church organization. However, the Session expressed "its entire sympathy with, and its loyal support of the social side of the life of the people in the Church and the community," and its recognition that those who made the proposal were sincere in their purpose.[7]

Since 1910, MacKay had consistently voted for Church Union. Union had seemed a certainty in 1914, but the war had interrupted discussions and this delay allowed opposition to grow. By 1918 the Presbyterian Church Association (PCA) was waging a bitter and divisive fight against Church Union. In December 1924, 70 people attended a meeting of the MacKay chapter of the PCA to hear a fire-breathing preacher accuse the unionists of every form of perfidy and deception. Nonetheless, when the vote was taken a month later, great care was taken to ensure it was fair and without rancour. When the congregation voted overwhelmingly in favour of Union, its leading opponent moved a vote of thanks to the returning officers. A number of opponents, including Margaret Askwith, the long-time president of the Ladies' Aid, left to join other Presbyterian churches in the early months of 1925, but others, including John T. McElroy, stayed with MacKay.[8] As it entered the United Church, MacKay also marked its golden jubilee with a gala affair that celebrated the achievements of a church that had grown from modest beginnings and had sunk deep roots in the community.

The previous year its minister had celebrated his twentieth anniversary in office and had been given a purse of gold by the congregation.[9] There was a steady turnover of church members in the years after the war. Many returned soldiers left New Edinburgh as they married, started families, and bought houses of their own in newly developing parts of a city that was being reshaped by the automobile, service industries, and mass culture. But the church attracted new people as New Edinburgh filled in, Lindenlea was developed as a planned suburb, and Rockcliffe began to grow. Church membership was 481 at the time of Church Union in 1925.

As they adjusted to peacetime, many of the returned soldiers carried the physical and mental scars of the war. Men who may have seen and done horrible things and faced unimaginable tests to their courage, now found themselves back in a church community that described them as heroes in terms that no longer had much meaning for them. For them and their families, recovery would take time. Some would never recover, and a few could be considered late casualties of the war.

Fred Jamieson had been gassed at Second Ypres in 1915. After a year of treatment he was still short of breath, unable to tolerate even moderate exertion, experiencing dizziness, numbness, tachycardia, and anxiety. He would marry and have children, but he would die at age 44 from lobar pneumonia. John Simpson, who had contracted double pneumonia and pleurisy in France,

Figure 25.2. 50th anniversary souvenir program.
Source: MacKay United Church.

never recovered his health, and in 1931 he would die of myocarditis and lung disease at the military hospital at Ste. Anne de Bellevue, Quebec. Clifford Erskine, a star athlete before the war, had been the victim in 1918 of a shell containing phosgene and mustard gas. He had been on the verge of death for weeks, and a medical board in January 1919 had starkly described his brown skin; hard, non-productive cough frequently followed by vomiting; shortness of breath; and tremors. He resumed his job in the City of Ottawa engineering department and would marry and have two children. He would move to Los Angeles in 1924 to try unsuccessfully to regain his health, and he would return to become superintendent of Ottawa sewers and maintenance. But he would die of pneumonia at age 48 in British Columbia and be buried in the Commonwealth war grave section of Royal Oak Burial Park, Saanich, British Columbia— "death due to service," says a note on his Circumstances of Death card. A similar note appears on the card for Norman Willson, whose hip had been severely injured in 1916, and who for 18 months thereafter would suffer bouts of shell shock.

Some men would have permanent disabilities. Thomas Isaac Jackson could not resume his former role as a contractor, nor could John MacKenzie, who had been gassed at Second Ypres, ever again be a policeman. Joseph Munro, wounded in both legs at St. Eloi in 1916, still had metal in his Achilles tendon, back, and both thighs after several operations, and he would always have a limp. Gordon Munro had been wounded in the hand and Douglas Munro had lost his thumb when it became septic after the war. John and George Powers had both been wounded (the latter four times). Jack McKenzie would bear facial scars for the rest of his life. Fred Stalker and Arthur Sproule would never fully regain the use of their right arms and hands. William Robertson and Gordon Halcro Clark would never fully recover from thoracic wounds. Jason Davidson, weak after a series of operations, was discharged with a disability. James Wallace McPhail had become "dangerously ill" in 1918 on the voyage to England with influenza and lobar pneumonia and would suffer from bronchial conditions for many years. Some men who had enlisted in poor health had their conditions exacerbated by the war. Robert Hill's chronic leg problems had become ulcerous and he spent most of 1917 and 1918 in treatment and convalescence; the muscles in his left calf had atrophied to the point that he could hardly walk without pain. Julius Hillas died at 53 of a heart attack. John Regan had to retire from the civil service in 1933 and became a patient at the Perley Veterans' Hospital. Frank Miles was permanently disabled with valvular heart disease. Robert Finter, who had enlisted on four occasions only to be discharged for health reasons each time, died in 1928 at age 38 of a cerebral embolism. These men had carried on with their lives, but in the end they paid a terrible price for their service.

Others would be luckier, recovering without disability from serious wounds or illness, even if these had involved weeks or months in hospital. Thomas Winton had been declared unfit for combat due to a suppurating bone in his leg, then varicose veins and phlebitis, but was able to continue service in England. Ray Tubman had lost parts of three fingers but carried on with sports and with his career. Robert Drake needed several operations to save his leg but returned in good health. Albert Kendall suffered no permanent disability after breaking his leg in a motorcycle accident. William Lanceley was shot in the hand and developed a crooked right leg, and while his childhood asthma was aggravated by dust and gas—he lived to be 64. Several others who had been seriously ill, like Shirley Slinn, George Sayles, Bruce Smith, and Alex Inch, lived long and generally healthy lives.

On the other hand, some veterans who had been healthy, even athletic, died at what we would today consider a young age, from a variety of causes: Alex Hobart Clark at age 31, Russell Muhlig and Douglas Stalker at 44, William Fixter Stevenson and Arthur Sproule at 47, Ernest Benedict at 50, Ernest Gardner at 56, and Thomas Nicholas Jackson at 58. Did drill, marching, hard labour, diet, stress, gas poisoning, pollution, cold and damp, infections, or bronchial conditions shorten their lives? Or was death at such an age more common, due to diet and to what are, today, curable diseases? One fact which may account for shorter lifespans, though not in each case, was that most soldiers and veterans were heavy smokers.

Harder to document, but nonetheless real, was the mental toll the war took on soldiers. Dr. Neil MacLeod had collapsed under the strain of 18 months without leave in field hospitals, under fire, at the front. "His condition is one of nervousness, and he is generally run down," wrote a medical board on his service file. "He is still unable to sleep properly, and cannot concentrate his mind on his work." Even after re-enlisting for home service in 1917, Alexander Masson continued to suffer general nervousness and inability to sleep. Several soldiers, like Russell White, Oscar May, Dalton McCarthy, and Gerald McLatchie, had been treated for battle fatigue. Others who had clearly reached their limit, like 40-year-old Reginald Elliott, a father of five who had survived the battle of Desire Trench, had been quietly posted to jobs behind the lines. Who knows what mental anguish a man like Sidney Mansell, one of a handful of soldiers in the Borden Motor Machine Gun Battery who survived the battle of March 24, 1918 (see Chapter 20), or the men who had lived through Desire Trench, Vimy, Passchendaele, and the Hundred Days, may have suffered? Many men probably experienced disturbed sleep, shakes and tremors, and harrowing memories, and their families undoubtedly also paid a price.

One man carried a different sort of scar. Alfred Philp had been with 4 CMR at the Battle of the St. Eloi Craters where a fierce German bombardment had all but wiped out the regiment, and the survivors who had taken shelter in a tunnel had found themselves with no alternative but surrender. Philp became the only prisoner of war among the MacKay soldiers. He appears not to have been badly mistreated; a medical examination in England after the war revealed a soft heart murmur, but he was otherwise well. But there was always a certain stigma attached to prisoners of war and former prisoners would find it difficult to tell their stories, even to other returned soldiers. How or whether this affected Philp we do not know; he started a new life in Winnipeg, and when he died in 1971 he would be buried in a military cemetery.

Some men undoubtedly found it difficult to settle down. Ray Tubman, having returned from Siberia, took off for the west, as did his brother Harry. Arthur Sproule went to Manitoba. All three returned to Ottawa (though Sproule later left for British Columbia) but most who left Ottawa, like William Fixter Stevenson and Gordon Clark who went west to ranch with the Tubmans, or others who went elsewhere in Ottawa or Canada, were gone for good. Robert Curtis returned to England with his English wife to the job he had left a decade ago before coming to Canada, and others also stayed in the old country.

How many men had "lost their faith" in the trenches, as one often hears descendants say today about their fathers or grandfathers? It is very difficult to answer this question with respect to a single church, much less about individual men, or even to know what this really meant in any given case. We do not know how broad and deep their faith was before the war, how far they subscribed to the doctrines of the church, or how regular was their attendance at church. Undoubtedly many men ceased to believe in the same things, or in the same way, as they had done before; whether this represented a complete "loss of faith" would differ with each man.

Yet most of those who had been regular church-goers before the war continued to do so for as long as they remained in New Edinburgh. This could have been for the sake of appearances or their families, or because they had not altogether abandoned some form of religious belief and retained the need for spiritual guidance and religious fellowship. But a large number of the returned soldiers appear to have held pretty much the same religious beliefs that they had before the war—indeed, the church was important to their reintegration in society. A few, like Alex Masson, joined the church when they came to New Edinburgh as wounded soldiers. Many returned men, like John MacKenzie, Herbert Love, Gerald McLatchie, the Jackson family, the Slinn brothers, the Jardine brothers, the Farmer brothers, Robert Drake, Elizabeth Ralph, Clifford Earl, John English, Clifford Erskine, and their families, were very active in the church over many years, and T. K. Gerard and John Powers occupied senior positions for decades. The fact that some returned soldiers left MacKay over Church Union shows that they took their religion seriously, and several played leadership roles in the Presbyterian churches to which they transferred. Many of those who left New Edinburgh became active members of other United or Presbyterian churches, or in some cases joined Anglican or even Catholic churches. Several men on the MacKay church

Honour Roll whose primary allegiance had been to other churches, such as St. Bartholomew's, remained active members of those churches. The Finter family converted to Baptism and became founding members of Eastview Baptist Church. For those who remained, and for new members, Reverend Peter Anderson's liberal, inclusive approach undoubtedly made people of different views feel comfortable at MacKay and there was a wide range of activities in which they could participate.

Some of these men had not displayed what pre-war Presbyterians would have considered exemplary behaviour while in the military. George Beardsley, a 37-year-old clerk with a wife and children, and three years' previous militia service, had just joined MacKay when he was among the first to enlist in 1914. Even before he left Canada and throughout his training in England, his record shows a lengthy series of forfeiture of pay, incarcerations, and field punishments for drunkenness, for being AWOL, even for desertion. This record of misbehaviour ended when we was sent to France in October 1916. There he suffered a hand injury and then, back in England, he contracted a serious illness which resulted in his return to Canada in May 1918. On his discharge certificate in October 1918 his character and conduct were listed as "Good." Robert Hill, who had been raised in an orphanage, signed up in March 1915, went to England in June as part of a reinforcing draft, and was sent to the Ypres Salient in August 1915 with less training than most recruits. In November 1915, he was given three days of Field Punishment No. 1 for "making improper replies to an N.C.O." In January 1916, he was sentenced to 14 days of FP No. 1 for "insolence to an N.C.O." When a pre-existing leg condition, periostitis, flared up, he was transferred to a labour battalion, where in November 1916 he was confined for three weeks awaiting courtmartial for being drunk and resisting an escort attempting to take charge of him, and was then sentenced to 45 days' Field Punishment No. 1—a sentence which because of its harshness had to be confirmed by the major-general commanding the division. By August 1917 his leg problems had become a chronic ulcer and, though he returned briefly to France, he spent most of 1918 being treated in England.

We do not have evidence that would allow us to ascertain what circumstances might have led to such indiscipline, as we do, for example, in the case of Arthur Hawke (Chapter 23). In general, however, the service records of MacKay soldiers show better than average conduct. On occasion, some of the independent, adventurous young athletes of 1914 found it difficult to accept arbitrary discipline or obey stupid orders, like George Powers who was punished for missing parades and using obscene language to a superior. Others were quite young, like Samuel Lindsay who was not yet 18 when he was sentenced to 10 days of Field Punishment No. 1 for having an "improperly protected light in his billet"—something that could have endangered his comrades by allowing their position to be spotted by artillery—but he matured and was later awarded a good conduct badge. Some men who had had good conduct records early in their service encountered problems later on as the stress of war began to tell, like Homère Joliat (chapter 20), or Dalton McCarthy who, after returning to service following treatment for battle fatigue, was sentenced to forfeit five days' pay for "hesitating to comply with an order." Some men who had been devout teetotallers before the war, like George Robertson, had now learned to "drink the rum," and a few men were disciplined for drunkenness. Heavy smoking among soldiers led to the abandonment of the church's prewar opposition to tobacco. The number of MacKay soldiers who fell victim to VD increased greatly in the last year of the war and the months after it. How many families knew this (late in the war military authorities had taken to cutting the pay of soldiers being treated for VD and informing their families of the reason why)? Would the returned men see the church's advocacy of Prohibition and its insistence on strict morality as hypocritical? Would they be able to settle down once they were back?

The evidence available indicates that for most of the returned men, what had happened at the front stayed at the front. The great majority reunited with their families, got married and started their own families, returned to their old jobs or embarked on new careers, and spent useful working lives as civil service clerks, managers, bank clerks, retail salesmen and service managers, small businessmen, railway and street railway workers, city employees, meter readers, postmen, printers, bricklayers, painters, carpenters and other skilled tradesmen, motor mechanics, and drivers.

And for some, the experience of war seemed to provide a spur to achievement. Dalton McCarthy resumed his civilian career as a barrister, becoming involved in service clubs and other organizations and even trying his hand at provincial politics. Dr. M. David Graham settled into half a century of practice as a much-beloved physician who, he once joked, had half the babies in New Edinburgh named after him. Shirley Slinn started a cartage business with his brother John (who died tragically in 1923) and was, like his father, active in many community organizations—in 1935-1936 he served a term as alderman for Rideau Ward. John Powers became a salesman, then an accountant, and ultimately a very successful businessman who was Chair of Trustees at MacKay in the 1950s and 1960s. In 1937 he succeeded Slinn as alderman, and he later served as a controller and chairman of Ottawa's department of health and recreation. George and William Farmer came back to work with their father and brothers in the family contracting business, married, and built houses for themselves in a family compound on Bertrand Street. Harold Short took a job in Arnprior with Kenwood Mills, a woollens factory which had just opened its doors, and rose to be its president as it became a leading producer of blankets, woollen fabrics, and high-quality felts; he was also president of the Ottawa Valley branch of the Canadian Manufacturers' Association. W. H. Milne became partner in a leading Montreal shipbuilding firm, was appointed director of shipbuilding for the Canadian government during the Second World War, and is recognized as one of the most important figures in the Canadian shipbuilding industry.[10]

Many of the returning men resumed athletic pursuits, in some cases despite war injuries. Charles Foad played on New Edinburgh sports teams even after he left New Edinburgh. Gordon and Douglas Munro played football and hockey, and John Powers and several others paddled for the Ottawa New Edinburgh Canoe Club. Doug Stalker and Ray and Reed Tubman resumed their careers as all-round athletes. Joe Tubman came into his own as a footballer and Milton Short also played on the Ottawa Rough Riders Grey Cup teams in the 1920s. Four wounds had ended the athletic career of George Powers, but he became a hockey referee in the Ottawa Valley, and in the 1930s he was volunteer equipment manager and then team manager with the Ottawa Rough Riders. Cleveland "Zeke" Stevenson developed an extraordinary career as an athletic trainer to a variety of amateur and later professional football and hockey teams through the 1920s and 1930s.

For most of these men, as they adjusted to civilian life, the experience of war was securely locked away in memory, as another life, in an alien world, that they could only talk about with others who had lived it. John Bothwell (according to his son) "never talked about his military service, though every year the Red Chevron society had an annual dinner."[11] George Robertson's son said that his father would never discuss the war; though in an interview shortly before his death at over 100, George recalled with pride his role as a sniper. John MacKenzie's grandson strongly believes that his physical injury, "along with the mental damage of having to come home while others remained to fight and not being able to restart his police career due to his injury, had a lifelong effect on him. [...] I never heard him speak one word about the War [...] My Grandfather left a large part of himself 'Over There.'"[12] For the men trying to return to normal lives, the happy memories of comradeship and life behind the lines were what they cherished, and all they would voluntarily share.

It is noteworthy that a number of the MacKay men continued being active in the military and ancillary organizations. Herbert Rolt found work as a mechanic for the fledgling RCAF at Rockcliffe air base. William Silsby also joined the RCAF and was in the service when war broke out again in 1939. Thomas Winton, Ernest Gardner, and James Leach continued as soldiers in the small permanent force that remained after the war. A number of veterans, especially those with disabilities, got jobs as clerks in war records or benefits sections of government departments. Many MacKay veterans, including

Fred Stalker, James Cairncross, Thomas Nicholas Jackson, Shirley Slinn, and George Robertson, served for years in militia regiments. A few, like Dr. Graham, George Robertson, John MacKenzie, William Silsby, and Samuel Kelly, served in the Second World War, in administrative, support, or training roles, and after the war MacKenzie joined the Canadian Corps of Commissionaires. Whatever they thought of the war, or of war generally, these men remained ready to serve when the call came again.

Epilogue

Time moved on, the church and the community evolved as they adapted to changing times. Life unfolded for the returned men and their families, and the Great War receded into the distance. Then the Great Depression cast a pall over the community and the church—Rev. Dr. John MacKay, who replaced Rev. Dr. Anderson in 1934, was told at one point that the church was within weeks of having to be closed—and then a new war drew 189 men and women from MacKay United Church, including some sons and daughters of veterans, into military service. Six died—two on active service in Ottawa, three in Royal Canadian Air Force squadrons based in England, one liberating the Netherlands. Many others did war service as public servants, diplomats, and other forms of auxiliary service.

After the war, the air base at Rockcliffe became a permanent fixture, and the opening of a new suburb in Manor Park, and growth in the older areas, provided homes for the greatly expanded public service of the welfare state that had emerged from the conflict. The mills and factories at Rideau Falls had long since been closed, and the businesses and buildings along Sussex Drive were cleared to make way for parks, the National Research Council central labs, the French Embassy, and the modernist Ottawa City Hall (now the John G. Diefenbaker Building). The last small industries like the mica factory closed in the 1950s, and streetcars vanished from Ottawa streets. The last CPR railway train ran through the village in 1964. The tracks were torn up, the warehouses and yards were closed, the right-of-way was replaced by a walking path along the Rideau River (New Edinburgh residents blocked an attempt to build a parkway which would have carried traffic from a bridge to Quebec to the highway system of Ontario), and in 1973 the Lester B. Pearson Building was built where the railway terminus had been. Only a few derelict piers in the Rideau River remain as evidence that the railway ever existed. Some of the older houses were replaced with more modern residences, apartments, and town houses. New Edinburgh had been transformed, but it remained a unique place with a mix of population, schools, small businesses and stores, and an ambience that is fondly remembered today by those who grew up there.

MacKay United Church saw unprecedented expansion. In 1952 a new Memorial Hall was built to provide space for meetings, clubs, theatre companies, Boy Scouts, bazaars, and many other activities, and to house the Sunday School which was now bursting with the children of the baby boom. Church services were held twice on Sunday and an exploding membership, including many veterans of both wars, required the expansion of the Sanctuary by the addition of a chancel carved out of the old 1890s Sunday School hall.

With time the memory of war, and its commemoration, changed. The country was full of memorials from the First World War, and after the Second World War there was extensive debate on how to honour the fallen. There was no doubt anywhere that this war had been necessary to rid the world of a monstrous evil. But paradoxically, or perhaps for that very reason, the sentiment prevailed that its memorials should not be cold, lifeless monuments or cenotaphs, but utilitarian spaces—hospitals, parks, arenas, libraries, galleries, churches, schools—that would embody what the men and women had fought for, that would be living, daily, reminders of their sacrifice, but would look to the promise of the future and not to the tragedy of the past.[1]

So it was at MacKay United Church. A framed, hand-lettered, illuminated list of those who served in the Second World War hangs in one corner of the Sanctuary. A bronze plaque, much smaller and plainer than those created after the First World War, honours the mercifully smaller number of dead from the Second. This plaque has no nationalist symbols but only the crest of the United Church of Canada. Rather than a verse from the Bible, it has a quotation from John Bunyan: "so he passed over and all the trumpets sounded for him on the other side." And besides honouring those who had fallen, its primary purpose was to mark the dedication of an organ in the church in their memory. The dedicatory plaque in the Memorial Hall remembers not only "those who went forth from this church in two World Wars, that we might continue to worship here in peace," but also of all those "whose labours made it possible for us to worship here."

Today at MacKay United Church there is no trace of the flag that was made in 1915 to honour the first 35 men who had enlisted, nor of the flags that once draped the memorial tablets, nor of the ribbons used by the Prince of Wales to unveil them, which some had wanted to preserve. The plaques with the names of fallen Sunday School and Young Peoples' Association members fell into disrepair in the church archives. The illuminated list of those who had enlisted up to June 1916 was found broken in two pieces in the back of a cupboard—if there was another list of the few who enlisted after that time, it has not survived.

By the 1990s, as with all United Churches, MacKay's membership was beginning to decline. In 2012, its manse was sold to a community organization. New Edinburgh, with its new and renovated homes, its parks, and its quiet streets, has become a favoured residence of senior public servants and professionals. One by one the stores and small businesses whose memory was cherished by their patrons have closed. The schools that taught generations of students have also closed, as has the orphanage on Rideau Terrace. St. David's Reformed Episcopal Church is now a private residence. Today, the MacKay United Church blends its rich history with an enhanced vocation as a spiritual space and community hub.

Each year on Remembrance Sunday, the church holds a solemn service of remembrance. Since 2015, I have been privileged at these services to tell the stories of the soldiers who fell in the First World War a century before, so that we might remember them—not only as names on a wall to be read out once a year, but as vibrant young men who "lived, felt dawn, saw sunset glow, loved and were loved." Today we do not remember these men, or those from the Second World War, as friends, husbands, fathers, or people most of us knew. We can no longer fully comprehend their experiences or share their worldview and their beliefs. Nor can we know what the future will bring for the church, the nation, or our memory of war. What we do remember, and celebrate, is the rich legacy they have bequeathed to us—the service and sacrifice of soldiers, and the faith, hope, courage, and resilience of the families who sat in the same pews during the dark days of war.

Bibliography

Primary Sources
Digitized information available through Ancestry.ca
Information such as birth, death, marriage, immigration, census records for Canada, UK, Scotland, Ireland, and the US, and some other information such as voters' lists, was accessed through ancestry.ca, which has partnered with repositories in these countries to digitize and make available microfilmed records. These include the following:

Archives of Ontario
Delayed Registrations of Births and Stillbirths, "90" Series, 1869–1911, 1913. MS 933, reels 1–64, 68. Evidence for Delayed Registrations of Births, 1861–1897. MS 946, 2 reels. Toronto, Ontario, Canada: Division Registrar Vital Statistics Records, 1858–1930. MS 940, reels 1–4, 10–15, 17–20, 22–25, 27–28. Registration of Births and Stillbirths, 1869–1917

MS 935, Registrations of Deaths, 1869–1948 (reels 1–694)

Delayed Registrations and Stillbirths, "50" Series, 1869–1911, 1913. MS 930, reels 1–67, 73–74

Registrations of Births and Stillbirths, 1869–1913. MS 929, reels 1–245

Registrations of Marriages, 1869–1928

Library and Archives Canada
Honours and Awards Citation Cards. Honours and Awards Citation Cards, 1900–1969 (Accession 2004–01505–5, volumes 1 to 75)

RG31-C-1, Statistics Canada Fonds,
    Census of Canada 1891. Microfilm reels: T-6290 to T-6427. http://www.bac-lac.gc.ca/eng/census/1891/Pages/about-census.aspx. or access individuals through ancestry.ca

    Census of Canada 1901. Microfilm reels T-6428 to T-6556. http://www.bac-lac.gc.ca/eng/census/1901/Pages/about-census.aspx or access individuals through ancestry.ca

    Census of Canada 1911. Microfilm reels T-20326 to T-20460. http://www.bac-lac.gc.ca/eng/census/1911/Pages/about-census.aspx or access individuals through ancestry.ca

    Census of Canada 1921. https://www.bac-lac.gc.ca/eng/census/1921/Pages/introduction.aspx or access individuals through ancestry.ca

RG 76-C. Department of Employment and Immigration Fonds, Canada, Incoming Passenger Lists, 1865-1935. Microfilm Publications T-479 to T-520, T-4689 to T-4874, T-14700 to T-14938, C-4511 to C-4542

Beechwood Cemetery, Ottawa, Canada

Beechwood Cemetery Interments, 5 vols. https://www.ancestry.ca/search/collections/2168/

Institut Généalogique Drouin, Gabriel Drouin, comp. Montreal, Quebec

Online as Quebec, Canada, Vital and Church Records (Drouin Collection), 1621–1968, https://www.ancestry.ca/search/?event=_catholic+church+drouin+collection&location=3243&priority=canada&viewMode=category

National Archives of the United States

Fifteenth Census of the United States, 1930. NARA microfilm publication T626, 2,667 rolls
Fourteenth Census of the United States, 1920. NARA microfilm publication T625, 2076 rolls. Records of the Bureau of the Census, Record Group 29
Passenger and Crew Lists of Vessels Arriving at New York, New York, 1897–1957. Microfilm Publication T715, 8892 rolls. NAI: 300346. Records of the Immigration and Naturalization Service
Sixteenth Census of the United States, 1940. NARA microfilm publication T627, 4,643 rolls

UK Public Record Office

Board of Trade: Commercial and Statistical Department and successors: Inwards Passenger Lists UK and Ireland, Incoming Passenger Lists 1878–1960
Census Returns of England and Wales
    1881. RG 11
    1891. RG12
    1901. RG13
    1911. RG14
Imaged by National Record Office and available through ancestry.ca
General Record Office, United Kingdom, England & Wales, Civil Registration Marriage Index, 1916–2005
Liverpool Record Office; Liverpool, England; Liverpool Church of England Parish Registers; Reference Number: 283 PAL/2/1 1848-1881
London Workhouse Admission and Discharge Registers held by the London Metropolitan Archives, London, England. Images produced by permission of the City of London Corporation; Reference Number: WEBG/ST/135/003, Edmonton Workhouse Register, 1897–1900
Records created or inherited by the War Office, Armed Forces, Judge Advocate General, and related bodies. Online as Ancestry.com. UK, British Army World War I Service Records, 1914–1920
UK Army, Register of Soldiers' Effects, 1901–1929

UK WWI Pension Record Cards and Ledgers
War Office: Soldiers' Documents, First World War 'Burnt Documents' (The National Archives Microfilm Publication WO363)

National Archives of Scotland

Census of Scotland 1881, 1891, 1901 (also available through official website Scotland's People, https://www.scotlandspeople.gov.uk/)
Scottish Birth, Death, Marriage Records (also available through official website Scotland's People, https://www.scotlandspeople.gov.uk/)

Digitized files from Library and Archives Canada:

RG 150, Service Files of the Canadian Expeditionary Force (CEF): Soldiers, nurses and chaplains, database https://www.bac-lac.gc.ca/eng/discover/military-heritage/first-world-war/personnel-records/Pages/search.aspx
John Fotheringham Askwith 475754
Horace E. Barnes 297549
George Frederick Beardsley 229
Ernest Benedict 318943
Levi D. Boston 345107
George Sulker [Selkirk] Bothwell 300204
John Robert Bothwell, Lt. [no service number]
A. Ivan Brunel 246555
Reginald Isambard Brunel 89200
James Cairncross 113124
Gordon Halcro Clark 506
Alex Hobart Clark 300036
George Victor Coker A410472
George Cruikshank 410479
Albert Henry Currie, Lt. [no service number]
William A. Currie 640166
Robert H. Curtis 1036071
Jason S. Davidson 246819
Robert Ludlow Drake 103
Clifford Earl 2590823
Angus Edwardson 1090307
Reginald Elliott 410088
George Bruce English 2043117
Clifford Leslie Erskine 89269
William J. Fallis 722267
George E. Farmer 40402
William I. Farmer 40403
Abraham Ferguson 805522
Henry W. Ferguson 2500012

William O. Finter 1036151
Robert H. Finter 40169, 144042, 2043007, 972
Charles T. Foad 319940
William Gaitens 514915
T. Ernest Gardner 113235
Thomas Knight Gerard 305604
Dr. David M. Graham [no service number]
Nairn Grant 342857
Arthur Frank Hawke 410504
Robert Hill 410451
Julius Hillas 410111
Gordon Hughes 3056080
Andrew Inch 1036057
Thomas Isaac Jackson 639677
Thomas Nicholas Jackson 541741
Fred J. Jamieson 40117
Andrew Jardine 633934
Arch. M. Jardine 633935
A. Reginald Johnston 2738543
Homer [Homère] Joliat 113329
Irwin Kelly 300073
Samuel John Kelly 2738545
Albert Richard Kendall 113334
Dr. Carson J. Kendall 377
William Henry Lanceley 144771
James Leach 144396
Walter Samuel Lindsay 89347
Percy Lister 2350337
Herbert Charles Love 410133
Dr. Neil MacLeod [no service number]
Sidney Bruce Mansell 113379
Percy Thomas Mansell 2266120
George Earl Marion 145022
Alexander Mason [Masson] 1013
Emile August Frank May 21498
Oscar Victor Albert May 7878
Henry J. Mayo 144122
Dalton McCarthy 342843
John McGillivray 410369
Alex. Lyon McKenzie 486567
John Langdale McKenzie 486566
D. Kenneth McKenzie 2738549
Gerald Farmer McLatchie 2266133
Archibald Stuart McLaurin 2085

James Wallace McPhail 3057294
Alfred Merritt 343856
Frank H. Miles 144373
William Harold Milne 345266
Elmer Allen Moodie 246374
Russell E. Muhlig 320992
Gordon James Campbell Munro 1260030
William Douglas Munro 1260031
Frederick Munro 3327553
Joseph A. Munro 113415
Olaf Olsen 343860
Erland D. Perney, Lt.
Alfred Philp 144827
Gordon M. Porteous 410175
Charles Powers 2265615
George Powers 113493
John Powers 113494
Cecil Eugene Putman 318856
Elizabeth Kirkland Ralph [no service number]
John Regan 2266122
Daniel Robertson Sr. 145841
Daniel Robertson Jr. 21510
George Robertson 220193
William Price Robertson 144887
Herbert Henry Rolt 510231
Mathew William Ryan 454510
Thomas E. Samways 49739
George A. Sayles 639747
Milton D. Short 110512
William Harold Armstrong Short 110513
George Henry Fred Silsby 514671
William Oliver Silsby 514672
John Simpson 145537
John Imrie Slinn 319950
Shirley Samuel Slinn 320030
William B. Slinn 50165
Robert Bruce Smith 305542
Arthur Sproule 343862
Benjamin Cleveland Stevenson 504943
William Fixter Stevenson 144416
Andrew Douglas Stalker, Lt. [no service number]
George Frederick Stalker 911889
Robert Alexander Stalker, Lt. [no service number]
Elmer Tubman 342854

Leslie Watters Tubman, Lt. [no service number]
Norman Harry Tubman 318944
Thomas Raymond Tubman, Lt. [no service number]
William Reed Tubman, Lt. [no service number]
Charles E. Trotter 145102
Arthur Kendall Watkins 536095
Edmund John Watkins 297030
Charles Albert Wendt 60043
Harry Wendt 4023075
Russell Gordon White 500095
Norman Keller Willson 302101
Arthur Samuel Wilson 30140
William Henry Wilson 410200
Thomas Winton 7920
Frederick Samuel Wright 246242

RG9-D-III-3, War Diaries of the First World War; https://www.bac-lac.gc.ca/eng/discover/military-heritage/first-world-war/Pages/war-diaries.aspx

War Diaries of the First Divisional Ammunition Column, 1915/11/01–1916/12/31, Volume number: 4978, Microfilm reel number: T-10806, T-10806, File number: 581, Item ID number: 2004809; https://recherche-collection-search.bac-lac.gc.ca/eng/home/record?app=fonandcol&IdNumber=2004809&new=-8585525277690145667

War Diaries of the 6th Brigade CFA, 1915/09/01–1917/07/31, Volume number: 4969, Microfilm reel number: T-10792--T-10793, File number: 543, File part: 1=1915/09/01–1916/09/30; 2=1916/10/01–1917/07/31, File no. (creator): 543, Item ID number: 2004756; https://recherche-collection-search.bac-lac.gc.ca/eng/home/record?app=fonandcol&IdNumber=2004756&new=-8585524380688390118

War Diaries of the 7th Brigade CFA, 1916/01/16–1917/02/28, Volume number: 4970, Microfilm reel number: T-10794, T-10794, File number: 546; https://recherche-collection-search.bac-lac.gc.ca/eng/home/record?app=fonandcol&IdNumber=2004758&new=-8585524383898861589

War Diaries of the 8th Infantry Battalion, 1914/10/18–1916/06/30, Volume number: 4918, Microfilm reel number: T-10710--T-10711, File number: 369, File part: 1=1914/10/18–1915/12/31; 2=1916/01/01–1916/06/30, Item ID number: 1883215; https://recherche-collection-search.bac-lac.gc.ca/eng/home/record?app=fonandcol&IdNumber=1883215&new=-8585511920082615774

War Diaries of the 12th Infantry Brigade 1916/10/01–1916/12/31, Volume number: 4907, Microfilm reel number: T-10698, T-10698, File number: 325, Item ID number: 1883189; https://recherche-collection-search.bac-lac.gc.ca/eng/home/record?app=fonandcol&IdNumber=1883189&new=-8585518752671899631

War Diaries of the 13th Infantry Battalion, 1918/07/18–1919/04/20, Volume number: 4922, Microfilm reel number: T-10716, File number: 385, File part: 1=1918/07/18–1918/10/31; 2=1918/11/01–1919/04/20, Item ID number: 2005902;

https://recherche-collection-search.bac-lac.gc.ca/eng/home/record?app=fonandcol&IdNumber=2005902&new=-8585511914421796083

War Diaries of the 24th Infantry Battalion, 1916/01/01–1917/08/31, Volume number: 4932, Microfilm reel number: T-10733, File number: 414, File part: 1=1916/01/01–1916/12/31; 2=1917/01/01–1917/08/31, Item ID number: 1883241; https://recherche-collection-search.bac-lac.gc.ca/eng/home/record?app=fonandcol&IdNumber=1883241&new=-8585518751470866407

War Diaries of the 38th Infantry Battalion 1916/08/13–1919/05/31, Volume number: 4938, Microfilm reel number: T-10743, T-10743, File number: 432, File part: 1=1916/08/13–1917/12/31; 2=1918/01/01–1919/05/31, Item ID number: 1883252; https://recherche-collection-search.bac-lac.gc.ca/eng/home/record?app=fonandcol&IdNumber=1883252&new=-8585518750265314979

War Diaries of the 50th Battalion 1916/08/10–1917/12/31, Volume number: 4941, Microfilm reel number: T-10747, T-10747--T-10748, File number: 441, File part: 1, Item ID number: 1883262; https://recherche-collection-search.bac-lac.gc.ca/eng/home/record?app=fonandcol&IdNumber=1883262&new=-8585518749650144888

War Diaries of the 87th Canadian Infantry Battalion 1916/08/11–1919/04/30, Volume number: 4944, File number: 455 00001134054; https://recherche-collection-search.bac-lac.gc.ca/eng/home/record?app=fonandcol&IdNumber=4919575&new=-8585518749015714681

War Diaries of the 102nd Canadian Infantry Battalion, 1916/08/12–1917/09/30, Volume number: 4944, Microfilm reel number: T-10752, T-10752, File number: 456 Item ID number: 1883279; https://recherche-collection-search.bac-lac.gc.ca/eng/home/record?app=fonandcol&IdNumber=1883279&new=-8585525113606240647

War Diaries of the Borden Motor Machine Gun Battery 1914/12/10–1918/06/08, Volume number: 4987, Microfilm reel number: T-10821, T-10821, File number: 630, File part: 1=1914/12/10–1917/04/30;2=1917/05/01–1918/06/08, File 630, Item ID number: 2004853; https://recherche-collection-search.bac-lac.gc.ca/eng/Home/Record?app=fonandcol&IdNumber=2004853&new=-8585894849610755025.

RG 150, 1992-93/314, Commonwealth War Graves Registers, First World War, Canada, War Graves Registers, Volumes 145 to 238, Circumstances of Death Registers; https://www.bac-lac.gc.ca/eng/discover/mass-digitized-archives/circumstances-death-registers/Pages/circumstances-death-registers.aspx

RG 38, Department of Veterans Affairs. Soldiers of the South African War, Land Grant Applications. (vols. 117–136) Vol. 117: land grants 0201–0295; https://www.bac-lac.gc.ca/eng/discover/military-heritage/south-african-war-1899-1902/Pages/item.aspx?IdNumber=5883&

Insurance plan of the city of Ottawa, Ontario, Volume 1, September 1902, revised 1912 Online MIKAN no. 3816030; https://recherche-collection-search.bac-lac.gc.ca/eng/home/record?app=fonandcol&IdNumber=3816030&new=-8585597058062255624

Online Sources

Bytown Museum www.bytownmuseum.com
Canada, Department of National Defence, Military History, Record of Service OMFC Medical Units: No 12. Canadian General Hospital Bramshott https://www.canada.ca/en/department-national-defence/services/military-history/history-heritage/official-military-history-lineages/ledgers/ww1-medical-units.html
Canadian Virtual War Memorial https://www.veterans.gc.ca/eng/remembrance/memorials/canadian-virtual-war-memorial
Commonwealth War Graves Commission https://www.cwgc.org/find-records/
The Gazette (UK) https://www.thegazette.co.uk/
Lost Ottawa www.lostottawa.ca
Manitoulin Roots https://manitoulinroots.ca/getperson.php?personID=I48103&tree=Manitoulin
Perth (Scotland) City Directories https://digital.nls.uk/directories/browse/archive/85711695
Royal Flying Corps Casualty Cards http://www.rafmuseumstoryvault.org.uk/archive.
Royal Flying Corps People Index http://www.airhistory.org.uk/rfc/people_index.html.
UK Forces War Records https://www.forces-war-records.co.uk

Archival Information

MacKay United Church Archives

Baptismal Registers
Communion Rolls
Deaths 1929–1937
Minutes of Annual General Meetings, 1889–1923
Minutes of Board of Managers 1913–1922
Minutes of Ladies' Aid 1902–1914, 1914–1924, 1924–1932
Minutes of Session 1902–1924
Register of Deaths 1907–1928
Register of Marriages

City of Ottawa Archives

Ernest Stitt Fonds MG101 7578
Interprovincial Rugby Football Union Fonds MG103 Accession 17 S 78, Box A2011-2050
Might's Ottawa Directories 1900–1935 (many of these are also available online through various portals)
New Edinburgh Canoe Club Fonds CA ON00075 MG 29
Ottawa Football Club Fonds CC-OSC, Accession 17 S 78 Box A-2011-0449 A-2011-2051, A-2011-2052

Provincial Archives of British Columbia

Executive Council of British Columbia Order in Council 437/1927, http://www.bclaws.ca/civix/document/id/oic/arc_oic/0437_1927

File GR-1483.463 – Stalker, Robert A. British Columbia Supreme Court (Prince Rupert), Microfilm B09395, Probate 441/1917

File GR-2202.5232 – Stalker, Robert. British Columbia Supreme Court (Vancouver), Accession number 87-0710, Microfilm B09033, Number Probate 33065

Series GR-2727 British Columbia Supreme Court orders, vol. 34, file 428

University of Toronto Archives

Robert Bothwell Fonds

Canadian War Museum Archives

Photo Archives 52C 2 6.2 control no 20050110-0: Tubman, Raymond, photo album of Vladivostok, Canadian War Museum, 09

UK National Archives, Kew

Catalogue Reference WO 339/105704, file Lt. John Henry RYAN, Royal Flying Corps

Catalogue Reference WO 339/78183, file 2/Lieutenant Erland Dauria PERNEY Royal Flying Corps (Special Reserve)

Catalogue Reference WO/339/58286, file Lt. Ewan BLACKLEDGE, RFC, copies provided to me by William Borland, Liverpool, England

St. John Lutheran Church, New Edinburgh, Archives

Church history and documents

Lisgar Collegiate, Ottawa, Archives

Student cards and alumni journals

Published Works

21st Battalion. 1919. *Historical Calendar 21st Canadian Infantry Battalion (Eastern Ontario Regiment) Belgium – France – Germany 1915–1919*. London. https://commons.wikimedia.org/wiki/File:Historical_calendar,_21st_Canadian_Infantry_Battalion_(Eastern_OntarioRegiment),_Belgium_-_France_-_Germany,_1915-1919_(1919)_(14802201193).jpg

77th Battalion. 1926. *An Historical Sketch of the 77th Overseas Battalion, Canadian Expeditionary Force*. Ottawa: War Publications, Ltd.

Adams, Annmarie. 1999. "Borrowed Buildings: Canada's Temporary Hospitals during World War I." *Bulletin canadien d'histoire de la santé = Canadian bulletin of health history* 16(1): 25–48. https://www.utpjournals.press/doi/abs/10.3138/cbmh.16.1.25.

Airhart, Phyllis. 2014. *A Church with the Soul of a Nation*. Montreal and Kingston: McGill-Queen's University Press.

Allen, Richard. 1973. *The Social Passion: Religion and Reform in Canada 1914–28*. Toronto: University of Toronto Press.

Allen, Richard. 2008. "Prologue." In *The View from Murney Tower: Salem Bland, the Late Victorian Controversies, and the Search for a New Christianity: Book One: Salem Bland: A Canadian Odyssey*. Toronto: University of Toronto Press, xv–xxxvii.

Anderson, Clara. 1923. *John Matheson: A Wholesome Human Story of Canadian Rural Life*. Toronto: Ryerson.
Anderson, Clara. 1911. *An Old Time Ladies' Aid Business Meeting at Mohawk Crossroads*. Ottawa: Hope.
Anderson, Clara. 1912. *Afternoon Tea in Friendly Village, 1862*. Ottawa: Hope.
Anderson, Clara. 1912. *Aunt Mary's Family Album*. Ottawa: Pattison.
Anderson, Clara. 1913. *The Minister's Bride*. Ottawa: Hope.
Anderson, Clara. 1915. *The Young Village Doctor*. Ottawa: Hope.
Anderson, Clara. 1917. *Aunt Susan's Visit*. Ottawa: s.n.
Anderson, Clara. 1920. *The Young Country Schoolm'am*. 2nd edition. Ottawa: Hope.
Anderson, Clara. c. 1920. *Martha Made Over*. Ottawa: Pattison.
Anderson, Clara. n.d. *The Joggsville Convention*. Ottawa: Progressive Printers.
Anderson, Clara. n.d. *Let Mary Lou Do It*. Ottawa: s.n.
Anderson, Clara. n.d. *Wanted: A Wife*. Ottawa: s.n.
Anderson, Clara. 192(?). *Marrying Anne?* Ottawa: s.n.
Anderson, Clara. 1933. *Aunt Sophia Speaks*. Ottawa: s.n.
Armstrong, Karen. 2014. *Fields of Blood: Religion and the History of Violence*. New York and Toronto: Knopf.
Bacic, Jadranka. 1998. *The Plague of the Spanish Flu*. Bytown Pamphlet Series (No. 63). Historical Society of Ottawa.
Badcock, G. E. 1925. *A History of the Transport Service of the Egyptian Expeditionary Force 1916–1917–1918*. London: Hugh Rees Ltd.
Bagnall, Kenneth. 1980. *The Little Immigrants: Orphans Who Came to Canada*. Toronto: Macmillan.
Baker, Chris. n.d. "The Army Service Corps in the First World War." The Long Long Trail. Accesed March 18, 2022. http://www.longlongtrail.co.uk/army/regiments-and-corps/the-army-service-corps-in-the-first-world-war/.
Bannerman, James. 1958. "The Year We Went Wild for the Prince of Wales." *Maclean's*, April 26, 1958.
Bashow, David L. 2000. *Knights of the Air: Canada's Fighter Pilots in the First World War*. Toronto: McArthur and Company.
Baswick, Daniel. 1997. "Social Evangelism, the Canadian Churches, and the Forward Movement, 1919–1920." *Ontario History*, 84(4): 303–320.
Bennett. Y. A., ed. 2009. *Kiss the Kids for Dad, Don't Forget to Write: The Wartime Letters of George Timmins, 1916–1918*. Vancouver: UBC Press.
Benson, Michael. 2000. "New Edinburgh Heritage Conservation District Study" published by the Ottawa Department of Urban Planning and Public Works in September 2000. Part I: "New Edinburgh Heritage Character and Significance," prepared by Benson and revised by P. B. Wear.
Berger, Carl. 1970. *The Sense of Power: Studies in the Ideas of Canadian Imperialism 1867–1914*. Toronto: University of Toronto Press.
Bernier, Jacques. 2003. *Disease, Medicine and Society in Canada: A Historical Overview*. Ottawa: The Canadian Historical Association. Historical Booklet Number 63.13.
Bird, Kym. 2022. *Blowing Up the Skirt of History: Recovered and Reanimated Plays by Early Canadian Women Dramatists, 1876–1920*. Montreal and Kingston: McGill-Queen's University Press.

Bird, Kym. 2004. *Redressing the Past: The Politics of Early English-Canadian Women's Drama. 1880–1930*. Montreal and Kingston: McGill-Queen's University Press.

Boucher, Frank, and Trent Frayne. 1973. *When the Rangers Were Young*. New York: Dodd, Mead

Bowker, Alan. 2014. *A Time Such as There Never Was Before: Canada After the Great War*. Toronto: Dundurn Press.

British Columbia Regiment. 1981. *Swift and Strong: The British Columbia Regiment (Duke of Connaught's Own): A Pictorial History*. Vancouver: British Columbia Regiment (Duke of Connaught's Own) Museum Society.

Broad, Graham. 2017. *One in a Thousand: The Life and Death of Captain Eddie McKay, Royal Flying Corps*. Toronto: University of Toronto Press.

Broadfoot, S. Rupert, K. C. 1941. *Holidaying in Canada on the Ottawa River*. Ottawa: Privately published.

Bruce, Anthony. 2013. *The Last Crusade: The Palestine Campaign in the First World War*. London: Thistle Publishing.

Burns, Lt. Gen. E. L. M. 1970. *General Mud*. Toronto: Clarke Irwin.

Bush, E. F. 2003. "McKAY, THOMAS," in *Dictionary of Canadian Biography*, vol. 8. Toronto: University of Toronto/Quebec City: Université Laval. http://www.biographi.ca/en/bio/mckay_thomas_8E.html.

Butler, Don. 2009. "A Very Different Strike in 1919." Ottawa *Citizen*, January 11, 2009.

Campbell, David. 2007. "Military Discipline, Punishment, and Leadership in the First World War: The Case of the 2nd Canadian Division." In *The Apathetic and the Defiant: Case Studies of Canadian Mutiny and Disobedience, 1812 to 1919*, edited by Craig Leslie Mantle, 297–342. Toronto: Dundurn.

Carkner, Thomas W. 2002. *Ottawa Germania: A History of the 19th Century Immigration and Settlement of Ottawa's German Community*. Self-published.

Cassel, Jay. 1987. *The Silent Plague: Venereal Disease in Canada, 1839–1939*. Toronto: University of Toronto Press.

Cassel, Jay. 1994. "Public Health in Canada." In *The History of Public Health and the Modern State*, edited by Dorothy Porter. Amsterdam and Atlanta: Editions Rodopi.

Christie, Nancy. 2000. *Engendering the State: Family, Work and Welfare in Canada*. Toronto: University of Toronto Press.

Christie, Nancy and Michael Gauvreau. 1996. *A Full-Orbed Christianity: The Protestant Churches and Social Welfare in Canada, 1900–1940*. Montreal and Kingston: McGill-Queen's University Press.

Christie, Norm. 2000. *The Canadians at Mount Sorrel June 2nd–14th, 1916. For King and Empire*, Volume III. Ottawa: CEF Books.

Christie, Norm. 1996. *The Canadians on the Somme 1916. For King and Empire*, Volume II. Ottawa: CEF Books.

Clarke, Nic. 2015. *Unwanted Warriors: The Rejected Volunteers of the Canadian Expeditionary Force*. Vancouver: UBC Press.

Comacchio, Cynthia. 1999. *The Infinite Bonds of Family: Domesticity in Canada, 1850–1940*. Toronto: University of Toronto Press.

Connor, Ralph [Charles W. Gordon]. 1919. *The Sky Pilot in No Man's Land*. New York: Doran.

Cook, Sharon Anne. 1995. *"Through Sunshine and Shadow": The Women's Christian Temperance Union, Evangelism, and Reform in Ontario, 1874–1930.* Montreal and Kingston: McGill-Queen's University Press.
Cook, Tim. 2000. "'More a Medicine than a Beverage': 'Demon Rum' and the Canadian Trench Soldier of the First World War." *Canadian Military History*, 9(1): 6-22.
Cook, Tim. 2007. *At the Sharp End: Canadians Fighting the Great War, 1914–1916, Volume One.* Toronto: Viking.
Cook, Tim. 2008. *Shock Troops: Canadians Fighting the Great War, 1917–1918, Volume Two.* Toronto: Viking.
Cook, Tim. 2016. "The Fire Plans: Guns, Machine Guns, and Mortars." In *Capturing Hill 70: Canada's Forgotten Battle of the First World War*, edited by Douglas E. Delaney and Serge Marc Durflinger, 102–136. Vancouver: UBC Press.
Cook, Tim. 2017. *Vimy: The Battle and the Legend.* Toronto: Allen Lane.
Cook, Tim. 2018. *The Secret History of Soldiers: How Canadians Survived the Great War.* Toronto: Allen Lane.
Cook, Tim. 2020. *The Fight for History: 75 Years of Forgetting, Remembering, and Remaking Canada's Second World War.* Toronto: Allen Lane.
Cooper, Jane, and David Way. 2014. *Private Sully Goes to War: An Eastern Ontario Boy Writes to His Girl From the Trenches in World War One.* Osgoode Township Museum.
Copp, Terry, Nick Lachance, Caitlin McWilliams, Matt Symes, and Mark Humphries. 2015. *The Canadian Battlefields of the First World War: A Visitor's Guide.* Waterloo, ON: Wilfrid Laurier University Press.
Copp, Terry. 2021. *Montreal at War 1914–1918.* Toronto: University of Toronto Press.
Crane, David. 2013. *Empires of the Dead: How One Man's Vision Led to the Creation of WWI's War Graves.* London: William Collins.
Crerar, Duff. 2014. *Padres in No Man's Land: Canadian Chaplains and the Great War.* 2nd ed. Montreal and Kingston: McGill-Queen's University Press.
Crooks, Sylvia. 2014. *Names on a Cenotaph: Kootenay Lake Men in World War I.* Vancouver: Granville Island Publishing.
Cross, L. D. 2004. *Ottawa Titans: Fortune and Fame in the Early Days of Canada's Capital.* Toronto: James Lorimer.
Cummings, H. R. and W. T. MacSkimming. 1971. *The City of Ottawa Public Schools: A Brief History.* Ottawa: Ottawa Board of Education.
Davidson, Melissa. 2019. "For God, King, and Country: The Canadian Churches and the Great War, 1914–1918." PhD thesis, University of Ottawa.
Davis, Donald F. 2001. "A Capital Crime? The Long Death of Ottawa's Electric Railway." In *Ottawa: Making a Capital. Construire une capital*, edited by Jeff Keshen and Nicole St. Onge, 349–382. Ottawa: University of Ottawa Press.
Delaney, Douglas E., and Serge Marc Durflinger, eds. 2016. *Capturing Hill 70: Canada's Forgotten Battle of the First World War.* Vancouver: UBC Press.
Dennis, Patrick M. 2017. *Reluctant Warriors: Canadian Conscription and the Great War.* Vancouver: UBC Press.
De Wolfe, J. H., comp. 1919. *Our Heroes in The Great World War.* Ottawa: Patriotic Publishing Co.
Dirks, Patricia. 2002. "Reinventing Christian Masculinity and Fatherhood: The Canadian Protestant Experience, 1900–1920." In *Households of Faith: Family, Gender, and*

Community in Canada, 1760–1969, edited by Nancy Christie, 290–316. Montreal and Kingston: McGill-Queen's University Press,
Dodds, R.V. 1980. *The Brave Young Wings*. Stittsville, ON: Canada's Wings.
Dougall, Charles. 2003. "RYERSON, GEORGE," in *Dictionary of Canadian Biography*, vol. 11. Toronto: University of Toronto/Quebec City: Université Laval.
Dutil, Patrice and David Mackenzie. 2017. *Embattled Nation: Canada's Wartime Election of 1917*. Toronto: Dundurn.
Edmond, Martha. 2005. *Rockcliffe Park: A History of the Village*. Ottawa: Friends of the Village of Rockcliffe Park Foundation.
Edwards, Margaret Bunel, ed. 1975. *Highlights from MacKay's History 1875–1975*. Ottawa: LoMor Printers.
Falls, Cyril, and A. F. Becke. 1930. *Official History of the Great War Military Operations: Egypt and Palestine II: From June 1917 to the End of the War*. London: HMSO.
Fetherstonhaugh, R. C. 1925. *The 13th Battalion Royal Highlanders of Canada 1914–1919*. The 13th Battalion Royal Highlanders of Canada.
Fletcher, Katharine. 2004. *Capital Walks: Walking Tours of Ottawa*. 2nd ed. Markham, ON: Fitzhenry and Whiteside.
Fowler, Michelle. 2003. "Keeping the faith: The Presbyterian press in peace and war, 1913– 1917." MA thesis, Wilfrid Laurier University. http://scholars.wlu.ca/etd/43.
Fowler, Michelle. 2006. "Faith, Hope and War: The Motivations of Lance Corporal Frederick Spratlin, MM and Bar, 3rd Battalion, CEF." *Canadian Military History*, 15(1): 45-50.
Fraser, Brian J. 1988. *The Social Uplifters: Presbyterian Progressives and the Social Gospel in Canada, 1875–1915*. Waterloo, ON: Published for the Canadian Corporation for Studies in Religion by Wilfrid Laurier University Press.
Gauvreau, Michael. 1990. *The Evangelical Century: College and Creed in English Canada From the Great Revival to the Great Depression*. Montreal and Kingston: McGill-Queen's University Press.
Gervais, Reginald A. 2014. *The Silent Sixtieth*. Winnipeg: FriesenPress.
Gidney, Catherine. 2004. *A Long Eclipse: The Liberal Protestant Establishment and the Canadian University 1920–1970*. Montreal and Kingston: McGill-Queen's University Press.
Gordon, Charles W. 1938. *Postscript to Adventure: The Autobiography of Ralph Connor*. New York: Farrar and Rinehart.
Gould, L. McLeod. 1919. *From B.C. to Baisieux: being the narrative history of the 102nd Canadian Infantry Battalion*. Victoria, B.C: T.R. Cusack. https://www.canadiana.ca/view/oocihm.71514/1?r=0&s=1.
Grafton, C. S. 1938. *The Canadian 'EMMA GEES': A History of the Canadian Machine Gun Corps*. London, ON: Canadian Machine Gun Corps Association.
Granatstein, J. L. 2001. *Canada's Army: Waging War and Keeping the Peace*. Toronto: University of Toronto Press.
Granatstein, J. L., and J. M. Hitsman. 1977. *Broken Promises: A History of Conscription in Canada*. Toronto: Oxford University Press.
Grass, Tim. 2017. *The Lord's Work: The History of the Catholic Apostolic Church*. Eugene, OR: Pickwick Publications.
Greenhous, B, ed. 1987. *A Rattle of Pebbles: The First World War Diaries of Two Canadian Airmen*. DND Historical directorate monograph no. 4.
Greenlee, Robert. 1988. *Sir Robert Falconer: A Biography*. Toronto: University of Toronto Press.

Grout, Derek. 2015. *Thunder in the Skies: A Canadian Gunner in the Great War*. Toronto: Dundurn.
Gwyn, Sandra. 1984. *The Private Capital: Ambition and Love in the Age of Macdonald and Laurier*. Toronto: McClelland and Stewart.
Gwyn, Sandra. 1992. *Tapestry of War: A Private View of Canadians in the Great War*. Toronto: HarperCollins.
Hallowell, Gerald. 1972. *Prohibition in Ontario, 1919–1923*. Ontario Historical Society Research Publication no. 2.
Hanna, Martha. 2020. *Anxious Days and Tearful Nights: Canadian Wives During the Great War*. Montreal and Kingston: McGill-Queen's University Press.
Harrison, Mark. 2010. *The Medical War: British Military Medicine in the First World War*. Oxford: Oxford University Press.
Harrison, Phyllis, ed. 1979. *The Home Children*. Winnipeg: Watson and Dwyer.
Hart, Peter. 2005. *Bloody April: Slaughter in the Skies over Arras, 1917*. London: Cassell.
Hartley, Harold E. 1971. *Up and at 'em*. Ed. Stanley M. Ulanoff. Garden City: Doubleday.
Heath, Gordon L, ed. 2014. *Canadian Churches and the First World War*. McMaster Divinity College Press, McMaster General Series 4. Eugene, OR: Pickwick Publications.
Historical Section, General Staff. 1926. *Narratives Covering Operations of The 1st Canadian Motor Machine Gun Brigade, The Canadian Independent Force, The Composite Brigade And Brutinel's Brigade During 1918*. Ottawa: September 1926.
Hodgetts, J. E. 2003. "BRUNEL, ALFRED," in *Dictionary of Canadian Biography*, vol. 11. Toronto: University of Toronto/Quebec City: Université Laval. http://www.biographi.ca/en/bio/brunel_alfred_11E.html.
Holden, Michael James. 2003. "Constantly Shifting and Constantly Adapting: The Tactical Exploits of the Canadian Motor Machine Gun Brigades, 1914–1918," MA thesis, University of New Brunswick.
Holt, Richard. 2017. *Filling the Ranks: Manpower in the Canadian Expeditionary Force, 1914–1918*. Montreal and Kingston: McGill-Queen's University Press
Hopkins, J. Castell. 1920. *The Canadian Annual Review of Public Affairs, 1919*. Toronto: The Canadian Annual Review Limited.
Horrocks, William, ed. 1993. *In Their Own Words*. Ottawa: Rideau Veterans' Home Residence Council.
Humphries, Mark Osborne. 2018. *A Weary Road: Shell Shock in the Canadian Expeditionary Force, 1914–1918*. Toronto: University of Toronto Press.
Iriam, Glenn R. 2008. *In the Trenches 1914–1918*. n.p.: Trafford.
Isitt, Benjamin. 2010. *From Victoria to Vladivostok: Canada's Siberian Expedition, 1917–19*. Vancouver: UBC Press.
Jenkins, Philip. 2014. *The Great and Holy War: How World War I Became a Religious Crusade*. New York: HarperOne.
Johnson, Rob. 2016. *The Great War and the Middle East*. New York: Oxford University Press.
Jones, H. A. 1928. *The War in the Air: being the story of the part played in the Great War by the Royal Air Force. Volume II*. Oxford: Clarendon Press.
Jones, H. A. 1931. *The War in the Air: Being the story of the part played in the Great War by the Royal Air Force. Volume III*. Oxford: Clarendon Press.

Jones, H. A. 1934. *The War in the Air: Being the story of the part played in the Great War by the Royal Air Force. Volume IV.* Oxford: Clarendon Press.

Kealey, Linda. 1998. *Enlisting Women for the Cause: Women, Labour, and the Left in Canada, 1890–1920.* Toronto: University of Toronto Press.

Kerr, W. B. 1929. *Shrieks and Crashes: Being Memories of Canada's Corps 1917.* Toronto: Hunter Rose.

Keshen, Jeff and Nicole St-Onge, eds. 2001. *Construire une capital Ottawa Making a Capital.* Ottawa: University of Ottawa Press.

King, Ross. 2010. *Defiant Spirits: The Modernist Revolution of the Group of Seven.* Vancouver: Douglas and McIntyre.

Kierstead, Robin Glen. 1982. "The Canadian Military Medical Experience During the Great War, 1914–1918." MA thesis, Queen's University.

Kilpatrick, T. B. 1917. *The War and the Christian Church.* Toronto: Presbyterian Church in Canada.

Kohli, Marjorie. 2003. *The Golden Bridge: Young Immigrants to Canada 1833–1939.* Toronto: National Heritage Books.

Laverdure, Paul. 1994. "Canada's Sunday: The Presbyterian Contribution, 1875–1950." In *The Burning Bush and a Few Acres of Snow: The Presbyterian Contribution to Canadian Life and Literature,* edited by William Klempa, 83–99. Carleton Library Series no 180. Ottawa: Carleton University Press.

Lee-Whiting, Brenda. 1985. *A Harvest of Stones: The German Settlement in Renfrew County.* Toronto: University of Toronto Press.

Lloyd, Nick. 2014. *The Hundred Days: The Campaign That Ended World War I.* New York: Basic Books.

Lloyd, Sheila. 1979. "The Ottawa Typhoid Epidemics of 1911 and 1912: A Case Study of Disease as a Catalyst for Urban Reform," *Urban History Review* 8(1): 66–80.

Lockwood, Glenn J., and Janet B. Uren. 2017. *Faithful: St. Bartholomew's Church Ottawa 1867–2017.* Ottawa: St. Bartholomew's Church.

Logan, H. T. et al. 1919. *History Of The Canadian Machine Gun Corps, C.E.F. Written, February – August, 1919, in Bonn, London and Ottawa by Major H.T. Logan, M.C. and Captain M.R. Levey, M.M. assisted by: Brig.-Gen. R. Brutinel, C.B. C.M.G. D.S.O. Major W.B. Forster, M.C. Lieut. W.M. Baker, Lieut. P.M. Humme.* Canadian War Narrative Section. Chateau val Fosse, France; London; Shorncliffe and Ottawa. Transcribed by members of the Canadian Expeditionary Force Study Group, 17 December, 2015. https://ia801305.us.archive.org/27/items/15HistoryCMGCFullManuscript17Dec-Final/15-HistoryCMGC-Full%20Manuscript-17Dec%20Final.pdf.

Love, David. 2012. *A Nation in Making: The Organization and Administration of the Canadian Military in World War One.* 2 vols. Ottawa: Service Publications.

Lynch, Alex. 2001. *The Glory of Their Times: 1st Canadian Motor Machine Gun Brigade, March 1918.* Kingston, ON: Lawrence Publications.

Lynch, Alex. 1978. *Dad, the Motors and the Fifth Army Show.* Kingston, ON: The Printing Factory.

MacBeth, Madge [writing as Gilbert Knox]. 1924. *The Land of Afternoon.* Ottawa: The Graphic Press.

Macdonald, Stuart. 2012. "Myth Meets Reality: Canadian Presbyterians and the Great War", *Canadian Society of Church History Papers,* 103–120.

Macdonald, Stuart. 2014. "For Empire and God: Canadian Presbyterians and the Great War." In *Canadian Churches and the First World War*, edited by Gordon L. Heath, 133–151. McMaster Divinity College Press, McMaster General Series 4. Eugene, OR: Pickwick Publications.

MacCulloch, Diarmaid. 2009. *Christianity: The First Three Thousand Years.* New York: Viking.

Mackersey, A. Ian. 2012. *No Empty Chairs: The Short and Heroic Lives of the Young Aviators who Fought and Died in the First World War.* London: Weidenfeld and Nicolson.

Marshall, David B. 1992. *Secularizing the Faith: Canadian Protestant Clergy and the Crisis of Belief, 1850–1940.* Toronto: University of Toronto Press.

Massey, Raymond. 1976. *When I Was Young.* Toronto: McClelland and Stewart.

Mathieson, William D., ed. 1981. *My Grandfather's War: Canadians Remember the First World War, 1914–1918.* Toronto: Macmillan.

Maurer, Maurer, ed. and comp. 1979. *The U. S. Air Force in World War I, Vol. IV: Postwar Review.* Washington, DC: Office of Air Force History Headquarters USAF.

McClintock, Alexander. 1917. *Best O' Luck: How a Fighting Kentuckian Won the Thanks of Britain's King.* New York: George H. Doran.

McCuaig, Katherine. 1999. *The Weariness, the Fever, and the Fret: The Campaign Against Tuberculosis in Canada 1900–1950.* Montreal and Kingston: McGill-Queen's.

McGee, David. 2017. *Lost Ottawa.* Ottawa: Ottawa Press and Publishing.

McGee, David. 2018. *Lost Ottawa Book Two.* Ottawa: Ottawa Press and Publishing.

McKeown, Bill. 2006. *Ottawa's Streetcars: An Illustrated History of Electric Railway Transit in Ottawa's Capital City.* Pickering, ON: Railfare DC Books.

McLaren, Roy. 1976. *Canadians in Russia, 1918–1919.* Toronto: Macmillan.

McKillop, A. B. 2001. "Introduction to the Carleton Library Edition." In *A Disciplined Intelligence: Critical Enquiry and Canadian Thought in the Victorian Era*, xiii–xxxii. Montreal and Kingston: McGill-Queen's University Press.

McMunn, George and Cyril Falls. 1928. *Military Operations: Egypt and Palestine from the Outbreak of war with Germany to June 1917.* London: HMSO.

Milberry, Larry. 1979. *Aviation in Canada.* McGraw-Hill-Ryerson.

Miller, Carman. 1993. *Painting the Map Red: Canada and the South African War 1899–1902.* Ottawa: Canadian War Museum and McGill-Queen's University Press.

Miller, Ian Hugh Maclean. 2002. *Our Glory and Our Grief: Torontonians and the Great War.* University of Toronto Press.

Morton, Desmond. 2004. *Fight or Pay: Soldiers' Families in the Great War.* Vancouver: UBC Press.

Morton, Desmond, and J. L. Granatstein. 1989. *Marching to Armageddon: Canadians and the Great War 1914–1919.* Toronto: Lester & Orpen Dennys.

Morton, Desmond. 1993. *When Your Number's Up: The Canadian Soldier in the First World War.* Toronto: Random House.

Morton, Desmond and Glenn Wright. 1987. *Winning the Second Battle: Canadian Veterans and the Return to Civilian Life 1915–1930.* Toronto: University of Toronto Press.

Morton, Desmond. 1978. "The Cadet Movement in the Moment of Canadian Militarism, 1909-1914." *Journal of Canadian Studies*, 13(2) (summer): 56–68.

Morton, Desmond. 1980. "'Kicking and Complaining': Demobilization Riots in the Canadian Expeditionary Force, 1918–19." *Canadian Historical Review* (61)3, 364–360.

Moss, Mark. 2001. *Manliness and Militarism: Educating Young Boys in Ontario for War.* Toronto: Oxford University Press.

Murphy, Brian. 2008. "Proposed Demolition of Three Rockcliffe Houses Opposed," *Heritage Ottawa Newsletter* vol. 35 no. 1. https://heritageottawa.org/sites/default/files/newsletter-pdfs/HerOttNews_2008_03.pdf.

Murray, W. W. 1947. *The History of the 2nd Canadian Battalion (East Ontario Regiment) Canadian expeditionary force in the Great War 1914–1919.* Ottawa: Historical Committee.

Nelles, H.V. 2003. "Keefer, Thomas Coltrin," in *Dictionary of Canadian Biography,* vol. 14. Toronto: University of Toronto/Quebec City: Université Laval. http://www.biographi.ca/en/bio/keefer_thomas_coltrin_14E.html.

Nicholson, G. W. L. [1962] 2015. *Canadian Expeditionary Force, 1914–1919: Official History of the Canadian Army in the First World War.* Montreal and Kingston: McGill-Queen's University Press.

Nicholson, G. W. L. 1967. *Gunners of Canada: The History of the Royal Regiment of Canadian Artillery, 1534–1919.* Toronto: McClelland and Stewart.

Nicol Stephen J. 2008. *Ordinary Heroes: Eastern Ontario's 21st Battalion C. E. F. in the Great War.* Privately published.

Overseas Service of the 18th Battalion, Canadian Field Artillery. [1919?]. N.p. https://archive.org/stream/overseasservice00nppp#page/n43/mode/2up.

Pettigrew, Eileen. 1983. *The Silent Enemy: Canada and the Deadly Flu of 1918.* Saskatoon: Western Producer Prairie Books.

Pitsula, James. 2008. *For All We Have and Are: Regina and the Experience of the Great War.* Winnipeg: University of Manitoba Press.

Pritchard, James. 2011. *A Bridge of Ships: Canadian Shipbuilding During the Second World War.* Montreal and Kingston: McGill-Queen's University Press.

Proulx, Ethel Sivyer. 1991. *Memories of New Edinburgh.* Ottawa: Privately published.

Proulx, Ethel Sivyer. 1999. *More Memories of New Edinburgh.* Ottawa: Privately published.

Pulsifer, Cameron. 2001. "Canada's First Armoured Unit: Raymond Brutinel and the Canadian Motor Machine Gun Brigades of the First World War." *Canadian Military History* 10(1), 43–57.

Pulsifer, Cameron. 2002. "Death at Licourt: An Historical and Visual Record of Five Fatalities in the 1st Canadian Motor Machine Gun Brigade, 25 March 1918." *Canadian Military History* 11(3), 48–64.

Report of the Work of the Invalided Soldiers' Commission Canada May 1918. Ottawa: King's Printer.

Rogan, Eugene. 2015. *The Fall of the Ottomans: The Great War in the Middle East.* New York: Basic Books.

Roy, Reginald, ed. 1998. *The Journal of Private Fraser Canadian Expeditionary Force 1914–1918.* Ottawa: CEF Books.

Rutherdale, Robert. 2005. *Hometown Heroes: Local Responses to Canada's Great War.* Vancouver: UBC Press.

Ryrie, Alec. 2017. *Protestants: The Faith That Made the Modern World.* New York: Viking.

Schroeder. Walter, n.d. "Memoir of Boyhood in New Edinburgh and Being a Pupil of 'Teacher Hartwick' in Primary School (1906–1913)," typescript.

Shaw, P. E. 1946. *The Catholic Apostolic Church. Sometimes Called Irvingite. A Historical Study.* New York: King's Crown Press.

Stacey, Charles P. 1977. *Canada and the Age of Conflict*. Volume I. Toronto: Macmillan.
St. John Lutheran. 1995. *Come Celebrate With Us: St. John Evangelical Lutheran Church 1895-1995*. Ottawa: Privately printed.
Sweeny, Alastair. 2022. *Thomas Mackay: The Laird of Rideau Hall and the Founding of Ottawa*. Ottawa: University of Ottawa Press.
Taylor, John H. 1986. *Ottawa: An Illustrated History*. Toronto: James Lorimer and the Canadian Museum of Civilization.
Tennyson, Brian Douglas. 2017. *Nova Scotia at War 1914–1919*. Halifax: Nimbus Publishing.
The Great War 1914–1918. "Arras Flying Services Memorial." Accessed April 2, 2022. http://www.greatwar.co.uk/french-flanders-artois/memorial-arras-flying-services-memorial.htm
Threinen, Norman J. 2006. *A Religious-Cultural Mosaic: A History of Lutherans in Canada*. Vulcan, AB: Today's Reformation Press.
Threinen, Norman J. 2014. "Canadian Lutheranism the First World War." In *Canadian Churches and the First World War*, edited by Gordon L. Heath, 197–217. McMaster Divinity College Press, McMaster General Series 4. Eugene, OR: Pickwick Publications.
Toman, Cynthia. 2016. *Sister Soldiers of the Great War: The Nurses of the Canadian Army Medical Corps*. Vancouver: UBC Press.
Toman, Cynthia. 2013. "'Help Us, Serve England': First World War Military Nursing and National Identities," *CBMH/BCHM* 30(31): 143–166.
Ulrichsen, Kristian Coates. 2014. *The First World War in the Middle East*. London: Hurst Publishers.
Valverde, Mariana. 1991. *The Age of Light, Soap and Water: Moral Reform in English Canada, 1885–1925*. Toronto: McClelland and Stewart.
Vance, Jonathan F. 1997. *Death So Noble: Memory, Meaning and the First World War*. Vancouver: UBC Press.
Vance, Jonathan F. 2018. *A Township at War*. Waterloo, ON: Wilfrid Laurier University Press.
Wert, Mike. 2000. "From Enlistment to the Grave: The Impact of the First World War on 52 Canadian Soldiers." *Canadian Military History* 9(2).
Wilson, Barbara, ed. 1977. *Ontario and the First World War 1914–1918: A Collection of Documents*. Toronto: The Champlain Society.
Wheeler, Victor. 2000. *The 50th Battalion in No-Man's Land*. Ottawa: CEF Books.
Wherrett, George Jasper. 1978. *The Miracle of the Empty Beds: A History of Tuberculosis in Canada*. Toronto: University of Toronto Press.
Wise, S. F. 1980. *Canadian Airmen and the First World War: The Official History of the Royal Canadian Air Force, Vol. 1*. Toronto: University of Toronto Press.
Woodward, David R. 2006. *Hell in the Holy Land: World War I in the Middle East*. Lexington: University Press of Kentucky.
Wright, Robert. 1992. *A World Mission: Canadian Protestantism and the Quest for a New International Order 1918–1939*. Montreal and Kingston: McGill-Queen's University Press.
Ziegler, Philip. 1990. *King Edward VIII: The Official Biography*. London: Collins.

Notes

Introduction
1. See Macdonald 2012 and 2014; Fowler 2003, 102–108, and 2006.
2. There is an extensive literature on Canadian churches. For Presbyterianism see McKillop 2001; Airhart 2014; Allen 1973; Marshall 1992; Gauvreau 1990; Christie and Gauvreau 1996; Fraser 1988.
3. See the works cited above and Bliss 1968; Marshall 1985; Crerar 2014; Heath 2014; Macdonald 2014; Fowler 2008, and Davidson 2019. For the role of religion in all the belligerent countries, see Jenkins 2014.
4. Berger 1970, 217; see especially chapter 9.
5. Macdonald 2012, 110. See also Macdonald 2014, 149; Fowler 2003, 14–24.
6. Tennyson 2017; Miller 2002; Copp 2021 and https://montrealatwar.com/; Blanchard 2010; Pitsula 2008; Rutherdale 2005; Gwyn 1992; Vance 2018; Crooks 2014.
7. The best general work on Imperial and Commonwealth war graves is Crane 2013. For Canadian battlefields, cemeteries, and monuments, see Copp et al. 2015; Norm Christie, *For King and Empire*. 11 vols. Ottawa: CEF Books, 1996–2003, and Cook 2017.
8. Exceptions are John Marshall, who was buried by his wife in a public cemetery in Perth, Scotland, and Arthur Hawke, who is buried in his family plot in Beechwood Cemetery, Ottawa.
9. See Cook 1995.
10. Morton 2004; Nancy Christie 2000. This study rather supports the viewpoint of Hanna 2020.
11. See Mike Wert's excellent article on returned soldiers (Wert 2000).
12. On memory see Vance 1997; Cook 2017; Bowker 2014, 86–92; and the closing chapters of Cook 2008.
13. A recent study that blends methodology with telling the story of an airman is Broad 2017.
14. His middle name is misspelled "Isnbard" on the In Memoriam plaque.
15. Spelled Miles on all written documentation.
16. His actual name was Alex Inch (Andrew Inch was his son, who did not serve).
17. His name was spelled MacLeod.
18. His name was spelled Norman K. Willson.
19. John K. Ryan on the plaque.
20. Spelled on all other documents as White.
21. His name was usually spelled Gardner.
22. Powers's name was added to the tablet sometime after its dedication in 1919.

Chapter 1: New Edinburgh
1. He spelled his name McKay, but after his death his family spelled it MacKay. Sweeney 2022, 7–8, argues that the correct family spelling was Mackay. When New Edinburgh Presbyterian Church changed its name to honour the family, it used the spelling MacKay, and it is this spelling that is used in this book.
2. Bush 2003; Sweeny 2022; Cross 2004, 50–61.

3. Nelles 2003.
4. McKeown 2006, 15–94. See also Davis 2001.
5. Source information for this chapter includes, besides city directories and census information, Benson 2002; Fletcher 2004, 105–130, 220–249; Taylor 1986.
6. The Edwards mills were sold in 1921 to the Gatineau Co. and in 1928 the federal government took over all these holdings.
7. Mica was used *inter alia* for electrical capacitors and resistors, windows for wood stoves, and later for radio tubes—and during the First World War, as eye-pieces for gas masks.
8. Lee-Whiting 1985.
9. Proulx 1991 and 1999; she is descended from the German community.
10. Boucher 1973, 45–46.
11. Schroeder n.d. (graciously provided to me by Janet Uren).
12. Boucher 1973, 46–47.
13. Besides city directories and 1911 census information, see Insurance plan of the city of Ottawa, Ontario, Volume 1, September 1902, revised 1912; Boucher 1973, 26.
14. St. John 1995, 15.
15. St. Luke website, http://www.stlukeottawa.org/story; Schroeder n.d.
16. As indicated earlier, Crichton Street at this period was usually spelled "Creighton Street." In later years this school would be known as the Crichton Street Public School.
17. Cummings and MacSkimming 1971, 55–56.
18. Ottawa Archives, Ernest Stitt Fonds, has membership lists of New Edinburgh Canoe Club, 1906–1908.
19. Boucher 1973, 29–30.
20. Boucher 1973, 42.
21. Bunel 1975, 119–122.
22. Ottawa *Citizen*, July 16, 1900, "Five of Ottawa's Heroes are Home," Ottawa *Journal*, July 14, 1900, "Returned Canadians Welcomed at Quebec."
23. Ottawa *Journal*, April 23, 1902, "Gave Them Drinking Cups."
24. See Moss 2001 and Morton 1978.
25. Lloyd 1979.
26. See Clarke 2015, especially chapter 1.
27. See McCuaig 1999; Wherrett 1978; and Cassel 1994, 294–295.
28. Bernier 2003, 13.

Chapter 2: MacKay Presbyterian Church

1. Ottawa *Journal*, February 17, 1900, "Merry Children: Annual New Edinburgh Presbyterian Church Sunday School Festival."
2. An invaluable source on all aspects of MacKay history is Edwards 1975.
3. Ottawa *Citizen*, February 4, 1969, "Ottawa resident for 100 years buried," and the attestation papers for Joseph and Frederick Munro.
4. Ottawa *Citizen*, January 22, 1912, "Obituary."
5. Gwyn 1984 and 1992.
6. Ottawa *Citizen*, March 14, 1925, "MacKay Presbyterian Church Golden Jubilee to be Celebrated With Fitting Ceremony by Congregation Sunday and Monday March 22–23."
7. Dr. David Graham (Edwards 1975, 137).

8. Minutes of AGM, 1910.
9. Anderson 1923, 9.
10. An extensive discussion of her life and plays, in the context of early women's theatre and maternal feminism, is found in Bird 2004, 138–193. One of her plays, *The Joggsville Convention,* is anthologized in Bird 2022, 179–212, and see introduction, 3–54.
11. Dirks 2002; Moss 2001.
12. Ottawa *Citizen,* November 14, 1904, "St David's Guild."
13. Ottawa *Citizen,* October 28, 1914, "The May Brothers."
14. Airhart 2014, 23.
15. Anderson 1923, 337, 339.
16. Anderson 1923, 333–334.
17. Ottawa *Citizen,* April 30, 1906, "The Oddfellows' Annual Service."
18. Fraser 1988, xiii.
19. Ottawa *Citizen,* April 30, 1906, "The Oddfellows' Annual Service."
20. Minutes of Session 1902–1924, 1909, p. 108.
21. Ottawa *Citizen,* November 21, 1910, "Christian City."
22. Valverde 1991, 54, views Shearer as "a man of limited intellect and narrow views" whose crusade against "white slavery" was based on little fact and less understanding.
23. Ottawa *Citizen,* December 29, 1913, "Presbyterian."
24. Ottawa *Citizen,* November 1, 1910, "Sunday Sermons."
25. Ottawa *Citizen,* April 8, 1913, "A Joint Banquet at MacKay Church."
26. Airhart 2014, chapter 1.
27. Minutes of Session 1902–1924, 1912, February 14, 1912, 135–136; Ottawa *Citizen,* November 27, 1915, "Church Union Carried Here."
28. Broadfoot [1941], 127–128.
29. Boucher 1973, 24–26.
30. Lockwood and Uren 2017, 78.
31. Of eleven men on the Honour Roll who appear on both lists, six appear to be more firmly Anglican, and five more strongly Presbyterian; and one of them is also on the St. David's Honour Roll.
32. St. John's, 1995, 12.
33. Broadfoot [1941], 127.
34. Airhart 2014, 23–24.
35. Ottawa *Citizen,* March 7, 1910, "First Services in New Church."

Chapter 3: A Church at War: 1914–1915

1. Gwyn 1992, 17–18, 47–49.
2. Jenkins 2014; MacCulloch 2017, 255–264.
3. Gwyn 1992, esp. chapter 2.
4. Ottawa *Citizen,* October 10, 1918, "Unveil Honor Roll St. David's Church."
5. Ottawa *Journal,* November 21, 1914, "Manifesto from President of Synod Makes This Point Clear to All." See Threinen 2014, 197–215.
6. St. John 1995, 15.
7. Ottawa *Journal,* March 12, 1915, "Alien-Enemies in Confinement at Fort Henry Well Treated and Fed."

8. Ottawa *Journal*, October 23, 1914, "Church League to Have Many Hockey Teams."
9. Cited in Fowler 2003, 34.
10. Ottawa *Citizen*, June 28, 1915, "Col. Herridge's Strong Appeal for Recruits." See also Davidson 2019, 96–102; Greenlee 1988, chapter 8; Marshall 1992, chapter 6; Crerar 2014; Fraser 1988, chapter 7; Macdonald 2014; Gordon 1938, and his war novels including *The Sky Pilot in No Man's Land* (Connor 1919).
11. The information on these men was gleaned from their service records, city directories, census documents, birth records, and church records.
12. Finter was discharged as medically unfit and returned to Canada in January 1915. He would enlist again in the 77th Battalion in June but is not counted twice.
13. Email from Bob Cleary, his grandson, December 12, 2020.
14. All his service documents give his name as Mason.
15. Ottawa *Journal*, March 8, 1915, "Patriotic Service at MacKay Street Church."
16. Ottawa *Journal*, March 8, 1915, "Patriotic Service at MacKay Street Church." Although the story refers to 35 men, it names 36, and these do not include all those who would eventually appear on the Honour Roll.
17. Ottawa *Journal*, March 24, 1915, "Mr. H. B. Brophy, M.P., on 'Britain and the War.'"
18. Ottawa *Citizen*, June 29, 1915, "MacKay Church in Patriotic Service."
19. Ottawa *Journal*, May 31, 1915, "Captain Chas McGee Was Killed in Action."
20. 77th Battalion 1926, 2.
21. 77th Battalion 1926, 1–14.
22. The PPCLI was part of the British Army until 1916 when it was transferred to the Third Canadian Division.
23. Ottawa *Journal*, January 20, 1916, "MacKay Church Has 65 Men in Khaki."
24. See Clarke 2015.
25. For context see Holt 2017.
26. Ottawa *Citizen*, June 29, 1915, "MacKay Church in Patriotic Service."

Chapter 4: Charles Albert Wendt: A German-Canadian Patriot

1. Information from Carkner 2002, and his website http://ottawa-germania.ca/ (consulted in 2015 and since discontinued).
2. Census of Canada 1901, Ontario, District 112, Russell, Sub-district New Edinburgh, lines 24–32.
3. See Miller 1993.
4. Ottawa *Citizen*, July 16, 1900, "Five of Ottawa's Heroes are Home," Ottawa *Journal*, July 14, 1900, "Returned Canadians Welcomed at Quebec."
5. Ottawa *Journal*, February 17, 1900, "Merry Children."
6. Ottawa *Journal* June 30, 1905, obituary, Mrs. William Wendt.
7. U. S. Census 1910, New York, Niagara, Niagara Falls Ward 9, District 0116, Sheet No. 7, lines 74–82.
8. The Raabe family appears in records under different spelling: Rabbi, Rabbie, Rabbe. Census of Canada 1911, Ontario, Russell, Ottawa, District 7, enumeration district 2, Rideau Ward, lines 39–43.
9. The adjoining house, 35 Ivy Street, was occupied by Frank Raabe, their uncle. Ottawa *Citizen*, December 2, 1915, "Charlie Wendt on Roll of Honour; Ottawa *Journal*, February 18, 1919, "Henry A. Wendt."
10. Nicol 2008, chapter 2.

11. Nicol 2008, chapters 3–4.
12. 21st Battalion 1919, 6.
13. Nicol 2008, chapter 5.
14. Roy 1998, 23–61.
15. 21st Battalion 1919, 26.
16. Ottawa *Citizen,* December 3, 1915, "Charlie Wendt on Roll of Honour."
17. Cook, 2007, 266–267, Nicol 2008, chapter 6.
18. Nicol 2008, chapter 6.
19. Roy 1998, 61.
20. Ottawa *Journal,* December 1, 1916, "Three Ottawa Men Died From Wounds."
21. Commonwealth War Graves Registers, Webber to Whitcutt, volume No., 3180_B016653, 133, 60043 Wendt Charles.
22. Ottawa *Citizen,* December 2, 1915, "Charlie Wendt on Roll of Honour."
23. Ottawa *Citizen,* November 15, 1916, "In Memoriam."
24. Archives of Ontario, Registrations of Marriages, 1869–1928, Carleton, 1918, reel 451, image 2162, 008013.
25. Ottawa *Journal,* February 15, 1919, "Henry A. Wendt." Archives of Ontario, Registration of Deaths, 1869–1948, MS935, Carleton, 1919, reel 253, image 276, 009895.
26. Lloyd 2014, 182–188.
27. Hebert C. W. Wendt, 1214395, New York State Archives; Albany, New York; Abstracts of National Guard Service in World War I, 1917–1919; Series: 13721; Box: 6; Volume: 17: 108th Infantry (3rd Inf NYNG) T-Z. National Archives at Washington D.C.; Washington D.C., USA; Applications for Headstones for U.S. Military Veterans, 1925–1941; NAID: A1, 2110-C; Record Group Number: 92; Record Group Title: Records of the Office of the Quartermaster General, Surname Range: Waters, George F-Wheeler, Edward Clifford: Herbert C. W. Wendt, 1214395.

Chapter 5: A Church at War: 1916

1. Minutes of the Ladies' Aid 1914–1924, 24–29.
2. Minutes of the Session, February 23, 1916.
3. Ottawa Citizen, May 3, 1916, "MacKay Church Young People in Playlet," Ottawa *Journal*, May 3, 1916, "MacKay Y. P. A. in Character Sketch."
4. Ottawa *Citizen,* April 18, 1916, "Privates George and Jack Powers of Ottawa in the Recent Fighting."
5. Iriam 2008, 135.
6. The Fifth Canadian Division was assembled in 1916 from troops in England. Its infantry brigades were not sent to the front and were instead broken up in February 1918 to reinforce the other four divisions. But its artillery, machine gun, service, and mechanical units were kept intact as Corps troops to be deployed where needed.
7. By the end of the war (including the Siberian Expedition) there would be 24 sets of two or more brothers, 6 of three or more, and 3 sets of fathers and sons or stepsons.
8. Morton 2004, 92–96, 117; see also Kealey 1998, 202–207.
9. Quoted in Fowler 2003, 56; see also Davidson 2019, chapter 3.
10. Ladies Aid Minutes, annual report for 1916, p. 43.

Chapter 6: Victor and Theresa Coker: A Good Man, a Christian Woman, and Her Two Sons at the Front

1. England and Wales, Civil Registration Birth Index, 1837–1915, Births Registered in July, August, and September 1877, page 101. Census Returns of England and Wales, 1881 England Census, London, Streatham, All, District 7, Class: RG11; Piece: 665; Folio: 47; Page: 34; GSU roll: 1341154 [shows him as three-years-old and one of six children]. 1891 England Census, Piece: 456; Folio: 42; Page: 28; GSU roll: 6095566, Enumeration District 13 [shows him as one of six children in the family, living in Streatham].
2. Coker Service Record, ADM—Records of the Admiralty, Naval Forces, Royal Marines, Coastguard, and related bodies; ADM 159—Admiralty: Royal Marines: Registers of Service, ADM 159/47 - 7025 - 7658.
3. Archives of Ontario, Registrations of Marriages 1826–1938, reel 146, image 185, Carleton County, 1910, 00700; and MacKay Presbyterian Church, Register of Marriages.
4. 1871 England Census, Piece 522, Folio 49, Page 4, GSU roll 823384, Enumeration District 3; 1881 England Census, Surrey, Richmond, District 11, Folio 37, Page 18, GSU roll 1341200; 1901 English census, Kent, Canterbury, District 17, folio 108, Page 14.
5. Frederick Corp married Annie Hupfeld in Bristol in 1897. Bristol Archives, Bristol Church of England Parish Registers, Marriages and Banns, 1754-1935, Reference: P/St TE/R/2/a, Eastvale, St. Thomas Parish Register 1889–1911, no 131; Henry Hupfeld is described in the marriage register as a "furniture broker." Census of Canada 1911, Ontario, District 118, Russell, Sub-district 7, page 4, lines 40–44.
6. LAC, Canada, Incoming Passenger Lists, 1865-1935, RG 76-C; Roll: T-4734 image 55, Halifax, 1908, December, Tunisian, Steerage.
7. Might's Ottawa Directory, 1910.
8. Their real ages are derived from British census information, Victor's attestation papers for the Royal Marines and the CEF (which make him one year older than his British birth record), and in Theresa's case the ship's register and her death certificate.
9. Census of Canada 1911, Ontario, District 118 Russell, Sub-district 7, page 3, lines 24–32, and city directories.
10. "Canadian Expeditionary Force, 38th Battalion, also 1st and 2nd reinforcing drafts, Non-Commissioned Officers, and Men," 1915. There is some indication in William's service file that he may have gone to join the 2nd Battalion without permission (perhaps to be with his stepfather?)
11. Murray 1947, 77–80.
12. Circumstances of death register, vol. 31829_B016730, pages 603–604, A10472, Coker, George Victor.
13. Ottawa *Citizen,* September 30, 1915, "Men From the 38th Were in the Trenches."
14. Census of Canada 1921, Russell, Ontario, District 125, Sub-district 38, page 2, lines 41–47.
15. Ottawa *Citizen,* August 7, 1956, "Mrs. T. E. Coker."

Chapter 7: The Bothwell Family: War Claims Lives and Destroys Families

1. See Ottawa *Citizen*, October 2, 1926, "Stories of Days When Wood Made Big Business on River from Greens Creek, Grenville," and Robert Bothwell, personal communication, November 1, 2015. In the Bothwell Fonds, Box 004, Bothwell Family, File 01 is a notebook with exercises in hydraulics and a Bothwell family tree (photos 1–6). Census of Canada 1911, Russell, Ontario, District 118, Sub-district 57, New Edinburgh, p. 9, lines 4–12.
2. Ottawa *Citizen,* September 7, 1907, "Fire Enquiry is Renewed."
3. Robert Bothwell, personal communication, November 1, 2015.
4. Census of Canada 1921, Ontario, District 125, Russell, Sub-district 37, p. 14, lines 35–42; Bothwell Fonds, Box 004, Files 02, 03, and 04 are books and records of loans, expenses, and properties; Box 008 has share certificates in the Lumsden Mining Co. Ottawa *Journal*, May 25, 1916, "Pte. Bothwell Killed"; Ottawa *Citizen*, April 7, 1928, Obituary; and April 10, 1928, "Pay Tribute to Captain Wm. Bothwell."
5. Bothwell Fonds, Box 004, file 009, book of pay in which William Bothwell records pay to Edwards employees; Census of Canada 1911; George Bothwell attestation papers.
6. Ottawa *Citizen,* November 1, 1910, "WFMS Convention"; and December 16, 1914, page 5, "Delightful Entertainment."
7. Ontario, Canada, Registrations of Marriages 1826–1938, Carleton, Ottawa, 1910, reel 146, image 168, 006952. According to an affidavit sworn by her father in 1929, she was born on November 27, 1892, in Ottawa. Ontario, RG 80-2902402, Delayed Registrations of Births and Stillbirths, "90" Series, 1869–1911, 1913, reel 18, image 119; age corroborated in the 1921 census.
8. War Diaries of the First Canadian Divisional Ammunition Column, 1915/11/01 to 1916/12/31, March and April.
9. Ottawa *Citizen,* May 26, 1916, "Sad Notice Came Just After Letter."
10. Circumstances of Death Registers, First World War, vol. 31829_B016721, pages 109–110, 300204 George Sulker [sic] Bothwell.
11. Ottawa *Citizen,* July 17, 1916, "Serving Guns in Flanders."
12. Ottawa *Citizen,* May 26, 1916, "Sad Notice Came Just After Letter."
13. Ottawa *Citizen,* June 9, 1916, "Honours Paid to Gunner Bothwell."
14. Archives of Ontario, Registrations of Marriages, 1869–1928; Carleton, Ottawa, 1917, reel 427, image 1516, 014379.
15. Bothwell Fonds, Box 004, File 01, notebook with hydraulic notes, and other information.
16. Census of Canada 1921, Ontario, District 110, Ottawa, Sub-district 54, Capital Ward, page 2, lines 25–30.
17. Bothwell Fonds, Box 012.
18. Bothwell Fonds, File 007.
19. Ottawa *Journal,* May 13, 1924, "George Earl Marion has disappeared."
20. Ottawa *Citizen,* June 5, 1924, "Had Suffered by His War Service."
21. LAC, Circumstances of Casualty, 1914–1948, vol. 256, file McCormack-Maynard, image 738, 145022 Marion George E.

22. Ottawa *Citizen,* June 5, 1924, "Late George Earl Marion; Ottawa *Journal,* June 5, 1924, "Hold Funeral George Marion."
23. Private communication from a descendant, September 13, 2016, and April 7, 2022.
24. Ottawa *Citizen,* April 7, 1928, "Veteran Ottawa River Navigator Died on Friday."
25. Bothwell Fonds, Box 06, file 15, Staff Pass for John R. Bothwell to the 1924 British Empire Exhibition.
26. Ottawa *Citizen,* February 17, 1943, "Mrs. J. R. Bothwell Dies in Hospital Here"; email from Robert Bothwell, November 3, 2015.
27. Information provided by Robert S. Bothwell (November 1, 2015). Bothwell Fonds Box 06, Files 013-016 concern the daughters. Box 05, File 42 is information on Katie's wedding.
28. Ottawa *Citizen,* March 16, 1929.
29. Ottawa *Citizen*, December 22, 1927, "Father-Son Banquet," and October 19, 1928, "MacKay Nedimac Group."
30. Ottawa *Citizen*, Obituary, May 4, 1984.
31. Bothwell Fonds Box 004, files 01721 contains information on the children and grandchildren.
32. Private communication from a descendant, September 8, 2016 and April 7, 2022.

Chapter 8: Charles Edward Trotter and the Jackson Family: "Lovable Disposition and Fine Character"

1. Census Returns of England and Wales, 1901, Yorkshire, York, Bootham, District 11, page 2.
2. UK, War Office: Soldiers' Documents, First World War, 24 May 1903, short service attestation for Charles Edward Trotter, bricklayer. Census of Canada 1911, Ontario, Gloucester, District 118, Sub-district 4, enumeration district 11, page 46, lines 47–50, 47, lines 1–8.
3. Ottawa *Citizen,* June 14, 1916, "Ottawa Names in Honour Roll."
4. "Proposed Demolition of Three Rockcliffe Houses Opposed," by Brian Murphy, *Heritage Ottawa Newsletter* Winter 2008, vol. 35 no. 1. Ottawa *Journal,* March 28, 1931, "Thomas I. Jackson."
5. Edmond 2005, 51. Census of Canada 1921, Ontario, Russell, District 125, Sub-district 18, page 2, lines 10–18.
6. See the excellent website https://60thbattalioncef.ca/history-of-the-battalion/ for full information including war diaries, compiled by Reginald Gervais.
7. Ottawa *Citizen,* June 15, 1916, "Pte Trotter's Last 'Turn.'"
8. Norm Christie 2000, 1.
9. See A. Y. Jackson's description of the battle in King 2010, 203–205. Jackson was evacuated to Étaples where he was admitted to the No. 1 Canadian General Hospital on June 4.
10. See Norm Christie 2000, 17–27; Gervais 2014, for brief information about Trotter, and chapters "May, 1916" and "June 1916"; Cook 2007, 361–362; Roy 1998, 146–156; Humphries 2018, 111–117.
11. The exact DOB is uncertain; he is not listed in a document on Jackson's service file dated October 6, 1916, but in the 1921 census his age is given as five years.
12. MacKay United Church Register of Deaths, 1931.

13. Ottawa *Journal*, January 8, 1955, "Thomas N. Jackson"; Ottawa *Journal*, January 4, 1955, "Cameron Veteran Thomas N. Jackson Dies in Hospital"; Ottawa *Citizen*, January 7, 1955, "Many Friends at Funeral of T. N. Jackson."
14. Beechwood Cemetery Interments, 1953–1982, p. 11.

Chapter 9: The Robertson Family: "There Is no Other Woman in Ottawa Who Has Given so Gloriously to the Cause"

1. National Records of Scotland, Statutory Registers: Births 490/113, 1868, Births in the Parish of Stirling in the Burgh of Stirling, page 38 no. 113; Marriages 644/3/423, 1887, Marriages in the District of Dennistoun in the County of Lanark, page 211, no. 423; Census 1901 520/4/25 page 25–26; 1911 Scottish census (National Records of Scotland, Census 622/2 6/14 p. 14). I am indebted to Ian and Linda Parker for providing copies of these and other documents from the National Records of Scotland.
2. Canada, Incoming Passenger Lists, 1865–1935, Roll T-4796, image 1136, Quebec, May 1913, *Letitia*, p. 45.
3. Recollections of George Robertson, age 99, in Horrocks 1993, pages 12–13.
4. Canada, Incoming Passenger Lists, 1865–1935, Roll T-4808, image 403, Quebec, May 1914, *Letitia*.
5. MacKay Presbyterian Church Communion Rolls. Beside his name is a later entry: "Killed in France, November 1916, reported January 10, 1917."
6. There is no record of either of the Robertson girls having jobs but they could have done so late in the war. Jean Robertson was described at age 15 as a "clerkess" on the incoming ship's register in 1914, but when she married in 1920, she was listed at age 22 as "at home." Annie was described as a "stenographer" when she married in 1921, but she would not have turned 16 until the middle of 1916.
7. National Records of Scotland, Statutory Registers of Births, 479/2 168, 1890: Births in the District of Falkirk, County of Stirling, 1890, page 56.
8. Fetherstonhaugh 1925, chapter 2.
9. Holt 2017, 210.
10. Quoted in Cook 2007, 146.
11. Cook 2007, 110–168.
12. War diary of the 8th Battalion, 13–15 June, 1916.
13. Circumstances of Death Registers, First World War, vol. 31829_B016704, pages 787–788, 21510 Robertson, Daniel.
14. Horrocks 1993, 12.
15. Wheeler 2000, 27.
16. Quoted in Cook 2007, 515.
17. Cook 2000.
18. Horrocks 1993, 13.
19. Cook 2007, 519; McClintock 1917. McClintock was in the 87th Battalion and was wounded at Desire Trench. His book is full of bravado but he committed suicide in 1918.
20. War diaries of the 87th Battalion, November 18, 1916.
21. Circumstances of Death Registers, First World War, vol. 31829_B016704, pages 789–790, 145841 Robertson, Daniel.

22. Ottawa *Journal*, December 21, 1916, "Is reported missing." This newspaper account is the only reference to her son James, who was serving in the Imperial forces, we do not know in what capacity.
23. Ottawa *Journal,* February 9, 1917, "Husband and Son Killed Mother Waits for News."
24. Horrocks, 1993; Ottawa *Journal,* February 11, 1997, "Ex-sniper wouldn't discuss war."
25. Census of Canada 1921, Ontario, District 110, Central Ward, Sub-district 33, Central Ward, p. 26, lines 44–45.
26. "Mrs. Mary Robertson," Ottawa *Journal,* November 18, 1952.

Chapter 10: Gordon Maynard Porteous: "Quite a Few Homes ... Will Be Sad After This"

1. Census of Canada 1911, Quebec, district 165 Labelle, Sub-district 39 Buckingham, p. 7, lines 46–50.
2. A caption on the picture notes that the "names on the back are Lillie (Sarah) b. 1888 Ethel (Mae), b. 1890 Laura, b. 1892 Gordon Maynard Porteous b. 1895." A boy, Daniel, had died in 1888 at age 2.
3. Census of Canada 1911, Quebec, district 165 Labelle, Sub-district 40 Buckingham, page 21, lines 33–35; Census of Canada 1921, New Brunswick, Westmoreland, District 49, Sub-district 49, Moncton, p. 12, lines 49–50, p. 13, lines 1–3.
4. Ottawa *Citizen,* May 29, 1915, "Nurses Given Their Medals."
5. Ottawa *Journal,* March 27, 1916, "All Are Eager to Get Into the Fight."
6. Letter published on March 3, 1916, in *Buckingham Post*; information supplied by Richard Porteous through Pat Allan. Ottawa *Journal*, February 23, 1916, "As if Snow is Something to Eat."
7. Ottawa *Journal,* November 8, 1916, "38th Battalion Boys Met Many Old Friends on Reaching New Front."
8. Wheeler 2000, 13–16; and McClintock 1917.
9. War Diaries of the 38th Battalion, August 13, 1916, to May 31, 1919; Cook 2007, 510–512.
10. Ottawa *Journal,* November 8, 1916, "38th Battalion Boys Met Many Old Friends [...]."
11. War diary of the 12th Brigade, October 1, 1916, to December 31, 1916, November 18, 1916.
12. Circumstances of Death Registers, vol. 31829_B016769, pages 207–208, 410175 Porteous, Gordon Maynard.
13. Cook 2007, 519.
14. MacKay church archives.
15. MacKay Presbyterian Church Communion Rolls and wedding register; see also AO, Register of Marriages, 1826–1938, reel 571, image 772, Carleton, May 10, 1921, Marriage of Laura Porteous to Noble Carruthers.
16. Ottawa *Journal*, July 17, 1941, "Funeral Mrs. Porteous." The depth of carving indicates that Gordon's name was added with his mother's in 1941.

Chapter 11: Henry James Mayo: A "Home Boy" Serves His Country

1. Biographical information provided by Jeanne Mayo and Colleen Mayo.
2. See Bagnall 1980; Harrison 1979; and Kohli 2003.

3. Kohli 2003, 119–131.
4. Canada, Incoming Passengers Lists, 1865-1935, reel T-4670, image 589, Quebec, 1909, May 29, *Corsican*.
5. From its letterhead. Additional information provided by Jeanne Mayo, and the 10th annual report of the home, 1918, found in the Ottawa City Archives. At one point its president was Dr. Dougall King, brother of Mackenzie King.
6. Ottawa *Journal*, January 13, 1917, "Ottawa Scouts will Assist Boys' Home." Ottawa *Citizen*, August 2, 1913, "Ottawa Boys' Home an Institution Worthy of Public Support." Ottawa *Journal*, March 13, 1917, "Splendid record is Made by Boys' Home."
7. Reference provided by Jeanne Mayo.
8. Ottawa *Journal*, January 20, 1917, "Service for Mayo held in St. Bart's."
9. Reference provided by Jeanne Mayo.
10. Ireland, Civil Registration Births Index, 1864–1958, vol. 2, page 765, record of birth of Mary Elizabeth Welford, July–Sep 1893, Naas, Ireland.
11. Information provided by Colleen Mayo.
12. National Archives of Ireland, Census 1911, Fermanagh, Drumrush, Tubrid, residents of a house. Drumrush today is a lodge, not far from Dora Kesh where May Mayo stayed for a time during the war. National Archives of Ireland, Census 1901, Tipperary, Cashel Urban, Cashel – John Street, Residents of a house 17 in Cashel – John Street.
13. Canada, Incoming Passenger Lists, 1965–1935, reel T-4790, image 78, Quebec, September 1, 1912, *Scandinavian*, p. 10.
14. This ad had run in the Ottawa *Citizen*, February 15, 1910, and again on March 13, 1911.
15. Ottawa *Journal*, March 28, 1957, "Tobin, Jean Frances Welford." An obituary for Henry Mayo in the Ottawa *Journal*, January 10, 1917, describes May as a niece of Mrs. J. Tobin.
16. Ottawa *Citizen*, August 2, 1913, "Ottawa Boys' Home an Institution Worthy of Public Support."
17. I am indebted to Jeanne Mayo for this information. It was not at that time mandatory to register births.
18. AO, Register of Marriages, 1826–1938, Carleton, 1914, reel 303, image 504.
19. AO, Registrations of Deaths, 1869–1948, Carleton, 1914, reel 196, image 204; "labourer" is the designation in the Beechwood Cemetery Register, though the address given is that of the Boys' Home.
20. There may have been another relative associated with MacKay church: a Mrs. T. Tobin is recorded on MacKay's communion rolls from 1916 on, presumably the wife of Thomas Tobin, a teacher.
21. AO, Registrations of Deaths, 1869-1948, Carleton, 1919: reel 253, image 228; Mary Jane Welford, 24 January 1919.
22. See Ottawa *Citizen* report, February 5, 1916; and interview with Colleen Mayo, March 5, 2020.
23. Birth announcement, Ottawa *Journal*, April 6, 1916.
24. See Morton 1993, 199–203; Cassel 1987; Kierstead 1982; 199–217; Cook 2018, 272–275.
25. See Bennett 2009, 38–44.

26. Hanna 2020, chapter 4.
27. U.K. and Ireland Incoming passenger lists, 1878–1960, Glasgow, Scotland, July 26, 1916, *Pretorian*. See Mayo's service file for addresses to which separation allowances and assigned pay were sent.
28. Wheeler 2000, 53 ff.
29. War diary of the 50th Infantry Battalion CEF, 1916/08/10–1917/12/31, December 1916, page 6; Circumstances of Death Registers, First World War, v. 31829_B016754, pages 685–686, 144122 Henry J. Mayo. Mayo appears to have died the same day as he was wounded, but this was not known to the battalion diarist. See Canada CEF Commonwealth War Graves Register, Mayall to Millens, 144122 Henry James Mayo.
30. See Hanna 2000, 140–146.
31. A note on Mayo's service file gives that address as of October 18, 1919.
32. Proulx 1999, 64 notes that Mayo was one of the original tenants in this row of townhouses constructed in 1921.
33. Interview with Colleen Mayo, March 5, 2020, supplemented by census, birth and marriage information and city directories; "Mayo, W. H. (Bill)," Ottawa *Citizen*, February 18, 1998. "Mayo, Percy W. (Bud)," Ottawa *Citizen*, November 21, 2001; Ottawa *Journal* March 3, 1975, Death notice: "Mayo, Mary Elizabeth."
34. Information provided by Jeanne Mayo.

Chapter 12: A Church at War: 1917

1. AO, Register of Marriages 1826–1938, reel 207, images 1470–1471, Carleton, 3 July 1912; wedding announcement in Ottawa *Journal*, July 8, 1912.
2. AO, Register of Deaths, 1869–1948, MS 935, reel 230, image 710, Carleton, 1917, 010999; Beechwood Cemetery Interments 1888–1921, pages 162–163.
3. MacBeth 1924 and Gwyn 1992, chapter 11.
4. Ottawa *Journal*, March 5, 1917, "MacKay Church Has Special Service."
5. Minutes of Session 1902–1934, 197, meeting of June 22, 1917; Minutes of Ladies' Aid 1914–1924, 45–64; quotations 56, 63.
6. Cited in Fowler 2003, 55–56.
7. Fowler 2003, 52–86; and Macdonald 2014, 138–142.
8. Kilpatrick 1917, 5–12; lengthy quotation 11–12.
9. Crerar 2014, chapter 7.
10. Clarke 2015, chapter 1.
11. Quoted in Fowler 2003, 74; see also Davidson 2019, chapter 5.
12. Dennis 2017, 42–43.
13. Granatstein 1977, 83–88.
14. Ottawa *Journal*, November 1, 1917; "Tribunal No. 238"; Ottawa *Journal*, November 14, 1917, "Tribunal No. 238."
15. Ottawa *Journal*, November 10, 1917, "Tribunal No 238."
16. Ottawa *Journal*, November 10, 1917, "Tribunal No. 238"; November 16, "He apologizes for Statement Made"; November 17, 1917, "Tribunal No. 238"; November 21, 1917, "Tribunal No. 238"; November 22, 1917, "Tribunal No. 238."

Chapter 13: The Stalker Family and the Many Faces of Courage

1. UK Public Record Office, Census Returns of England and Wales, 1881. RG 11, Piece: 1376; Folio: 26; Page 46; GSU roll: 1341335. UK Public Record Office,

Census Returns of England and Wales, 1851, HO107; Piece: 1480; Folio: 800; Page: 15; GSU roll: 87804-87805.
2. Dictionary of architects in Canada, http://dictionaryofarchitectsincanada.org/node/2222.
3. Ottawa *Journal,* August 24, 1895, "Died in a Cab."
4. Personal notes in Ottawa *Journal,* May 20, 1898, and January 13, 1899.
5. Beechwood Cemetery Interments, 1873–1898, 7190.
6. Ottawa *Journal,* December 5, 1899, "Arrived Too Late."
7. Ottawa *Journal* February 27, 1904, "Obituary: Clara M. Stalker."
8. Information provided by Deborah Wawryk, who is Fred Stalker's granddaughter.
9. British Columbia, Death Index 1872–1990, Mary Anna Stalker, May 3, 1913; Registration number 1913-09-220108; BCA Number B13113; GSU Number 1927141.
10. Information provided by Mrs. B. Sheppard, Robert Stalker's granddaughter.
11. Ottawa *Journal,* January 28, 1898, from a report on the Annual General Meeting of the New Edinburgh Presbyterian Church, and April 2, 1897, "Temperance Debate." Ottawa *Journal,* February 17, 1900, "Merry Children."
12. Ottawa *Citizen,* November 19, 1897, "New Woman's Guild." Ottawa *Journal,* November 17, 1899, "The Tennyson Evening," and Ottawa *Citizen,* December 15, 1899, "St. David's Y. P. Society." Interestingly, the other members active in organizing activities were all young women. Ottawa *Journal,* April 28, 1904, "Y. P. Guild, St. David's;" Ottawa *Citizen,* November 14, 1904, "St David's Guild." Ottawa *Citizen,* November 9, 1904, "New Edinburgh."
13. Ottawa *Citizen,* December 13, 1912, "City Clerk's Office", and January 10, 1946, "Fellow Employees to Honor Moray Stalker"; Ottawa *Journal,* September 30, 1937, "A. D. Stalker Was Popular Civic Official"; Ottawa *Citizen,* September 30, 1937, "Late A. D. Stalker Popular Officer in Waterworks Dept."
14. British Columbia Regiment 1981.
15. Neither he nor any of the other officers was assigned a service number.
16. British Columbia Regiment 1981, 107, 72.
17. Gould 1919, 18, 19.
18. General Record Office, United Kingdom, England & Wales, Civil Registration Marriage Index, 1916–2005, Volume 6b, page 630, 1916 Q4-Oct-Nov-Dec, letter S.
19. 1881 Census Returns of England and Wales, Class: RG11; Piece: 3685; Folio: 60; Page: 9; GSU roll: 1341882, Lancashire, Kirkdale, Enumeration District: H M Prison, line 24; 1891 Census Returns of England and Wales: Piece: 4287; Folio: 122; Page: 3; GSU roll: 6099397. Cumberland, St. Cuthberts; District: Her Majesty's Prison, page 3 line 6; 1881 Census Returns of England and Wales, Piece: 3691; Folio: 109; Page: 15; GSU roll: 1341884; Enumeration District: 27, Lancashire, Bootle cum Linacre, Household 69; 1891 Census Returns of England and Wales, Piece: 2982; Folio: 19; Page: 32; GSU roll: 6098092, Enumeration District: 1, Lancashire, Great Crosby, household 172. Edith's mother died in 1893. A record of a London workhouse (London Workhouse Admission and Discharge Registers Edmonton Workhouse Register, 1897–1900, page 36) in 1899 shows an Edith Boult entering on June 13, 1899; a son Frederick born June 24 and dying August 10; and Edith discharged at her own request on August 16, 1899. It cannot be corroborated that this is the same Edith Boult.

20. New York, Passenger and Crew Lists (including Castle Garden and Ellis Island) 1820–1957, Year: 1902; Arrival: New York, New York, USA; Microfilm Serial: T715, 1897–1957; Line: 1; Page: 74. Record of Detained alien passengers, SS *Lucania*, from Liverpool, arrived May 31, 1902; Massachusetts Vital Records, 1840–1911. New England Historic Genealogical Society, Boston, Massachusetts, Massachusetts Vital Records, 1911–1915. New England Historic Genealogical Society, Boston, Massachusetts, Marriages registered in the city of Fall River for the Year 1904, page 24, no. 418.
21. Census Returns of England and Wales, 1911, Enumeration District: 32 London, Islington, Highbury lines 1, 2. This is one of the few times Edith correctly reported her age, as corroborated by her birth record, November 2, 1879: Liverpool Church of England Parish Registers, 1848–1881, page 359.
22. Canada, Incoming Passenger Lists, 1865–1935, reel T-4756, image 25, Halifax, Nova Scotia, May 1917, register of her landing in Halifax in May 1917, where she declares that she had been in Canada before, in Prince Rupert, for two years, presumably since 1914.
23. Gould 1919, chapter 3.
24. Gould 1919, chapter 4.
25. War diary of the 102nd Infantry Battalion, 1916/08/12–1917/09/30, April 1917, pp. 9–11. British Columbia Regiment 1981, 109. See Cook 2008, chapter 8, and Cook 2017, 96–113.
26. Cook 2008, 330–339; Nicholson [1962] 2015, 318–320.
27. Cook 2008, chapter 22, and war diary of the 38th Battalion, 1916/08/13–1917/12/31, especially October 30.
28. Ottawa *Citizen,* September 30, 1937, "Late A. D. Stalker Popular Officer in Waterworks Dept.,"; and Ottawa *Journal,* September 30, 1937, "A. D. Stalker Was Popular Civic Official."
29. War diary of the 38th Infantry Battalion, 1918/01/01–1919/05/31; Appendix I to August 1918 diary.
30. Cook 2008, 483.
31. Ottawa *Journal,* June 16, 1919, "How 'Red' Nunney Won Three Honours."
32. War diary of the 38th Infantry Battalion, 1918/01/01–1919/05/31, "38th Canadian Infantry Battalion Report on Scarpe Operations, 30th August to 3rd September 1918."
33. Canada, Incoming Passenger Lists, Halifax, SS *Olympic*, roll T-4756, image 17, May 1917.
34. Archives of British Columbia, Victoria, File GR-2202.523 - Stalker, Robert. Accession 87-0710. Reel B09033, Number Probate 33065. GR-1483.463 – Stalker, Robert A. Reel 09395, Probate 441/1917, Documents concerning probate of the will of Robert A. Stalker, Prince Rupert.
35. Prince Rupert *Daily News*, September 10, 1917; copy of a clipping provided by Mrs. Sheppard. See also a clipping provided by her from a different newspaper, dated September 12, recording that she had won her case.
36. In the Supreme Court of British Columbia. In the Matter of Nora Jean Stalker, Norman Douglas Stalker, Robert Fred Stalker, and Margaret Stalker, Infants, Before the Honourable Mr. Justice MacDonald, in Chambers, Wednesday the 12th day of September, 1917. Provincial Archives of British Columbia, Series GR-2727 British Columbia Supreme Court orders, vol. 34, file 428.

37. British Columbia. Division of Vital Statistics, Marriage Registrations 059173 to 059585. 18-C9-188416, Marriage Certificate No. 47, Colin James Morris and Edith Stalker.
38. Archives of Ontario, Register of Marriages; 1826–1938, reel 563, image 4765; York County, June 15, 1921; Francis John Beattie Cox and Edith Lillian Morris.
39. British Columbia Order in Council 437/1927.
40. MacKay Presbyterian Church, Minutes of Ladies Aid 1914–1924, 62.
41. Ottawa *Journal*, November 13, 1917, "Tribunal No. 238," Rideau Ward. Ottawa *Citizen*, October 2, 1918, "Stalker Out of It."
42. Ottawa *Journal*, June 7, 1940, "Major G. F. Stalker Dies in 64th Year"; Ottawa *Journal*, June 10, 1940, "Many Mourn Major Stalker." Semi-military honours means that the casket was draped at the funeral home and in the procession with a Union Flag, but there was no Last Post or volley at the cemetery.
43. Ottawa *Journal* September 30, 1937, "A. D. Stalker Was Popular Civic Official Death Occurs of Waterworks Engineer."
44. Ottawa *Citizen*, January 10, 1946, "Fellow Employees to Honour Moray Stalker." Ottawa *Citizen*, August 20, 1970, "Obituary."
45. Ottawa Citizen, October 4, 1954, "Arthur P. Stalker, Carpenter, Dies."

Chapter 14: The Ryan Family: "Who Played the Game Through"

1. Mathew William does not appear to have been too concerned with accuracy when reporting his birth date. His attestation papers show him as being born on October 28, 1882 in Montreal; the 1901 census gives his birthdate as October 16, 1883; the 1911 census gives his birthdate as November 1882.
2. Census of Canada 1901, District 112, Russell, Ontario, Sub-district 57, New Edinburgh Page:13, lines 33–37.
3. Ottawa *Journal*, March 4, 1903, "Sixteenth Annual Meeting of W. F. M. S."
4. Census of Canada 1911, District 112, Ontario, Russell, Sub-district 57, Page: 10, lines 2–5.
5. Cathryn Crocker, personal communication, January 24, 2021.
6. Ottawa *Citizen*, July 29, 1907, "Regatta Notes," and many other reports.
7. Ottawa *Citizen*, November 17, 1958, "W. Crowe, Electric Firm Head, Dies"; Ottawa *Citizen*, September 10, 1913, "Electrical Firm Doing Good Work."
8. Ottawa *Citizen*, September 4, 1916, "To Pte. H. W. [sic] Ryan."
9. In April 1902 the British requested 2,000 more mounted troops for South Africa. Four battalions were recruited including the 3rd Canadian Mounted Rifles (CMR) from Ottawa. 3 CMR exceeded its targets and some recruits, including Ryan, did not go at once to South Africa. LAC, South African War, 1899–1902, Medals and Land Applications, file 263 vol. 117, series A1b, item no, 5883, Vol. 117, land grants 0201–0295.
10. Ottawa *Citizen*, May 5, 1917, "Ottawa Ski Club is Also in Mourning".
11. Ottawa *Journal*, 14 November 1911, "Toronto Opinion."
12. Ottawa City Archives, Interprovincial Rugby Football Union Fonds, Minute Book, 1907–1928, minutes for 1908, record of special meeting of Board of Governors, October 23, 1908.

13. Ottawa *Journal*, September 28, 1909, "Jack Ryan's Fate Will Be Decided Friday Night"; Ottawa *Journal*, December 14, 1911, "Vics Still Claim Ryan Can't Play"; Ottawa *Citizen*, December 14, 1911, "Miscellaneous Sport." The question of amateur status even dogged him in rowing for the NECC.
14. War diaries of the 24th Battalion, 1916/01/01–1917/08/31, Volume number: 4932, Microfilm reel number: T-10733, File number: 414, image 195, August 1916, page 3; Circumstances of Death Registers, First World War, vol. 31829_B016703, Rowland to Ryrie, pages 639–640.
15. No CEF service record has been located for him, but on a list of MacKay soldiers, his name appears with others who enlisted in early 1915, and his picture appears to show him in a militia uniform.
16. Ottawa *Citizen*, May 5, 1917, "Ottawa Ski Club is Also in Mourning."
17. Greenhous 1987, 53n; Wise 1980, 23–35; Dodds 1980, 13.
18. Broad 2017, 30–31 describes the training of a Canadian pilot at a Wright School in Ohio.
19. Ottawa *Citizen*, October 29, 1915. Ryan may or may not have gone to Bermuda because he was accepted for the RFC in late 1915.
20. Ottawa *Citizen*, December 30, 1916, "Football-Aviator Presented with Pipe By Registration Branch Employes [sic]."
21. Background on aviation and training is found in Milberry 1979, 10–19; 175–187; Hartley 1971; Dodds 1980, 13; and the diary of Don Brophy in Greenhous 1987.
22. See Greenhous 1987, xii–xiii.
23. Mackersey 2012, 2.
24. See Hart 2005, chapter 1.
25. See "Royal Flying Corps People Index," Ryan, J. H.; Greenhous 1987, 105.
26. Greenhous 1987, xviii–xix; Bashow 2000, 56; Mackersey 2012, chapter 14; Jones 1928, 147–313.
27. Ottawa *Citizen*, October 28, 1916.
28. Greenhous 1987, 102n; Ottawa *Citizen*, September 13, 1916, "Ottawa Boys Are Doing Their Share in the Flying Corps"; Ottawa *Citizen*, January 2, 1917, "'Flying is Fascinating Game', Wrote Late Lieut. Don Brophy a Few Days Before His Death."
29. Jones 1931, 251–301 (re. solo hours 297); Jones 1935, 424.
30. Jones 1931, 413.
31. Hart 2005, chapter 2.
32. Jones 1931, 332–379; Mackersey 2012, chapter 14; Wise 1980, 398–400; Hart 2005, chapter 5.
33. Jones 1931, 369.
34. National Archives, Kew, UK, Catalogue Ref WO 339/105704, file Lt. John Henry Ryan, RFC, casualty report. There are inconsistent accounts of how Ryan died. Hart 2005, chapter 5, suggests from a German account that four F.E.2ds, not two, were shot down behind German lines. The commander of 57 Squadron told Mabel McElroy that Ryan's engine had overheated and he had crashed in a shell hole (Ottawa *Journal*, May 25, 1917, "Jack Ryan's Aeroplane Fell into Shell Hole"). The service file of Ryan's Observer, B. Soutten, says that he suffered multiple gunshot wounds, which would not be consistent with a flying accident; but he appears to have survived.

35. Ottawa *Citizen,* May 8, 1917, miscellaneous notes; Ottawa *Journal,* May 4, 1917, "Jack Ryan Pays Supreme Sacrifice"; Ottawa *Journal,* May 3, "Jack Ryan Was Best Flying Wing in Game."
36. Ottawa *Journal,* May 5, 1917, editorial.
37. Ryan's service file from the UK National Archives consists for the most part of these documents generated following his death.
38. Beechwood Cemetery Interments, 1898–1921, page 469, no. 16695.
39. Ottawa *Journal,* July 24, 1918, "Mrs. John T. McElroy."
40. Ottawa *Journal,* March 7, 1947, "Mrs. William T. Crowe Dies in Ottawa"; March 11, 1947, "Pay Last Tribute to Mrs. W. T. Crowe."
41. Ottawa *Citizen,* November 17, 1958, "W. Crowe, Electric Firm Head, Dies."

Chapter 15: Reginald Isambard Brunel: Engineer and Artilleryman

1. Census of Canada 1911, Ontario, District 118, Russell, Sub-district 7, Rideau Ward, page 1, lines 12–17.
2. Census of Canada 1891, district 103 Wellington Ward, Ottawa City, Ontario, page 12, Canada, Roll: T-6359, Family No: 48.
3. Drouin Collection, Ottawa, Registry of Paroisse St. Joseph, 1882–1901, 387, 467.
4. AO, Register of Deaths, 1869–1948, #133 MS935, reel: 124, image 120, Carleton, 1906, 008063.
5. AO, Registrations of Marriages, 1869–1929, reel 127, image 509, Carleton, 1907, no. 176.
6. I am grateful to Joy Heft, archivist at Lisgar Collegiate, for providing copies of Brunel's transcripts at OCI.
7. Nicholson 1967, 240.
8. War diary of the 7th Brigade CFA, January 1916 to February 1917.
9. See Nicholson 1967, 209; Grout 2015; Kerr 1929, 81–108.
10. War diary of the 7th Brigade CFA; Nicholson 1967, 258–279.
11. War diary, 6th Brigade CFA, April 1, 1917.
12. Cook 2017, 43–47, 65–69; war diary, 6th Brigade CFA, April 9, 1917.
13. Grout 2015, 258, 259; Nicholson 1967, 287–291.
14. Circumstances of Death Register, Vol. 31829_B016724, Brubacher to Bunyan, page 73.
15. His first wife had died in 1915. Drouin Collection, Register of Basilique Notre Dame 1916–1920, 2.
16. AO, Registrations of Marriages, 1869–1928; reel: 450, image 940, Carleton, 1918.
17. Minutes of Session, 1902–1924, 256–257.
18. Edwards 1975, 89–91.
19. Ottawa *Journal,* August 28, 1972, "Dr. David Graham"; Ottawa *Citizen,* April 9, 1973, October 1977, "Dr. David Graham."

Chapter 16: The Tubman Families: "Conspicuous Gallantry and Devotion to Duty"

1. Ottawa *Journal,* November 6, 1959, "WESTWICK: Ray Liked to Recall the Joliat Story."

2. Murray 1947, 174; Ottawa *Citizen,* June 30, 1917, "Officer's tribute to late Les Tubman." A clipping of this article was saved by William Bothwell and is in the Robert Bothwell Fonds.
3. Ottawa *Citizen,* June 25, 1923, "Late Mrs. W. Tubman is Mourned by Many." Thomas Tubman's house was kitty corner from a large grocery store owned by his brother William, who died in 1902. Other branches of the Tubman family gradually left New Edinburgh.
4. Ottawa *Citizen,* April 25, 1922, "Late W. J. Tubman." Ottawa *Citizen,* January 3, 1934, obituary for Robert James Tubman.
5. Census of Canada 1901, Ontario, District 100, Ottawa City, Sub-district 6, St. George's Ward, page 10, lines 15–21; Census of Canada 1911, Ontario, District 118, Russell, Sub-district 7, page 1, lines 48–50, page 2, lines 1–10.
6. Ottawa *Journal,* October 10, 1918, "Unveil the Honor Roll of St. David's Church."
7. Ottawa *Citizen,* April 25, 1922, "Late W. J. Tubman"; Ottawa *Journal,* November 16, 1954, "Mrs. Robt. J. Tubman Dies at Age 87."
8. Ottawa *Citizen,* June 11, 1912, "Montreal Gets It," and May 23, 1912, "Y. M. C. A. Men Enter."
9. Information on the family members provided by Joy Heft, archivist at Lisgar Collegiate; see also the OCI magazine *Vox Lycei* of 1918, and newspaper accounts.
10. Ottawa *Citizen,* July 18, 1911, "Carelessness Cause of Fire."
11. Ottawa *Citizen,* April 29, 1920, "Tubman to Try For Olympic Team."
12. Murray 1947, 2; Cook 2007, 39.
13. Cook 2007, 135–159; Murray 1947, 35–60.
14. Murray 1947, 128.
15. Cook 2007, 426–429.
16. Murray 1947, 153–154.
17. Murray 1947, 157–159.
18. Murray 1947, 160–161.
19. London *Gazette,* Fourth Supplement, May 26, 1917.
20. Murray 1947, 165–166; Ottawa *Citizen,* May 10, 1917, "Lt. Leslie Tubman Killed in Action."
21. Ottawa *Citizen,* June 30, 1917, "Officer's tribute to late Les Tubman."
22. Ottawa *Citizen,* June 30, 1917, "Officer's Tribute."
23. Murray 1947, 180–181.
24. Ottawa *Citizen,* June 30, 1917, "Officer's Tribute."
25. "The Officers and Men of Infantry in Haig Dispatch," Ottawa *Citizen,* June 2, 1917.
26. Ottawa *Citizen,* June 30, 1917, "Officer's Tribute." See also June 26, 1917, "Tells How Ottawans Died in France."
27. Cook 2008, 105.
28. Grout 2015, 289–297, quote 292.
29. Ottawa *Citizen,* May 1, 1917, "Lt. Leslie Tubman Killed in Action."
30. Ottawa *Citizen,* October 27, 1917, "In the Sporting World."
31. Ottawa *Journal,* April 25, 1922, death notice.
32. Ottawa *Citizen,* January 10, 1986, obituary for Edith Mary Tubman.
33. Ottawa *Journal,* May 26, 1955, "Many Sportsmen Pay Last Honours to Reed Tubman"; Ottawa *Journal,* May 24, 1955, death notice; Ottawa *Journal,* May 24, 1955, "Reed Tubman, Noted Runner, Football Player, Dies at 65"; Ottawa *Citizen,* May 24, 1955, "W. Reed Tubman Dies Was Former Athlete."

34. Ottawa *Citizen,* April 8, 1920, "Ottawa Losing Star Athlete." In the 1921 census Harry was recorded as a lodger on the Bow River Valley farm of another MacKay soldier, William Fixter Stevenson. Census of Canada 1921, Alberta, District 2, Bow River, Sub-district 24, page 10, line 1, and page 9, line 50.
35. Ottawa *Journal,* January 11, 1936, "Banquet Is Given For Ray Tubman by Friends Here; Ottawa *Journal,* November 5, 1959, "Ray Tubman Dies at 63 Suddenly"; Ottawa *Citizen,* November 5, 1959, "Outstanding Citizen, Theatre Manager Dies"; November 6, 1959, editorial, and Bob Blackburn, column.
36. Ottawa *Journal,* June 5, 1936, "Death Mourned of R. A. Tubman"; Ottawa *Citizen,* June 5, 1936, "R. Arnold Tubman Died in Ottawa Yesterday."
37. Ottawa *Journal,* August 11, 1922, "Start Efforts to Obtain Sums Wrongly Paid"; September 14, 1922, "Judgment Given Against Tubman in Test Action."
38. Ottawa *Citizen,* December 1, 1975, "Former football great dies at 78."

Chapter 17: Erland Dauria Perney: "Sorrow Which Is Almost Intolerable"

1. Ottawa *Citizen,* July 16, 1909, "Scholarship Winners."
2. Census of Canada 1911, Ontario, District 118, Russell, Sub-district 7, Rideau Ward, page 37, lines 11–14.
3. Cummings and MacSkimming 1971, 68.
4. Ottawa *Citizen,* February 14, 1917, "Bilingualism and School Position."
5. Student card provided by Joy Heft, archivist at Lisgar Collegiate.
6. Ottawa *Citizen,* November 19, 1919, "Ottawa Ski Club to Hold Meeting on November 27"; November 30, 1917, "Lt. Erland Perney Reported Missing."
7. Ottawa *Citizen,* July 12, 1916, "Art. Officers For England."
8. UK National Archives, catalogue reference: WO 339/78183, file 2/Lieutenant Erland Dauria PERNEY Royal Flying Corps (Special Reserve), hereinafter cited as Kew, Perney file: 87/Instruction/73 (A.o.l.b), Major Hausburg for Director of Air Organization to Commandant, School of Military Aeronautics, Reading. "This officer has been selected in Canada for a commission in the Royal Flying Corps Special Reserve, under the conditions laid down in the War Office letter dated the 4th October, 1916."
9. Wise 1980, 34–43.
10. See, besides the general sources for flying services, Broad 2017, chapter 4; and Hart 2005, chapter 4.
11. Damage report, in a file of documents collected by William Borland of Liverpool from Blackledge's service file in UK National Archives, Kew, WO339/58286, hereinafter referred to as Kew, Blackledge file.
12. Jones 1934, 227–259; Wise 1980, 443–444.
13. From Royal Flying Corps People Index, and Casualty Card for Perney E. D.
14. Kew, Perney file; 14 November, 1918, Frank Perney to Mewburn; 18 November, 1918, Fiset to Secretary, Air Ministry; 21 November 1918, R. C. Fowler to the Secretary, Militia Council Headquarters, Ottawa.
15. Kew, Perney file; August 2, 1918, and 17 October 1918, Deputy Minister of Militia and Defence in Ottawa to The Military Secretary, Whitehall, England.
16. Maurer 1979, 225, and note 81b, 553. I am indebted to "Regular 122" on The Aerodrome Forum, theaerodrome.com, who posted this reference in response to my inquiry on E. D. Perney, March 29, 2021.

17. Kew, Perney file; Margret E Perney letter September 7, 1918, in response to letter to her of August 17, 1918; from R. C. Fowler. See also Margaret Perney's letter of September 10 and Frank Perney's letter of January 18, 1919, to the Air Ministry.
18. Kew, Blackledge file; War Office (contracts department) to C. G. Evans; Air Ministry, 8 August 1918; R. G. Fowler of Casualties Department to Blackledge, 9 July 1918; Blackledge to War Office, 6 July 1918; Fowler to Deputy Adjutant General, Third Division, BEF, 5 June 1918.
19. Kew, Perney file; 4 October 1917, W. B. Grindle to Mrs. Perney.
20. Kew, Blackledge and Perney files both have copies of 4 October 1918, letter to The Secretary, Prisoners of War Department, C.2.Casualties 13067/4; and 13 December 1918, diplomatic note from Netherland Legation (British Section) at Berlin to British Embassy in the Hague; Kew, Perney file; Fowler to Mrs. Perney, 27 January 1919.
21. Kew, Blackledge file; Captain P.M. Miller to Blackledge, 26 December 1918; Blackledge to War Office, 2 January 1919; War Office to Blackledge, 8 January 1919; Blackledge to Secretary of War, 1 February 1919; War Office to Blackledge, 5 April 1919.
22. Jones 1935, 246.
23. Ottawa *Citizen,* March 10, 1919, "Met Death in a Plucky Attempt to Save Regiment."
24. Kew, Perney file; Frank Perney to War Office, March 14, 1919.
25. In the midst of this correspondence was a letter to the Air Ministry from a Miss A. Walton of Glasgow: Kew, Perney file; 23 April 1919, Miss A. Walton to the Military Secretary; War Office, referring to previous correspondence on February 13, 1919. "Needless to say, any news of his whereabouts will be gladly received by me." A reply on February 21, 1919, from B. Grindle to Miss Walton was a standard restatement of the facts. Her identity and relation to Perney is not known.
26. Kew, Perney file; April 25, 1919, Grindle to McKeever; April 30, 1919, Frank Perney to McKeever.
27. Kew, Perney file; Fiset to Secretary, Air Ministry, 24 March, 1919.
28. Kew, Perney file; 25 March 1919, Grindle to Mrs. Perney; 25 April 1919, C. B.B. Cubitt, War Ministry (casualties) to Mrs. Perney.
29. Kew, Blackledge file; 10 June 2019, Diplomatic Note No B.1083, Netherlands Embassy (British Section) to British Legation, Hague.
30. Kew, Perney file; June 16, 1919, Perney to Corcoran; June 28, 1919, J. A. Corcoran to Perney.
31. Kew, Perney file; 30 June 1919, minute to the Adjutant-General, Headquarters Canadian Air Force in London, from the Secretary of the Casualties Section, Air Ministry; July 1, 1919, Mrs. Perney to War Office.
32. Kew, Perney file, 20 August 1919, Frank Perney to J. A. Corcoran, War Office.
33. Kew, Perney file, 29 September 1919, Grindle to Perney.
34. See Perney's CEF service file.
35. Kew, Blackledge file, 23 August 1919, Blackledge to War Office, and 6 September 1919, War Office to Blackledge.
36. Kew, Blackledge file, 29 November 1919, Army Council to Blackledge.
37. Source: Commonwealth War Graves Commission, Caring for the Fallen, "Remembering Bloody April," https://www.cwgc.org/our-work/blog/

remembering-bloody-april/; and The Great War, 1914–1918, "Arras Flying Services Memorial, Arras," http://www.greatwar.co.uk/french-flanders-artois/memorial-arras-flying-services-memorial.htm.
38. See https://www.lsuc.on.ca/uploadedFiles/PDC/CR_and_A/PF58(1).pdf, and history of WLAO, https://wlao.on.ca/about/history/. Ottawa *Journal*, January 5, 1950, page 2, "Margaret Perney, Formerly of Ottawa, Among 39 New KC's."
39. Ottawa *Journal*, July 24, 1919. I am grateful to Alan McCullough of ONEC for the additional information.

Chapter 18: A Church at War: 1918

1. Kealey 1998, 203–204.
2. Minutes of Session, 213.
3. The Death Register erroneously records August 27.
4. Bacic 1998.
5. Pettigrew 1983, 101.
6. See Ottawa *Citizen,* November 11, 1918, "Thankfulness Expressed by City Pastors on Kaiser's Abdication," and Ottawa *Journal,* same date.
7. Minutes of the Ladies' Aid 1914–1924, 78.

Chapter 19: John Marshall: A Chauffeur in Egypt

1. Census of Scotland, 1881, Roll cssct1881_86, Reg. No. 282/4, District St. Andrew, Dundee, Enumeration District 8, household number 100, line 1; Census of Scotland 1891, Roll CSSCT1891_88, Reg. No. 282/1, Registration district St. Peter, Civil Parish Liff and Benvie, County Angus, Enumeration District 32, Household number 164, line 10; Census of Scotland 1901, Roll CSSCT1901_124, Reg. No. 387, Registration District, Perth, Civil Parish Perth, County Perthshire, Enumeration District 4, Household No. 17, Line 23; Perth Directory for 1905-6; Dundee City Directory 1910 (which lists Archibald Marshall as a "lorryman").
2. Scottish BDM 387/204 for marriage of John Marshall to Catherine Nicol Birss Dec 6, 1901, Perth SCT.
3. LAC, Canada, Incoming Passenger Lists, 1865-1935, Roll T-4768, image 2009, Quebec, June 27, 1910, *Dominion,* page 6; Census of Canada 1911, Ontario, district 104, South Ontario, Sub-district 39, Whitby town, page 1, lines 16–18.
4. AO Registration of Births and Stillbirths 1869–1917, MS 929, Reel 248, RG 80-2, Carleton 1914–1915, image 62, January 28, 1914.
5. Ottawa *Journal,* April 27, 1918, "Ottawa Man Dies of Sunstrioke Got in Egypt."
6. Ottawa *Journal,* July 22, 1916, "Many Country Boys Make Good Drivers."
7. Holt 2017, 46. Holt says that this recruitment took place in October of 1916, but it is clear from the source materials cited that it was one year earlier. Marshall's obituary gives this date and church records show that he did not attend after 1914. See Ottawa *Journal,* March 27, 1916, "What Ottawa and Capital District Have Done for the Cause of the Empire": "Small squads of men for the Dental Corps, Veterinary Corps, Cyclist, Imperial Motor Transport, Aviation, and other smaller units have drawn their quota of men from the city."

8. UK National Archives, Board of Trade: Commercial and Statistical Department and successors: Inwards Passenger Lists; Class: BT26; Piece: 619; Item: 70; UK and Ireland, Incoming Passenger Lists 1878–1960, Glasgow, Scotland, 1916, January.
9. Badcock 1925, 218–221.
10. See Woodward 2006, 33–157; Bruce 2014, 94–223; Rogan 2015, 311–353; Ulrichsen 2014, 97–118; Johnson 2016, 60–84, 109–131, 189–203; Falls and Becke 1930; McMunn and Falls 1928.
11. Quoted in Badcock 1925, 248.
12. Woodward 2006, 23.
13. Ulrichsen 2014, 34–35; Woodward 2006, 22–24, 34–41, 208; Johnson 2016, 116–117; Rogan 2015, 314; Bruce 2014, 97–98; McMunn and Falls 1928, 138, 176–178, 243.
14. Ottawa *Journal,* April 27, 1918, "Ottawa Man Dies of Sunstroke Got in Egypt;" UK WWI Pension Record Cards and Ledgers, Other Ranks Died, Marshall F-Marshall T, Reference Number 1/Wm/3184 [which says that Marshall died from "Exhaustion from Depressive Manic Insanity Agg. by A. S."]; Harrison 2010, 277. After the fall of 1917 the Palestine campaign was fought in cooler, rainy weather.
15. Paul Climey, "Asylums in Glasgow: The buildings where madness was managed."
16. Gary Thomson, curator of the Dundee memorial website, examined the Dundee City Directories and electoral lists for the war years. Personal communication from Gary Thomson, March, 16, 2018 and March 18, 2018.
17. British Army, Register of Soldiers' Effects, 1901-1929, for John Marshall 1914–1915; Woolwich and Blackheath, 674501-676000, image 69, He is listed as SAC MT Pvte, M2152731. Account Woolwich 4/18 credits.
18. Scottish BDM 387/236 marriage of Catherine to James Clark, July 18, 1919. The Commonwealth War Graves register entry for "Marshall, Pte. John, M2/152731 M. T. Coy. Royal Army Service Corps" refers to her as "Catherine Birrs Clark Marshall of 2, Hill St., Crastonhill, Glasgow."

Chapter 20: Homère Joliat: "A Brave Soldier, Having Won the Military Medal"

1. Ottawa *Journal,* August 27, 1931, "New Police Chief Skilled Athlete in His Early Days."
2. His name was spelled Aurel in the English language media.
3. Homère joined by Profession of Faith in 1914; Alice in 1916; and Aurèle in 1918; Although Émile was a Presbyterian and had probably been attending MacKay for some time, he, Azilda, and René Joliat did not formally join until March 23, 1917.
4. "Felix Cornu", Ottawa *Citizen,* February 6, 1934.
5. Ottawa *Journal,* August 27, 1931, "New Police Chief Has Had Thrilling and Romantic Life."
6. See Ottawa *Journal,* March 24, 1952, "Retired Chief Émile Joliat Given Impressive Last Tributes"; Henri is described in some sources as his nephew, in others as a brother or half-brother. Émile and his brothers were not the only Joliats to emigrate to Canada. A distant cousin, also Émile Joliat, emigrated from Switzerland just before the war to farm in Manitoba. He enlisted in 1916, was wounded at Passchendaele, died of wounds in 1918, and is buried in Switzerland.

7. "Death Notice," Ottawa *Journal*, March 17, 1959.
8. Drouin Collection, Notre Dame de Grace Church Register, 1886-1900, 4 February 1892.
9. Ottawa *Journal*, March 17, 1910, "Police Reorganization has become a reality"; Ottawa *Journal*, August 27, 1931, "New Chief of Police Skilled Athlete in His Early Days"; Ottawa *Journal*, August 27, 1931, "New Police Chief Has Had Thrilling and Romantic Life." See also Ottawa *Journal*, March 20, 1952, "Emile Joliat Former Police Chief Dies."
10. Ottawa *Journal*, April 5, 1918, "Wounds Are Fatal to L-Corp. Joliat."
11. Logan et al. 1919, 22–28.
12. LAC, war diary of the Borden Machine Gun Battery, 1914/12/10–1917/04/30, April 6, 1916.
13. Ottawa *Citizen*, May 4, 1916, "Machine Gun Men in the Thick of the Fight."
14. Logan et al. 1919, 148–184; Pulsifer 2001; Cook 2007, 88–89; Morton and Granatstein 1989, 277; Holden 2003, 35–47; Grafton 1938.
15. War diary, September 26, 1916.
16. Cook 2016, 112–114.
17. Morton 1993, 83–84. See also Campbell 2007, 307–316.
18. Lynch 2001, 6.
19. Reminiscences of Pte. Richard Wm. Mercer, 911016; provided to me by Dwight Mercer, 6/25/2018. Lynch 2001, 16–17; Logan et al. 1919, 185–232.
20. Canada, Military Honours and Awards Citation Cards, 1900–1960, Johnston, G. H. to Kelsey; H. G. London *Gazette* 3057, March 12, 1918. Neither the citation nor the December 13 war diary entry give any specific reason for this award. A newspaper article at the time says it was "for his splendid work with the battery, and for his devotion to duty in carrying of dispatches in and from the front lines" (Ottawa *Journal* January 16, 1918, "L.-Corp Joliat Decorated)."
21. Holden 2003, 48. Lynch 2001, 16–17; Logan et al. 1919, 185–232.
22. Ottawa *Journal* January 16, 1918, "L.-Corp Joliat Decorated."
23. Lynch 2001, 16, 19. Pulsifer 2002. The inspection is not recorded in the Battery's war diary.
24. Cook 2008, 390.
25. Pulsifer 2002.
26. Logan et al. 1919; Grafton 1938, 123–138; Holden 2003.
27. Cook 2008, 392–393; Pulsifer 2002; *Narratives Covering Operations Of The 1st Canadian Motor Machine Gun Brigade, The Canadian Independent Force, The Composite Brigade And Brutinel's Brigade During 1918*. Historical Section, General Staff. OTTAWA, Canada, September, 1926, 10.
28. Holden 2003, 66. Logan et al. 1919, 243–245; Lynch 2001, 47–52; Holden 2003, 63–66; Lynch 1978. *Narratives Covering Operations of the 1st Canadian Motor Machine Gun Brigade*, 30.
29. Circumstances of Death Registers, vol. 31829_B016692, pages 9–10, 113329 Homer [*sic*] Joliat.
30. Lynch 2001, 115–117.
31. December 23, page 13.
32. Ottawa *Journal*, October 29, 1924, "Mrs. Emile Joliat passes away here."

33. Census of Canada 1921, Ontario, District 125, Russell, Sub-district 37, Rideau Ward, page 1, lines 26–31.
34. Ottawa *Journal*, August 27, 1931, "New Police Chief Has Had Thrilling and Romantic Life."

Chapter 21: Irwin Kelly: "Blessed Are Those that Have Not Seen, and Yet Have Believed"

1. Archives of Ontario, Registrations of Marriages, 1869–1928; reel: 53, image 55, Frontenac, 1886, 003335, marriage of Samuel Kelly and Olivia Irwin.
2. Census of Canada 1901, Ontario, district 100, Ottawa City, Sub-district 3, Dalhousie Ward, page 15, lines 20–26; Census of Canada 1911, Ontario, District 118, Russell, Sub-district 7, Rideau Ward, Page 3, lines 44–50; Census of Canada 1921, Ontario, District 125, Russell, Sub-district 39, Rideau Ward, page 16, line 50, page 17, lines 1–3.
3. See McCulloch 2009, 829, 911; Grass 2017; Shaw 1946; Dougall 2003.
4. Ottawa *Citizen*, May 5, 1906, "Labor Men Hear Questions of Vital Interest Debated."
5. Might's Ottawa Directories, 1900–1909; Ottawa *Citizen*, January 14, 1924, "Late Samuel J. Kelly."
6. Ottawa *Journal*, September 18, 1918, "Gunner Irwin Kelly is Among the Killed"
7. War diaries of the 7th Brigade CFA, January 1916 to February 1917.
8. Nicholson 1967, 258–279.
9. His service file says this happened on the 19th, but the war diary records "I Kelly" wounded and evacuated on the 18th.
10. Ottawa *Citizen*, September 18, 1918, "Gr. Irwin Kelly is killed in action."
11. The 7th Brigade had been broken up as part of a reorganization.
12. *Overseas Service* [1919], 6.
13. *Overseas Service* [1919], 6.
14. Cook 2008, chapter 31.
15. *Overseas Service* [1919], 10.
16. *Overseas Service* [1919], 11.
17. Circumstances of Death Registers, vol. 31829_B016705, pages 571–572, 300073 Kelly; Irwin.
18. Ottawa *Citizen*, August 17, 1931, "Kelly-Clark."
19. Ottawa *Citizen*, January 14, 1924, "Late Samuel J. Kelly."
20. Death announcement, Ottawa *Journal*, February 10, 1970.
21. Ottawa *Journal*, June 2, 1964, "Mark Anniversary"; Ottawa *Journal*, December 27, 1973, obituary for Percy Lister; Ottawa *Journal*, August 4, 1970, obituary for Sarah Lister.
22. Ottawa *Journal*, February 19, 1946, "Pay Last Respects to Miss C. Kelly."

Chapter 22: The McKenzie Brothers: Service and Sacrifice

1. Archives of Ontario, Registrations of Marriages 1826–1938, reel 57, image 4, Grenville, Edwardsburgh, 1887, p. 278, entry 006452.
2. Census of Canada 1901, Ontario, District 100, Ottawa, Sub-district 13, Central Ward, p. 18, lines 48–50, and p. 19 lines 1–5; Census of Canada 1911, District 118, Sub-district 57, Ottawa, Russell, Rideau Ward, p. 3 lines 33–39.
3. Ontario, Registrations of Deaths 1869–1948, Reel: 134, Carleton, 1908, no. 299.

4. "Through the Years, Vol. II, No. 11, September 1985, p. 13 - More Heroes Return January 1919." *The Recorder*, Gore Bay, Thursday, October 17, 1918, "Honor Roll," reporting Sandy's death. Found on a website https://wc.rootsweb.com/trees/615434/I13543/johnlangsdale-mckenzie/individual.
5. Fetherstonhaugh 1925, 86–87.
6. Fetherstonhaugh, 1925, chapter 7.
7. Fetherstonhaugh, 1925, 130–131.
8. Cook 2008, 276–278; Fetherstonhaugh 1925, chapter 14.
9. Cooper and Way 2014.
10. Cook 2008, 414–426; Fetherstonhaugh 1925, chapter 20.
11. Cook 2008, 485–488.
12. Cook 2008, 505–534, quote 540.
13. Circumstances of Death Registers, First World War, vol. 31829_B016761, pages 363–364, 486567 McKenzie, Alex Lyon.
14. LAC, Canada, Military Honours and Awards Citation Cards, 1900–1961, McKaig; Albert William – McMordie, H. C., image 341: 486567 Sgt. McKenzie A. L., 13th Batt.; war diary of the 13th Battalion.
15. On June 18, 1919 (when Kenneth was safely back from Siberia); Dora McKenzie swore an Official Return of Birth declaring that Donald Kenneth McKenzie was born on September 7, 1901. Archives of Ontario, Delayed Registrations of Births and Stillbirths, "90" Series, 1869–1911, 1913; reel 34, image 26, RG 80-2, Carleton 1900–1906. This is corroborated by census data.
16. "John Langsdale McKenzie," in Manitoulin Roots, online.
17. MacKay Register of Deaths.
18. Archives of Ontario, Registrations of Marriages, 1826–1938, reel 709, image 568, Carleton, 1925, no. 007821.
19. Death notice, Ottawa *Citizen*, October 23, 1975.

Chapter 23: Arthur Frank Hawke and the War Against TB

1. This information is drawn from Carkner 2002 and his website (consulted in 2015 and since discontinued), and information on ancestry.ca. Besides Johann's father (d. 1889) and his sister, his mother Carolina (c. 1826–1915) and his brothers Carl (c. 1862–1952) and Heinrich (1872–1936) came to Canada about the same time.
2. Census of Canada 1891, Ontario, District 115, Russell, Sub-district New Edinburgh, page 4, lines 18–22, Roll: T-6367.
3. Archives of Ontario, RG 80-2, Delayed Registrations of Births and Stillbirths, "90" Series, 1869–1911, 1913; reel 15, image 17; Russell, 1889–1890, 90173 [a sworn affidavit by Matilda Haak on November 27, 1918, probably to secure Arthur Hawke's military benefits].
4. Beechwood Cemetery Register 1873–1898, 6281.
5. The 1901, 1911, and 1921 censuses all give different dates of immigration: 1890, 1892, or 1894. Census of Canada 1901, Ontario, District 118 Russell, Sub-district, New Edinburgh, page 17, lines 1–7; Archives of Ontario, Registrations of Marriages, 1869–1928, reel 88, image 86, Carleton, 1896, 002258.
6. Archives of Ontario, MS935, Registrations of Deaths, 1869–1948, Carleton, 1905, reel 119, image 94, page 171.

7. See Census of Canada 1921, Ontario, Folder Number: 85; District 125, Russell, Sub-district 39, Rideau Ward, page 19, lines 33–36.
8. Archives of Ontario, Registrations of Marriages, 1869–1928, reel 427, image 1244, Carleton, 1917: 0148457.
9. "Mrs. Bertha Jacques," Ottawa *Journal*, July 12, 1919.
10. Census of Canada 1911, Ontario, District 118 Russell, 58 Ottawa, Sub-district 7, Rideau Ward, page 14, lines 34–50.
11. Ottawa *Journal*, February 11, 1914, "Surprise Party and Birthday Present to Miss E. Haak."
12. "Three Alleged Thieves," Ottawa *Journal*, April 12, 1913; Ottawa *Journal*, April 15, 1913, "Guilty of Theft."
13. Richard's attestation papers describe him as a "farmer," which suggests that he may have gone to Renfrew County, where his wife had roots. Sandusky, who had previously enlisted and been discharged, was assigned to the Railway Troops where he had serious disciplinary issues. In March 1918 Haak and Gromoll were taken out of the artillery and transferred to the Canadian Forestry Corps in Carlisle, with a notation on both files: "Caty A.C. Not to proceed overseas," referencing "Auth HQ INT 917/45 pf 10 6 18 and A. G. 3.B. 10-3-9."
14. Archives of Ontario, Registrations of Deaths, 1869–1948, Carleton, 1925, reel 323, image 595, 010326; reel 542, image 1314, Carleton, 1936, 010857; reel 253, image 489, Carleton, 1919, 010507; reel 461, image 1056, Carleton, 1933, 010589; reel 346, image 352, Carleton, 1927, 010368; reel 207, image 143, Carleton, 1915, 009603; reel 219, image 406, Carleton, 1916, 011540.
15. Archives of Ontario, Registrations of Deaths, 1869–1948, Carleton, 1916, reel 219, image 161, 010106.
16. Adams 1999. See Morton and Wright 1987, 25–27.
17. Archives of Ontario, Registrations of Marriages, 1869–1928, Carleton, 1917, reel 427, image 1244, 014857.
18. *Report of the Work of the Invalided Soldiers' Commission Canada May 1918*. Ottawa: King's Printer, 1918, 25–28.
19. Archives of Ontario, Registrations of Deaths, 1869–1948, reel 242, image 176, Frontenac, 1918, 449.
20. McCuaig 1977; Morton and Wright 1987, chapter 2.
21. Wolf H. Heick, quoted in Threinen 2014, 215.
22. Sandusky became a much-loved letter carrier in Rockcliffe. In 1922 Richard Haak was secretary of the Rockcliffe Athletic Association and Sandusky was vice-president (Ottawa *Journal*, August 16, 1922). "Rene Gromoll" was witness at Richard Hack's wedding in 1920, and he was an active member of St. Luke Lutheran church.
23. Archives of Ontario, Registrations of Marriages, 1869–1928, reel 537, image 49, Russell, 1920, 016438.
24. Ottawa *Journal*, March 4, 1927, "'Pied Piper' Invades Ottawa's Main Drag."
25. On the document reporting this she is referred to for the first time as "Haak."
26. Ottawa *Journal*, March 27, 1947.

Chapter 24: 1919: The Men Come Home

1. Ziegler 1990, 115–133; Bannerman 1958; Hopkins 1920, 272.

2. Ottawa *Citizen*, November 10, 1919, "Unveiling of Memorial Window at St. Bartholomew's Church and of Two Tablets at MacKay."
3. Isitt 2010; McLaren, 125–244; Stacey 1977, 276–284.
4. Further evidence that their conscription was an anomaly is that their service numbers fall within a block that is listed in the Regimental Number List of the Canadian Expeditionary Force as "unallocated."
5. Massey 1976, 73–83.
6. Sixty-six out of the 112 whose files can be traced.
7. Ottawa *Citizen*, March 31, 1919, "Morrison Most Popular General in France, Writes Ottawa Gunner."
8. Ottawa *Citizen*, December 18, 1918, "Varied War Trophies."
9. MacKay United Church; Minutes of the Session 1902–1924, letters included in the minutes for 1919, 23 Sep. 1919; Anderson to Acting Private Secretary to GG.
10. October 2, 1919, Lionel Halsey to Anderson.
11. October 9, 1919, Anderson to Halsey.
12. Ottawa *Citizen*, November 10, 1919, "Unveiling of Memorial Window at St. Bartholomew's Church and of Two Tablets at MacKay."
13. Email from Museum Manager, Clifton Springs Historical Society, March 26, 2021.
14. Toman 2016, 68–69; Ottawa *Citizen*, March 27, 1916, "Nurses for Overseas."
15. Toman 2103, 143–166.
16. Record of Service OMFC Medical Units: No 12, Canadian General Hospital Bramshott.
17. US Department of Labour; Application for U. S. citizenship by Elizabeth Kirkland Ralph, July 1927. I am indebted to Melanie Morin-Pelletier for providing a copy of this document. In 1936 Elizabeth applied for naturalization under her married name, giving her date of permanent arrival as 1933 and claiming that she had never before applied for naturalization.
18. Ottawa *Citizen*, February 4, 1929, "House Wedding of Much Charm."
19. New York *Herald,* February 10, 1922, "Peter B. Olney, Tweed Ring Foe, Passes Away". Census of the United States, 1920, Roll: T625_1128; Hempstead, Nassau, New York, Enumeration District 40, page 9A, lines 43–50 (his brother Sigourney B, 31, who lived in the same compound, was also a lawyer). Boston *Globe,* September 24, 1968, "Peter Butler Olney, Federal Official, at 87". Census of the United States, 1930, FHL microfilm: 2341395; Census Place: Ossining, Westchester, New York, Enumeration District 0292, page 6B, lines 77–81. Census of the United States, 1940, Roll: m-t0627-02805, Census Place: Ossining, Westchester, New York; Enumeration District 60–253, page 16A, lines 17–20. National Archives and Records Administration; Washington, D.C.; Petitions for Naturalization from the U.S. District Court for the Southern District of New York, 1897–1944; Series: M1972; Roll: 1033, Petition No· 274848 –Petition No· 275186: Petition No, 274920. Ottawa *Citizen,* December 3, 1947, "Mrs. P. B. Olney Dies in New York." "Referee's Wife Dies", Daily Times, Mamaroneck, NY, December 5, 1947. Personal correspondence from Stephen Ralph Olney, June, 2023.

Chapter 25: Aftermath

1. Ottawa *Citizen*, March 15, 1920, "Moderator Pringle at M'Kay Church."
2. Macdonald 2014, 147.

3. Ottawa *Citizen*, April 12, 1920, "Unveiled Tablets to Men of M'Kay Who Fell in War."
4. Baswick 1997, 308.
5. Minutes of Annual General Meetings 1889–1923, 1921 AGM, Report of the Session.
6. Butler 2009.
7. Minutes of Session 1902–1924, 58.
8. Ottawa *Journal*, January 8, 1925, "Calvin, Glebe, MacKay Congregations Vote to Stay in Union."
9. Ottawa *Citizen*, March 14, 1925, "MacKay Presbyterian Church Golden Jubilee to be Celebrated with Fitting Ceremony by Congregation Sunday and Monday, March 22–23."
10. Pritchard 2011, 37; Ottawa *Journal*, July 19, 1974, "Milne, W. Harold."
11. Private communication, Robert Bothwell, November 3, 2015. The Chevron Society was for men who enlisted in 1914.
12. Private communication, Bob Cleary, December 12, 2020.

Epilogue
1. Cook 2020, esp. 88–92.

Index

Page references with *f* denote a figure. References to endnotes show both the page number and the note number (365n33).

A

Achiet-le-Grand, France, 59*f*, 204, 208
Achiet-le-Grand Military Cemetery, 204–205, 208–209, 210*f*
Ahearn, Thomas, 18, 31, 83
Airhart, Phyllis, 45, 49
Allman, David B., 116
Amiens, 59*f*, 184, 231, 255–256, 274*f*, 275, 284*f*, 293
ammunition columns, 83, 86, 88, 89, 107–108, 108*f*, 110, 169
Anderson, Clara Rothwell, 40–42, 41*f*, 42*f*, 46, 50*f*, 58, 81, 101, 164, 195, 254
Anderson, Peter, 39–40, 39*f*, 42*f*, 46–47, 49, 50–51, 51*f*, 54–55, 62–63, 81, 93, 164, 165, 197, 253, 257, 276, 300, 305, 315, 316, 321, 325, 334
Anglican churches
  St. Bartholomew's, 24, 38, 50, 53, 97, 153, 156, 222, 281, 306, 314, 334
  St. David's Reformed Episcopal, 24, 43–44, 50, 53, 104, 106, 176–178, 222, 340, 365n31
Arnold, Jack, 226
Arnoldi, Jack, 109
Arras, 59*f*, 274*f*, 284*f*
Arras Sector, 6, 158, 163, 180, 184, 185, 195, 241, 248
Askwith, Bessie Hill, 38, 61
Askwith, John Fotheringham, 14, 67, 91*f*, 256
Askwith, Leonard, 309
Askwith, Margaret, 42, 81, 257–258, 329
No. 1 Australian General Hospital (Rouen), 283

B

Bailleul, France, 59*f*, 76
Bailleul Communal Cemetery Extension, 76, 79, 79*f*, 80*f*, 140
Ballantyne, Henry F., 51
Barnardo, Thomas, 153
Barnes, Gladys, 37, 42
Barnes, Horace E., 14, 86, 91*f*
Barnes, Rachel, 37
BASC. *See* British Army Service Corps (BASC)
Bath War Hospital, 183
battalions. *See* forestry battalions (224th and 238th); infantry battalions
batteries, artillery
  1st Battery CFA, 57
  2nd Battery CFA, 57,
  18th Battery CFA, 283–285
  21st Battery CFA, 89
  25th Battery CFA, 66, 214–217
  32nd Battery CFA, 67, 282
  50th (Queen's) Battery CFA, 87, 88, 231
  51st Battery, CFA, 87–88
  52nd Battery CFA, 87–88, 231
  53rd Battery, CFA, 88
  72nd Battery, CFA, 88–89, 232, 241, 301
  73rd Battery, CFA, 88
  74th Battery CFA, 170, 255
  80th Depot Battery, 88
battles
  Bourlon Wood, battle at, 99, 242–243, 245
  Canal du Nord, battle of, 137–138, 231, 255, 256, 289, 293, 296
  Courcelette, battle of, 92, 137, 150, 225, 271
  Desire Trench, battle of, 92, 139, 147, 149–150, 151*f*, 158, 167, 216, 283, 332, 372n19
  Drocourt-Quéant Line, battle of, 6, 185, 231, 255–256, 285, 288, 293

Festubert, battle of, 63, 224
Fresnoy, battle of, 163, 227, 283
Mount Sorrel, battle of, 82, 108, 121, 122–123, 135, 199, 224, 271, 291–292
Paardeberg, battle at, 71
Passchendaele, battle of, 9, 171–173, 175, 183–184, 231, 253, 272, 283, 292, 332, 384n6
Second Ypres, battle of, 63, 69, 97, 134, 224, 290, 329, 331
St. Eloi, battle of, 82, 108, 124, 164, 179, 181, 199, 256, 271, 331, 332
St. Quentin, battle of, 77
Vimy Ridge, battle of, 137, 158, 161, 164, 230, 283
Beagley, Jane. *See* Coker, Jane (Beagley)
Beardsley, George Frederick, 14, 57, 91*f*, 334
Beechwood Cemetery, 12, 13, 16, 29, 126, 164, 191, 192, 205, 209, 211, 257, 286, 305, 306, 307*f*, 361n8, 371n19
Bell, Clarinda. *See* Stalker, Clarinda (née Bell)
Bellamy, Joseph William, 209
Benedict, Ernest, 14, 88, 90, 91*f*, 332
Bennett, Dora (McKenzie). *See* McKenzie, Dora (née Bennett)
Berger, Carl, 4
Birrs, Catherine Nicol. *See* Marshall, Catherine Nicol (née Birrs)
Birt, Louisa, 153, 154
Blackledge, Ewan J., 243–247, 249
Blomfield, Sir Reginald, 109, 142, 181, 220, 235
Boehmer, Herbert, 173, 174
Boer War, 4, 28, 45, 71, 79, 84, 107, 197, 201, 318
Bolduan, Matilda. *See* Haak, Matilda (née Bolduan)
Booth, John, 200
Bordat, Ernest, 179
Borden, Sir Robert, 75, 172, 173, 311, 312

Borden Motor Machine Gun Battery (Borden Battery), 6, 60, 173, 269–272, 275, 332
Boston, Levi D., 14, 170
Bothwell, Adelia (née Gale), 103, 106, 110, 112, 113, 115, 116
Bothwell, Agnes, 103, 104, 104*f*, 106, 116
Bothwell, Emma, 103, 104, 104*f*, 106, 116
Bothwell, Frederick Henry, 106, 110, 112, 113*f*, 116
Bothwell, George Selkirk, 14, 67, 82, 86, 91*f*, 103, 104, 105*f*, 106–109, 107*f*, 113*f*, 116
Bothwell, Helen Eleanor ("Ella") (née Robinson), 9, 106, 109, 110, 112–114, 117
Bothwell, John Robert, 14, 57, 91*f*, 103–104, 105*f*, 106*f*, 107, 109, 113*f*, 114–116, 115*f*, 314, 336
Bothwell, Katie (Allman), 103, 104, 104*f*, 106, 106*f*, 116
Bothwell, Lois Helen, 106, 110, 112, 113*f*, 116
Bothwell, Mary Pauline (née Rutherford), 116
Bothwell, Robert, 116
Bothwell, William, 37, 38, 57, 103, 106, 109, 110, 112, 113*f*, 114, 115, 225, 225*f*
Bothwell, William Alexander, 106, 110, 112, 113*f*, 116
Boucher, Billy, 277
Boucher, Frank, 21–22, 25–26, 27, 49
Boucher, George, 27*f*
Boult, Edith. *See* Stalker, Edith (née Boult)
Boult, Rawlinson ("Rollo"), 179, 186, 187
Bourlon Wood, battle at, 99, 242–243, 245
Boyle, Joe, 269
Boys' Home, Ottawa, 153, 155–157
Bray, Art, 109

Brigades, artillery
  3rd Brigade CFA, 232, 293
  5th Brigade CFA, 283
  6th Brigade CFA, 217
  7th Brigade CFA, 66, 214–216, 283
  8th Brigade CFA, 67, 106, 282–283
  9th Brigade CFA, 283
  13th Brigade CFA, 87, 88, 231
Brigades, infantry
  11th Brigade, 137, 138, 149, 179, 180
  12th Brigade, 92, 149–150, 184–185
British Army Service Corps (BASC), 6, 67, 97, 254, 259, 260, 261
British Empire, 4, 7, 50*f*, 53, 63, 261, 309
No. 6 British Red Cross Hospital (Étaples), 123, 291
Brophy, Don, 200, 203
Brophy, H. B., 63
Brunel, A. Ivan, 14, 213, 217, 218
Brunel, Alfred, 213
Brunel, Frances Maud (née Gaynor), 43, 213, 214, 217–218, 328
Brunel, Gertrude (née Finley), 213–214
Brunel, Henry, 213–214, 217, 218
Brunel, Hope, 213, 214, 217
Brunel, Ivan, 85
Brunel, John Erskine, 217, 218
Brunel, Olive Marie (Graham), 170, 213, 214, 218
Brunel, Reginald Isambard, 14, 66, 91*f*, 163, 173, 213, 214, 216–217, 220, 220*f*
Brunel, Troilus, 213
Brunel, William Troyless, 213
Brutinel, Raymond, 269
Byng, Julian, 123, 242, 326

C

CAC. *See* Catholic Apostolic Church (CAC)
Cairncross, James, 14, 60, 91*f*, 256, 336–337
Calgary Rifles, 67

Cambrai, France, 171, 231, 242, 243, 255, 284*f*, 285, 286, 293, 296
CAMC. *See* Canadian Army Medical Corps (CAMC)
Cameron, Norman, 14, 62, 91*f*
Cameron Highlanders (militia), 127, 142, 191
Campbell, Jim, 227
Canadian Army Medical Corps (CAMC), 9, 58, 89, 107, 170, 217, 317–318, 320–321
Canadian Army Service Corps (CASC), 57, 67, 89, 97, 133, 170, 260, 294
Canadian Army Veterinary Corps (CAVC), 62
Canadian Casualty Assembly Centre (Hastings), 283, 292
Canadian Convalescent Hospital (Woodcote, Epsom), 230, 231, 271, 294
Canadian Corps, 64, 75, 81–82, 92, 123, 137, 158, 163, 171, 185, 226, 229, 242, 269, 271, 274, 285, 286, 293, 309, 314
  ammunition columns (*See* ammunition columns)
  brigades (*See* artillery brigades, infantry brigades)
  divisions (*See* divisions)
  forestry battalions (*See* forestry battalions)
  infantry battalions (*See* infantry battalions)
  railway troops (*See* railway troops)
  tank battalions, 255
Canadian Engineers, 58, 62, 67, 83, 124, 125, 156, 170, 233, 255
Canadian Expeditionary Force (CEF), 53, 56, 57, 74, 97, 119, 131, 169, 178, 301, 303, 305, 376n15, 387n4
  records, 8, 11–12
  2nd Battalion, 223
  11th Battalion, 57, 133, 134
  38th Battalion, 147

80th Battalion, 136
Canadian Expeditionary Force
 (Siberia), 221, 233, 295,
 311–312, 313f
Canadian Field Ambulance, 76, 83, 89,
 109–110, 160, 165, 184, 231,
 273, 291, 303
Canadian Field Artillery (CFA), 57,
 64–67
 batteries (*See* batteries)
 brigades (*See* brigades, artillery)
Canadian General Hospital
 (Bramshott), 321
Canadian Machine Gun Corps,
 142, 269
Canadian Motor Machine Gun Brigade
 (1CMMGB), 269–270, 270f,
 271–275, 276f
Canadian Mounted Rifles (CMR)
 3rd (3 CMR), 197, 375n9
 4th (4 CMR), 64, 82, 332
 8th (8 CMR), 59, 60, 269
Canal du Nord, battle of, 137–138, 231,
 255, 256, 289, 293, 296
CASC. *See* Canadian Army Service
 Corps (CASC)
Casualty Clearing Stations (CCS), 76,
 123, 204, 303, 320
Catholic Apostolic Church (CAC), 49,
 281, 286
CAVC. *See* Canadian Army Veterinary
 Corps (CAVC)
CCS. *See* Casualty Clearing Stations
 (CCS)
CEF. *See* Canadian Expeditionary
 Force (CEF)
cemeteries
 about, 7
 Achiet-le-Grand Military Cemetery,
 204–205, 208–209, 210f
 Bailleul Communal Cemetery
 Extension, 76, 79, 79f, 80f, 140
 Beechwood Cemetery, 12, 13, 16, 29,
 126, 164, 191, 192, 205, 209,
 211, 257, 286, 305, 306, 307f,
 361n8, 371n19

Dickebusch New Military Cemetery,
 208, 208f, 209f
Écoivres Military Cemetery, 219f,
 220, 220f
Étaples Military Cemetery, 128, 128f,
 129f, 130f
Faubourg d'Amiens Cemetery,
 247–248, 248f
Poperinghe New Military Cemetery,
 109–110, 111f
R. E. Farm Cemetery, 99, 100f
Sains-les-Marquion British Cemetery,
 296–297, 296f, 297f, 298f
Ste. Catherine British Cemetery, 235,
 236f, 237f
St. Pierre Cemetery, Amiens, 277,
 278f, 279f, 280f
Tigris Lane Cemetery, 286, 287f, 288f
Villers Station Cemetery, 161, 162f,
 181, 182f
Wellshill Cemetery (Perth, Scotland),
 263–264, 264f, 265f, 266f
Chabot, Dr. John Léo, 173, 217, 218
Cherry, William, 38
Christie, Nancy, 9
Christie, Norm, 122
Chrysler, Captain, 225
churches
 Anglican (*See* Anglican churches)
 Lutheran (*See* Lutheran churches)
 See MacKay Presbyterian / United
 Church; *specific churches (e.g., St.
 Bartholomew's)*
Church Union, 33, 49, 209, 267, 329, 333
Clark, Alex Hobart, 67, 91f, 332
Clark, Alex O., 14
Clark, Catherine. *See* Marshall,
 Catherine Nicol (née Birss)
Clark, Gordon Halcro, 14, 58, 91f,
 163–164, 331, 333
Clark, James, 265, 382n18
Clarke, Nic, 30
Cléry, France, 274f, 275
Coker, Frederick, 95
Coker, George Victor, 6, 14, 57, 61, 81,
 91f, 95–98, 96f, 99, 366n8

Coker, Jane (Beagley), 95
Coker, Theresa Elizabeth (Wilson) (née Hupfeld), 38, 61, 81, 95, 96–97, 98, 101, 101*f*, 366n8
Connaught, Duke of, 179, 314–315
Connaught Military Hospital, 158
Connor, Ralph, 54
conscription, 77, 90, 172–173, 190, 232, 253, 254, 255, 311, 312, 314, 387n4
Cook, Bill, 27
Cook, Bun, 27
Cook, Tim, 185, 274, 275
Cornu, Félix, 267, 277
Cornu, Jules, 277
Corp, Annie (née Hupfeld), 96
Corp, Frederick, 96
Costello and Crowe, 195, 209
Courcelette, battle of, 92, 137, 150, 225, 271
Courcelette, France, 59*f*
Creighton Street. *See* Crichton Street
Creighton (Crichton) Street Public School, 25, 28–29, 37, 43, 89, 116, 160, 176, 214, 223, 239–240, 268–269, 282, 362n16
Crichton Street, 18–20, 24, 25, 37, 98, 133, 170, 190, 195, 196, 218, 221, 234
Crowe, Lena (née Ryan). *See* Ryan, Margaret Lena (Crowe)
Crowe, William, 195, 209, 211
Cruikshank, George, 14, 61, 91*f*, 163
Currie, Albert H., 14, 84, 91*f*
Currie, General Sir Arthur, 227, 273, 273*f*, 275–276, 293
Currie, William A., 14, 62, 91*f*
Curtis, Robert Henry, 14, 86, 91*f*, 333

D

Dalton, George Francis, 296
Dalton, Jessie (née McKenzie). *See* McKenzie, Jessie (Dalton)
Davidson, Jason S., 14, 169, 331
Dawson, Ethel, 42, 81

Dawson, Frederick, 38
Delahey, Donald Murray, 296
Delahey, Ellen (née McKenzie). *See* McKenzie, Ellen (Delahey)
Desire Trench, battle of, 92, 139, 147, 149–150, 151*f*, 158, 167, 216, 283, 332, 370n19
Devonshire, Duke of, 316
Dick, William Reif, 248
Dickebusch, Belgium, 59*f*, 75, 199, 208, 216, 283
Dickebusch New Military Cemetery, 208, 208*f*, 209*f*
divisions
  First Division, 63, 64–65, 86, 88, 89, 97, 99, 107–108, 110, 134, 216, 223, 225, 290, 313–314
  Second Division, 60, 64–65, 66, 75, 82, 86, 97, 134, 199, 214, 216, 270, 271–272, 283, 313–314
  Third Division, 60, 64–65, 67, 81, 83, 88, 97, 121, 122, 148, 169, 216, 364n22
  Fourth Division, 92, 97, 137–139, 149, 158–159, 179, 180, 183, 216
  Fifth Division, 88, 365n6
Doane, Gyp, 227
Drake, Robert Ludlow, 14, 58, 91*f*, 92, 332, 333
Drake, W. F., 38
Drocourt-Quéant Line, battle of, 6, 185, 231, 255–256, 285, 288, 293
Duke of Connaught's Own Rifles, 178
Duke of Cornwall's Own Rifles (Regiment) (militia), 28, 137, 147, 299
Dykebar Military Hospital (Paisley, Scotland), 263

E

Earl, Clifford E., 14, 170, 333
Earl Grey's Own Rifles (Regiment) (militia), 178
Eastview, 22–23, 36, 38, 60, 110, 113, 114, 255

Eastview Baptist Church, 334
Eaton Battery, 269
Écoivres Military Cemetery, 219*f*, 220, 220*f*
Edward, Prince of Wales, 6, 151, 309, 310*f*, 314–317, 340
Edwards, Gordon, 37, 103
Edwards, John, 14, 58, 91*f*
Edwardson, Angus, 14, 164, 170, 256
Edwardson, Elizabeth. *See* Lamb, Elizabeth (née Edwardson)
Edward VIII, King, 151
Egypt, 254, 259, 260–263, 262*f*
elections
    1917 federal election, 173–174
    1921 federal election, 218
    1926 federal election, 37, 218
Elliott, Reginald, 14, 61, 91*f*, 332
Elmsley, James, 311, 312
English, F. W. P., 38
English, George Bruce, 14, 170, 256
English, John, 333
Erskine, Clifford Leslie, 14, 66, 91*f*, 256, 330–331, 333
Esdale, David, 38, 326
Esdale, George, 173
Étaples, France, 59*f*, 123, 139, 291, 303, 368n9
Étaples Military Cemetery, 128, 128*f*, 129*f*, 130*f*
Evans, Annie, 97, 98, 101

F

Fallis, William J., 14, 85, 91*f*
Farmer, George E., 14, 37, 38, 57, 91*f*, 333, 335
Farmer, William (father), 57, 335
Farmer, William J., 14, 57, 91*f*, 333, 335
Faubourg d'Amiens Cemetery, 247–248, 248*f*
federal elections. *See* elections
Ferguson, Abraham, 14, 84, 91*f*, 165
Ferguson, Henry Warren, 14, 255
Festubert, battle of, 63, 224
Fettercairn Island convalescent facility, 140, 141*f*

Finley, Gertrude (Brunel). *See* Brunel, Gertrude (née Finley)
Finter, Robert H., 14, 57, 64, 91*f*, 169, 254, 331, 364n12
Finter, William O., 14, 86, 91*f*, 165
Fisher, Harold, 257
Fleming Hospital, Ottawa, 112, 126, 140, 164, 183, 190, 254, 256
Flying Services Memorial, 247–249, 248*f*, 249*f*, 250*f*
Foad, Charles T., 14, 88, 91*f*, 336
forestry battalions, 8, 64, 85, 86, 87*f*, 90, 165
Forse, Ethel May (née Porteous). *See* Porteous, Ethel May (Forse)
Forse, William Henry, 147
Fraser, Brian, 47
Fraser, Donald, 75, 76
Fresnoy, battle of, 163, 227, 283
Fresnoy, France, 59*f*

G

Gaitens, Agnes, 142
Gaitens, Daniel Robertson, 133
Gaitens, William, 14, 89, 91*f*, 133, 142
Gale, Adelia. *See* Bothwell, Adelia (née Gale)
Gardner, T. Ernest (Gardiner on the Honour Roll), 14, 60, 91*f*, 332, 336, 361n21
Garvock, W. B., 40
Gaynor, Frances Maud. *See* Brunel, Frances Maud (née Gaynor)
No. 3 General Hospital (Le Tréport), 183
George V, King, 45, 128, 214
Gerard, Eddie, 27, 28*f*, 233
Gerard, Thomas Knight, 14, 67, 86, 91*f*, 333
Gerard, William, 37
Goforth, Alex, 213
gonorrhea. *See* venereal diseases (gonorrhea, syphilis)
Gordon, Charles W., 54
Gott, Frank, 178
Gough, General Sir Hubert, 274, 275

Governor General's Foot Guards (militia), 28, 44
Graham, Dr. David Malcolm, 14, 170, 217, 218, 335, 337
Graham, Olive Marie (née Brunel). *See* Brunel, Olive Marie (Graham)
Grandcourt Trench, 139, 150
Grant, Donald Nairn, 14, 88–89, 313–314
Gromoll, Reinhold, 301, 386n13, 386n22
Gwyn, Sandra, 38, 165

H

Haak family, 9, 31, 299, 300*f*, 307*f*
Haak, Augusta (Schroeder), 299
Haak, Augusta (sister), 299
Haak, August Frank Heinrich. *See* Hawke, Arthur Frank
Haak, Augustus, 302
Haak, Bertha, 299, 300, 301, 303
Haak, Charles, 299, 306
Haak, Elizabeth, 299, 300–301, 302
Haak, Johannah (née Miller), 299
Haak, Johann Albert, 299
Haak, John, 299, 306
Haak, Mary, 299, 300, 301
Haak, Matilda (née Bolduan), 299, 300, 306, 385n3
Haak, Richard, 299, 301, 306, 386n13, 386n22
Haig, Field Marshall Sir Douglas, 128, 139
Haley, R. G., 225, 225*f*
Hawke, Arthur Frank (August Frank Heinrich Haak), 13, 14, 61, 257, 299, 300, 300*f*, 302–303, 304*f*, 305, 306, 307*f*, 334, 361n8
Heatstroke, 7, 259, 263
Herridge, Rev. W. T., 54
Hill, Bessie. *See* Askwith, Bessie Hill
Hill, Robert, 14, 61, 91*f*, 331, 334
Hillas, Julius (Joseph A. Hillas on the Honour Roll), 14, 61, 91*f*, 331
Hockey Hall of Fame, 27, 233, 277
Hodges, Rev. A. V., 76

Holt, Richard, 260, 382n7
"home children," 153–154, 155–156
Hooper, R., 121
Hope, James, 37, 38
Horsey, Rev. Captain H. I., 167
hospitals
  No. 1 Australian General Hospital (Rouen), 283
  Bath War Hospital, 183
  No. 6 British Red Cross Hospital (Étaples), 123, 291
  Canadian Casualty Assembly Centre (Hastings), 283, 292
  Canadian Convalescent Hospital (Woodcote, Epsom), 230, 231, 271, 294
  Canadian General Hospital (Bramshott), 321
  Connaught Military Hospital, 158
  Dykebar Military Hospital (Paisley, Scotland), 263
  Fleming Hospital, Ottawa, 112, 126, 140, 164, 183, 190, 254, 256
  No. 3 General Hospital (Le Tréport), 183
  No. 2 Hospital Amiens, 254
  "Mrs. Pollock's Hospital," 180
  Ontario Military Hospital (Orpington), 303
  Ottawa Military Base Hospital, 173
  Perley Veterans' Hospital, 331
  Petawawa Military Hospital, 170
  Protestant Hospital (Rideau Street, Ottawa), 31, 35, 147, 150, 178, 192
  Queen's Military Hospital, 126, 140, 164
  Sir Oliver Mowat Memorial Hospital (Kingston), 303, 305
  No. 42 Stationary Hospital (Amiens), 275
  No. 32 Stationary Hospital (Wimereux), 230
  War Hospital (Reading), 283
Housman, A. E., 251
Hughes, John Gordon, 14, 255

Hughes, Sir Sam, 49, 56, 74, 75, 134,
    148, 179, 224*f*
Hughes, Lt. Col. William
    St. Pierre, 74
Hundred Days, 6, 9, 99, 125, 175, 184,
    221, 231, 255, 275, 284, 284*f*,
    296, 332
Hupfeld, Annie (née Susman), 96
Hupfeld, Henry, 96, 366n5
Hupfeld, Theresa Elizabeth. *See* Coker,
    Theresa Elizabeth (Wilson)
    (née Hupfeld)

I

Inch, Alex, 14, 86, 91*f*, 332, 361n16
Inch, Andrew, 14, 361n16
infantry battalions
    2nd, 56, 61, 97–99, 159, 223–229,
        224*f*, 225*f*, 228*f*, 368n10
    8th, 83, 134–135, 144
    11th, 57, 133, 134
    13th, 290–293, 294*f*
    14th, 293
    21st, 58, 74–76
    24th, 62, 199
    27th, 60
    29th, 270
    37th (Algonquin Rifles), 67, 290
    38th, 59, 60–61, 61*f*, 81, 92, 97, 139,
        147–150, 167, 183–185, 190, 302
    46th, 183
    50th, 83, 158–160
    59th, 62, 135, 198–199
    60th, 64, 121–123
    75th, 136, 137
    77th, 63–64, 65*f*, 69, 81, 83, 84*f*, 85,
        110, 121, 137, 157–158, 169,
        364n12
    80th, 136
    87th, 83, 92, 137, 139, 149–150,
        370n19
    102nd, 85, 178–181, 181*f*, 199
    108th, 85
    136th, 84
    139th, 85, 229

    154th, 84
    156th, 62, 84, 124
    196th Western Universities Overseas
        Battalion, 85, 181, 183
    207th, 85, 169, 183, 217
    240th, 301
    253rd, 170
    Princess Patricia's Canadian Light
        Infantry, 53, 57, 67, 122, 315*f*
influenza, 9, 158, 160, 257, 299
    See also Spanish Flu

J

Jackson family, 120*f*, 121, 121*f*
Jackson, A.Y., 123, 368n9
Jackson, Betty, 124
Jackson, Charles Edward, 124,
    127–128, 130
Jackson, Gordon, 124
Jackson, Henrietta (daughter), 124, 127
Jackson, Henrietta (née Schayltz), 119,
    121, 124, 128, 130
Jackson, Joseph, 124
Jackson, Manfred, 119, 121, 124, 127
Jackson, Marjorie, 121, 124, 127
Jackson, Mary, 124
Jackson, Ryland, 124
Jackson, Thomas Isaac (father),
    14, 37, 84, 91*f*, 119, 121,
    124–125, 125*f*, 126, 127*f*,
    130, 256, 331
Jackson, Thomas Nicholas (son), 14, 67,
    91*f*, 92, 119, 124, 125–126, 126*f*,
    127, 332, 336–337
James, Fred, 227, 228, 229
Jamieson, Fred J., 14, 57, 69, 91*f*, 329
Jardine, Andrew, 14, 84, 91*f*, 163, 333
Jardine, Archibald M., 14, 84, 91*f*,
    256, 333
Johnston, Arthur Reginald, 14, 311, 312
Johnston, Lancelot, 311
Joliat, Alice, 267, 269, 277, 382n3
Joliat, Aurèle, 27, 30, 267, 269, 277,
    278*f*, 382n3

Joliat, Azilda (née Lavictoire), 267, 268, 276, 382n3
Joliat, Émile, 267–268, 268*f*, 276, 277, 301, 382n3, 382n6
Joliat, Henri, 267, 276, 382n6
Joliat, Homère (Homer), 6, 14, 60, 91*f*, 172, 254, 267, 268–269, 270–273, 273*f*, 275–276, 277, 280*f*, 382n3
Joliat, Jeanne, 267, 269, 276, 277
Joliat, René Robert ("Bobby"), 267, 269, 277, 382n3

K
Keefer, Annie (MacKinnon), 33
Keefer, Thomas Coltrin, 17–18, 213
Kelly, Catherine, 281, 286
Kelly, Irwin, 6, 14, 67, 91*f*, 92, 256, 281, 282–284, 282*f*, 285, 286, 288, 288*f*
Kelly, Lillian, 282, 285, 286
Kelly, Olivia Irwin, 281, 286
Kelly, Samuel, Jr., 281, 282, 285–286, 311, 337
Kelly, Samuel John, Sr., 14, 281–282, 286
Kelly, Sarah (Lister), 282, 285, 286
Kendall, Albert Richard, 14, 27*f*, 60, 91*f*, 163–164, 269, 332
Kendall, Carson J., 14, 58, 60, 91*f*
Kenny, Martha, 176, 178, 185–187, 188–189, 188*f*
Kenny, Mary Anna (Stalker), 176, 176*f*, 187
Kenny, Nora, 187
Kilpatrick, Thomas, 168
King, Dougall, 40, 371n5
Kitchener, Lord, 75, 214
Knowlton Distributing Home, 154, 155, 155*f*

L
Ladies' Aid (MacKay Presbyterian / United Church)
  about, 34, 42–43, 49, 52, 69, 167, 254, 328, 329
  members, 38, 40, 81, 95, 101, 101*f*, 106, 115, 178, 192, 289, 296
  records, 11, 12, 41*f*, 62, 93, 163, 187, 257–258
Lamb, Elizabeth (née Edwardson), 9, 164
Lamb, James, 164
Lanceley, William Henry, 14, 64, 91*f*, 332
Laurier, Sir Wilfrid, 172
Lavictoire, Azilda. *See* Joliat, Azilda (née Lavictoire)
Law, Bonar, 75
Leach, James, 14, 64, 83, 91*f*, 336
Lindsay, Walter Samuel, 14, 66, 68, 86, 91*f*, 334
Lisgar Collegiate. *See* Ottawa Collegiate Institute (OCI) (Lisgar Collegiate)
Lister, Percy, 14, 170, 282, 285, 286
Lister, Sarah (née Kelly). *See* Kelly, Sarah (Lister)
Love, Herbert Charles, 14, 61, 91*f*, 333
Ludendorff, General Erich, 255
lumber industries, 6, 16–17, 19, 19*f*, 20*f*, 32, 86, 103, 105*f*, 222
Lumsden family, 28*f*, 36, 326
Lunan, William, 38
Lutheran churches, 53–54, 305
  St. John Evangelical, 24, 50, 54
  St. Paul, 24, 299
Lutyens, Sir Edwin, 128, 247, 248, 277

M
Macbeth, Madge, 42, 165
Macdonald, Blyth, 81
Macdonald, Mrs. Blyth, 81
Macdonald, Douglas Henry, 38, 328
Macdonald, Sir John A., 17
Macdonald, Stuart, 4, 10, 325
Macdonald, W. A., 187, 374n12
MacKay, Annie, 17, 33
MacKay, Christina, 33, 34*f*
MacKay, John, 339
MacKay, Thomas. *See* McKay, Thomas
MacKay Estate, 17, 18*f*, 24, 33

MacKay Presbyterian / United Church
  about, 15, 33–36, 34f, 35f, 51–52, 51f, 52f
  administration, 39–40, 39f, 46–48, 48f
  athletics, 43–44, 44f
  choir, 41f, 43
  congregation, 6, 8–9, 34, 36–38, 36f, 49–51, 50f, 67–69
  Ladies' Aid (*See* Ladies' Aid [MacKay Presbyterian / United Church])
  Sunday School, 35, 40, 41f, 52
  and the war, 3, 5, 6–7, 44–45, 166f, 316f
Mackenzie, Donald, 37
MacKenzie, John (McKenzie on the Honour Roll), 14, 57, 83, 91f, 331, 333, 336, 337
Mackersey, Ian, 201
MacKinnon, Annie (née MacKay), 17
MacKinnon, John, 16, 17
MacKinnon, William, 33
MacLean, Lt. Col. Charles Wesley, 85, 183, 217
MacLeod, Dr. Neil (McLeod on the Honour Roll), 14, 27f, 57, 83, 91f, 92, 332, 361n17
MacNeil, Grant, 328
Macpherson, Annie, 153–154
Maginnes, Alexander, 38
Malone, Pat, 227
Mansell, Percy Thomas, 14, 171
Mansell, Sidney Bruce, 14, 60, 91f, 173, 254, 269, 275, 332
Mansell, Thomas Henry, 37
Marion, Ella, 112–114, 117
  See also Bothwell, Helen Eleanor ("Ella") (née Robinson)
Marion, George Earl, 110, 112–113, 114
Marion, Marguerite, 112, 114, 117
Marion, William, 112, 114, 117
Marshall, Archibald, 259
Marshall, Catherine Nicol (née Birss), 254, 259, 260, 263, 265
Marshall, John, 6–7, 14, 67, 91f, 254, 259–261, 263, 264, 265, 266f, 361n8, 382n7

Marshall, John Roy, 259, 263
Marshall, Margaret (mother of John), 259
Marshall, Margaret (daughter), 259, 263
Massey, Raymond, 312
Masson, Alexander, 14, 57, 83, 91f, 332, 333
Mathieson, Chas. G. R., 14, 91f
May, Emile August Frank, 14, 44, 45, 57, 91f, 165
May, Oscar Victor Albert, 14, 44, 56–57, 91f, 92, 165, 332
Mayo, Frank, 153, 159
Mayo, Frank, Jr., 153, 159
Mayo, Henry James, 14, 64, 83, 91f, 153, 154, 154f, 155, 156–159, 160, 161, 163, 181, 372n29
Mayo, Margaret Georgina (née Murphy), 153
Mayo, Mary Elizabeth ("May") (née Welford), 9, 156–157, 159, 160–161, 371n12
Mayo, Percy, 153, 159
Mayo, Percy Welford ("Bud"), 158, 159, 160–161
Mayo, William Henry ("Bill"), 157, 159, 160
McCarthy, Dalton, 14, 88–89, 332, 335
McCreery, William, 20
McElroy, John, Jr., 27f, 195, 196, 196f, 197, 207, 209, 233, 245, 329
McElroy, John, Sr., 196
McElroy, John M. ("Jack"), 209
McElroy, Mabel (née Ryan). *See* Ryan, Mabel
McElroy, Margaret Mabel, 209
McGillivray, John, 14, 61, 91f
McGowan, John, 14, 67, 91f
McIntosh, Scott, 227
McKay, Thomas, 15–17, 33
McKeever, Captain, 243, 245
McKenzie, Alexander Lyon ("Sandy"), 14, 44f, 67, 91f, 92, 256, 289, 290–293, 290f, 294, 294f, 295, 296, 297, 298f
McKenzie, Alexander Sr., 256, 289, 295, 296

McKenzie, D. Kenneth, 14
McKenzie, Dora ("Dollie"), 289, 296
McKenzie, Dora (née Bennett), 289, 296
McKenzie, Ellen (Delahey), 289, 295–296
McKenzie, Evelyn (née Purvis), 295
McKenzie, Jessie (Dalton), 289, 295–296
McKenzie, John. *See* MacKenzie, John
McKenzie, John Langsdale ("Jack"), 14, 67, 82, 91*f*, 289, 290–291, 291*f*, 294, 295, 295*f*, 331
McKenzie, Kenneth, 289, 295, 296, 311
McLatchie, Gerald Farmer, 14, 171, 332, 333
McLaurin, A. Stuart, 14, 57, 91*f*, 256
McLaurin, Mrs. Graham (née Lumsden), 326
McLeod, Dr. Neil. *See* MacLeod, Dr. Neil
McPhail, James Wallace (K. Wallace McPhail on the Honour Roll), 14, 244, 331
Melville, Mrs. Gordon, 179
Menin Gate, Ypres, 7, 142–144, 143*f*, 144*f*, 145*f*
Merritt, Alfred (Merrit on the Honour Roll), 14, 88
Michael, Herb, 225, 225*f*
Miles, Frank Henry (Myles on the Honour Roll), 14, 64, 83, 91*f*, 165, 331, 361n15
military cemeteries. *See* cemeteries
militia
  103rd Calgary Rifles, 67
  Cameron Highlanders, 127, 142, 191
  Duke of Connaught's Own Rifles, 178
  Duke of Cornwall's Own Rifles (Regiment), 28, 137, 147, 229
  Earl Grey's Own Rifles (Regiment) (militia), 178
  107th (East Kootenay) Regiment, 178
  Governor General's Foot Guards, 28, 44
  43rd Ottawa and Carlton Rifles, 178

Miller, Ian, 10
Miller, Johannah. *See* Haak, Johannah (née Miller)
Miller, Sarah Jane ("Jennie"). *See* Porteous, Sarah Jane ("Jennie") (Miller)
Milne, William H., 14, 255, 336
Montgomery, Clara Bell. *See* Stalker, Clara Bell (Montgomery)
Moodie, Elmer Allen, 14, 85
Morel, Ronin, 108–109
Morenz, Howie, 277
Morrison, Edward, 326
Morton, Desmond, 8–9, 92
Mount Sorrel, battle of, 82, 108, 121, 122–123, 135, 224, 271, 291–292
Mount Sorrel, France, 59*f*
"Mrs. Pollock's Hospital," 180
Muhlig, Russell E., 14, 88, 91*f*, 332
Munro, Christina, 37
Munro, Fred, 14, 255
Munro, Gordon James Campbell, 14, 88, 91*f*, 256, 331, 336
Munro, John, 37
Munro, Joseph A., 14, 60, 82, 91*f*, 164, 165, 331
Munro, Margaret, 37, 60, 165
Munro, William Douglas, 14, 88, 91*f*, 331, 336
Murphy, Charles, 174
Murphy, Margaret Georgina. *See* Mayo, Margaret Georgina (née Murphy)
Myles, F. H. *See* Miles, Frank Henry

N

Naismith, Annie Isobel, 190
NECC. *See* Ottawa New Edinburgh Canoe Club (NECC / ONECC)
New Edinburgh, Ottawa
  about, 6, 15, 16–17, 16*f*, 18–20, 18*f*, 21*f*, 22–23, 22*f*
  athletics, 25–29, 26*f*, 27*f*, 28*f*
  Boer War, 4

challenges in, 29–31
churches, 24 (*See also* MacKay Presbyterian / United Church)
population, 20–21, 23–24
schools, 24–25
New Edinburgh Canoe Club. *See* Ottawa New Edinburgh Canoe Club (NECC / ONECC)
Nichol, Alex, 81
HMCS *Niobe*, 57
Nunney, "Red," 185

O

OCI. *See* Ottawa Collegiate Institute (OCI) (Lisgar Collegiate)
Odlum, General Victor, 138
OER. *See* Ottawa Electric Railway (OER)
O'Leary, Daniel, 73–74
O'Leary, Louise (née Wendt). *See* Wendt, Louise (O'Leary)
Olney, Elizabeth (née Ralph). *See* Ralph, Elizabeth (Olney)
Olney, Peter Butler, 321, 322
Olney, Peter Butler III, 323*f*
Olney, Richard, 322
Olsen, Olaf, 14, 88, 91*f*
ONECC. *See* Ottawa New Edinburgh Canoe Club (NECC / ONECC)
Operation Michael (German offensive), 273–274, 274*f*
Orange Lodge, 28, 45, 71
Ottawa Boys' Home, 153, 155–157
Ottawa Collegiate Institute (OCI) (Lisgar Collegiate), 25, 214, 222–223, 240, 249
Ottawa Electric Railway (OER), 18, 20, 23, 64, 71, 83, 88, 195, 200, 299, 327
Ottawa Football Club, 197, 223
Ottawa Military Base Hospital, 173
Ottawa New Edinburgh Canoe Club (NECC / ONECC), 25, 27, 43, 178, 197, 222–223, 234, 239, 241, 250–251, 251*f*, 252*f*, 282, 289, 336
Ottawa Rough Riders, 27, 190, 191*f*, 221, 233, 234, 235, 267, 336
Ottawa Senators, 27

P

Paardeberg, battle at, 71
Passchendaele, battle of, 9, 59*f*, 171–173, 175, 183–184, 231, 253, 272, 283, 292, 332, 382n6
Patriotic Fund (PF), 8, 68–69, 92–93, 110, 133, 159, 183
Perney, Erland Dauria, 14, 89, 91*f*, 239, 240–241, 240*f*, 242, 243–246, 247, 250, 250*f*, 251, 251*f*, 252*f*
Perney, Frank, 37, 38, 43, 239–240, 245–246, 249, 250
Perney, Margaret, 9, 239, 240, 247, 250
Perney, Margaret (daughter), 239, 249–250
Petawawa Military Hospital, 170
PF. *See* Patriotic Fund (PF)
Philp, Alfred, 14, 64, 82, 91*f*, 122, 167, 332–333
Poperinghe, Belgium, 59*f*, 109–110
Poperinghe New Military Cemetery, 109–110, 111*f*
Porteous, David, 147, 150–151
Porteous, Ethel May (Forse), 147, 148*f*
Porteous, Gordon Maynard, 6, 14, 61, 92, 147, 148–149, 148*f*, 150, 151–152, 152*f*
Porteous, Laura, 147, 148*f*, 150–151
Porteous, Lillian, 147, 148*f*, 150–151
Porteous, Sarah Jane ("Jennie") (Miller), 147, 150–151, 152
Powers, Charles William, 14, 171, 361n22
Powers, George, 14, 60, 82, 91*f*, 163–164, 331, 334, 336
Powers, John, 14, 60, 82–83, 91*f*, 164, 166, 256, 331, 333, 335, 336
Price, Mary. *See* Robertson, Mary (née Price / Pryce)

Prince of Wales. *See* Edward, Prince of Wales
Princess Patricia's Canadian Light Infantry, 53, 57, 67, 122, 315*f*
Protestant Hospital (Rideau Street, Ottawa), 31, 35, 147, 150, 178, 192
public health, 30–31, 305
Purvis, Evelyn (McKenzie). *See* McKenzie, Evelyn (née Purvis)
Putman, Cecil Eugene, 14, 88
Putman, J. H., 239

Q

Queen Alexandra's Imperial Nursing Service (QAINS), 89, 318, 320
Queen's Military Hospital, 126, 140, 164
Queen's University, 85, 87, 170, 178, 183, 239

R

Raabe, Augusta (Wendt). *See* Wendt, Augusta (née Raabe)
Raabe, Carolina, 73
Raabe, William, 73
railway troops, 83, 90, 124–125, 256, 386n13
Ralph, Edna, 319*f*
Ralph, Elizabeth (Olney), 9, 14, 89, 91*f*, 315, 317–318, 319*f*, 320–323, 320*f*, 322*f*, 323*f*, 333, 387n17
Ralph, Eugenia, 81
Ralph, Isabel, 42–43, 319*f*, 321
Ralph, William Allan, 277
R. E. Farm Cemetery, 99, 100*f*
Regan, John, 14, 171, 331
Regina Trench, 92, 137, 139, 216, 283
Reid, Elizabeth, 43
RFC. *See* Royal Flying Corps (RFC)
Richthofen, Manfred von ("Red Baron"), 202, 243
Rideau Hall, 4, 6, 15, 17, 17*f*, 23, 24, 25, 27–28, 32, 38, 64, 71, 88, 221, 309, 314, 316

Robertson, Annie, 133, 142, 371n6
Robertson, Daniel (father of Daniel Sr.), 131
Robertson, Daniel, Jr., 14, 57, 63, 92, 131–133, 132*f*, 134–135, 134*f*, 140, 142, 144, 163
Robertson, Daniel, Sr., 6, 14, 83, 92, 131–133, 132*f*, 137, 138–139, 138*f*, 140, 142, 144, 149, 163
Robertson, George, 14, 62, 131, 133, 135–137, 136*f*, 138–139, 142, 335, 336–337
Robertson, James, 131, 133
Robertson, Jennie, 133, 142, 369n6
Robertson, Mary (née Price / Pryce), 9, 83, 131, 133, 140, 141*f*, 142
Robertson, Mary Jane (Wendt), 78
Robertson, Peter, 133
Robertson, William Price, 14, 64, 92, 131, 133, 137, 139, 140, 141*f*, 149, 331
Robinson, Helen Eleanor. *See* Bothwell, Helen Eleanor ("Ella") (née Robinson)
Rockcliffe, 6, 15–18, 18*f*, 23, 31–32, 36–37, 57, 64, 119, 120*f*, 121*f*, 173–174, 197, 253, 327, 329, 336, 339, 386n22
Rodgers, Jimmy, 76
Rolt, Herbert Henry, 14, 67, 91*f*, 336
Royal Canadian Air Force, 339
Royal Canadian Dragoons, 57
Royal Canadian Mint, 37, 45, 58, 60, 277
Royal Canadian Navy, 8, 57
Royal Canadian Regiment (RCR), 71, 147–148
Royal Flying Corps (RFC), 6, 8, 12, 89, 200–201, 205, 241–242, 242*f*, 244, 246, 248, 260
Russell, Rev. C. Edward, 43–44
Rutherford, Mary Pauline. *See* Bothwell, Mary Pauline (née Rutherford)
Ryan, John, 195

Ryan, John Henry ("Jack") ("Rufus"), 6, 27, 27f, 28f, 50f, 89, 91f, 92, 163, 195, 196–198, 198f, 200–203, 200f, 204–207, 207f, 208–209, 211, 223, 376n34
Ryan, Mabel (McElroy), 195, 196, 205, 207, 209, 376n34
Ryan, Margaret Lena (Crowe), 195, 207, 209, 211
Ryan, Mathew William ("Billy"), 6, 62, 90, 91f, 92, 195, 197, 198–199, 199f, 207–208, 211, 375n1
Ryan, Susanah, 195

S

Sains-les-Marquion, France, 293
Sains-les-Marquion British Cemetery, 296–297, 296f, 297f, 298f
Samways, Thomas E., 14, 62, 91f
Sandusky, Michael, 301, 386n13, 386n22
Sargent, Bert, 217
Sayles, George A., 14, 84, 91f, 256, 332
Schayltz, Henrietta (Jackson). *See* Jackson, Henrietta (née Schayltz)
Schroeder, Albert Christian, 299
Schroeder, Augusta. *See* Haak, Augusta (Schroeder)
Schroeder, Charles, 300
Schroeder, Rosie, 300–301
Seaforth Highlanders (Scotland), 57
Second Ypres, battle of, 63, 69, 97, 134, 224, 290, 329, 331
Shearer, John George, 47–48, 48f, 363n22
Sheppard, A. E., 328
Short, Maria, 50
Short, Milton D., 14, 60, 91f, 336
Short, William, 50
Short, William Harold Armstrong, 14, 60, 91f, 335–336
Siberia, 233, 234, 295, 311–312, 313f
Signals Corps, 89, 169, 171, 256, 311–312
Silsby, George Henry Fred, 14, 170
Silsby, William Oliver, 14, 170, 336–337
Simons, Joe, 226, 227
Simpson, John E. J., 14, 64, 83, 256, 329–330
Sinai campaign, 261–263, 262f
Sir Oliver Mowat Memorial Hospital (Kingston), 303, 305
Slinn, Breary, 20, 38, 58, 335
Slinn, John Imrie, 14, 88, 91f, 333, 335
Slinn, Nan, 42
Slinn, S. Shirley, 14, 88, 91f, 332, 333, 335, 337
Slinn, William B., 14, 58, 91f
Smith, Goldwin, 31
Smith, Robert Bruce, 14, 67, 91f, 165, 332
Somme, the, 6, 59f, 77, 89, 92, 98, 137, 139, 149–150, 151f, 158, 159, 200, 203, 209, 216, 225, 241, 271, 274–275, 283, 292, 303, 309
Soper, Eddy, 200
Soper, Warren, 18, 23
Spanish Flu, 6, 77, 231, 254, 255, 256–257, 299, 305, 312, 314
Sproule, Arthur Henry, 14, 88, 256, 331, 332, 333
Stalker family, 36, 36f, 175, 176f
Stalker, Alexander, 85
Stalker, Andrew Douglas ("Doug"), 14, 27f, 85, 91f, 174, 175, 176, 176f, 178, 183–185, 184f, 186f, 189–190, 191–192, 191f, 332, 336
Stalker, Arthur, 27f, 173, 175, 176f, 178, 187, 190, 192, 193f
Stalker, Clara ("Daisy"), 175–176, 176f, 178
Stalker, Clara Belle (Montgomery), 176, 176f, 181, 183, 189
Stalker, Clarinda (née Bell), 9, 163, 175, 176f, 178, 187, 192
Stalker, Edith (née Boult), 179–180, 186–187, 373n19
Stalker, George Frederick ("Fred"), 14, 85, 90, 91f, 172, 175, 176, 176f,

178, 181, 183, 189–191, 192*f*, 331, 336–337
Stalker, Ivy Eveline, 175–176, 176*f*
Stalker, Jean Belle ("Queenie"), 175–176, 176*f*, 178
Stalker, Margaret, 176*f*, 187, 188–189, 188*f*
Stalker, Moray, 175, 176*f*, 178, 187, 192, 193*f*
Stalker, Nora Jean, 176*f*, 187, 188–189, 188*f*
Stalker, Norman Douglas, 176*f*, 187, 188*f*, 189*f*
Stalker, Robert Alexander, 14, 85, 90, 91*f*, 92, 175, 176, 176*f*, 177*f*, 178–181, 181*f*, 185–186
Stalker, Robert Fred, 176*f*, 187, 188*f*, 189*f*
Stalker, Violet, 175–176, 176*f*
Stanley Cup, 27, 277
St. Bartholomew's Anglican Church, 24, 38, 50, 53, 97, 153, 156, 222, 281, 306, 314
St. David's Reformed Episcopal Church, 24, 43–44, 50, 53, 104, 106, 176–178, 222, 340, 363n31
Ste. Catherine British Cemetery, 235, 236*f*, 237*f*
St. Eloi, 59*f*, 124
St. Eloi, battle of, 82, 108, 164, 179, 181, 199, 256, 271, 331, 332
Stevenson, Benjamin Cleveland ("Zeke"), 14, 89, 91*f*, 336
Stevenson, William Fixter, 14, 64, 83, 91*f*, 332, 333
Stitt, A. E., 28*f*, 37
St. John Evangelical Lutheran Church, 24, 50, 54
St. Pierre Cemetery, Amiens, 277, 278*f*, 279*f*, 280*f*
St. Quentin, battle of, 77
Sunstroke. *See* heatstroke
Suicide Road, 76
Susman, Annie (Hupfeld), 96

T

tank battalion, 255
TB. *See* tuberculosis (TB)
Thompson, Lt. Col. A. T., 63, 69
Thompson, Major the Rev. B. W., 166
Tigris Lane Cemetery, 286, 287*f*, 288*f*
Tobin, Joshua, 157, 159, 160
Tobin, Mrs. J, 371n15
Tobin, Mrs. T., 371n20
Tobin, Thomas, 371n20
Trenchard, Major-General (later Air Marshall Lord) Hugh, 202, 248
Trotter, Charles Edward, 14, 64, 82, 91*f*, 119, 120*f*, 121–122, 122*f*, 123, 124, 128, 130, 130*f*, 135
Trotter, Elizabeth, 119
Trotter, William, 119
tuberculosis (TB), 6, 9, 30–31, 175, 213, 257, 299, 301–303, 305–306
Tubman family, 36, 36*f*, 221, 222*f*
Tubman, Caroline Rebecca, 221, 222, 222*f*, 232, 234
Tubman, Edith Mary ("May"), 222*f*, 223, 232
Tubman, Elmer ("Joe"), 14, 27, 30, 88–89, 221, 222, 222*f*, 223, 232, 232*f*, 235, 336
Tubman, Jean, 222, 222*f*, 223, 235
Tubman, Jennie Watters, 9, 222, 222*f*, 232, 234
Tubman, Leslie Watters, 6, 14, 36*f*, 56, 91*f*, 163, 174, 221, 222*f*, 223–229, 225*f*, 228*f*, 229*f*, 235, 250–251, 251*f*, 252*f*
Tubman, Mary, 222*f*, 234
Tubman, Norman Harry ("Harry"), 14, 88, 91*f*, 222*f*, 223, 231, 235
Tubman, Robert James, 221, 222, 222*f*, 232, 234
Tubman, Russell Arnold, 221–222, 222*f*, 235
Tubman, Thomas, 222*f*
Tubman, Thomas Raymond ("Ray"), 14, 27*f*, 85, 91*f*, 163, 164, 174, 221, 222*f*, 223, 229–231,

230f, 233, 234, 311–312, 313f, 331–332, 333, 336
Tubman, William John, 20, 221, 222, 222f, 232, 234, 250
Tubman, William Reed, 14, 90, 221, 222–223, 222f, 232, 233, 233f, 234, 255, 336
Tunstead, Sarah. *See* Wendt, Sarah (née Tunstead)
Twyman, Harriet, 98, 101

V

Valcartier Camp, 56, 56f, 58, 97, 133, 134, 169, 214, 223–224
Vance, Jonathan, 10
VD. *See* venereal diseases (gonorrhea, syphilis)
venereal diseases (gonorrhea, syphilis), 30, 99, 110, 158, 190, 273, 321, 335
Villers-au-Bois, France, 161
Villers Station Cemetery, 161, 162f, 181, 182f
Vimy, France, 9, 59f, 137, 158–159, 161, 163, 164, 175, 180–181, 203, 216–217, 220, 221, 226–228, 229–230, 273–274, 311
Vimy Memorial, 7, 144, 145f, 146f, 151–152, 152f, 180
Vimy Ridge, battle of, 137, 158, 161, 164, 230, 283

W

War Hospital (Reading), 283
Watkins, Arthur Kendall, 14, 89
Watkins, Edmund John, 14, 86, 91f
Watson, George T., 14, 58, 91f
W. C. Edwards Companies (Rideau Falls industrial complex), 17, 18–19, 20f, 37–38, 57, 66, 86, 89, 103, 105f, 115, 150, 222, 327–328, 362n6
Welford, Mary Elizabeth. *See* Mayo, Mary Elizabeth ("May") (née Welford)

Welford, Mary Jane (née Beck), 156–157
Welford, William, 157
Wellshill Cemetery (Perth, Scotland), 263–264, 264f, 265f, 266f
Wendt family, 72f
Wendt, Albert Charles, 78, 78f
Wendt, Archie, 173
Wendt, Augusta (née Raabe), 71, 72f
Wendt, Charles Albert ("Charlie"), 14, 58, 69, 71, 72f, 73, 74, 75, 76–77, 78–79, 306
Wendt, Heinrich, 71, 72f
Wendt, Henry, 71, 72f, 73, 76–77
Wendt, Herbert, 71, 72f, 77–78, 79
Wendt, Johann ("John"), 71
Wendt, Louise (O'Leary), 71, 72f, 73–74
Wendt, Margaret, 71, 72f, 74
Wendt, Mary Jane (née Robertson), 78
Wendt, Sarah (née Tunstead), 73
Wendt, Wilhelm ("Billy"), 28, 45, 71, 72f, 73, 73f, 79
western front, 59f, 63, 79, 86, 171, 227, 253, 260, 273, 311
Wheeler, Victor, 137–138, 159
White, Russell (Whyte on the Honour Roll), 14, 62, 92, 164–165, 166, 332, 361n20
Williams, Stanley, 14, 58, 91f
Williams, William A., 14, 45, 57, 91f
Willson, Norman Keller (Wilson on the Honour Roll), 14, 45, 58, 91f, 92, 256, 331, 361n18
Wilson, A. John, 14
Wilson, Arthur S., 14, 57, 91f, 95, 97, 99, 101
Wilson, Dora, 95
Wilson, Jessie, 95, 98, 101
Wilson, Katie, 95, 98, 101
Wilson, Theresa Elizabeth. *See* Coker, Theresa Elizabeth (Wilson) (née Hupfeld)
Wilson, William H., 96
Wilson, William Henry, 14, 61, 91f, 95, 97, 98–99, 101

Winton, Thomas, 14, 56, 91*f*, 331, 336
Woods, Mark, 38
Wright, Frederick Samuel, 14, 85, 91*f*, 165
Wulvergem, Belgium, 59*f*, 98, 99

Y

Ypres Salient, 63, 75, 77, 79, 83, 95, 97, 107, 121, 134–135, 137, 140, 143, 149, 179, 199, 223, 270, 274*f*, 283, 334
Yukon Battery, 269

MERCURY SERIES/COLLECTION MERCURE

The best resource on the history, archaeology, and culture of Canada is proudly published by the Canadian Museum of History and the University of Ottawa Press.

Le Musée canadien de l'histoire et Les Presses de l'Université d'Ottawa publient avec fierté la meilleure ressource en ce qui a trait à l'histoire, à l'archéologie et à la culture canadiennes.

Series Editor/Direction de la collection: Pierre M. Desrosiers
Editorial Committee/Comité éditorial: Laura Sanchini, Janet Young
Managing Editor/Responsable de l'édition: Robyn Jeffrey
Coordination: Pascal Scallon-Chouinard

Strikingly Canadian and highly specialized, the *Mercury Series* presents works in the research domain of the Canadian Museum of History and benefits from the publishing expertise of the University of Ottawa Press. Created in 1972, the series is in line with the Canadian Museum of History's strategic directions. The *Mercury Series* consists of peer-reviewed academic research, and includes numerous landmark contributions in the disciplines of Canadian history, archaeology, culture, and ethnology. Books in the series are published in at least one of Canada's official languages, and may appear in other languages.

Remarquablement canadienne et hautement spécialisée, la *collection Mercure* réunit des ouvrages portant sur les domaines de recherches du Musée canadien de l'histoire et s'appuie sur le savoir-faire des Presses de l'Université d'Ottawa. Fondée en 1972, elle répond aux orientations stratégiques du Musée canadien de l'histoire. La *collection Mercure* propose des recherches scientifiques évaluées par les pairs et regroupe de nombreuses contributions majeures à l'histoire, à l'archéologie, à la culture et à l'ethnologie canadiennes. Les ouvrages sont publiés dans au moins une des langues officielles du Canada, avec possibilité de parution dans d'autres langues.

The Mercury Series/La collection Mercure

Yves Frenette, Marc St-Hilaire et Marie-Ève Harton, dir., *Déploiements canadiens-français et métis en Amérique du Nord (18e-20e siècle)*, 2023.

Ronald F. Williamson and Robert von Bitter, *The History and Archaeology of the Iroquois du Nord*, 2023.

Frances M. Slaney, *Marius Barbeau's Vitalist Ethnology*, 2023.

Kenneth R. Holyoke and M. Gabriel Hrynick, *The Far Northeast: 3000 BP to Contact*, 2022.

Stacey J. Barker, Krista Cooke, and Molly McCullough, *Material Traces of War: Stories of Canadian Women and Conflict, 1914–1945*, 2021.

Michael K. Hawes, Andrew C. Holman, and Christopher Kirkey, eds., *1968 in Canada: A Year and Its Legacies*, 2021.

Steven Schwinghamer and Jan Raska, *Pier 21: A History*, 2020.

Steven Schwinghamer et Jan Raska, *Quai 21 : Une histoire*, 2020.

Robert Sweeny, ed., *Sharing Spaces: Essays in Honour of Sherry Olson*, 2020.

Matthew Betts, *Place-Making in the Pretty Harbour: The Archaeology of Port Joli, Nova Scotia*, 2019.

Lauriane Bourgeon, *Préhistoire béringienne : étude archéologique des Grottes du Poisson-Bleu (Yukon)*, 2018.

Jenny Ellison and Jennifer Anderson, eds., *Hockey: Challenging Canada's Game – Au-delà du sport national*, 2018.

Myron Momryk, *Mike Starr of Oshawa: A Political Biography*, 2018.

John Willis, ed., *Tu sais, mon vieux Jean-Pierre: Essays on the Archaeology and History of New France and Canadian Culture in Honour of Jean-Pierre Chrestien*, 2017.

Anna Kearney Guigne, *The Forgotten Songs of the Newfoundland Outports: As Taken from Kenneth Peacock's Newfoundland Field Collection, 1951–1961*, 2016.

Ian Dyck, *The Life and Work of W. B. Nickerson (1865–1926): Scientific Archaeology in Central North America*, 2016.

Brad Loewen and Claude Chapdelaine, eds., *Contact in the 16th Century: Networks Among Fishers, Foragers and Farmers*, 2016.

Mauro Peressini, *Choosing Buddhism*, 2016.

Pierre Bibeau, David Denton, André Burroughs, dir., *Ce que la rivière nous procurait : archéologie et histoire du réservoir de l'Eastmain-1*, 2015.

Charles Garrad, *Petun to Wyandot: The Ontario Petun from the Sixteenth Century*, 2014.

Gabriel M. Yanicki, *Old Man's Playing Ground: Gaming and Trade on the Plains/Plateau Frontier*, 2014.

Jean-François Blanchette, *Du coq à l'âme : l'art populaire au Québec*, 2014.

Terence N. Clark, *Rewriting Marpole: The Path to Cultural Complexity in the Gulf of Georgia*, 2013.

Michel Plourde, *L'exploitation du phoque à l'embouchure du Saguenay par les Iroquoiens de 1000 à 1534*, 2013.

Stuart E. Jenness, *Stefansson, Dr. Anderson and the Canadian Arctic Expedition, 1913–1918: A Story of Exploration, Science and Sovereignty*, 2011.

Co-published by the Canadian Museum of History and the University of Ottawa Press.
Publié conjointement par le Musée canadien de l'histoire et Les Presses de l'Université d'Ottawa.

For a complete list of the University of Ottawa Press titles, visit:
Pour une liste complète des titres des Presses de l'Université d'Ottawa, voir :
www.Press.uOttawa.ca

Milton Keynes UK
Ingram Content Group UK Ltd.
UKHW050621140424
441033UK00004B/22